EXPRESS TO THE TOEFL iBT® TEST

Tammy LeRoi Gilbert
Dorothy E. Zemach

Express to the TOEFL iBT® Test

Pearson Education, 10 Bank Street, White Plains, NY 10606

Staff credits: The people who made up the ***Express to the TOEFL iBT® Test*** team, representing editorial, production, design, and manufacturing, are: Pietro Alongi, Aerin Csigay, Dave Dickey, Christine Edmonds, Eddi Edwards, Pam Fishman, Nancy Flaggman, Jennifer McAliney, Barbara Perez, and Joan Poole.

Cover design: Gary Rose
Text composition: TSI Graphics
Text font: 11/14 pt. Helvetica Neue 55
Text art: Kenneth Batelman
Photo credits: Page 93 Caro/Alamy; p. 96 senior images/Alamy; p. 97 Tomas Rodriguez/age fotostock; p. 99 Ice Tea Media/Alamy; p. 102 Alexander Raths/Shutterstock; p. 103 UpperCut Images/age fotostock; p. 104 amana images inc./Alamy; p. 107 & 108 Monkey Business Images/Getty Images; p. 111 Blend Images/Alamy; p. 112 David R. Frazier Photolibrary, Inc./Alamy; p. 114 & 115 Angela Hampton Picture Library/Alamy; p. 118 Corbis Bridge/Alamy; p. 119 Angela Hampton Picture Library/Alamy; p. 121 GoGo Images Corporation/Alamy; p. 125 West Coast Surfer/age fotostock; p. 128 Golden Pixels LLC/Shutterstock; p. 129 Tissiana Bowman/Shutterstock; p. 131 Stuart Forster/Alamy; p. 135 Tetra Images/Alamy; p. 136 Asiaselects/Alamy; p. 137 Fancy Collection/SuperStock; p. 140 Fancy Collection/SuperStock; p. 141 Gogo Images/Glow Images; p. 143 moodboard/Alamy; p. 145 Bubbles Photolibrary/Alamy; p. 146 Golden Pixels LLC/Alamy; p. 148 ZouZou/Shutterstock; p. 183 Monkey Business Images/Shutterstock; p. 195 The Photo Works/Alamy; p. 196 ONOKY - Photononstop/Alamy; p. 200 Customimages/Glow Images; p. 214 Edwin Remsberg/Alamy; p. 215 ImageSource/Glow Images; p. 218 UpperCut Images/Alamy; p. 227 (top) MBI/Alamy, (bottom) Ianni Dimitrov/Alamy; p. 230 Fancy/Alamy; p. 238 (top) Rachel Epstein/PhotoEdit, (bottom) Rubberball/Glow Images; p. 242 MBI/Alamy; p. 243 PureStock/Glow Images; p. 244 Mary Kate Denny/PhotoEdit; p. 245 Ryan McVay/Getty Images; p. 305 AISPIX by Image Source/Shutterstock; p. 306 Golden Pixels LLC/Alamy; p. 308 DURIS Guillaume/Fotolia; p. 310 ONOKY - Photononstop/Alamy; p. 311 Radius Images/Alamy; p. 313 Ilene MacDonald/Alamy; p. 317 Alix Minde/age fotostock; p. 319 fotomy/Alamy; p. 320 Robert Kneschke/Shutterstock.

Library of Congress Cataloging-in-Publication Data

Gilbert, Tammy LeRoi.
Express to the TOEFL iBT test / Tammy LeRoi Gilbert, Dorothy E. Zemach.
p. cm.
ISBN 978-0-13-286162-5
1. Test of English as a Foreign Language--Study guides. 2. English language--Textbooks for foreign speakers. 3. English language--Examinations--Study guides. I. Zemach, Dorothy E. II. Title.
PE1128.G523 2013
428.0076--dc23

2012031658

ISBN-10: 0-13-286162-3
ISBN-13: 978-0-13-286162-5

Printed in the United States of America
1 2 3 4 5 6 7 8 9 10–V011–16 15 14 13 12

ACKNOWLEDGMENTS

Special Thanks from Tammy to:

My dear friend, Nancy Douglas, whose wisdom and many years of support and friendship have been vital to my professional, mental, and emotional survival.

Another dear friend, Stuart Silberman, whose long lists of creative topic ideas gave me the necessary inspiration to keep writing and made me smile.

Special Thanks to Our Reviewers:

Deborah Bobobza, Buffalo Public Schools; **Marta Dmytrenko-Ahrabian**, English Language Institute, Wayne State University; **Wil Fennell**, Kyoto Bukkyu University; **Joseph Granitto**, English Language Institute, LIU/CW Post College; **Christopher Kilmer**, Colorado School of English; **Mike Lindsay**, University of Arizona; **Michael Luchuk**, ELT Consultant; **Helen Roland**, Miami Dade College; **Mario Souza**, Baruch College, CUNY Language & Test Preparation Programs; **Bill Walker**, American English Institute, University of Oregon.

CONTENTS

Writing

Practice Test

Scoring Charts

INTRODUCTION

The TOEFL iBT® Test is an exam offered by the Educational Testing Service (ETS) that tests the abilities of nonnative English-speakers to understand and use academic English in four skill areas: Reading, Listening, Speaking, and Writing. Universities and colleges in North America use the TOEFL iBT Test scores to evaluate applicants' readiness to enroll in their institutions.

Comprehensive yet compact, *Express to the TOEFL iBT® Test* allows you to completely cover all of the skills and question types found on the TOEFL iBT Test in a much shorter amount of time than is possible with standard TOEFL iBT Test preparation textbooks. You'll learn the format and style of the test, progressively build specific skills in all four areas tested, gain valuable practice, evaluate your own strengths and areas for improvement, and learn numerous test-taking tips and strategies. In addition to the carefully scaffolded skills instruction and exercises, *Express to the TOEFL iBT® Test* includes three full practice tests. The textbook includes one full Practice Test, while the CD-ROM also includes this Practice Test from the book as well as the four Post-Tests from the book combined to form a complete test, for students who choose not to take each Post-Test section independently. There is also free access to a complete online Pearson iTest, which contains special features, including the ability to e-mail results to the instructor, print scores, and retake the test as necessary for review. In addition, detailed explanations are provided for both the correct and the incorrect answers. (See the inside front cover for information to access your free Pearson iTest.)

This is not a general English course; if your English level is too low for academic study, then we recommend that you continue your language studies before taking the TOEFL iBT Test. However, if you are ready to take college or university courses in a North American institution, then *Express to the TOEFL iBT® Test* will teach you the style, format, and content of the exam most commonly used to determine entrance and placement for international students. This course will help ensure that your test scores accurately reflect the full range of your English abilities.

Because *Express to the TOEFL iBT® Test* offers a concise and engaging coverage of all testing materials, it is appropriate for intensive test preparation courses of about a month or longer, or for independent study. You will learn the specific skills you need to get a high score on the TOEFL iBT Test and get ample opportunities to practice these skills with authentic test-type passages and questions. While it is important to become familiar with the test, taking dozens of practice tests alone will not raise your score. Instead, you first need to know what exactly is being tested by the TOEFL iBT Test and how well you can perform in those areas. In addition, unless you understand *why* you missed a particular item, you are likely to continue repeating the same mistake. For that reason, this course provides you with tools for evaluation as well as detailed answer keys.

Express to the TOEFL iBT® Test provides step-by-step instruction to help you develop the skills needed to recognize and answer the questions found on the TOEFL iBT Test. Like the test itself, the book is divided into four sections: Reading, Listening, Speaking, and Writing. Each section is broken down into questions types and skills. You may work through the sections in any order, or work only on the sections in which you feel you need the most improvement.

- **Brief yet complete explanations** and computer screen pictures of each question type clearly show you exactly what you will see on the day of the test.
- **Skill Builders** first provide you with fully supported lessons to help you learn the most important skills and strategies necessary to answer each specific question type.
- **Authentic Practice** of the skills then allows you to apply what you have learned in the Skill Builders by providing sample test items in the TOEFL iBT Test style. The passages and question types prepare you with engaging and accessible materials.
- **Express Tips** offer useful suggestions and essential strategies for answering questions correctly.
- **Comprehensive Review** sections **combine** and **expand skills practice** with full-length test items.
- **Self-evaluations for the Speaking and Writing Sections** that don't have any one "correct" answer are included so you can evaluate your strengths and formulate a plan to improve specific skills.
- **Post-Tests** for each section provide you with additional practice and provide an opportunity for you to practice all of the skills needed for each section.
- A **full Practice Test** simulates the test in content and length, further preparing you for success.
- A comprehensive **CD-ROM** is included. It features:
  - **Two interactive practice tests:** one created from the Student Book Practice Test and one created from the Student Book Post-Tests. You have the option of taking the tests in practice mode or timed mode.
  - **An answer key with comprehensive answer explanations** for all questions in the textbook that offer you the opportunity to understand why answers are correct or incorrect. The answer key also includes samples for Speaking and Writing answers.
  - **A full MP3 audio program and audioscript**

Used alone or in conjunction with its comprehensive multimedia program, *Express to the TOEFL iBT® Test* is an ideal way for you to quickly and thoroughly prepare for the TOEFL iBT Test.

About the TOEFL iBT Test

The TOEFL iBT Test is administered by the Educational Testing Service (ETS) and is taken on a computer. The TOEFL iBT Test is not given online, although the test is Internet-based; to take the test, you must travel to a test center, where you will take the test on a computer. In addition to completing the multiple-choice sections found in the Reading and Listening sections, you will type your essays for the Writing section using a word processor, and will record answers for the Speaking section with equipment provided by the testing center. Check the ETS website for information about location, cost, schedules, and how to register.

The entire test will take about 3–4 hours, and there is one break. You are not allowed to bring materials into the actual computer testing area at the testing centers such as a calculator, cell phone, dictionary, books, food, and so on. Many testing centers have lockers where you can leave such items, and you can also store a snack and water that you may access from the locker during the break. Check with the individual testing center that you will be using for more details.

Testing centers have strict security to make sure that scores are accurate and fair. You should be prepared to get your ID checked, be photographed, get searched, and be asked to leave any items in a locker. Most testing centers also have video cameras filming test takers at all times.

To register for the test, go to http://www.ets.org/toefl/.

Here is the order in which the sections of the TOEFL iBT Test are administered. (Explanations of all question types are offered in the individual sections in this book.)

TOEFL iBT Test Format

Section	Number of Items/Questions	Timing
Reading	3–4 passages; approximately 600–700 words per passage 12–14 question per passage; 39 total questions	60–80 minutes
Listening	4–6 lectures, each with 6 questions 2–3 conversations, each with 5 questions 34 total questions	60–90 minutes
BREAK	Required	10 minutes
Speaking	6 tasks: 2 independent and 4 integrated	20 minutes
Writing	2 tasks: 1 integrated and 1 independent	20 minutes (integrated) 30 minutes (independent)
TOTAL TIME	3.5 to 4 hours	

Please note: ETS does change the test periodically, or may include special items for field-testing; therefore, not all item types in this textbook may be on the test. However, working on every item type will improve your overall ability to score well on the TOEFL iBT Test.

Score Ranges and Total Score

The Reading, Listening, Speaking, and Writing sections of the test all have a possible score range of 0–30, with a total score of 120 possible for the complete test.

A score range of 22–30 indicates an advanced level in each particular section. A score range of 15–21 indicates an intermediate level of performance, and a score range of 0–14 indicates a low level.

See the score conversion charts for scoring the Post-Tests and the Practice Test (on pages 325–330) if you wish to take them in the textbook. You may also take these tests on the CD-ROM which will automatically score them for you.

EXPRESS TIP

You should practice taking the test on a computer. This will help you understand and feel comfortable with the computer-based TOEFL iBT Test.

Tips for Taking the TOEFL iBT Test

NOTE: The following tips are based on what many former students who studied for and took the TOEFL iBT Test and their teachers told us about their experiences with the test. We hope that with this information and our own experience, we can help make the TOEFL iBT Test easier for you.

Before Taking the TOEFL iBT Test:

1. Go to the official TOEFL website at http://www.ets.org/toefl/ to download the *TOEFL iBT® Registration Bulletins* (not currently available in print form). They will provide detailed instructions for registration, forms, identification (ID) requirements, score reporting information, policies, and procedures. Read the Bulletin completely. If you don't understand the information or have questions about it, ask your English teacher or an English-speaking friend to help you.
2. Schedule your TOEFL iBT Test early. Some test centers fill up quickly, and you might not be able to take the test on a date or at a time that is convenient for you if you wait to sign up. Schedule your test so the institutions, colleges, or universities that need your scores will get them on time.
3. If possible, take a practice trip to the test center before the day of your test. You need to know where it is and how long it will take you to get there by car, bus, or train. Travel close to the actual time of your test appointment. This will help you understand how traffic conditions will affect your arrival time. If you drive, check for parking in the area. This is very important! You don't want to worry about getting lost or being late on the day of your test.
4. Study plan:
   - Take a TOEFL iBT Test preparation class and complete all activities in this textbook.
   - Learn to take good notes in class, and review your notes and the material covered in the textbook every day after class.
   - Plan a regular time to study every day. Do not try to "cram" or study for the TOEFL iBT Test in a short amount of time.
   - Study in a quiet place where you can focus and concentrate.
   - Take the Practice Test in this book under "real" conditions (timed).
   - Constantly assess your progress. If you don't have much time, focus on the skills that are more difficult for you. Assessment will help you understand which skills you need to study.
   - Practice the taking the TOEFL iBT Test on the CD-ROM included in *Express to the TOEFL iBT® Test* and the Pearson iTest online so you know what it looks like and how it works. Be familiar with the directions, so you don't waste time reading them on the day of the test. The more comfortable you are with the computer, the more relaxed you will be when you take the actual test.
   - Use flashcards to learn and expand your vocabulary and grammar.
   - Study with other TOEFL students. It's more fun and will help you remember if you read the dialogues aloud to each other and test each other.
   - Eat well, get sufficient exercise, and get enough sleep.

- Stop studying completely the night before and the day of the test. Relax with friends or family, eat well, and get a good night's sleep.
- In your mind, create a picture of yourself doing well on the test. Keep telling yourself that YOU CAN DO IT! Encourage yourself! Stop bad thoughts about the test and stay away from people who are too nervous about the test. Practice relaxing.

On the Day of the Test:

- Eat a good breakfast or lunch. Relax! Look in the mirror and tell yourself that you are going to do very well on the test. Remember to think positive.
- Dress in comfortable clothes that allow you to adjust to any room temperature. If it's cold, bring a sweater with you.
- Think about bringing earplugs. The testing room can be noisy. You can also keep the headphones for the Listening Section on during the whole test. If it is really noisy, you may want to use both the earplugs and the headphones.
- Remember to bring:
  - your passport and/or a valid identification (please see the TOEFL iBT website for more information on what is considered acceptable identification)
  - your TOEFL iBT Registration Confirmation (you can print this out from your TOEFL iBT Online Profile at the official TOEFL iBT website)
- Get to the test center early. You need to be there 30 to 45 minutes before your scheduled test time.
- Get a drink of water and go to the restroom before you start the actual test. If you leave during the test, the test clock will keep running and you will lose time needed for the test.
- After you sit down to take the test:
  - change the height of the computer chair so your feet are flat on the floor
  - adjust the back of the chair so you are sitting straight up
  - move the computer monitor (screen) up or down or side to side so it is at eye-level
  - ask someone at the test center to clean the screen if it is dirty
  - change the contrast or the brightness of the screen by using the button on the front of the computer monitor. Ask someone at the test center if you don't know how to do this.
  - arrange the headphones comfortably on your head and ears

During the Test:

- Focus your attention. Don't worry about what other people in the testing room are doing.
- Think about only one question at a time.
- Answer all the questions.
- If you do not know the answer to a question, use the process of elimination or guess.
- If you start to feel nervous because you can't answer a question:
  - tell yourself that you already studied for it and the answer is in your mind somewhere
  - take a few deep breaths, close your eyes for a few seconds, and then go back to the question

- Remember that you must *click two times* to get to the next question in the Listening section: click once on **Next**, and then, click a second time on **OK** to confirm your answers. Think: "click, click!" Once you click on **OK**, you will go to the next question and cannot go back. Some students say that they forget to click on the **OK** icon and lose valuable time waiting for the next question. Practice taking the TOEFL iBT Test to become familiar with this section.
- Pace yourself. Check the time on the computer screen and don't spend too much time on one question.
- Every 10 to 15 minutes, do some exercises to relax your eyes, neck, shoulders, and hands.
- If you have trouble during the test (with equipment not functioning, for example), raise your hand and someone from the testing center will help you. Avoid using the "Help" icon on your computer screen, because the clock will continue to count down while you are waiting for help, and you will lose precious time.
- Use the 10-minute break between the Reading and Listening sections and the Speaking and Writing sections to relax. Have a snack and something to drink, sit back, close your eyes, think of nothing, and breathe deeply.

After the Test:

- Don't worry about how you did on the test. Sometimes it's difficult to know exactly how well you did right after taking the test.
- Go out and do something fun. Celebrate! You did it, and it's finished!
- If you did not get the score you need, study in the needed areas and take the test again. There is no limit to how many times you can take the TOEFL iBT Test.

EXPRESS TO THE TOEFL iBT® TEST

PART 1 • READING

READING OVERVIEW

The Reading section tests your ability to read and understand the academic English that you would typically find in college-level textbooks.

The reading passages on the TOEFL iBT® Test are typically organized in one of the following ways:

- by category or class
- cause/effect
- chronologically or by steps in a process
- comparison/contrast
- problem/solution

The passages include a wide variety of academic topics such as science, history, art, literature, economics, and biography. However, you do not have to be familiar with the topics in order to answer the questions correctly. The topic in a reading passage will be explained, be presented as an argument (often with several different points of view), or involve a historical perspective.

On the actual test, you will read three or four separate passages that are approximately 600 to 700 words long. Each passage will be followed by 12 to 14 questions. You are allowed 60 to 80 minutes to complete the entire Reading section. The different parts of the Reading section are not timed separately; this means that you can move back and forth throughout the entire Reading section.

You will be given a pencil and paper to use. You may not need to, but you *can* take notes during the Reading section (and during all other sections as well). You may use your notes when you answer the questions. The notes are not scored or seen by anyone else, but you may not take them out of the testing center. They will be collected at the end of the test. (See pages 87–91 for Note-Taking Skills.)

Most questions in the Reading section are multiple-choice; however, there are summary and chart completion questions as well. These will be covered in more detail in the Skills units in this section. (See pages 53–67, Reading Skills 9 and 10, "Constructing a Summary" and "Table Completion," for more information.)

Another question type you will see, "insert the sentence," requires you to click on a black square in the passage where you wish to add a **bolded** sentence provided in the question. (See pages 21–27, Reading Skill 4, "Inserting a Sentence into the Passage," for more information.)

Specific words, phrases, or sentences will be highlighted for vocabulary, pronoun referent, and paraphrasing questions in the passage.

The TOEFL iBT Test also includes a **Glossary** feature. This means you can click on blue **underlined** words to see definitions which will appear on the lower left-hand side of the screen after you click on them.

For example, you will see in the reading passage on the right side of the computer screen:

> Tulips, a member of the *Liliaceae* family, are a simple-looking plant: growing from a **bulb**, they normally have one brightly colored flower whose shape resembles a cup, atop a long stem, and a few straight green leaves that grow nearly vertically.

When you click on the blue underlined word, you will see the definition at the bottom of the left side of the screen:

Glossary
bulb: A short, thick, underground stem of some plants.

Here are the different types of questions:

- Vocabulary
- Paraphrasing a Sentence
- Referent (a noun or noun phrase to which a pronoun refers)
- Inserting a Sentence into the Passage
- Detail and Fact
- Negative Fact
- Inference
- Rhetorical Purpose (why specific information was included)
- Summary
- Table Completion

Tool Bar for the Reading Section

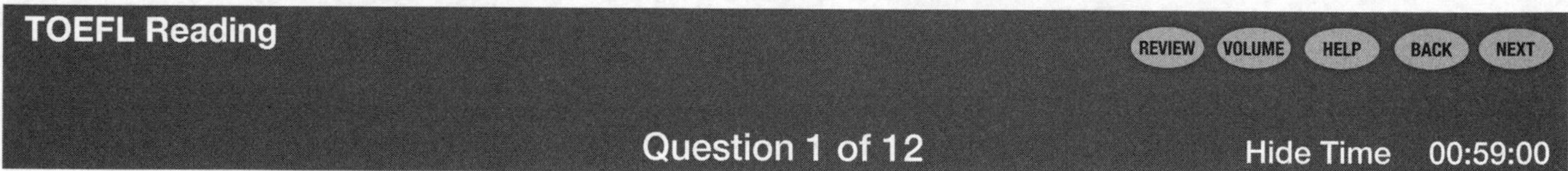

The section you are in and the question you are answering will always be displayed on the tool bar at the top of the computer screen.

Volume—Enables you to change the volume during the test.
Help—Offers the help you need when you click on this button. However, we recommend that you avoid using it because the clock doesn't stop when you use it and you will waste precious time.
Hide Time—Hides the clock any time during the test when you click on this button. However, we recommend that you do *not* use it; you need to pay attention to how much time you have left on the clock.

Next—Allows you to go to the next question.
Back—Enables you to return at any time to a previous question.
Review—Takes you to a screen where you can see a list of all the questions and your answers. The screen will indicate whether or not you have answered a question. To answer a question you skipped or to change an answer, click on that question in the "Review" screen and then click on the "Go to the Question" button. When you are finished, click on the "Return to Where I Was" button to go back to where you were previously.

The Reading section of the TOEFL iBT Test is administered as follows:

1. The general directions for the Reading section will appear on the computer screen. However, you should already be familiar with the directions, so don't waste time reading them; immediately click on "Continue" to move to the first reading passage.
2. You must read the passage *to the end* or scroll down to the end of each passage using the scroll bar (on the right edge of the screen) before the questions and answer choices will appear on the left-hand side of the screen. Once you see the questions and answer choices, the reading passage will appear on the right side of the screen and the questions and answers will come up on the left side.
3. You may also see "Paragraph (#) is marked with an arrow" on the left-hand side of the screen. There will be an arrow (→) next to the paragraph in the right-hand side of the screen where you can find the information needed to answer the question.
4. After you answer the question, click the "Next" button at the top of the screen to move to the next question.
5. To go back to review or answer a previous question, click on the "Back" button.
6. You may also use the convenient "Review" feature to return to a question. To do so, click on the "Review" button the top of the screen.

EXPRESS TIP

You are allowed to skip questions in the Reading section, but remember to go back to answer them before you finish the section. You can also change your answers at any time during this section of the test.

In the individual Skills units of this section, you will see examples of the computer screens used for each type of question.

Improving Your Reading Skills

Reading is a skill that you can easily practice on your own. The key to learning to read faster and comprehend more is to practice reading something *every day* and, if possible, several times a day. Try some or all of the following suggestions:

- Read online or on a computer screen so that you get used to it and are ready to do so on the TOEFL iBT Test.
- Check out academic textbooks from a library, find academic articles in magazines, or read online in as many different fields (biology, Earth science, geology, etc.) as possible. Read a little from a different field each day.
- When you are finished reading a selected part of a text, write a short summary of what you read. You can practice on paragraphs as well as texts as long as ones on the TOEFL iBT Test.
- Skim (read quickly for general information) the materials you have chosen. Try to determine the general idea of the reading. Then read the material again more carefully and create an outline of the main ideas and the most important details and facts.
- Choose a newspaper or online news story that interests you. Write down the *wh*-question words: *who*, *where*, *why*, *when*, *what*, and *how*. Then quickly scan (read only for specific information you need) the article and write a short answer for each *wh*-question word.
- Try to determine how the material you are reading is organized (cause/effect, steps in a process, comparison/contrast, etc.). Understanding the organization will help you search for information more quickly and answer the questions more accurately.
- While you are reading, guess the meaning of unfamiliar words from the context. Use a dictionary afterwards to see if you guessed the meanings correctly.
- Search for pronouns (*she*, *him*, *they*, *them*, *those*) in the materials you are reading and highlight or underline them in online materials or circle them in print materials if possible. Find the nouns or noun phrases to which the pronouns refer.
- Work with a partner and choose some sentences from your reading materials. Practice paraphrasing (stating the idea in another way) the sentences in your own words.
- Read fiction (for example, short stories or novels) that you enjoy. This will inspire you to continue reading on a regular basis.

READING SKILLS 1 AND 2

UNDERSTANDING VOCABULARY FROM CONTEXT; PARAPHRASING A SENTENCE

Reading Skill 1: Understanding Vocabulary from Context

Vocabulary questions in the reading section test your ability to figure out the meaning of a word you don't know. Therefore, do not worry if you don't already know the word! There will be clues in the passage to help you guess its meaning. Check the other words in the sentence, and also the sentences just before and after the one with the highlighted word.

Some words in English have several meanings. Even if you are already familiar with one meaning of the word, check the sentence carefully to see which meaning is appropriate for that passage. Pay attention to the part of speech (i.e., noun, verb, adjective, or adverb).

- The *cast* of the play was comprised of only male actors. (*cast* = noun, meaning the group of players who act in a theatrical production)
- The fisherman on the boat *cast* his nets into the water. (*cast* = verb, meaning "to throw")

EXPRESS TIP

One type of common clue is a contrast clue, which shows the unknown word in contrast to a more familiar word. Check for words and phrases such as *unlike*, *instead of*, and *on the other hand*.

Rats are active at night. The mongoose, on the other hand, is diurnal. (*diurnal* = "awake and active during the day")

The vocabulary questions will ask you about the word directly, and show you where to find it by highlighting it in the passage:

- *The phrase on the clock in the passage is* ***closest in meaning to***
- *The word unseemly in the passage could* ***best be replaced by***

The correct answer will be a synonym (or phrase) for the word (or expression) that could be used in the same place in the passage.

EXPRESS TIP

After you have selected an answer, mentally put it into the sentence, and "read" the sentence with your replacement to double-check that it makes sense.

You must wear your uniform as long as you are on the clock. = "at work"

You must wear your uniform as long as you are at work. √

Look at this example of a vocabulary question from the TOEFL iBT Test on a computer screen.

EXAMPLE: Understanding Vocabulary from Context Question

TOEFL Reading

REVIEW VOLUME HELP BACK NEXT

Question 1 of 12

Hide Time 00:59:00

1. The word pseudonym in the passage is closest in meaning to
   - false name
   - married name
   - nickname
   - middle name

Agatha Christie

1 Agatha Christie is perhaps the best-known writer of mystery and detective novels in the English language. In fact, she is the best-selling writer of books of all time. She wrote romances using the pseudonym Mary Westmacott, and an autobiographical account of her travels with her archaeologist husband using her married name, Agatha Christie Mallowan. However, it is her mystery and detective novels, short stories, and plays for which she is most famous.

SKILL BUILDER

Directions: *Work with a partner. Read the paragraph and the questions. Discuss the clues in the paragraph that tell you the answers. Circle the contrast word in the paragraph that helps you figure out the answer to #2. Then mark the correct answers.*

Agatha Christie

1 Agatha Christie is perhaps the best-known writer of mystery and detective novels in the English language. In fact, she is the best-selling writer of books of all time. She wrote romances using the the pseudonym Mary Westmacott, and an autobiographical account of her travels with her archaeologist husband using her married name, Agatha Christie Mallowan. However, it is her mystery and detective novels, short stories, and plays for which she is most famous.

2 Agatha was painfully shy as a child. Perhaps as result of this, her mother decided that she would not receive a formal education, but would instead be taught at home. She taught herself to read by age five, and had lessons from part-time tutors. She was interested in the arts from a young age, first music and then storytelling and writing. At age 16, she was sent to Paris to study singing and piano. However, because of her shyness, she never became a performing musician. Perhaps her shyness is partly to thank for her choice of writing as her favorite form of artistic expression as an adult.

---

1. The word pseudonym in the passage is closest in meaning to
   Ⓐ false name
   Ⓑ married name
   Ⓒ nickname
   Ⓓ middle name

2. The word formal in the second paragraph could best be replaced by
   Ⓐ expensive
   Ⓑ fancy
   Ⓒ traditional
   Ⓓ free

EXPRESS TIP

You can also look at the word itself for clues to its meaning. Check to see if the word has any of these elements:

- word roots you recognize [*teleport*: *tele~* (far) you might recognize from *telephone*; *port~* (carry) you might recognize from *porter* or *transport*]
- prefixes that change the word's meaning, such as *re~* (again) or *un~* (not)

Skill Builder Answers:

1. **Answer A is correct.** The word "pseudonym" means "false name." The clues in the passage that tell you this are the presence of her real name (Agatha Christie) and the word "using" that comes before "the pseudonym Mary Westmacott." Answer B is incorrect because her married name is given as Agatha Christie Mallowan. Answer C is incorrect because a nickname is a shortened form of a person's first name. Answer D is incorrect because a middle name is the second name of three.

2. **Answer C is correct.** The word "formal" here is contrasted by the word "instead" to "taught at home"—so a "formal education" is opposite to being taught at home. Answer A is incorrect because there is no mention in the paragraph about price or cost. Answer B is incorrect because "fancy" (although it is a possible definition of the word "formal" in other contexts) is not the opposite of "taught at home." Answer D is incorrect because there is no mention of cost or price.

PRACTICE

Directions: *Read the passages. Then mark the correct answers to the questions.*

Passage 1 (Questions 1–2)

The Four-Color Theorem

1 How many different colors would you have to use to color a map so that no two countries next to each other are the same color? It sounds like a simple question, and yet it wasn't until 1976 that the answer—four—was proven, by mathematicians Kenneth Appel and Wolfgang Haken, who were working together at a university in Illinois. The theorem was additionally significant because it was the first to be proven through the use of a computer. The four-color conjecture was first proposed in 1852, but no definitive proof, or mathematical answer, could be demonstrated.

continued . . .

2 The theory is of more interest to mathematicians than to mapmakers, who have used colors to show significant features such as climate, population, system of government, or other such features. Furthermore, although a map is the usual example given to help people visualize the four-color theorem, it is necessary to define countries as being only one landmass. This means, for example, that in the case of the United States, one would consider only the continental United States, and not states such as Alaska and Hawaii that are not contiguous but are separated from the rest of the country by water.

1. The word conjecture in the first paragraph is closest in meaning to
   Ⓐ proof
   Ⓑ assumption
   Ⓒ mathematician
   Ⓓ program

2. The word contiguous in the second paragraph could best be replaced by
   Ⓐ large
   Ⓑ distant
   Ⓒ visible
   Ⓓ neighboring

Passage 2 (Questions 3–4)

Airport Codes in the United States

1 In the early 1900s, the aviation industry adopted the system of the National Weather Service for indicating cities, using two letters. Sometimes the letters were the first two letters of the city name (such as JA for **Ja**cksonville, Florida), and sometimes the first letter of each word of a two-word city were used (such as LA for **L**os **A**ngeles). However, as air travel became more popular, more airports were built, some in places that didn't have a National Weather Service letter code. Therefore, the decision was made to add a third letter—in many cases, the letter X. Thus, the airport at Jacksonville became JAX and the Los Angeles airport became LAX. Other cities, such as Savannah, Georgia (SAV), and Boise, Idaho (BOI), used the first three letters of their name.

2 However, special restrictions kept some letters from being used. Because radio stations east of the Mississippi River began with the letter W, and those west of the Mississippi with the letter K, it was decided not to let any airport codes commence with W or K, although those letters can be placed second or third. The Navy then reserved all of the N codes for the military airbases that served them. Q and Z have also been reserved for special purposes. Some cities, therefore, use internal letters, such as Newark, New Jersey (EWR), and some are even named for places that no longer exist—the New Orleans, Louisiana, airport code MSY comes from the old **M**oisant **S**tock **Y**ards.

3. The word aviation in paragraph 1 could best be replaced by
   Ⓐ weather
   Ⓑ city
   Ⓒ airline
   Ⓓ code

4. The phrase commence with in paragraph 2 is closest in meaning to
   Ⓐ begin with
   Ⓑ contain
   Ⓒ start to use
   Ⓓ repeat

Reading Skill 2: Paraphrasing a Sentence

Paraphrasing means to say the same idea in another way. This type of question asks you to choose the best restatement of a highlighted sentence from the reading passage. The restatement has the same meaning, but it is expressed in a simpler way, and with synonyms for key words. To find the correct answer, first make sure that you understand the highlighted sentence. Then read the four restatements.

One type of restatement leaves out unimportant details. However, the main idea and important supporting information from the original sentence must be present in the restatement.

An incorrect restatement will contradict part or all of the highlighted sentence.

A question of this type will be phrased as follows:

Which of the sentences below best expresses the essential information in the highlighted sentence in paragraph 2?

Look at this example of a paraphrasing question on a computer screen.

EXAMPLE: Paraphrasing a Sentence Question

TOEFL Reading

REVIEW VOLUME HELP BACK NEXT

Question 2 of 12

Hide Time 00:59:00

2. Which of the sentences below best expresses the essential information in the highlighted sentence in paragraph 1?
   - The Quechua Indians of Peru got jobs by selling quinine as a drug to treat malaria.
   - Quinine can be made in the laboratory now, but it is more expensive than quinine from the cinchona tree.
   - Natural quinine was used to combat malaria until more effective drugs were created.
   - In the seventeenth century, people used quinine to fight malaria.

Quinine

2 The first effective drug to fight malaria was quinine, made from the bark of the cinchona tree, a native of South America. Long used by the Quechua Indians of Peru, quinine was employed as an antimalarial from the seventeenth century to the middle of the twentieth century, at which time it was largely replaced by more effective laboratory-created drugs. Nowadays, it is possible to create quinine itself entirely in the laboratory, although it is still less expensive to extract it from its natural plant source. However, quinine is no longer seen as one of the more effective drugs for the treatment of malaria.

SKILL BUILDER

Directions: *Work with a partner. Read the passage. Then, on the next page, match the answer choice in the left-hand column to its evaluation in the right-hand column.*

Quinine

1 Malaria is a disease caused by parasites and spread by mosquitoes. The existence of different strains of the disease means that it must be combated by different drugs and treatments. In addition, strains of malaria become resistant to some drugs over time, necessitating the development of new treatments.

2 The first effective drug to fight malaria was quinine, made from the bark of the cinchona tree, a native of South America. Long used by the Quechua Indians of Peru, quinine was employed as an antimalarial from the seventeenth century to the middle of the twentieth century, at which time it was largely replaced by more effective laboratory-created drugs. Nowadays, it is possible to create quinine itself entirely in the laboratory, although it is still less expensive to extract it from its natural plant source. However, quinine is no longer seen as one of the more effective drugs for the treatment of malaria.

Which of the sentences below best expresses the essential information in the highlighted sentence in paragraph 2?

___ 1. The Quechua Indians of Peru got jobs by selling quinine as a drug to treat malaria.

___ 2. Quinine can be made in a laboratory now, but it is more expensive than quinine from the cinchona tree.

___ 3. Natural quinine was used to combat malaria until more effective drugs were created.

___ 4. In the seventeenth century, people used quinine to fight malaria.

Ⓐ The information is accurate, but it does not include the most important ideas.

Ⓑ This is the best restatement of the highlighted sentence.

Ⓒ The information isn't an accurate restatement.

Ⓓ The information is accurate, but is from a different sentence.

The highlighted sentence from the passage is long, and almost always is made up of several clauses and phrases. To understand its meaning, follow these steps:

- Examine one part of the sentence at a time.
- Make a mental note of what each part means.
- Eliminate words or phrases that don't communicate important information.

In the Skill Builder text about quinine, look at how this sentence can be divided:

Nowadays, it is possible to create quinine itself entirely in the laboratory, although it is still cheaper to extract it from its natural plant source.

Nowadays	(not very important)
it is possible to create quinine entirely in the laboratory	you can make quinine in a lab
although it is still less expensive to extract it from its natural plant source	but it's cheaper from plants

EXPRESS TIP

To logically divide a sentence into smaller pieces:

- check before and after commas
- consider prepositional phrases (*of the more effective drugs; for the treatment of malaria*)

Skill Builder Answers: 1. c; 2. d; 3. b; 4. a

PRACTICE

Directions: *Read the passages. Then mark the correct answers to the questions.*

Passage 1 (Questions 1–2)

Tulip Mania

1 Tulips, a member of the *Liliaceae* family, are a simple-looking plant: growing from a **bulb**, they normally have one brightly colored flower whose shape resembles a cup, atop a long stem, and a few straight green leaves that grow nearly vertically. A simple plant, perhaps, but one with a history as colorful as its blooms.

2 Even today, tulips are associated with Holland, a region in the Netherlands, although they were first cultivated by the Ottoman Empire (today's Turkey and, at its height, several neighboring countries). The exact date of the introduction of the tulip to northwestern Europe isn't known, although we do know it occurred around the latter half of the sixteenth century. 1594 is commonly accepted as the year when tulips first bloomed in Holland, however, and they caught on quickly. Gardeners became obsessed with cultivating new colors and patterns, especially stripes. The trend spread to the middle and upper classes. Prices for tulips soared, reaching thousands and even tens of thousands of dollars for a single bulb of the more desired varieties. People bought and sold items using tulip bulbs as a form of currency, and tulips were listed on the **Amsterdam** stock exchange. Some people sold their homes in order to have sufficient amounts of money available to invest in tulip trading.

3 By 1636, though, prices began to fall. Now people couldn't sell their tulips for the amounts of money they had anticipated. Not only individuals, but the economy of Holland suffered and did not recover for several years.

Glossary

bulb: A short, thick, underground stem of some plants.

Amsterdam: Capital city of the Netherlands.

1. Which of the sentences below best expresses the essential information in the highlighted sentence in paragraph 1?
   Ⓐ The history of tulips is simple.
   Ⓑ Tulips have an interesting history.
   Ⓒ The more colorful a flower is, the more interesting its history is.
   Ⓓ Tulips are not as simple as they first appear.

2. Which of the sentences below best expresses the essential information in the highlighted sentence in paragraph 2?
   Ⓐ People preferred to buy the more expensive types of tulips.
   Ⓑ Striped tulips cost more than any other variety.
   Ⓒ The cost of some tulip bulbs became surprisingly expensive.
   Ⓓ Having many different kinds of tulip bulbs became increasingly important.

Passage 2 (Questions 3–4)

Day Traders

1 Day traders are individuals who buy and sell a variety of financial instruments such as stocks, **futures**, and currencies. Their transactions begin and end during a single business day. Depending on the personality of the trader and the types of trades made, day traders may make only a few trades per day or several hundred.

2 Originally, most day traders worked for companies such as banks, which had access to market data and sophisticated equipment; such a trader is called an institutional trader. However, the decrease in price and the increase in speed and power of personal computers have made this type of work more available to more people, leading to a boom in the number of independent day traders, or retail traders. A retail trader generally uses his or her own capital, although some also manage money for other people. Some countries limit the amount of others' money that a retail trader can handle and how they may advertise.

3 A subgroup of traders are the auto-traders, so called because they engage in automated trading through the use of sophisticated computer software. This type of trading is also known as high-frequency trading (because of the speed at which transactions occur) or **algorithmic** trading (because of its use of computer algorithms).

Glossary

futures: Contracts traded on an exchange in which someone agrees to buy or sell a quantity of a bulk commodity (such as corn) in the future at an agreed-upon date and price.

algorithmic: Following a complex set of rules to calculate a function.

3. Which of the sentences below best expresses the essential information in the highlighted sentence in paragraph 2?
   (A) Cheaper and faster computers increased the number of retail traders.
   (B) These days, people can choose whether to be independent traders or retail traders.
   (C) Computers are less expensive and more efficient than they used to be.
   (D) Independent day traders have learned to carry out the work on their own, without depending on computers.

4. Which of the sentences below best expresses the essential information in the highlighted sentence in paragraph 3?
   (A) Most day traders have become overly dependent on automated means of trading.
   (B) Day trading in the automotive industry is almost entirely done by computer.
   (C) Most traders who are working today are auto-traders.
   (D) Some day traders carry out all of their transactions automatically by computer.

SKILLS REVIEW

Reading Skills 1 and 2: Understanding Vocabulary from Context and Paraphrasing a Sentence

Directions: *Read the passage. Then mark the correct answers to the questions.*

Frescoes

1 Fresco, from the Italian word *affresco*, meaning "fresh," refers to painting techniques used on plaster. Popular during the Renaissance period (around A.D. 1300–1600), especially in Italy, frescos were used to decorate walls and ceilings of churches, public buildings, and private homes with expansive murals.

2 The purest type of fresco painting, also known as *buon fresco*, or "true fresco," involves mixing pigments directly with wet plaster. The color is thus actually part of the material, rather than a coating on top of it, as is the case with *fresco a secco* ("dry fresco") or with regular painting. Famous examples of true fresco include the Bull-Leaping Fresco in the Great Palace in Knossos, Crete (created by an anonymous artist), and Michelangelo's frescoes on the ceiling and back wall of the Sistine Chapel in Vatican City.

3 The colors of a true fresco are especially vibrant and long lasting; the Bull-Leaping Fresco was created sometime during the seventeenth to fifteenth century B.C., but the colors are still clear today. However, this technique is not without its unique disadvantages. For one thing, colors look different when they are wet from how they do when they are dry. Artists of the time typically mixed their own plaster and color mixtures, and made up one batch at a time, working quickly to finish a section of a mural before the plaster dried. The mixture they created the next time might be a slightly different shade. If you look carefully at the frescoes on the Sistine Chapel, you can see which sections must have been completed in a single session by the faint differences in colors.

4 *Fresco a secco* requires something to be added to the paint to make it stick to the dry plaster; common binders include egg, oil, or glue. This technique is sometimes used to repair a *buon fresco* that has been damaged, although the colors are generally not as bright. However, some colors actually worked better with the dry fresco. During the Renaissance period, the available pigments for creating blue did not mix well with wet plaster; for this reason, skies, water, and blue clothing sometimes were painted as *secco* frescoes after the *buon* fresco had dried.

5 Given that with a fresco, the painting and the wall are now the same thing, naturally any damage to a wall will damage or destroy the fresco as well. Perhaps the most notable modern example of this was the destruction of the frescos by Giotto in the **basilica** of St. Francis in Assisi, Italy, in an earthquake in 1997. Chunks of plaster fell from the ceilings and walls, and many people judged the damage to the frescoes irreparable. However, a team of 150 restorers, many of whom were volunteers, spent five years gathering the pieces that they could find and assembling them, much like a giant jigsaw puzzle. The restoration, completed in 2002, featured 60,000 pieces of plaster set back into place, much like a mosaic. About 35 percent of the fresco remains incomplete.

Glossary

basilica: A shape of building, often used as a church, with a rounded central area at one or both ends and a long middle section.

1. The word expansive in the passage is closest in meaning to
   Ⓐ ancient
   Ⓑ large
   Ⓒ public
   Ⓓ costly

2. The word vibrant in the passage could best be replaced by
   Ⓐ bright
   Ⓑ moving
   Ⓒ watery
   Ⓓ rare

3. Which of the sentences below best expresses the essential information in the highlighted sentence in paragraph 3?
   Ⓐ Fresco mixtures dried quickly, so they were made in small amounts.
   Ⓑ Painters took a long time creating their unique colors.
   Ⓒ *Buon fresco* is more difficult for the artist than *secco fresco*.
   Ⓓ After a mixture of fresco dried, it couldn't be used.

4. The word notable in the passage is closest in meaning to
   Ⓐ fighting
   Ⓑ misunderstood
   Ⓒ satisfying
   Ⓓ significant

5. Which of the sentences below best expresses the essential information in the highlighted sentence in paragraph 5?
   Ⓐ Five years after the earthquake, the fresco looked like new.
   Ⓑ Most of the people who worked on the project were not paid.
   Ⓒ A group of people were eventually able to repair most of the damage.
   Ⓓ The repair process was too confusing to be successful.

READING SKILLS 3 AND 4

RECOGNIZING REFERENTS; INSERTING A SENTENCE INTO THE PASSAGE

Reading Skill 3: Recognizing Referents

A referent is a word that *refers to* another word or phrase.

The TOEFL iBT Test asks you to look at a highlighted pronoun in the reading passage and find the noun or noun phrase to which it refers, or its referent. In other words, the referent noun means the same thing as the pronoun. For example, in the following sentence, the pronoun "they" refers back to the plural noun "Americans":

Referent NOUN **pronoun**

Americans today sleep 20 percent less than ***they*** *did in the past.*

The highlighted pronoun will usually refer back to a noun or noun phrase that comes **before** it in the passage. Note that the noun or noun phrase might *not* be *the closest one* to the pronoun in the sentence. It might, in fact, be located in previous sentences. In the following example, you will notice that the pronoun "them" refers back to the noun phrase "Mormyrid fish" in the previous sentence:

Mormyrid fish create a field of electricity around their bodies. This helps guide ***them*** *through the water.*

All types of pronouns may be highlighted in the passages, including:

- reflexive (*itself/herself/themselves*)
- possessive (*its/hers/theirs*)
- demonstrative (*this/that/these/those*)
- indefinite (*one/few/many/some/others*)
- relative (*who/whose/which/that*)
- possessive adjectives (*his/hers/its/theirs*)

Other referent expressions may also be used: *then* = time *there* = place

Generally, there will be only one or two questions about referents per passage. Some passages might not contain any. A question about a referent includes the verb "refers to":

- The word **she** in paragraph 1 *refers to*
- The word **who** in paragraph 2 *refers to*
- The word **there** in paragraph 3 *refers to*
- The phrase **the other one** in paragraph 4 *refers to*

To find the correct answer, scan backwards from the highlighted pronoun in the passage and try to replace it with the noun or noun phrase that means the same thing. Use the context around the pronoun to help you choose the best answer.

EXPRESS TIP

When the highlighted pronoun is plural, it refers to a plural noun (more than one person, thing, or action). Remember that a plural noun referent can consist of two or more singular nouns connected with "and":

*A topic sentence consists of a general idea and a controlling idea. **These** are the essential parts needed to create a good essay.*

Look at this example of a referent question on a computer screen:

EXAMPLE: Referent Question

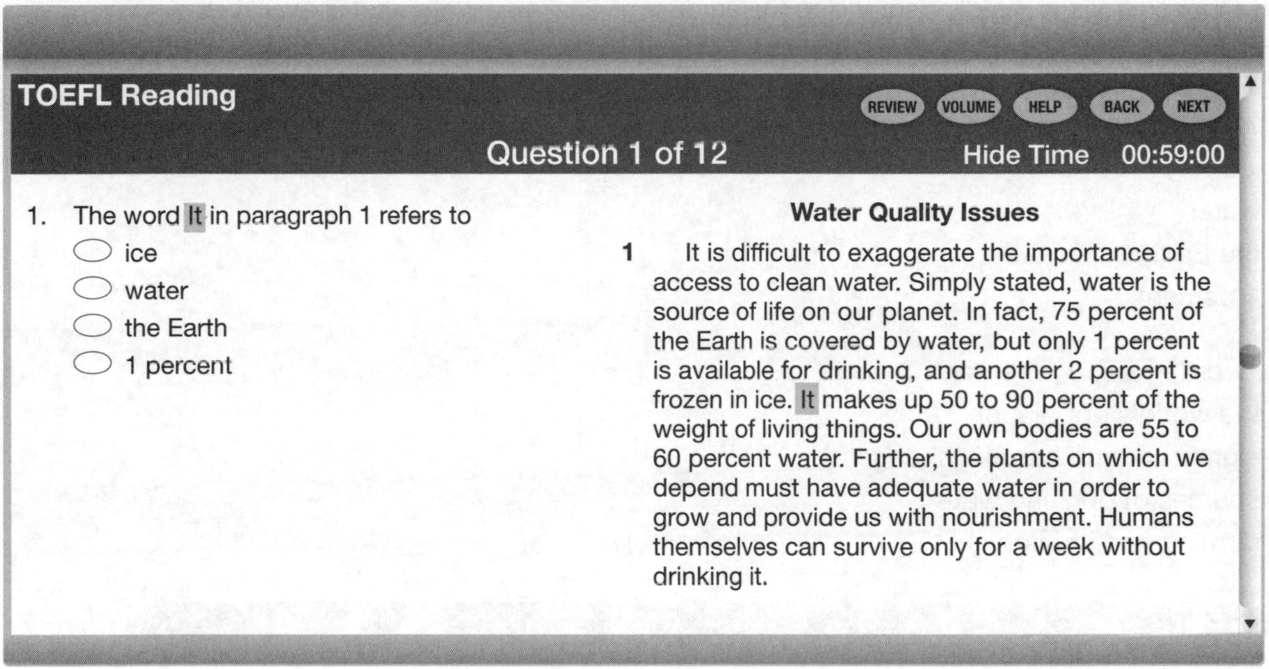
TOEFL Reading
REVIEW
VOLUME
HELP
BACK
NEXT
Question 1 of 12
Hide Time 00:59:00
1. The word It in paragraph 1 refers to
ice
water
the Earth
1 percent
Water Quality Issues
1 It is difficult to exaggerate the importance of access to clean water. Simply stated, water is the source of life on our planet. In fact, 75 percent of the Earth is covered by water, but only 1 percent is available for drinking, and another 2 percent is frozen in ice. It makes up 50 to 90 percent of the weight of living things. Our own bodies are 55 to 60 percent water. Further, the plants on which we depend must have adequate water in order to grow and provide us with nourishment. Humans themselves can survive only for a week without drinking it.

SKILL BUILDER

Directions: *Work with a partner. Read the passage and the questions. Circle the nouns or noun phrases in the passage below that the highlighted pronouns refer to. Then mark the correct answers.*

Water Quality Issues

1 It is difficult to exaggerate the importance of access to clean water. Simply stated, water is the source of life on our planet. In fact, 75 percent of the Earth is covered by water, but only 1 percent is available for drinking, and another 2 percent is frozen in ice. It makes up 50 to 90 percent of the weight of living things. Our own bodies are 55 to 60 percent water. Further, the plants on which we depend must have adequate water in order to grow and provide us with nourishment. Humans themselves can survive only for a week without drinking it.

2 However, as the world's population continues to grow, the need for more water increases. Farming and industry, which are using more water than ever before, are responsible for significant and harmful changes in the quality of water. Pollution from these and other sources is rapidly decreasing the amount of drinkable water that is available.

---

1. The word It in paragraph 1 refers to
   Ⓐ ice
   Ⓑ water
   Ⓒ the Earth
   Ⓓ 1 percent

2. The word these in paragraph 2 refers to
   Ⓐ the world's population
   Ⓑ significant and harmful changes
   Ⓒ sources of drinking water
   Ⓓ farming and industry

EXPRESS TIP

A longer phrase can also be used to refer back to a noun. For example:

Some teachers use "peer review" in their classrooms. *This approach* involves asking students to look at and comment on each others' work.

pronoun + noun = *this approach*
(refers back to the noun phrase "peer review")

Similar phrases include *his approach, another approach, their approaches.*

Skill Builder Answers:

1. **Answer B is correct** because the pronoun "It" refers back to "water" in the second sentence of paragraph 1. It does not make sense in the context of the sentence that "ice," "the Earth," or "1 percent" (answers A, C, and D) would make up "50 to 90 percent of the weight of living things."

2. **Answer D is correct** because "these" refers back to "farming and industry" in the second sentence of paragraph 2. Answer A is located too far away from the referent noun. Answers B and C do not make sense in the context of the sentence.

PRACTICE

Directions: *Read the passages. Then mark the correct answers to the questions.*

Passage 1 (Questions 1–3)

Wayne Thiebaud's Food Paintings

1 Wayne Thiebaud (pronounced "Tee-bow"), an American master of figurative painting, first gained an international reputation in the 1960s with his still-life paintings of food. Like many artists of the Pop Art period, such as Andy Warhol, he chose unusual subjects to portray. He is noted for **his** artistic power to take common, everyday objects and transform **them** into dramatic representations of modern popular culture. For example, a single ice-cream cone, removed from its ordinary surroundings and placed upon Thiebaud's canvas with rich, thick paint, suddenly takes on new importance and meaning.

2 In fact, Thiebaud's depictions of food, composed of simple shapes and painted in bold, brilliant colors, are among the most recognized of his paintings. Famous works such as *Pies, Pies, Pies* (1961) and *Around the Cake* (1962) easily appeal to viewers with **their** light humor, warmth, and sense of fun. However, it should not be forgotten that Thiebaud is considered by art critics to be a highly skilled painter in terms of his use of composition, brushstroke, color, and light and shadow.

---

1. The word **his** in paragraph 1 refers to
   - Ⓐ a reputation
   - Ⓑ Andy Warhol
   - Ⓒ an American
   - Ⓓ Wayne Thiebaud

2. The word **them** in paragraph 1 refers to
   - Ⓐ unusual subjects
   - Ⓑ paintings of food
   - Ⓒ common objects
   - Ⓓ dramatic representations

3. The word **their** in paragraph 2 refers to
   - Ⓐ famous works
   - Ⓑ brilliant colors
   - Ⓒ depictions of food
   - Ⓓ the viewers

Passage 2 (Questions 4–7)

The Silk Road

1 More than 2,000 years ago, early traders from Western Europe faced many hardships as they made their way along trade routes to the East. For these traders, most existing land routes made travel extremely slow and problematic. However, a system of roads was opened from the West to the East that made travel easier for many. This approximately 7,000-mile-long network of connecting roads came to be known as the Silk Road, so named by Western peoples because the silk carried on the route was what they most valued. Beginning near the Mediterranean coast and stretching all the way to China, it was the first transcontinental highway in the ancient world to link such a large number of different cultures. A variety of precious goods besides silk was also carried on the long, dangerous journey over the road—everything from gold, glass, and iron to exotic plants and animals.

2 This route, opened in the second century B.C., cut through boiling hot deserts and rugged mountains. The Silk Road crossed through a number of independent lands, but the Parthian territories were especially troubling. Once the traders arrived there, the local government made them pay large amounts of money to pass through. In addition, a single group could not make the whole trip, so several merchants carried the goods for trading at different stages along the Silk Road. A merchant might take goods from one trading station to another and return home, or travel a longer distance to an established town. Each one, of course, charged a price, thus raising the final cost of the goods. Although the Silk Road didn't offer the easiest journey, it did manage to prosper until more efficient sea-trading routes came into use in the seventeenth century.

---

4. The word many in paragraph 1 refers to
   - Ⓐ hardships
   - Ⓑ land routes
   - Ⓒ traders
   - Ⓓ trade routes

5. The phrase this route in paragraph 2 refers to
   - Ⓐ the journey
   - Ⓑ the Mediterranean coast
   - Ⓒ the ancient world
   - Ⓓ the Silk Road

6. The word there in paragraph 2 refers to
   Ⓐ hot deserts
   Ⓑ Parthian territories
   Ⓒ rugged mountains
   Ⓓ China

7. The phrase Each one in paragraph 2 refers to
   Ⓐ a merchant
   Ⓑ a group
   Ⓒ a trading station
   Ⓓ a town

Reading Skill 4: Inserting a Sentence into the Passage

On the TOEFL iBT Test, you will be asked to insert a sentence into the passage in a specific location. The question will present **an additional sentence, not in the paragraph,** that you must add to the passage. On the computer screen, you will see four small black boxes or squares [■] between the sentences in one paragraph of the reading passage. To answer the question, click on the square [■] where you think the **bolded sentence** should be added. That sentence will appear there. You can move the sentence by clicking on another black square [■] in a different location.

When a reading passage does include a sentence insertion question, there is usually only one per passage. The following is an example of this type of question:

> *Look at the four squares [■] that indicate where the following sentence could be added to the passage.*
>
> ***Xxxxx xx xxxxxx xxxxx xxxxx.***
> **(sentence to be added in bold)**
>
> *Where would the sentence best fit into the passage/paragraph? Click on a square [■] to add the sentence to the passage/paragraph.*

To find the correct answer, read the **bolded** sentence in the question, and scan the sentences **before** and **after** the squares [■] to find clues in the organization and context.

Finding the best place to add the sentence depends on the surrounding context and other clues. Understanding how a reading passage is organized is also very helpful. Most passages have a logical order of information: what comes first, second, third, and so on. The sentence you choose as the correct answer should logically connect an idea in that sentence to the ideas in other sentences before and after it.

Use connectors or other types of signal words that show relationships between ideas to decide where to insert the bolded sentence.

- Time or a sequence of steps: *first*, *second*, *then*, *next*, *before*, *after*, *finally*, *since*, *when*, *as a result of*, *consequently*, *therefore*
- Comparison: *compared to*, *both*, *like*, *the same as*, *similarly*, *equal to*, *more than*, *less than*
- Contrast: *unlike*, *not*, *but*, *although*, *despite*, *however*, *in contrast*, *on the other hand*, *instead*

Look at how connectors can help you understand where to insert the bolded sentence:

The human eye has one set of lenses, and they do <u>the same</u> job <u>as</u> the camera's lens. **<u>In contrast</u>, insects have "compound" eyes that contain many tiny lenses.** They are clustered together and each lens "sees" a small part of the scene. <u>Consequently</u>, the insect's brain must bring all of these thousands of tiny pictures together to form an image.

EXPRESS TIP

Scan the sentences before and after the squares [■] to find synonyms, repeated words, and pronouns that refer to nouns or noun phrases (referents) that match words in the **bolded sentence**. Look at how all these clues can work together to help you find the right location to insert the sentence:

<u>Teepees</u> look like large *tents.* ***Teepees are made up of long sticks of wood crossed together in the center and covered with buffalo skins.*** *Because of* their *simple design, <u>teepees</u> are very lightweight.*

Look at this example of a sentence insertion question on a computer screen:

EXAMPLE: Inserting a Sentence into the Passage Question

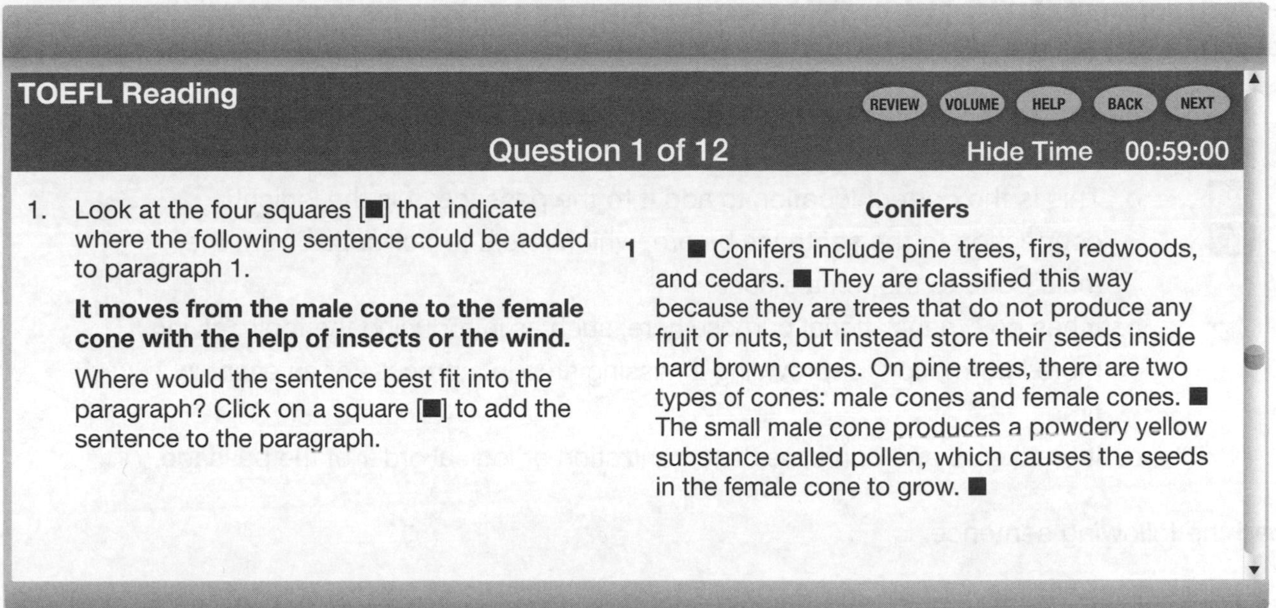

SKILL BUILDER

Directions: *Work with a partner. Read the passage. Look at the exercises that follow. Discuss why or why not the inserted sentence could fit in each square, and then answer the questions.*

Conifers

1 **1A** Conifers include pine trees, firs, redwoods, and cedars. **1B** They are classified this way because they are trees that do not produce any fruit or nuts, but instead store their seeds inside hard brown cones. On pine trees, there are two types of cones: male cones and female cones. **1C** The small male cone produces a powdery yellow substance called pollen, which causes the seeds in the female cone to grow. **1D**

2 It usually takes two or three years for the seeds inside a cone to develop completely. When the seeds are ready, the pinecone opens, allowing its seeds to fall out. **2A** A pinecone will open only at certain times of the year because pine tree seeds distribute best in good weather. **2B** However, pinecones close in wet or rainy conditions, keeping their seeds inside. **2C** In some cases, the cones of certain species of pines will open only during a forest fire, because the fire will clear away other plants that might compete with a young pine tree. **2D**

---

1. Read the following sentence:

   It moves from the male cone to the female cone with the help of insects or the wind.

   For each square (1A, 1B, 1C, or 1D), decide whether the sentence fits there. Match the reason with the square.

   ___ 1A
   ___ 1B
   ___ 1C
   ___ 1D

   a. It does not contain grammatical or contextual clues to connect it to the sentence before or after.
   b. This is the correct location to add it to the passage; it is the logical connection to the sentence before, which refers to pollination from the male cone to the female cone.
   c. It has no organizational purpose here, such as introducing the topic, giving more information, or providing a missing step in a process or an event in time.
   d. It breaks up and confuses the organization or logical order of the passage.

2. Read the following sentence:

   When it is warm and dry, the cone will open, allowing the wind to carry the seeds away.

   For each square (2A, 2B, 2C, or 2D), decide whether the sentence fits there. Match the reason with the square.

   ___ 2A
   ___ 2B
   ___ 2C
   ___ 2D

   a. It does not contain grammatical or contextual clues to connect it to the sentence before or after.
   b. This is the correct location to add it to the passage; it is the logical connection to the sentence before, which refers to the pinecone opening, and the sentence after, which refers to certain times of the year with good weather.
   c. It has no organizational purpose here, such as introducing the topic, giving more information, or providing a missing step in a process or an event in time.
   d. It breaks up and confuses the organization or logical order of the passage.

EXPRESS TIP

Check your answer to make sure it fits logically into the passage: Quickly read the sentence *before* the inserted sentence, then *the inserted sentence*, and finally the sentence *after*.

Skill Builder Answers:

1A – c   1B – a   1C – d   1D – b
2A – b   2B – a   2C – d   2D – c

PRACTICE

Directions: *Read the passages. Then mark the correct answers to the questions.*

Passage 1 (Questions 1–2)

Bengal Tigers

1 Bengal tigers, the largest members of the cat family, are magnificent creatures. They live in India, where they are the most common tiger. [1A] They can weigh up to 583 pounds (264 kilograms) and live as long as 26 years in the wild. [1B] Their vision is six times better than a human's. [1C] One of the reasons for this is the mirror-like layer in the back of their eyes that reflects extra light. However, hearing is their sharpest sense. [1D] In addition, the unique pattern of stripes on their bodies acts as camouflage, making it difficult for their prey to see them in the shadows of tall grasses. This enables the tigers to hide very effectively.

2 All these physical advantages make Bengal tigers extremely powerful and clever hunters. [2A] Then, at the last minute, they spring and launch a surprise attack. [2B] These tigers are absolute carnivores; they hunt medium- to large-sized animals, such as goats, deer, or buffalo. It is estimated that they can eat as much as 60 pounds (27 kilograms) in a single night. [2C] Unfortunately, however, their numbers have been greatly reduced in the wild due to hunting by humans and the loss of natural habitat. [2D]

---

1. Look at the four squares [■] that indicate where the following sentence could be added to paragraph 1.

   The tigers' rather large, cup-shaped ears allow them to concentrate on even the softest sounds from far away, giving them extremely sensitive hearing.

   Where would the sentence best fit into the paragraph? Circle the square [1A], [1B], [1C], or [1D] where the sentence should be added to the paragraph.

2. Look at the four squares [■] that indicate where the following sentence could be added to paragraph 2.

   Like most cats, they move very slowly and quietly toward their prey until they are very close.

   Where would the sentence best fit into the paragraph? Circle the square [2A], [2B], [2C], or [2D] where the sentence should be added to the paragraph.

Passage 2 (Questions 3–5)

Motivation

1 **3A** Motivation is the force that inspires us to do something: pass an examination, get a better job, or climb the highest mountain in the world. Psychology offers us many theoretical approaches for explaining what motivates us. At the most basic level is the "drive-reduction approach." **3B** We usually try to reduce these needs by finding ways to fulfill them. If you are hungry before dinnertime, you might eat a snack to relieve that feeling of hunger. **3C** However, this approach does not sufficiently explain the motivation behind more complex behaviors. **3D**

2 "Cognitive approaches" propose that we do things because of the way we think about the world, the goals we wish to achieve, and our expectations. **4A** There are two separate types of behavior related to the cognitive approaches: *intrinsic motivation* and *extrinsic motivation*. The former motivation means that we do something just because we like doing it, not because we think it will lead to some kind of future reward, praise, or honor. **4B** For example, an intrinsically motivated student might read extra materials not to get better grades, but just because the topic is interesting. **4C** This can be seen in the case of an extrinsically motivated employee who agrees to relocate for higher wages even though it means living in a new city that he doesn't particularly like. **4D**

3 **5A** Interestingly, psychological studies suggest that we are more likely to push ourselves harder and do our best work when we do it for our own enjoyment or simply because it is interesting or personally challenging to us. **5B** That is, when we are intrinsically motivated. However, it is believed that if we become more extrinsically motivated by external rewards, we may find that our intrinsic motivation is significantly lowered. This is especially true when a person thinks that the extrinsic motivators—better job conditions or more vacation time—are controlled by other people. **5C** For instance, when an employee discovers that to get an important promotion, his boss insists that he work very long hours, he may begin to lose motivation. **5D**

---

3. Look at the four squares [■] that indicate where the following sentence could be added to paragraph 1.

   This approach relates to our most fundamental biological needs: hunger, thirst, sleep, and so on.

   Where would the sentence best fit into the paragraph? Circle the square **3A**, **3B**, **3C**, or **3D** where the sentence should be added to the paragraph.

4. Look at the four squares [■] that indicate where the following sentence could be added to paragraph 2.

   On the other hand, extrinsic motivation compels us to do something because there *is* an external reward: a better test score or more money.

   Where would the sentence best fit into the paragraph? Circle the square **4A**, **4B**, **4C**, or **4D** where the sentence should be added to the paragraph.

5. Look at the four squares [■] that indicate where the following sentence could be added to paragraph 3.

The result of this employee's lost motivation is that his job performance may suffer.

Where would the sentence best fit into the paragraph? Circle the square 5A, 5B, 5C, or 5D where the sentence should be added to the paragraph.

SKILLS REVIEW

Reading Skills 3 and 4: Recognizing Referents and Inserting a Sentence into the Passage

Directions: *Read the passage. Then mark the correct answers to the questions.*

Frank Lloyd Wright's Guggenheim Museum in New York City

1 Born in 1867, Frank Lloyd Wright, one of the most famous American architects, had already designed his first building in 1886 at the age of 19. 1A His ability to incorporate natural, organic elements into the design of interior and exterior spaces transformed the field of architecture. One his most notable and innovative projects, completed in 1939, was Fallingwater, a home built over a waterfall and surrounded by a mountain forest. A significant challenge came in 1943, however, when he was asked to build a museum in New York City for displaying Solomon R. Guggenheim's art collection. 1B By this time in his long career, Wright had a well-developed architectural style and philosophy. 1C Therefore, he was not pleased about designing a museum to be built in New York City because he thought it was already too crowded with people. 1D In his opinion, there were too many buildings in the city, many of them with little architectural value.

2 However, a corner location at Fifth Avenue and 89th Street was eventually chosen as the site for the Guggenheim Museum. Wright favored this location because it was close to the natural setting of Central Park. It would not be as noisy and populated as other parts of the city. 2A Once the location was chosen, Wright began creating a unique design that reflected both nature and bold modern forms. The project immediately became a complex and difficult struggle. In contrast to Wright's courageous and adventuresome client, Mr. Guggenheim, there were many, from city officials and art critics, who did not particularly like Wright's plan for the museum. 2B Some worried that the building's unusual arrangement and powerful design would compete with the art for the viewer's attention. 2C In other words, the reason for this fear was that people would pay more attention to the museum's architecture than they would to the art. 2D

continued . . .

3 The Guggenheim Museum, unlike the 1880s Metropolitan Museum of Art at the eastern edge of Central Park, is not a typical, square-shaped art museum with separate rooms or galleries for displaying art. 3A From the outside, it looks like a thin piece of paper winding around and around or like the layers of a cake, one on top of the other. 3B Inside the building, the floors are not separated in the usual way by stairs. In fact, there aren't any to climb; art viewers in the Guggenheim move on a flat, circular ramp or walkway around the curved walls of the building where the art is hung. 3C They can see the art from different angles as they slowly wind to the top. The center area, which the ramp twists around, is an open space or well. 3D The roof of the Guggenheim Museum is capped by a multi-paned, round glass dome which allows natural light into the building.

4 4A He died at age 92 in 1959 only a few months before the construction was finished. 4B Despite his critics and the controversy that surrounded the museum's design, Wright broke away from the traditions of fixed, geometric design by using an "organic" style that flowed naturally and blended more easily with the environment in Central Park. This strong-willed architect was able to create a building that was like no other in its time. 4C Today, the Guggenheim Museum is considered to be one of Wright's most expressive buildings, and definitely the most important evidence of his architectural genius during the last years of his career. 4D

---

1. The phrase this time in paragraph 1 refers to
   Ⓐ 1867
   Ⓑ 1886
   Ⓒ 1939
   Ⓓ 1943

2. Look at the four squares [■] that indicate where the following sentence could be added to paragraph 1.

   According to these long-held approaches and ideas, he strongly believed that buildings should be constructed in a natural setting and fit into the nature around them.

   Where would the sentence best fit into the paragraph? Circle the square 1A, 1B, 1C, or 1D where the sentence should be added to the paragraph.

3. The word who in paragraph 2 refers to
   Ⓐ Frank Lloyd Wright
   Ⓑ Mr. Guggenheim
   Ⓒ city officials and art critics
   Ⓓ a client

4. Look at the four squares [■] that indicate where the following sentence could be added to paragraph 2.

   Among the general public, too, there was considerable disagreement about the plan.

   Where would the sentence best fit into the paragraph? Circle the square 2A, 2B, 2C, or 2D where the sentence should be added to the paragraph.

5. The word any in paragraph 3 refers to
   Ⓐ layers
   Ⓑ stairs
   Ⓒ walls
   Ⓓ floors

6. Look at the four squares [■] that indicate where the following sentence could be added to paragraph 3.

   Instead of the box-shaped and traditional structures of such museums, the Guggenheim, completed in 1959, is a round, bowl-shaped building.

   Where would the sentence best fit into the paragraph? Circle the square 3A, 3B, 3C, or 3D where the sentence should be added to the paragraph.

7. The word other in paragraph 4 refers to
   Ⓐ an architect
   Ⓑ a building
   Ⓒ an environment
   Ⓓ a style

8. Look at the four squares [■] that indicate where the following sentence could be added to paragraph 4.

   Unfortunately, Wright never saw the completed museum.

   Where would the sentence best fit into the paragraph? Circle the square 4A, 4B, 4C, or 4D where the sentence should be added to the paragraph.

READING SKILLS 5 AND 6

UNDERSTANDING DETAIL AND FACT QUESTIONS; UNDERSTANDING NEGATIVE FACT QUESTIONS

Reading Skill 5: Understanding Detail and Fact Questions

Detail and *fact* questions ask you to find true, specific information given in the passage.

They do *not* ask you to draw conclusions or make inferences.

There are more detail and fact questions than other types on the TOEFL iBT Test. They appear in the order in which the information is mentioned in the passage; that is, a question about information in the first paragraph will come before a question about information in the second paragraph. Often (although not always), the question will tell you where the answer is located:

- ***According to*** *paragraph 1, . . .*
- *It is* ***mentioned*** *in paragraph 2 that . . .*
- *What is* ***stated*** *in paragraph 3 about . . .*
- *It is* ***indicated*** *in paragraph 4 that . . .*

The correct answer choice does not always give the information in exactly the same words. It may use synonyms for key words, or state the same information in a different way. You need to find the same *meaning* in the original passage, but not necessarily the same *words*.

EXPRESS TIP

Detail and fact questions are very specific. They ask questions about dates, numbers, names, and reasons, *not* main ideas.

How many species of wolves are currently endangered?

Look at this example of a detail and fact question on a computer screen.

EXAMPLE: Detail and Fact Question

TOEFL Reading

REVIEW VOLUME HELP BACK NEXT

Question 1 of 12

Hide Time 00:59:00

1. According to paragraph 1, why do Americans sleep less today than in the past?
   - They aren't as healthy as they used to be.
   - People today don't need as much sleep.
   - They suffer from more stress.
   - They eat later at night.

Sleep

1 Some scientists claim that Americans today sleep 20 percent less than they did in the past. A few reasons for this lack of sleep are that Americans now work longer hours and are driving longer distances to get to their jobs. This can cause stress that makes it difficult for them to sleep well. In addition, it leads to bad habits such as drinking too much coffee to stay awake or having a late meal.

SKILL BUILDER

Directions: *Work with a partner. Read the passage and the questions. Underline the sentence(s) in the passage that tell you the answers. Then mark the correct answers.*

Sleep

1 Some scientists claim that Americans today sleep 20 percent less than they did in the past. A few reasons for this lack of sleep are that Americans now work longer hours and are driving longer distances to get to their jobs. This can cause stress that makes it difficult for them to sleep well. In addition, it leads to bad habits such as drinking too much coffee to stay awake or having a late meal.

2 Doctors recommend that people get at least seven hours of sleep every night, but not everyone is sure how to get it. In fact, surveys show that many people get only six hours a night or even less. However, there are few recommendations that can help people get the sleep they need. You can reduce any stress that might keep you awake by listening to music or relaxing your muscles before sleeping. You will also sleep better if you don't eat anything heavy or drink coffee too close to your bedtime.

---

1. According to paragraph 1, why do Americans sleep less today than in the past?
   Ⓐ They aren't as healthy as they used to be.
   Ⓑ People today don't need as much sleep.
   Ⓒ They suffer from more stress.
   Ⓓ They eat later at night.

2. It is mentioned in paragraph 2 that most people need to sleep every night for
   Ⓐ six hours or less
   Ⓑ seven hours or more
   Ⓒ at least eight hours
   Ⓓ about ten hours

EXPRESS TIP

Remember that the correct answer is one that is given in the passage. Do not rely on your general knowledge! Use only information from the passage.

Skill Builder Answers:

1. **Answer C is correct.** The passage states "A few reasons for this lack of sleep are that Americans now work longer hours and are driving longer distances to get to their jobs. This can cause stress that makes it difficult for them to sleep." Answer A is incorrect because the passage states that not enough sleep leads to poor health—not that poor health leads to not sleeping as much. Answer B is incorrect because the passage says only that Americans do sleep less, not that they don't need as much sleep. In fact, much of the passage discusses how to get more sleep. Answer D is incorrect because although the passage does warn that eating heavy meals close to bedtime could interfere with your sleep, it does not state that Americans do this more now than in the past.

2. **Answer B is correct.** The passage states that "Doctors recommend that people get at least seven hours of sleep every night." "At least seven" means the same as "seven or more." Answer A is incorrect because six hours is less than the recommended seven. Answer C is incorrect because the passage states "at least seven," not "at least eight." Answer D is incorrect because seven hours or any amount over seven hours is recommended, but not only around ten hours.

PRACTICE

Directions: *Read the passages. Then mark the correct answers to the questions.*

Passage 1 (Questions 1–2)

Deserts

1 Deserts cover about one-third of the Earth and are growing larger each year. The largest hot desert in the world, measuring about 3.5 million square miles (about 9 million square kilometers), is the Sahara Desert in North Africa. However, deserts are not just places full of sand with extremely high temperatures. The Antarctic Desert is 5.4 million square miles (about 14 million square kilometers) and is covered by ice and snow. What determines a desert is how dry it is. Deserts are defined by the fact that they have little or no rainfall and, thus, don't have many plants growing in them. They receive less than 10 inches (25.4 centimeters) of rain in a year.

2 There are four major types of deserts: subtropical, coastal, winter, and polar. A subtropical desert, such as the Kalahari in Africa, is the hottest kind. Coastal deserts, like the Atacama in Chile, are cool due to the nearby ocean winds blowing onto the shore. The Taklamakan Desert in China is a good example of a winter desert. Temperatures in winter deserts vary widely by the season, from 100 degrees Fahrenheit (37.5 degrees Celsius) in the summer to 10 degrees Fahrenheit (–12.2 degrees Celsius) in the winter. Both the North and South Poles contain polar deserts. The Arctic Desert in the North Pole is very dry and cold because the water is locked up in ice.

---

1. It is stated in paragraph 1 that the Sahara Desert
   - Ⓐ covers one-third of Africa
   - Ⓑ is the largest hot desert
   - Ⓒ is 5.4 million square miles
   - Ⓓ is characterized by its cold temperatures

2. According to paragraph 2, why are some polar regions deserts?
   - Ⓐ They are located too far north to receive rain.
   - Ⓑ Ocean breezes blow away the moisture.
   - Ⓒ The temperature varies too greatly.
   - Ⓓ All the water is held inside ice.

Passage 2 (Questions 3–4)

Camera Movement

1 The brothers Louis and Auguste Lumière created the first films ever shown. These films of people doing ordinary, everyday tasks, such as working in their yards, might seem boring by today's standards because of their simplistic themes and camera movement. However, the first audience to view these films at an 1895 exhibition in Paris was amazed and excited by this new invention. Today, films or movies are so common worldwide that we no longer respond to them with the surprise of discovery. Usually, we don't even think about the camera movement that produces the action on the screen.

2 Camera movement during the filming of a movie happens in a number of ways. First, the camera itself is not actually moved, but rather, the focus of the lens is changed. The lens can change the focus from one character standing in the foreground to another character in the background. The lens can also zoom in to make distant objects appear larger and closer. In addition, the body of the camera can also be moved in relation to some kind of fixed supporting structure. *Panning*, for example, means the camera follows a moving person or an object in a sweep from left to right or right to left. *Tilting* refers to the vertical movement of the camera, from up to down or down to up. Other elements in movie camera movement are achieved when both the camera and the support system are moved around. Dollies, or small carts with wheels, are used to create a free-flowing movement. However, sometimes when the action is fast, filming may require an automobile or a large truck to move the camera around a larger area at a faster speed. Finally, for smoothly filming a large area, a specially designed crane or movable arm called a boom is used. The boom supports the camera, the camera operators, and the director as they move up and down, across, close in, or farther away while filming a scene.

---

3. According to paragraph 1, who was the audience for the first films ever shown?

   Ⓐ People working in their yards
   Ⓑ The Lumière brothers, Louis and Auguste
   Ⓒ Attendees at an exhibition in Paris in 1895
   Ⓓ People who don't think about camera movement

4. What ability of a camera lens is mentioned in paragraph 2?

   Ⓐ Making a small object seem bigger
   Ⓑ Following a moving person or animal
   Ⓒ Creating a free-flowing movement
   Ⓓ Following very fast action

Reading Skill 6: Understanding Negative Fact Questions

Negative fact questions ask you to find information in the reading passage that is

1. not mentioned, or
2. not true

The questions are easy to recognize because words such as NOT and EXCEPT are written in capital letters. The question will usually tell you which paragraph contains the information you need to answer the question.

- ***According** to paragraph 1, it is NOT true that telegraph wires*
- *What is NOT **indicated** in paragraph 2 about the fishing season?*
- ***All of the following** are true about Dorothy Sayers EXCEPT*
- *It is **indicated** in paragraph 4 that honey is NOT*

There are two types of incorrect answers for negative fact questions: those that include information not mentioned, and those that give information that isn't true.

Information not mentioned

The first type of negative fact question is not more difficult than other questions, but it can take longer to answer because you might have to check each answer choice to see if it's mentioned in the passage. You cannot just find one answer that is mentioned in the paragraph and be finished.

To find the correct answer, you must look for all of the answer choices in the original passage. If you find one, then it is *not* the correct answer. After you have found three, then you know that the single remaining answer choice is the correct one.

EXPRESS TIP

Be careful to answer based only on what is in the passage. An answer choice could be true, but still not mentioned.

Information that is not true

This second type of negative fact question usually tests details. The incorrect answers will be true, and the correct answer will be false.

These questions are a little faster to answer because as soon as you find information in an answer choice that is false, you have found the correct answer. However, you may still need to check several answer choices before you find the correct one.

Look at this example of a negative fact question on a computer screen.

EXAMPLE: Negative Fact Question

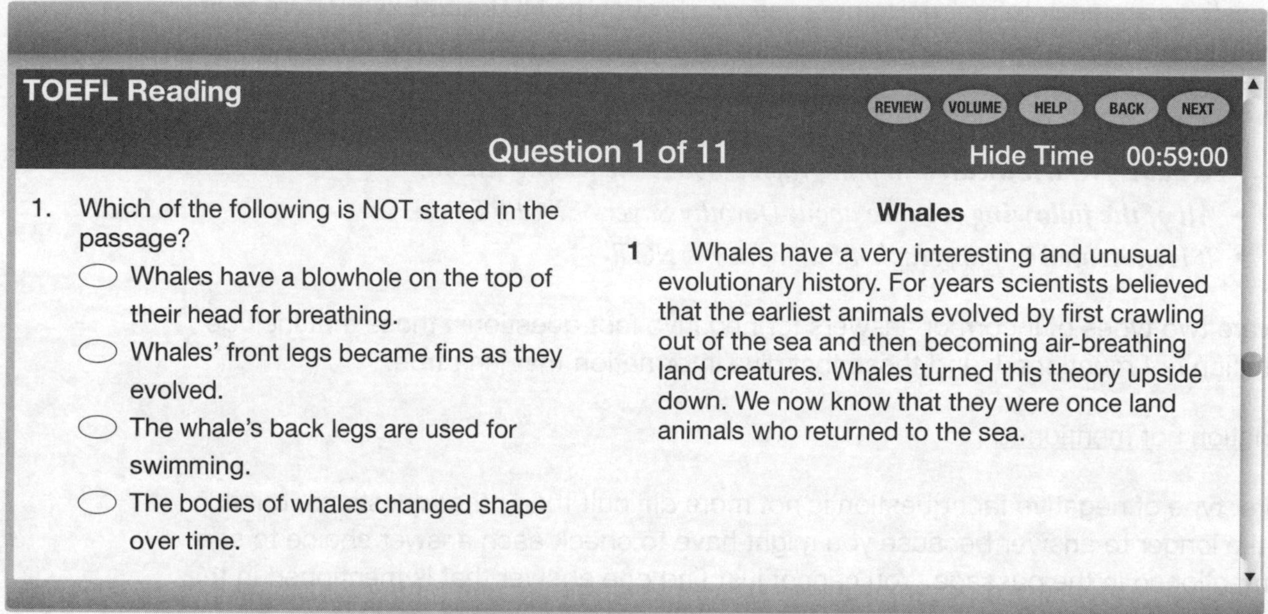

SKILL BUILDER

Directions: *Work with a partner. Read the passage and the questions. For #1, find the three answer choices that ARE mentioned in the passage, and underline the information in the passage. Then mark the correct answers for both questions.*

Whales

1 Whales have a very interesting and unusual evolutionary history. For years scientists believed that the earliest animals evolved by first crawling out of the sea and then becoming air-breathing land creatures. Whales turned this theory upside down. We now know that they were once land animals who returned to the sea.

2 The earliest ancestors of whales who walked on land were four-legged, meat-eating animals covered with fur or fine hair. However, nearly 50 million years ago, they learned to swim and eventually became giant ocean-dwelling creatures. Over a long period of time, whales' bodies grew longer and more fish-like in appearance. Their front legs grew shorter and became fins adapted for swimming, and their back legs disappeared from sight. It is interesting to note that even today, whales retain the tiny bones of their previous back legs inside their bodies. The nostrils in their noses moved to the top of their heads and became an air hole. The position of the air hole, or blowhole, allows the whale to barely break the surface of the water and get air without stopping or lifting its head out of the water.

---

1. Which of the following is NOT stated in the passage?

   Ⓐ Whales have a blowhole on the top of their head for breathing.
   Ⓑ Whales' front legs became fins as they evolved.
   Ⓒ The whale's back legs are used for swimming.
   Ⓓ The bodies of whales changed shape over time.

2. All of the following are true EXCEPT

   Ⓐ early ancestors of whales walked on four legs
   Ⓑ whales reversed scientific beliefs by returning to the land
   Ⓒ ancient whale-like animals learned to swim 50 million years ago
   Ⓓ the ancestors of whales ate meat

EXPRESS TIP

Don't just look for the same words in the answer choices and the passage. Sometimes different words are used to express the same meaning.

Whales have long been hunted as a source of meat and raw materials. =
People have killed whales for food and other substances.

hunted = killed
meat = food
raw materials = other substances

Skill Builder Answers:

1. **Answer C is correct.** The passage says only ". . . their back legs disappeared from sight," but does not say the back legs were ever used for swimming. Answer A is incorrect because the passage states, "The nostrils in their noses moved to the top of their heads and became an air hole. The position of the air hole, or blowhole, allows the whale to barely break the surface of the water and get air." Answer B is incorrect because the passage states "Over a long period of time . . . [t]heir front legs grew shorter and became fins adapted for swimming." Answer D is incorrect because the passage states, "Over a long period of time, whales' bodies grew longer and more fish-like in appearance."

2. **Answer B is correct.** The passage states, "We now know that they [whales] were once land animals who returned to the sea," not sea animals who returned to the land. Answer A is incorrect because the passage talks about "[t]he earliest ancestors of whales who walked on land . . ." Answer C is incorrect because the passage states, " . . . nearly 50 million years ago, they learned to swim . . ," Answer D is incorrect because the passage states "The earliest ancestors of whales who walked on land were . . . meat-eating animals . . ."

PRACTICE

Directions: *Read the passages. Then mark the correct answers to the questions.*

Passage 1 (Questions 1–2)

The Larynx

1 Our ability to speak depends to a large degree on the way we are built, on our unique human anatomy. Our mouth, lips, and tongue are very important physical features for producing the complicated sounds in words. They allow us more movement and flexibility than other species for shaping and producing specific sounds. In addition, our larynx (also known as the voice box), along with the epiglottis, which stops food from going down the windpipe, are essential for human speech. These bodily structures not only help us to make very exact sounds, but also let in a maximum amount of air. The larynx is responsible for the pitch (how high or low a sound is) and the volume (how loud a sound is). Unlike the larynx in other animals, the human larynx is situated low in the throat, which increases the type and variety of sounds that we can make, such as soft vowel sounds. However, it isn't always a perfect arrangement. Because the larynx is so low in our throats, we risk serious physical harm if we accidentally try to breathe and eat at the same time.

---

1. The passage mentions all of the following EXCEPT
   Ⓐ our mouth as an important part of our ability to make sounds
   Ⓑ the human tongue as an element in sound production
   Ⓒ the role of air movement in our nose for producing words
   Ⓓ the flexibility of our lips that allows us to shape specific sounds

2. Which of the following is NOT true?
   Ⓐ The larynx and the epiglottis are both vital for speech.
   Ⓑ The human voice box produces lower sounds than the voice box in other animals.
   Ⓒ The position of the human larynx makes certain vowel sounds possible.
   Ⓓ The epiglottis prevents food from going down our windpipe.

Passage 2 (Questions 3–4)

Rosemary

1 The rosemary plant (Latin name: *Rosmarinus officinalis*) commonly grows wild outdoors and is also a favorite among gardeners. Although rosemary originated in the area around the Mediterranean Sea, it grows in many countries throughout the world today. It is an upright evergreen bush that can grow to be over six feet tall. Its woody base has stiff, solid branches and rough skin. The leaves are long and thin, like small needles. Large numbers of the leaves grow closely together out of the branches. The pointed leaves are two-toned, dark green on the top and silver-white on the bottom. Rosemary also produces beautiful tiny pale blue or purple flowers. In warmer climates, rosemary can bloom all year long. Rosemary doesn't need much water, making it popular in dry areas; in fact, too much water can damage the plant.

2 Traditionally the rosemary plant was important for its role in homemade medicine that was used for treating many different kinds of illnesses. The leaves and flowers of the rosemary plant were used medicinally for muscle pain, headaches, stomach problems, memory loss, and to promote hair growth. It was once believed that sleeping with a bit of rosemary under one's pillow would prevent bad dreams. Today, the distinctive-smelling rosemary plant is widely used for adding fragrance to soap and other cosmetics and as a flavoring in cooking.

---

3. Which of the following is NOT mentioned as a characteristic of the rosemary plant?
   - Ⓐ It can withstand very hot weather.
   - Ⓑ It first grew in the Mediterranean.
   - Ⓒ Its leaves stay green all year.
   - Ⓓ The bush's flowers are blue or purple.

4. All of the following are true EXCEPT
   - Ⓐ its scent is used in modern cosmetics
   - Ⓑ people use rosemary to add flavor to food
   - Ⓒ both the leaves and flowers were used for medicines
   - Ⓓ eating too much rosemary can cause hair loss

SKILLS REVIEW

Reading Skills 5 and 6: Detail, Fact, and Negative Fact Questions

Directions: *Read the passage. Then mark the correct answers to the questions.*

History of the Computer

1 The first "computer," called an *abacus*, was invented 5,000 years ago. Still used by the Chinese today, this device allows the user to add or subtract numbers easily by moving beads on wires up and down. Like the abacus, all of the first "computers" could be considered calculators because they were designed to help people do math quickly without making many mistakes. Other early "computers" were invented in Europe by men like Blaise Pascal in 1642 and Charles Xavier Thomas de Colmar in 1694, both from France. Pascal's invention could add many large numbers together, and Colmar's machine could do all four of the basic mathematical operations; that is, it could add, subtract, multiply, and divide. As with all computers, the basic principle of these early machines was of turning mathematical language, such as numbers and equations, into mechanical and, later, electronic movements.

2 Charles Babbage's "analytical engine," designed in Britain in the 1830s, is thought to be the first real computer due to the fact that it could be given instructions. This made the "analytical engine" more functional and flexible than a calculator. The instructions—what we now call the computer's program—were originally paper cards with holes in them. The idea of using punched cards was borrowed from the French cloth-weaving industry, and the cards could be called the first computer software. The introduction of software is considered a very important addition because the software made the computer able to perform more tasks. Many of the major advances since then have involved enabling computers to do more varied jobs using an increasingly generalized set of instructions. The other important aspect of improvements in computers has involved the actual parts used to make them, called the hardware.

3 As computers of the twentieth century changed from being made mostly of mechanical parts, like gears and wheels, to being composed of electronic circuits, they became smaller. Computers built in the 1940s with **vacuum tubes** were enormous—large enough to fill half a soccer stadium—and those manufactured in the 1950s with **transistors** still occupied a large room. Transistors were next replaced with quartz microchips, which could store thousands of times more information in a very tiny space. This was an important innovation because it permitted the design of computers small enough to be used in the home on a desk. Finally, in 1981, IBM introduced the first personal computers, or PCs, and the reduced size and price of the computer made it attractive to individual consumers.

4 Nowadays, millions of companies and people use computers for many aspects of their personal and professional lives. In the future, with further advances in artificial intelligence, computers may become even less like machines and more like living creatures and even friends.

Glossary

vacuum tube: A sealed glass tube that allows the free passage of electric current.

transistor: A device that regulates current or voltage flow and acts as a switch or gate for electronic signals.

1. Which of the following is NOT mentioned about the abacus?
   Ⓐ Electronic versions are still used today.
   Ⓑ It was invented about 5,000 years ago.
   Ⓒ It was a type of calculator.
   Ⓓ People used it to calculate mathematical problems very quickly.

2. What is true about Colmar's machine, according to paragraph 1?
   Ⓐ It is still used in China today.
   Ⓑ It could perform the four basic functions necessary for math.
   Ⓒ It was used by moving beads up and down wires.
   Ⓓ It relied on electronic movements.

3. According to the passage, when was the first real computer probably invented?
   Ⓐ 1642
   Ⓑ 1694
   Ⓒ The 1830s
   Ⓓ The 1940s

4. According to paragraph 2, what was the first computer software?
   Ⓐ A specific set of instructions
   Ⓑ Moving parts
   Ⓒ Cloth with holes in it
   Ⓓ Paper cards

5. What is NOT stated in the passage as an advantage of electronic circuits over mechanical parts?
   Ⓐ They were much smaller in physical size.
   Ⓑ They allowed calculations to be made more quickly.
   Ⓒ They made it possible for a computer to sit on a desk.
   Ⓓ They caused the price of computers to fall.

READING SKILLS 7 AND 8

INFERRING INFORMATION; UNDERSTANDING RHETORICAL PURPOSE

Reading Skill 7: Inferring Information

Sometimes an idea is not stated directly in the reading passage. Instead, you must look at evidence that is given—facts, reasons, examples—and draw a conclusion based on that evidence. This is called *making an inference* or *inferring* information.

Be careful not to draw conclusions based on your own prior knowledge or opinions. Even though the information is not directly given, there is still some basis for the inference in the text itself. There is some logical reason to draw the inference.

For example, the sentence

The man put on a jacket, hat, and scarf because he was going outside.

implies that it is cold outside. That's why the man needs to put on extra warm clothes.

However, be careful not to infer too much. In the sentence above, we cannot infer that the season is winter. It could be a chilly day in another season, or the man might live somewhere that is cold even in summer.

The answer is only a reasonable and logical assumption based on the information you have. Don't, therefore, argue your way out of the correct answer. In the example sentence, it is possible—although highly unlikely—that someone told the man, "I will pay you $100 to put these things on and then go outside." But it is not a reasonable inference.

EXPRESS TIP

The same skills you use when figuring out the meaning of a vocabulary word from context can help you infer meaning from a sentence or several sentences. (See Unit 1.)

Inference questions on the TOEFL iBT Test use forms of words such as *likely*, *probably*, *infer*, *suggest*, or *imply* in constructions like these:

- *Which of the following can be* ***inferred*** *from paragraph 1?*
- *It can be* ***inferred*** *from paragraph 1 that sea lions*
- *What does the author* ***suggest*** *about sea lions?*
- *What do sea lions* ***probably*** *do in winter?*
- *What is* ***implied*** *about the hunting of sea lions?*

EXPRESS TIP

The correct answer might be active if the information in the passage is passive, or passive if the information in the passage is active. The same is true for positive and negative statements.

Sea lions can be found in both northern and southern oceans, with the exception of the northern Atlantic Ocean. (passive and positive) = *The Atlantic Ocean does not support sea lions.* (active and negative)

Look at this example of an inference question on a computer screen.

EXAMPLE: Inference Question

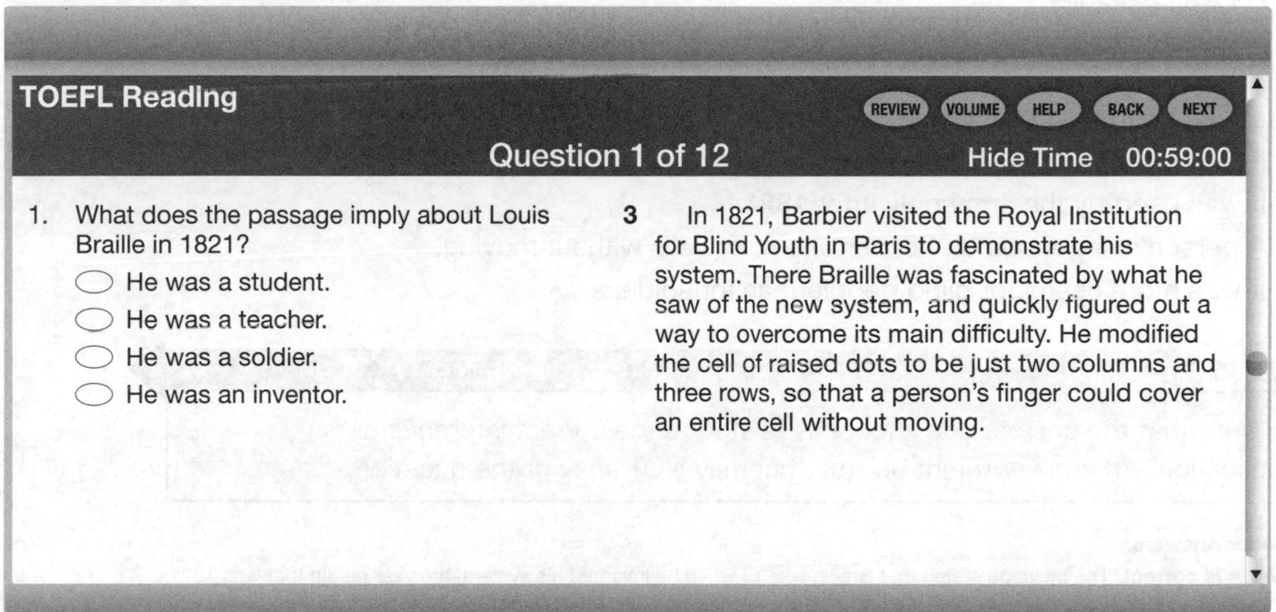
TOEFL Reading
REVIEW
VOLUME
HELP
BACK
NEXT
Question 1 of 12
Hide Time 00:59:00
1. What does the passage imply about Louis Braille in 1821?
He was a student.
He was a teacher.
He was a soldier.
He was an inventor.
3 In 1821, Barbier visited the Royal Institution for Blind Youth in Paris to demonstrate his system. There Braille was fascinated by what he saw of the new system, and quickly figured out a way to overcome its main difficulty. He modified the cell of raised dots to be just two columns and three rows, so that a person's finger could cover an entire cell without moving.

SKILL BUILDER

Directions: *Work with a partner. Read the passage and the questions. Underline the clues in the passage that tell you the answers. Then mark the correct answers.*

Braille

1 The Braille system of reading and writing, widely used by blind people all over the world, was devised by Frenchman Louis Braille when he was only fifteen. Blind himself, Braille took his idea from the earlier work of Charles Barbier.

2 As a soldier in Napoleon's army, Barbier created a code to help soldiers pass secret messages to each other at night. Barbier's system used a cell of raised dots in two columns and up to six rows. Different combinations of dots in the columns and rows represented the different letters of the alphabet. However, his system was rejected by the army as being too difficult for soldiers.

continued . . .

3 In 1821, Barbier visited the Royal Institution for Blind Youth in Paris to demonstrate his system. There Braille was fascinated by what he saw of the new system, and quickly figured out a way to overcome its main difficulty. He modified the cell of raised dots to be just two columns and three rows, so that a person's finger could cover an entire cell without moving. The modern Braille system is divided into different grades: in Grade 1 Braille, one cell represents one letter or punctuation mark. In higher grades, there are cells that stand for short words, such as *and* and *but*, and also for common combinations of letters, such as ~*tion*.

---

1. What does the passage imply about Louis Braille in 1821?
   Ⓐ He was a student.
   Ⓑ He was a teacher.
   Ⓒ He was a soldier.
   Ⓓ He was an inventor.

2. What can be inferred about the code that Barbier created?
   Ⓐ It was more difficult to write than it was to read.
   Ⓑ It was used by the army only after 1821.
   Ⓒ A person's finger couldn't cover one of its cells without moving.
   Ⓓ It was more useful for blind people than for soldiers.

EXPRESS TIP

Be sure that the answer you choose is related to the correct inference or implication. An answer might be true, but may NOT answer the question.

Skill Builder Answers:

1. **Answer A is correct.** The passage states that Braille was 15 when he invented his system; the year he did that was 1821, when he was staying at a school. From this, we can reasonably infer that he was a student. Answer B is incorrect because it is not reasonable to assume that a 15-year-old was a teacher at the school. Answer C is incorrect because he was not only too young to be a soldier, but wouldn't have been living at a school if he were a soldier. Answer D is incorrect because there is no information that implies Braille invented anything before the writing system for the blind, so he was not already an inventor.

2. **Answer C is correct.** The passage states, "Braille . . . quickly figured out a way to overcome its main difficulty. He modified the cell of raised dots to be just two columns and three rows, so that a person's finger could cover an entire cell without moving." This implies that the difficulty he solved was that a person's finger couldn't cover the cell without moving. Answer A is incorrect because there is no information about how difficult it was to write. Answer B is incorrect because the passage states that Barbier first invented a code, and then later came to the Royal Institution for Blind Youth in 1821, at which point Braille overcame the difficulty that the soldiers had objected to—therefore, the soldiers must have experienced the difficulty before 1821. Answer D is incorrect because the passage does not say whether Barbier's system had been tried by blind people.

PRACTICE

Directions: *Read the passages. Then mark the correct answers to the questions.*

Passage 1 (Questions 1–2)

The Angry Young Men

1 The Angry Young Men is a name given to a group of authors in Great Britain in the 1950s. The name is a reference to the title of a play, *Look Back in Anger*, by John Osborne. Other novelists and playwrights considered in this group include John Wain, Kingsley Amis, Philip Larkin, John Braine, Harold Pinter, and Alan Sillitoe.

2 Not a formal group by any means, the Angry Young Men were generally all from working-class backgrounds. A common theme in their writing was dissatisfaction with both traditional and contemporary social organizations and social structures, particularly the middle and upper British classes. However, their political views, especially with regard to coping with social issues, were varied—to the point that some of them didn't wish to have stories published in the same collection with other members of this group. Most of the members, in fact, rejected the name Angry Young Men, though it continues even today to be used by literary critics. This movement is seen as influencing the filmmaking trend in the 1950s and 1960s known as British New Wave, a direct translation of the French term *nouvelle vague*.

---

1. What does the passage imply about Osborne, Wain, Amis, Larkin, Braine, Pinter, and Sillitoe?
   Ⓐ Not all of them were British.
   Ⓑ They were the first members of the Angry Young Men.
   Ⓒ They refused to allow female members.
   Ⓓ They were only some of the Angry Young Men.

2. What can be inferred about the views of the Angry Young Men?
   Ⓐ They agreed about social problems, but not solutions.
   Ⓑ They were not interested in filmmaking.
   Ⓒ They didn't think British society could be improved.
   Ⓓ Most British readers didn't agree with them.

Passage 2 (Questions 3–4)

Brass

1 It's as bright and almost as pretty as gold, but it's cheaper and more practical. Brass is not a single metal but an alloy (or combination) of copper and zinc. Using different proportions of copper and zinc produces brasses with different qualities. Furthermore, the addition of other metals such as tin, iron, or aluminum can give different qualities to brass; these metals are generally added to make the brass stronger or more practical for special applications. Aluminum, for example, makes brass not only stronger but also more resistant to corrosion.

2 Brass is softer than most metals and melts at a relatively low temperature, which makes it popular for decorative uses. Many cultures create vases, plates, candlesticks, and ornaments out of brass. Several common musical instruments such as the trumpet, saxophone, and French horn are fashioned from brass. Brass is used for items such as doorknobs and light fixtures, but not for structural supports or the construction of bridges, buildings, or cars, which are generally made from steel.

3 These days almost all brass is recycled. A magnet is used to separate and remove other metals, such as iron, and the brass scraps that remain are melted down and re-formed into new products.

---

3. What does the author imply about steel in paragraph 2?
   Ⓐ Ornaments are never made from steel.
   Ⓑ It is a stronger metal than brass.
   Ⓒ It is less attractive than brass.
   Ⓓ Steel is not an alloy.

4. Which of the following can be inferred from paragraph 3?
   Ⓐ Brass is not attracted by magnets.
   Ⓑ Iron is more valuable than brass.
   Ⓒ Recycling is more expensive that making new brass.
   Ⓓ Almost all iron is also recycled.

Reading Skill 8: Understanding Rhetorical Purpose

Questions of rhetorical purpose ask you *why* the author included something in a text, such as an idea, argument, example, or even a specific word. The correct answer will complete the sentence "The author included this in the text in order to. . . ."

You might also be asked *what* the author's main purpose for writing the text was. The correct answer in this case will complete the sentence "The author wrote this text in order to. . . ."

A similar type of question asks you how the author accomplishes something: for example, how the author supports an argument, how the author emphasizes a certain fact or point, or how the author explains a process.

In all of these cases, you are being asked to figure out the author's purpose for writing something.

Rhetorical purpose questions look like this (note that special terms are sometimes highlighted; they will also be highlighted in the passage):

- *Why does the author **discuss** the history of coffee production?*
- *The author **mentions** pesticides in order to*
- *What are butterflies and moths **examples** of?*
- *How does the author **justify** the higher cost of shade-grown coffee?*
- *What does the author **compare** coffee to in terms of popularity?*

EXPRESS TIP

Try to answer the question in your own words before you read the answer choices. If you can easily do this, then choose the answer that best matches your own idea.

Look at this example of a rhetorical purpose question on a computer screen.

EXAMPLE: Rhetorical Purpose Question

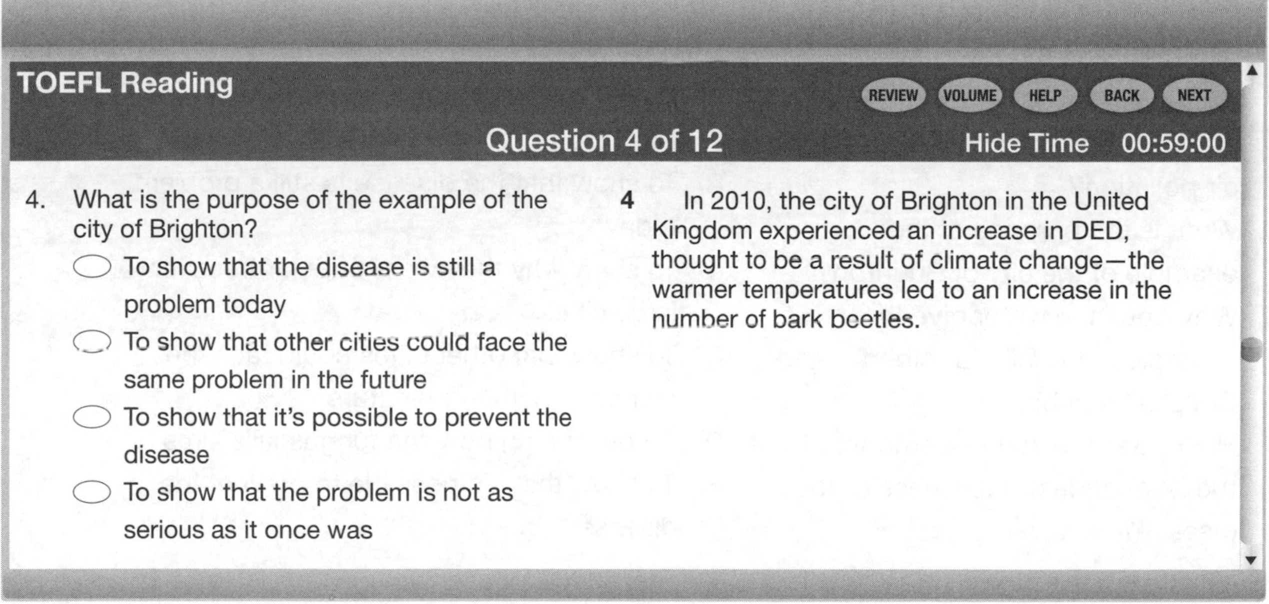
TOEFL Reading
REVIEW
VOLUME
HELP
BACK
NEXT
Question 4 of 12
Hide Time 00:59:00
4. What is the purpose of the example of the city of Brighton?
To show that the disease is still a problem today
To show that other cities could face the same problem in the future
To show that it's possible to prevent the disease
To show that the problem is not as serious as it once was
4 In 2010, the city of Brighton in the United Kingdom experienced an increase in DED, thought to be a result of climate change—the warmer temperatures led to an increase in the number of bark beetles.

SKILL BUILDER

Directions: *Work with a partner. Read the passage. Then match the question on the left with the rhetorical purpose on the right. Two rhetorical purposes are not used.*

Dutch Elm Disease

1 Tall, attractive, rapid-growing, and resistant to air pollution, elms became a popular tree for city plantings in Europe and North America around the beginning of the eighteenth century. Elms were especially common lining streets and avenues, but were also planted in parks and public gardens, and were prized as a shade tree that grew well in a variety of soils and climates.

2 However, the population of elms was drastically reduced by Dutch Elm Disease (DED). This fungus, carried by beetles that feed off the bark of elm trees, destroyed great quantities of elms: nearly three-quarters of the elm trees in Great Britain and 80 percent of the elms in Toronto, Canada, have been eliminated by DED. The only continent not affected at all has been Australia, due to its efforts to keep the bark beetles from reaching its shores. The Canadian provinces of Alberta and British Columbia are also free of DED.

3 Originating in Asia, where many of the varieties of elm have developed some resistance to the disease, DED first arrived in Europe in 1910 and North America in 1928. A second more destructive type of DED was discovered in Europe in the 1960s. Since the 1990s, elm trees have been slowly coming back to European and North American cities, thanks to aggressive programs to isolate and treat the disease.

4 In 2010, the city of Brighton in the United Kingdom experienced an increase in DED, thought to be a result of climate change—the warmer temperatures led to an increase in the number of bark beetles.

___ 1. Why does the writer describe elms as rapid-growing and resistant to air pollution?

___ 2. What is the purpose of the example of the city of Brighton?

___ 3. Why does the writer give the examples of Australia, Alberta, and British Columbia?

___ 4. How does the author demonstrate the level of destructiveness of the disease?

Ⓐ By using statistics to show how many trees died

Ⓑ To show that the disease is still a problem today

Ⓒ To show why they were popular trees for large cities

Ⓓ To show that other cities could face the same problem in the future

Ⓔ By describing how the fungus kills elms

Ⓕ To show that it's possible to prevent the disease

EXPRESS TIP

If the question asks about overall purpose or organization, reread the topic sentences in each paragraph. This can help you see connections and relationships between main ideas, which point to the writer's purpose.

Skill Builder Answers:

1. c; 2. d; 3. f; 4. a. These answers all show the rhetorical purpose of the statements. Choices b and e do not match the purpose of any of the statements.

PRACTICE

Directions: *Read the passages. Then mark the correct answers to the questions.*

Passage 1 (Questions 1–2)

Types of Diamonds

1 While the very name "diamond" makes most people think of jewelry and decorations, there are actually two major types of diamonds, known as gem-grade and industrial-grade. Gem-grade diamonds are used for decorative purposes, while the industrial-grade ones are used to create tools that cut, grind, or polish. Diamonds are particularly valuable because of their exceptional hardness.

2 Diamonds of either type come from two sources: They are mined from the ground or they are created in a laboratory. The qualities desired in gem-quality stones are usually aesthetic, such as clarity (having no imperfections) and color (clearer gems are more valuable). However, these qualities are not important in industry, one reason that only about 20 percent of mined diamonds are eventually classified as gem-grade. Lab-created diamonds are made by applying high pressure to carbon (simulating the forces that occur in nature) or through a low-pressure method known as chemical vapor deposition (CVD). While it is possible to create gem-quality diamonds in a lab, this is not common, probably due to pressure from the diamond market. However, because most lab-created diamonds are colored, and less than 1 percent of mined diamonds are colored, if you see a colored diamond in a piece of jewelry, it is probably synthetic.

---

1. Why does the writer use the word exceptional in paragraph 1?
   - Ⓐ To describe the beauty of diamonds
   - Ⓑ To point out how rare diamonds are
   - Ⓒ To emphasize how hard diamonds are
   - Ⓓ To show how unusual it is to find a diamond

2. How does the writer compare gem-grade and industrial-grade diamonds?
   - Ⓐ By discussing their cost and their color
   - Ⓑ By discussing their origin and their uses
   - Ⓒ By discussing their hardness and their beauty
   - Ⓓ By discussing their value and their popularity

Passage 2 (Questions 3–4)

The Dodo

1 If you know the dodo at all, it's probably either as an expression ("Dead as a dodo") or as a prime example of a recent animal extinction. The dodo was found only on Mauritius, an island in the Indian Ocean. Discovered by the Portuguese in 1598, this large flightless bird, somewhat similar in appearance to a duck or a goose (though actually more closely related to pigeons and doves), had never encountered humans before and had no natural fear of them.

2 By 1681, less than a hundred years later, the dodos were gone. It was thought at one time that people hunted them for food, which would have been easy, given their lack of fear and inability to fly. However, early written accounts describe dodo meat as bad tasting. The more likely reason for the dodo's extinction was that sailors brought with them animals such as cats, dogs, rats, and pigs, which ate both the birds and their nests on the ground.

3 Without the dodo, the Mauritian calvaria tree also faced extinction. It turned out that the calvaria seeds would only sprout after having passed through the digestive system of the dodo. And that's the real lesson—that everything is interconnected. Introduce new predators, and a species can become extinct; and one extinction can cause another. Perhaps the dodo can live on as a reminder of that crucial realization.

---

3. Why does the writer mention doves?
   - Ⓐ They are a similar species to the dodo.
   - Ⓑ They are also extinct on Mauritius.
   - Ⓒ They look similar to the dodo.
   - Ⓓ They were a food source for the dodo.

4. The author mentions calvaria trees in order to show
   - Ⓐ that plants as well as animals can become extinct
   - Ⓑ why a species' extinction matters
   - Ⓒ that they reproduced in an unusual way
   - Ⓓ that the plant and animal life on Mauritius was unique

SKILLS REVIEW

Reading Skills 7 and 8: Inferring Information and Understanding Rhetorical Purpose

Directions: *Read the passage. Then mark the correct answers to the questions.*

Socotra

1 Socotra, an island in the Indian Ocean belonging to the country of Yemen, is one of the most isolated pieces of land on Earth not of volcanic origin. The name "Socotra" actually refers to a group of four separate islands. Only about 1,400 square miles (3,625 square kilometers) in size, the main island, also known as Socotra, includes three different types of geographical terrain: inland mountains, a limestone plateau, and the coastal plains, which include both rocky and sandy beaches at the ocean's edge.

2 Conditions on Socotra are mostly dry—it is classified as a semi-desert climate, although the average annual rainfall of 7.7 inches (195 millimeters) is more or less evenly distributed throughout the months. Temperatures range from the low 70s°F (low 20s°C) in January to the low 90s°F (low 30s°C) in May, with average temperatures in the lower 80s°F (upper 20s°C). Monsoons (heavy rains and winds) over the surrounding oceans from June to September make boat and air travel to Socotra difficult during those months.

3 Its mild temperatures and geographical isolation have made Socotra home to some of the most unusual and rare plants and animals on Earth. Around 35 percent of the plants there are unique to the island; only the Hawaiian Islands and the Galápagos Islands have a higher such percentage. One of these endemic trees, the striking *Dracaena cinnabari*, or dragon's blood tree, has become a symbol of Socotra, featured on travel posters and coins. Often compared to a large sun umbrella or even a stalk of broccoli, the dragon's blood trees produce a red sap called cinnabar that is used as a dye and also for medicinal purposes. Other native trees whose saps are used for medicines and perfumes include frankincense and myrrh.

4 Socotra is also inhabited by rare birds, some native only to the island; the only native mammals, however, are bats, which live in Socotra's many limestone cliff caves and feed off insects, and the zabad cat, which is not a cat at all but a type of civet. It is thought that scientists might not yet have discovered the extent of the rich **endemic** insect and marine life associated with the islands.

5 The island is not densely populated or heavily visited. Around 33,000 residents live on Socotra, supporting themselves mostly through fishing and light agriculture. While there is interest in building Socotra's tourist industry, care is being taken to preserve the natural environment. No resort hotels have been built, and at the beach areas, tourists stay at low-impact campsites. Over 70 percent of the island has been set aside as national parkland and is off-limits to visitors.

continued . . .

6 In spite of these efforts, however, people still pose a threat to the island's native plants and animals. One significant threat is the introduction of nonnative animals. Residents raise cattle and goats for food; goats in particular are a growing problem for the island, as they are allowed to wander more or less freely, eating the available plants. Other animals, such as escaped house cats brought over as pets, eat the birds, which are unused to dealing with such predators. Climate change and pollution also put many plants (including the iconic dragon's blood trees) at risk; currently twenty-seven species of plants are listed as endangered and three species as critically endangered.

Glossary

endemic: Belonging to a certain area or population.

1. Why does the author discuss the weather of Socotra in paragraph 2?
   Ⓐ To show the extent of climate change in the area
   Ⓑ To persuade more tourists to visit the island
   Ⓒ To explain how conditions affected the plants and animals there
   Ⓓ To demonstrate how an island climate differs from a continental climate

2. In paragraph 3, what does the author imply about the number of unique plants and animals?
   Ⓐ It is unusually high.
   Ⓑ It is typical for a group of islands.
   Ⓒ It has significantly decreased.
   Ⓓ The reasons for it are not well understood.

3. Why does the author describe the dragon's blood trees as striking?
   Ⓐ They have been hard hit by global warming.
   Ⓑ People cut them down to manufacture medicines.
   Ⓒ This type of tree is especially strong.
   Ⓓ He wants to emphasize their unusual appearance.

4. It can be inferred from paragraph 4 that
   Ⓐ there aren't any insects that are unique to Socotra
   Ⓑ some unique species of sea life and insects have already been identified
   Ⓒ fish could be a source of income for the residents of Socotra
   Ⓓ it is impossible to tell if insect species on Socotra are also found elsewhere

5. What animal does the author use as an example of something that is harming native vegetation?
   Ⓐ Bats
   Ⓑ Civets
   Ⓒ Cattle
   Ⓓ Goats

READING SKILLS 9 AND 10

CONSTRUCTING A SUMMARY; TABLE COMPLETION

Reading Skill 9: Constructing a Summary

A *summary* is a short report given using the fewest words possible. It includes only the most important information about something you saw, heard, or read.

The summary question asks you to determine which ideas are important and which ideas are not important. The TOEFL iBT Test will provide an introductory sentence that includes the general topic of the reading passage. You will then see six possible answers and you will be asked to choose three of these that have the correct main ideas that support the general topic. You will be given points for this type of question as follows:

3 correct answers = 2 points
2 correct answers = 1 point
0 or 1 correct answer = 0 points

You must understand how the passage is **organized**: cause/effect, comparison/contrast, chronological order, process, or definition. To determine the pattern of organization, quickly skim each paragraph before you do a thorough reading. The correct answers are paraphrases of the important information in the passage. (See Reading Skill 2, pages 9–13.)

Look first at the introductory topic sentence. Make sure that you understand it completely; every answer you choose must be connected to and support the introductory sentence. Then identify key words in the answers and scan the passage to find them.

Do **not** choose answers that are:

- only small details or minor ideas
- not exact or not true according to the passage
- not related to or discussed in the passage

A summary question (or a table completion question) is almost always the last question in a passage. The question asking you to summarize the information will look like this:

Directions: *An introductory sentence for a brief summary of the passage is provided below. Complete the summary by selecting THREE answer choices that express the most important ideas in the passage. Some sentences do not belong in the summary because they express ideas that are not presented in the passage or are minor ideas in the passage.* **This question is worth 2 points.**

Introductory Sentence

•
•
•

Answer choices: (choose 3)

Xxx xxxxx xxxxxxxx xx xxxx xx xxxxx xxxxxxxx xxxx xxx xxxxxx.
Xxx xxxxx xxxxxxxx xx xxxx xx xxxxx xxxxxxxx xxxx xxx xxxxxx.
Xxx xxxxx xxxxxxxx xx xxxx xx xxxxx xxxxxxxx xxxx xxx xxxxxx.
Xxx xxxxx xxxxxxxx xx xxxx xx xxxxx xxxxxxxx xxxx xxx xxxxxx.
Xxx xxxxx xxxxxxxx xx xxxx xx xxxxx xxxxxxxx xxxx xxx xxxxxx.
Xxx xxxxx xxxxxxxx xx xxxx xx xxxxx xxxxxxxx xxxx xxx xxxxxx.

When you are ready to answer, click on the answer choices and drag them to the summary chart. It doesn't matter what order you put them in. Note that the reading passage is on a separate computer screen. However, you can click back and forth between the passage screen and the question screen.

Look at this example of a summary completion question on a computer screen.

EXAMPLE: Summary Completion Question

Screen 1

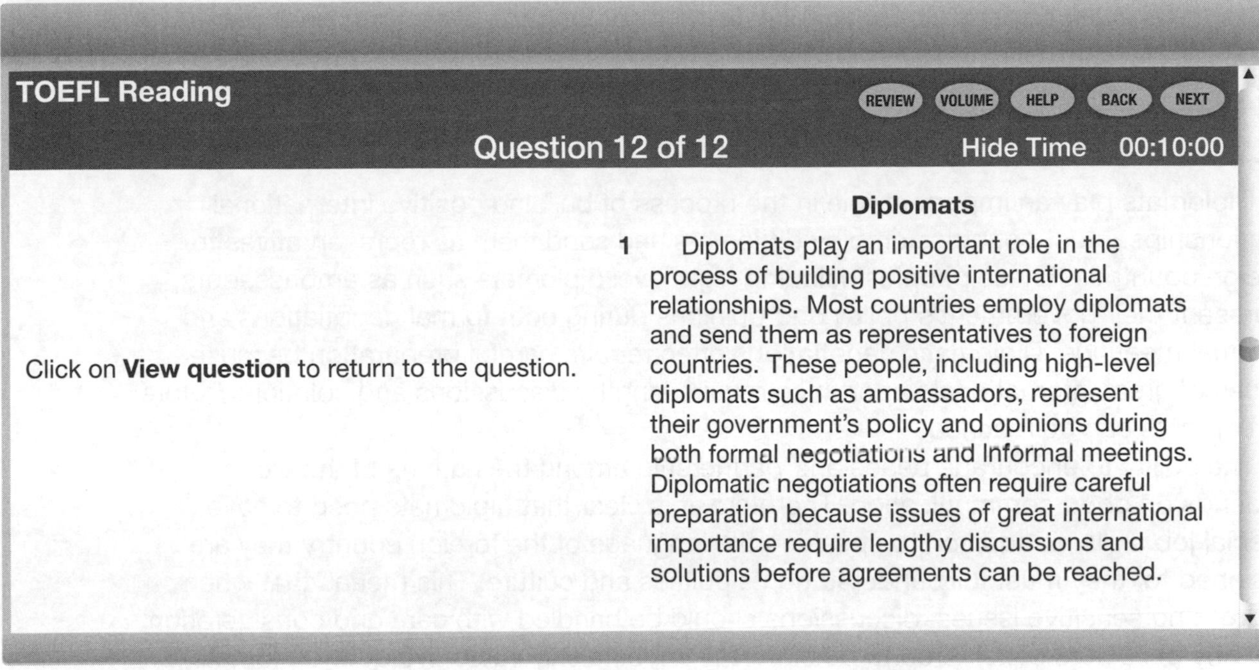
TOEFL Reading
REVIEW
VOLUME
HELP
BACK
NEXT
Question 12 of 12
Hide Time 00:10:00
Click on **View question** to return to the question.
Diplomats
1 Diplomats play an important role in the process of building positive international relationships. Most countries employ diplomats and send them as representatives to foreign countries. These people, including high-level diplomats such as ambassadors, represent their government's policy and opinions during both formal negotiations and Informal meetings. Diplomatic negotiations often require careful preparation because issues of great international importance require lengthy discussions and solutions before agreements can be reached.

Screen 2

TOEFL Reading

REVIEW VOLUME HELP BACK NEXT

Question 12 of 12 Hide Time 00:10:00

Directions: *An introductory sentence for a brief summary of the passage is provided below. Complete the summary by selecting THREE answer choices that express the most important ideas in the passage. Some sentences do not belong in the summary because they express ideas that are not presented in the passage or are minor ideas in the passage.* **This question is worth 2 points.**

Diplomats must have specific skills in order to build successful international relationships.

-
-
-

Answer choices: (choose 3)
They should be familiar with the policies and customs of the country they are in.
They should not talk about sensitive issues and always be polite.
They are required to speak two foreign languages wherever they travel.
They need to be aware of others' feelings and tolerant throughout negotiations.
They must be open-minded and willing to change their viewpoints when necessary.
They should be prepared to compromise in order to reach an agreement quickly.

SKILL BUILDER

Directions: *Work with a partner. Read the passage. Then read the introductory topic sentence after the passage and* <u>*underline*</u> *the phrases or sentences in the passage that: 1. State the most important ideas in the passage. 2. Support the introductory sentence. Then mark the correct answers.*

Diplomats

1 Diplomats play an important role in the process of building positive international relationships. Most countries employ diplomats and send them as representatives to foreign countries. These people, including high-level diplomats such as ambassadors, represent their government's policy and opinions during both formal negotiations and informal meetings. Diplomatic negotiations often require careful preparation because issues of great international importance require lengthy discussions and solutions before agreements can be reached.

2 The ability to encourage peace and partnership among the nations of the world depends on good communication. Therefore, it is clear that diplomats need to have special job skills. In addition to speaking the language of the foreign country they are assigned to, they must fully understand its politics and culture. This means that when addressing sensitive issues, discussions should be handled with care and consideration, and any behaviors considered to be culturally impolite should be avoided. Diplomats are also required to be both focused and patient during long and complicated negotiations. Most importantly, they need to be flexible by responding quickly to changes and modifying their positions to fit the current situation. Diplomats often have the difficult task of convincing those who don't have the same opinion to come to some type of agreement or compromise. It is not always an easy job to get people on different sides of an issue to give something up in order to solve the problem.

Directions: *An introductory sentence for a brief summary of the passage is provided below. Complete the summary by selecting THREE answer choices that express the most important ideas in the passage. Some sentences do not belong in the summary because they express ideas that are not presented in the passage or are minor ideas in the passage.* **This question is worth 2 points.**

Diplomats must have specific skills in order to build successful international relationships.

•
•
•

Answer choices: (choose 3)

1. They should be familiar with the policies and customs of the country they are in.
2. They should not talk about sensitive issues and always be polite.

3. They are required to speak two foreign languages wherever they travel.
4. They need to be aware of others' feelings and tolerant throughout negotiations.
5. They must be open-minded and willing to change their viewpoints when necessary.
6. They should be prepared to compromise in order to reach an agreement quickly.

EXPRESS TIP

Taking very brief notes is useful for answering summary questions. As you read, write down the number of each paragraph and a few words that describe its main idea. You can then compare your notes to the answer choices and, if needed, click back to the reading passage and use your notes to find the specific paragraph you want to review.

Skill Builder Answers:

Answers #1, #4, and #5 are correct. Answer #1 correctly summarizes one of the main ideas in paragraph 2: "In addition to speaking the language of the foreign country they [diplomats] are assigned to, they must fully understand its politics and culture." Answer #4 correctly summarizes two of the main ideas in paragraph 2: "This means that when addressing sensitive issues, discussions should be handled with care and consideration, and any behaviors considered to be culturally impolite should be avoided. Diplomats are also required to be both focused and patient during long and complicated negotiations." Answer #5 correctly summarizes one of the main ideas in paragraph 2: "Most importantly, they need to be flexible by responding quickly to changes and modifying their positions to fit the current situation." Answer #2 is incorrect because the passage says "sensitive issues" *are* discussed, but in a careful and considerate manner. Answer #3 is incorrect because the passage does *not* state that diplomats must speak *two* foreign languages *wherever* they travel, but rather it states that diplomats must have the skill of ". . . speaking the language of the foreign country they are assigned to . . ." Answer #6 is incorrect because the passage does *not* say diplomats must *compromise in order to reach an agreement quickly*. The passage states that the process is a "long and complicated" one.

PRACTICE

Directions: *Read the passages. Then mark the correct answers to the questions.*

Passage 1 (Question 1)

Product Development

1 Many companies try to expand their share of the market by creating new products. However, a large percentage of new products lose money and must be taken off the market. Some analysts estimate that 80 percent of the most recently introduced products no longer exist today. Others estimate that only one in three products ever succeeds in making it to market.

2 New product development is a difficult challenge for many reasons. At the very beginning of the process, some companies have trouble finding a completely new product that is useful and for which there is a real need. Even if a company decides to develop a new product by improving one that they already have, it may be difficult to come up with a unique way to make it better and, thereby, increase sales. It can cost as much as $50 million to design and get a new product to market. Many companies just don't have this kind of money for research, development, manufacturing, and marketing.

continued . . .

3 In addition, today's markets are fast-moving and require a company to get a product out as soon as possible. However, companies don't always have the time to do the necessary research. Without proper research, companies don't have enough information to predict whether or not the product will sell. When companies are in a hurry, mistakes can be made. Sometimes, in the rush to get a product to the buyers, it is badly designed. Further, a poorly advertised product or one that is priced too high might not sell. All of these mistakes can allow competing companies to offer a similar product with a better design or at a lower price. This means the company that originally introduced the product will not reach the goal of expanding its market share and increasing its profits.

Directions: *An introductory sentence for a brief summary of the passage is provided below. Complete the summary by selecting THREE answer choices that express the most important ideas in the passage. Some sentences do not belong in the summary because they express ideas that are not presented in the passage or are minor ideas in the passage.* **This question is worth 2 points.**

Companies face many problems when trying to develop a new product.

•
•
•

Answer choices: (choose 3)

1. Companies increase their market share by introducing a large number of products.
2. Creating a new product or improving an old one is problematic and expensive.
3. Developing a new product involves a long, detailed analysis of the market.
4. A company's lack of adequate research can lead to bad decisions.
5. Researchers need to find a new way to produce cheaper products.
6. Competitors can take advantage of poor product design and pricing errors.

Passage 2 (Question 2)

Sense of Taste

1 Scientific theories about how and what we taste have changed significantly as more discoveries have been made. Traditionally, although our sense of smell is actively involved, science focused on the taste buds as the primary sense organs responsible for our ability to taste the food we eat. The taste buds are the nearly 10,000 little bumps, located on the tongue, on the roof of the mouth, and in the throat. It was thought that the taste buds could generally perceive only four basic tastes: sweet, sour, salty, and bitter. However, a fifth taste, *umami*, became widely known and accepted in 1985. Named by the Japanese scientist Kikunae Ikeda, *umami* is probably closest in meaning to "meaty" or "savory." It is found in such foods as seaweed, mushrooms, aged cheeses, and meat broths.

continued . . .

2 In addition, early ideas about how each set of taste-specific buds function have been found to be inaccurate. In the past, taste was represented visually by a "tongue map." This map indicated that taste buds in each different part of the mouth, tongue, and throat were responsible for perceiving only one of the basic tastes. For example, the tip of the tongue was believed to pick up only sweet tastes. It is now known that our sense of taste is far more complex than just perceiving one type of taste at a time. Instead, the flavors of a majority of foods we eat are a combination of all basic tastes. Taste buds, no matter where they are, can sense all of the basic five tastes. However, while all taste buds can respond to the basic tastes to some degree, they still respond best to one specific taste.

3 As the scientific study of **genes** has made major advances, recent studies have begun to discover why people react differently to the same foods. It is believed these differences that determine our preferences for specific foods are based on our taste genes. If, for example, your mother was highly sensitive to sour foods such as lemons, you might also be sensitive to them. Likewise, some people, especially those from South America, Africa, and Asia, may have a gene that produces a high number of taste buds. These people, known as "supertasters," can experience the flavor of food more strongly than others and can detect flavors in common food that others can't. It is estimated that around 25 percent of people are supertasters and, of that percentage, women are more likely to be supertasters than men. However, while it may sound like a good thing to be able to taste so well, many supertasters feel that it limits what they eat. They complain that even common foods or drinks, such as coffee and ice cream, taste either too bitter or too sweet for them to enjoy eating.

Glossary

genes: A part in every cell of living things that controls how it develops. Parents pass genes to their children for such traits as eye color.

Directions: *An introductory sentence for a brief summary of the passage is provided below. Complete the summary by selecting THREE answer choices that express the most important ideas in the passage. Some sentences do not belong in the summary because they express ideas that are not presented in the passage or are minor ideas in the passage.* **This question is worth 2 points.**

Theories about our sense of taste have changed over time.

•
•
•

Answer choices: (choose 3)

1. The main sense organs used to determine taste are considered to be the taste buds.
2. A new set of taste buds was discovered by a professor in Japan.
3. It is generally recognized that there is an additional basic taste.
4. Supertasters are more common among women than among men.
5. The taste buds can react to more than one of the basic tastes.
6. Some people may be more sensitive to one or to many tastes than others.

Reading Skill 10: Table Completion

The TOEFL iBT Test contains table questions that require you to complete an outline of a passage by deciding in which category information should be placed. For the table questions, you are given a table with the most important ideas from the passage. Underneath the table are 7–9 answer choices. You must choose either 5 or 7 correct answers for each category in the chart. That means there will be always be **2 answers** that you will not choose. You will be given points for this type of question as follows.

In a table asking for 5 answers (total of 3 points possible):

- **5 correct answers = 3 points**
- **4 correct answers = 2 points**
- **3 correct answers = 1 point**
- **0, 1, or 2 correct answers = 0 points**

In a table asking for 7 answers (total of 4 points possible):

- **7 correct answers = 4 points**
- **6 correct answers = 3 points**
- **5 correct answers = 2 points**
- **4 correct answers = 1 point**
- **0, 1, 2 or 3 correct answers = 0 points**

As with summary questions, to find the correct answers for the table question, determine how the passage is organized. Look first at the information provided for you in the table. Depending on the table, you will be given two or three different categories, such as classes or types of things. Next, identify key words in the answers and scan the passage to find them. Make sure that the answers you choose belong in the category where you put them; check to make sure that they are directly related to the category and provide essential support for it. An answer is *not* necessarily correct just because it includes the same words or phrases as those in the passage.

Do **not** choose answers that are:

- only small details or minor ideas
- not exact or not true according to the passage
- not related to or discussed in the passage

A table completion question (or a summary completion question) is almost always the last question in a passage. The question looks like this:

Directions: *Select the appropriate phrases from the answer choices, and match them to the type of xxxxx to which they relate. TWO of the answers will not be used.* **This question is worth 3 points.**

xxxxxxxxxx (category 1)	• • •
xxxxxxx (category 2)	• •

Answer choices: (choose 5)

Xxx xxxxx xxxxxxxx xx xxxx xx xxxxx xxxxxxxx xxxx xxx xxxxxx.
Xxx xxxxx xxxxxxxx xx xxxx xx xxxxx xxxxxxxx xxxx xxx xxxxxx.
Xxx xxxxx xxxxxxxx xx xxxx xx xxxxx xxxxxxxx xxxx xxx xxxxxx.
Xxx xxxxx xxxxxxxx xx xxxx xx xxxxx xxxxxxxx xxxx xxx xxxxxx.
Xxx xxxxx xxxxxxxx xx xxxx xx xxxxx xxxxxxxx xxxx xxx xxxxxx.
Xxx xxxxx xxxxxxxx xx xxxx xx xxxxx xxxxxxxx xxxx xxx xxxxxx.
Xxx xxxxx xxxxxxxx xx xxxx xx xxxxx xxxxxxxx xxxx xxx xxxxxx.

When you are ready to answer, click on the answer choices and drag them to the bulleted location next to the correct category in the table. Note that the reading passage is on a separate computer screen. However, you can click back and forth between the passage screen and the question screen.

Look at this example of a table completion question on a computer screen.

EXAMPLE: Table Completion Question

Screen 1

TOEFL Reading

REVIEW VOLUME HELP BACK NEXT

Question 12 of 12

Hide Time 00:02:15

Click on **View question** to return to the question.

All That Glitters Is Not Gold

1 Throughout the centuries, people have been fooled into thinking they've found a fortune in gold. However, the glittering mineral they've discovered has turned out in many cases to be pyrite, or what is appropriately known as "fool's gold." Geologically speaking, there are several distinct ways to tell the difference between real gold and the much less valuable pyrite.

2 While both are minerals and shine like metal, gold is a more truly golden color or a silvery yellow. Pyrite, on the other hand, is a lighter yellow, sometimes tarnishing and turning black. Geologists can also distinguish between the two minerals based on hardness, on how easily they can be shaped or bent without breaking, and on magnetic attraction. Gold is softer than pyrite and flattens out or changes its shape if hit with a steel hammer. On the other hand, . . .

Screen 2

TOEFL Reading

REVIEW VOLUME HELP BACK NEXT

Question 12 of 12

Hide Time 00:02:15

Directions: *Select the appropriate phrases from the answer choices, and match them to the type of mineral to which they relate. TWO of the answers will not be used.* **This question is worth 3 points.**

gold	• •
pyrite	• • •

Answer choices: (choose 5)

Contains shiny, valuable minerals
Is lighter colored or tarnished
Has a silvery yellow color
Will scratch metal
Can be shaped without breaking
Burns steel when struck
Is magnetic

SKILL BUILDER

Directions: *Look at the two abbreviated categories (G = gold and P = pyrite) listed after the passage. Then read the passage and take short notes based on what you read about each category. List the most important points that match each category. Discuss your points with a partner. Then choose the correct answers on page 64 for each category in the chart and write your answers in the chart.*

All That Glitters Is Not Gold

1 Throughout the centuries, people have been fooled into thinking they've found a fortune in gold. However, the glittering mineral they've discovered has turned out in many cases to be pyrite, or what is appropriately known as "fool's gold." Geologically speaking, there are several distinct ways to tell the difference between real gold and the much less valuable pyrite.

2 While both are minerals and shine like metal, gold is a more truly golden color or a silvery yellow. Pyrite, on the other hand, is a lighter yellow, sometimes tarnishing and turning black. Geologists can also distinguish between the two minerals based on hardness, on how easily they can be shaped or bent without breaking, and on magnetic attraction. Gold is softer than pyrite and flattens out or changes its shape if hit with a steel hammer. On the other hand, pyrite will spark if you strike it with hammer. If a piece of this much harder mineral is used to scratch a metal object like cooper or steel, it will leave a mark. Finally, a magnet can be used to test the difference. Pure gold does not have iron in it, while pyrite does. Therefore, gold will not be attracted to a **magnet**, but the fool's gold will be.

Glossary

magnet: A piece of iron or steel metal that can make other objects move toward it, and hold or move them.

Types of Minerals	**Your Notes:**
G	
P	

Directions: *Select the appropriate phrases from the answer choices, and match them to the type of mineral to which they relate. TWO of the answers will not be used.* **This question is worth 3 points.**

gold	• •
pyrite	• • •

Answer choices: (choose 5)
1. Contains shiny, valuable minerals
2. Is lighter colored or tarnished
3. Has a silvery yellow color
4. Will scratch metal
5. Can be shaped without breaking
6. Burns steel when struck
7. Is magnetic

EXPRESS TIP

In table questions, comparison/contrast is frequently used as the pattern of organization. Check for the following words or phrases to identify the important points for the categories in a table:

Comparison: *like, the same as, compared to, similarly*
Contrast: *although, despite, however, in contrast, on the other hand, instead*

There may also be other patterns such as problem/solution or alternative arguments (two different theories, three different approaches, and so on).

Skill Builder Answers:

Answers #3 and #5 are correct for gold. Answers #3 and #5 are paraphrased in paragraph 2: "…gold is a more truly golden color or a silvery yellow" and "Gold is softer than pyrite and flattens out or changes its shape if hit with a steel hammer." **Answers #2, #4, and #7 are correct for pyrite.** Answers #2, #4, and #7 are paraphrased in paragraph 2: "Pyrite, on the other hand, is a lighter yellow, sometimes tarnishing and turning black"; "If a piece of this much harder mineral [pyrite] is used to scratch a metal object like cooper or steel, it will leave a mark"; and "Therefore, gold will not be attracted to a magnet, but the fool's gold will be."

PRACTICE

Directions: *Read the passages. Then mark the correct answers to the questions.*

Passage 1 (Question 1)

Sunspots and Solar Activity

1 Scientists observe sunspots in an effort to understand and predict some of the effects of solar activity on the Earth. Sunspots, regions on the Sun's surface that are darker and cooler than other areas, form when the Sun's magnetic field sends currents of gases up from the solar surface. These sunspots are enormous magnetic "storms" which release energy that can sometimes greatly increase the strength of the "solar wind"—a stream of fast-moving, electrically charged particles from the Sun. As a result, the intensified solar wind can have a direct impact on the Earth.

continued . . .

2 Scientists know that sunspots follow an eleven-year solar cycle, going from periods of low activity to periods of high activity and back to low again. Periods of minimum activity typically occur at the beginning or end of a cycle. During this time, few sunspots are observed, and the output of solar wind is within normal range. While a direct connection between Earth's climate and periods of low activity has not been proven, a dramatic drop in temperatures was experienced in the period from 1650 to 1710, known as the Maunder Minimum. Very few sunspots appeared on the surface of the Sun at that time, signaling a decline in the Sun's activity. The result was that large areas of the planet experienced extremely cold weather.

3 On the other hand, periods of high activity occur at the midpoint in the solar cycle. At this stage in the cycle, the highest numbers of sunspots occur, and there is an increase in the solar winds reaching Earth. This can interfere with the Earth's own magnetic field by causing magnetic storms in our atmosphere. One result is the Northern or Southern Lights: fantastic and beautiful auroras, or glowing multicolored lights in the skies in areas around the North and South Poles. However, the impact during a maximum activity of sunspots can have negative effects. The magnetic storms can interrupt radio reception and the electrical network. In 1989, at a peak level of solar activity, 6 million people in Quebec, Canada, lost electrical power for nine hours due to a solar storm.

Directions: *Select the appropriate phrases from the answer choices, and match them to the solar activity to which they relate. TWO of the answers will not be used.* **This question is worth 3 points.**

minimum activity	• •
maximum activity	• • •

Answer choices: (choose 5)

1. A small number of sunspots are seen at the start or end of a cycle.
2. Sunspots appear during magnetic storms every eleven years.
3. Magnetic storms may disrupt communication and power systems.
4. The solar wind is at an average level.
5. There are many sunspots in the middle of a cycle.
6. Extreme temperature changes occur on Earth.
7. There is a stronger solar wind.

Passage 2 (Question 2)

A Short History of Pens

1 As long ago as 4000 B.C., writing instruments were made from the hollow stems of reeds or other plants, cut at one end to form a sharp point. Some type of writing liquid or ink was then poured into the empty space inside, and the stem was squeezed to make the liquid come out of the sharp end. Next came the quill pen around 500 B.C. It was perhaps the most widely used pen for over a thousand years until new designs caused its decline in the nineteenth century. This type of pen was fashioned from a bird feather, or quill, also sharpened to a point at the end. Similar to previous writing instruments, ink had to be poured into the hollow shaft of the feather. However, sometimes these pens were also dipped in a container of ink because the shaft didn't hold much ink. The flow of ink was difficult to control, and the ink occasionally spilled out. In addition, quill pens wore out very quickly.

2 Other materials, such as wood and silver, were used for the body of pens, and stronger steel tips called nibs were added in the early 1800s. However, the metal nib-tipped pen still required the writer to dip it in an ink container, making it inconvenient to carry around. In the late 1800s, a completely new type of nib-tipped pen, the fountain pen, became widely available. The fountain pen was quite popular because it had its own interior ink container, or cartridge; there was no longer a need to bring along an extra supply of ink. At first, the cartridge had to be refilled, although later replaceable throw-away cartridges were used. Early versions sometimes leaked ink and left marks from the writer's hands on the paper.

3 The next major revolution came with the creation of the ballpoint pen. Two Hungarian brothers, Laszlo and George Biro, are usually credited with inventing the first one in 1938. They decided to use a thicker type of newspaper-print ink that couldn't be used in other pens. It dried very quickly and was nearly waterproof. Writers no longer had to wait to send documents, and the process was cleaner. However, this ink required a new type of pen design. The brothers fit the tip of the pen with a tiny ball to control the flow of ink. The ball rolled around smoothly, taking up a small amount of ink from the cartridge and leaving it on the paper. People could now write faster with more control, and the paper would be free from ink spots. Better yet, the cartridge didn't need to be constantly refilled; it would last for months. It was a cheaper, more reliable, and repair-free pen in every way. Today, the ballpoint pen is used worldwide as one of the most common writing instruments.

Directions: *Select the appropriate phrases from the answer choices, and match them to pens in the time period to which they relate. TWO of the answers will not be used.* **This question is worth 4 points.**

the earliest pens	• •
pens in the 1800s	• • •
pens in the 1900s	• • •

Answer choices: (choose 7)

1. The body and the nibs are shaped using wood and silver.
2. They are made from plants and pressed to force the ink out the sharpened end.
3. They have cartridges, but still need to be dipped in ink.
4. Quills don't last very long, are messy, and store limited amounts of ink.
5. Special tips are attached to the ends to keep them from wearing out.
6. The tip allows for the ink to be delivered in a controlled and clean way.
7. A separate source of ink is still necessary.
8. The cartridges of ballpoints contain fast-drying ink that eliminates stains.
9. Fountain pens have nibs and replaceable cartridges.

SKILLS REVIEW

Reading Skills 9 and 10: Summaries and Table Completion

Directions: *Read the passage. Then mark the correct answers to the questions.*

Bridge Design

1 Engineers must consider many factors when designing a bridge. For instance, they have to calculate how much weight it will need to carry and how long the span (the distance between the two ends of the bridge) needs to be. The way in which these factors have been successfully addressed can be seen in two of the most common bridge designs, suspension and cable-stay. Both of these elegant bridge designs have one or two towers rising from the midsection. When they must carry heavy traffic, they also have a roadway structure that hangs securely from very strong steel ropes called cables. However, the two bridges differ in a few important ways.

2 The concept of hanging or suspending a bridge is an ancient one. More than 600 years ago, the Inca civilization in Peru suspended bridges made of thick ropes and pieces of wood over river valleys. Today, suspension bridges remain the ideal engineering solution when a long distance over water needs to be crossed. Because they are light and strong, they can span distances far greater than any other type of bridge. These distances range from 2,000 feet (609.6 meters) to as much as 7,000 feet (2,133.6 meters). A suspension bridge has at least two enormous horizontal cables that reach from one end of the bridge to the other and usually pass through holes in the tops of the towers. These main cables are connected to support structures built into solid rock or concrete at both ends of the bridge. The weight of the load on a suspension bridge is carried by these structures. In addition, the roadway is not directly supported by the main cables or the towers, but rather by a series of many thinner cables. These smaller cables hang down vertically from the main cables and attach to the roadway. This system of bridge cables resembles a widely spaced fence. This "fence" makes a long, graceful "M" shape as the cables sweep up to and down from each tower.

3 For bridges needing a medium-length span, between 500 and 3,000 feet (152.4–914.4 meters), cable-stay bridges are becoming a popular choice. The roadway on a cable-stay bridge, unlike that on suspension bridge, hangs directly from the top of each tower by a "fan" of cables. These cables run down from the towers and attach to the roadway, creating the characteristic "A" shape. There are no additional vertical cables along the span. The towers on cable-stay bridges are not linked to each other by cables or to underground structures on land. Therefore, the weight is carried directly by the towers.

4 Besides the obvious advantage of being the only kind of bridge to effectively span very long distances, suspension bridges can be built high enough over the water to allow very tall ships to pass safely underneath. In terms of construction cost, however, they can be quite expensive to build because they require large amounts of cable, construction materials, and time. In contrast, cable-stay bridges require less cable and can usually be constructed much faster and at a lower cost. In addition, cable-stay bridge design reduces bending in the middle section of the roadway; therefore, it can actually be supported by only one tower, unlike a suspension bridge. While shorter than suspension bridges, cable-stay bridges are stronger and will support more weight.

Directions: *An introductory sentence for a brief summary of the passage is provided below. Complete the summary by selecting THREE answer choices that express the most important ideas in the passage. Some sentences do not belong in the summary because they express ideas that are not presented in the passage or are minor ideas in the passage.* **This question is worth 2 points.**

Bridges are designed in different ways depending on their uses and locations.

•
•
•

Answer choices: (choose 3)

1. Suspension bridges are constructed to span broad waterways.
2. Cable-stay and suspension bridges both have towers and roadways.
3. Suspension bridges are less commonly built than cable-stay bridges.
4. Cable-stay bridges are designed for crossing shorter distances than suspension bridges.
5. There are design advantages and disadvantages for both types of bridges.
6. Cable-stay bridges are built to support a medium amount of traffic.

Directions: *Select the appropriate phrases from the answer choices, and match them to the bridges to which they relate. TWO of the answers will not be used.* **This question is worth 3 points.**

suspension	• • •
cable-stay	• •

Answer choices: (choose 5)

1. The cables transfer the weight of the load to underground structures.
2. The roadway is not attached to the bridge.
3. The weight on the roadway is supported by towers.
4. A series of vertical cables holds the roadway far above the water.
5. The construction is costly and time-consuming.
6. The "M"-shaped towers are cheaper to build.
7. There is no need for two towers.

Note: Scoring information for this Reading Post-Test is available on page 325. Keep track of your score on this Reading Post-Test and add it to your scores for the Listening, Speaking, and Writing Post-Tests. The Reading Post-Test can also be taken on the CD-ROM, where it is combined with the other Post-Tests into one full test. It can be taken on the CD-ROM in either the "Practice Mode" (not timed; you can work at your own pace) or the "Timed Mode" (TOEFL iBT® Test timing; you will not be able to pause). On the CD-ROM, the Reading Post-Test will automatically be scored for you. If you want to see how you would score on an authentic TOEFL iBT® Test, take the test on the CD-ROM in the "Timed Mode."

READING POST-TEST

Directions:

The Reading Section of the TOEFL iBT® Test measures your understanding of academic passages and your ability to answer questions about them. It contains three passages and a set of questions about each passage. You have 60 minutes in which to complete the Reading Section.

The majority of questions are worth 1 point; however, the last question (summary or table completion) for each passage is worth more than 1 point. Please read the directions for the last question so you know how many points are possible.

When words or phrases are blue and underlined, definitions appear at the end of the reading in the glossary.

(Note: On the actual TOEFL iBT Test, the words will be blue and underlined, and definitions for them will appear when you click on them.)

As soon as you have finished one question, move on to the next one. You may skip questions and come back to them later, and change your answers if you want.

When you have finished reading these directions, go on to the first reading.

Reading Passage 1

Read the following passage and mark the correct answers.

Questions 1–12

The Formation of Domes in Yosemite National Park

1 Yosemite National Park in east-central California offers a wealth of breathtaking natural beauty, from Yosemite Falls, waterfalls that tumble down thousands of feet, to the world's largest trees, giant sequoias, which have survived for thousands of years. However, it is perhaps most famous for its unique and spectacular rock formations, and among the most unusual of the geological formations in Yosemite Valley are the domes. These onion-shaped giants rise above the valley floor to heights of nearly 5,000 feet (1,524 meters), amazing the millions of visitors who come to enjoy the natural wonders of Yosemite every year.

2 Domes are very rare structures and the ones in Yosemite, such as Half Dome, Basket Dome, North Dome, Sentinel Dome, and Liberty Cap, reveal a very ancient geological story; they did not simply spring up. The area that was to become Yosemite Valley, like most of the western United States, lay beneath a shallow sea 500 to 150 million years ago. Sedimentary rock, formed from layers of silt, mud, and marine organisms, was slowly lifted above the ancient sea level.

3 In the next stage of the valley's evolution, **magma** bubbled up through the Earth's crust and formed a chain of volcanoes. Intense internal pressure caused the overlying sedimentary and volcanic rock to crumple into folds and form mountains. The original source material of what would later become Yosemite's domes was the molten rock at the roots of these volcanoes. At an estimated 5 to 10 miles (8–16 kilometers) below the surface, it cooled slowly under intense pressure and crystallized into granite between 140 and 85 million years ago. Gradually, the ancient layer of sedimentary and volcanic rocks weathered and eroded away, thus exposing the salt-and-pepper colored granite rocks. Out of the seven types of granite which constitute the rims and walls of Yosemite Valley, only two of these can form domes.

4 The dome granite is very hard and behaves differently than other rock types when it is under pressure. As the plates of the Earth move and shift, thrusting up mountains, there is an enormous amount of pressure on the rocks being uplifted. The rock must release this tension. Normally, the rock being pushed up releases the outward pressure along many tiny cracks in surfaces. It then breaks off in chunks or pieces. However, the granite that forms the domes in Yosemite is very durable, massive, and has very few internal cracks. The crack or fracture systems that do exist within the rock are formed in enormous sheets, essentially parallel to the surface. Thus, when the forces within the Earth drive this rock formation upward, new cracks form in an unusual way beneath the surface of the granite and push outward to release pressure.

continued . . .

5 [9A] The process by which the dome granite releases pressure is responsible for the dome shape. [9B] As the pressure builds, the dome granite peels off, removing irregular surfaces and creating longer, more smoothly curved cracks underneath when the next internal pressure is released. [9C] As these leaf-like, **concentric** layers fall off in increasingly larger, longer curving layers, a smooth, rounded surface is left behind. [9D]

6 In other words, this "sheeting" process eliminates the corners or sharp angles of the original rock and replaces them with curves. As each succeeding layer drops off, the curves become progressively gentler until the final dome shape develops. The Royal Arches, a cliff below North Dome in Yosemite, illustrates this geological process in its series of granite arches, one seemingly carved within another. Too far below the surface to form the top of domes, it is as if nature had conveniently sculpted arches in the side of the cliff to reveal the process in a cross-section of exfoliated sheets up to 200 feet (61 meters) thick.

7 Even today the Earth continues to thrust the rocks of Yosemite Valley upward, and as the granite relieves pressure and peels away, bald rocks are exposed and new domes are still being created.

Glossary

magma: Extremely hot liquid rock found deep within the Earth which forms igneous rock, such as granite, after it cools.

concentric: Circles of different sizes with the same center; for example, a standard target used for bow and arrow practice has concentric circles.

1. According to the passage, for which of the following features is Yosemite National Park best known?
   Ⓐ Giant mountain onions
   Ⓑ High waterfalls
   Ⓒ The world's oldest trees
   Ⓓ Impressive rock structures

2. The phrase spring up in paragraph 2 is closest in meaning to
   Ⓐ rise slowly
   Ⓑ appear suddenly
   Ⓒ move according to season
   Ⓓ explode with great force

3. It is implied in the passage that
   Ⓐ there are only five domes in the world
   Ⓑ domes are not common
   Ⓒ there are only two types of granite
   Ⓓ domes are formed at the bottom the valley

4. Why does the author give details in paragraph 3 about the formation of volcanoes in Yosemite Valley?
   Ⓐ To illustrate how extreme pressure forms sedimentary rock
   Ⓑ To explain how magma is formed over millions of years
   Ⓒ To show how volcanic rock forms a series of mountains
   Ⓓ To indicate where the dome granite came from in the beginning

5. The word **these** in paragraph 3 refers to
   Ⓐ rims and walls
   Ⓑ volcanic rocks
   Ⓒ types of granite
   Ⓓ domes

6. According to the passage, how does rock usually release pressure?
   Ⓐ By breaking into pieces where there are very small openings in the surface
   Ⓑ By continuing to grow upward with the movement of the Earth's crust
   Ⓒ By falling apart in short, thin layers along large cracks in the surface
   Ⓓ By allowing the heat caused from pressure to melt away surface area

7. Which of the following is NOT true?
   Ⓐ The domes in Yosemite are made of very solid, strong rock.
   Ⓑ The rock in Yosemite's domes doesn't break into pieces or chunks.
   Ⓒ The granite in Yosemite's domes has many curved cracks inside.
   Ⓓ The shape of the Yosemite domes is caused when long rock layers fall off.

8. The word **it** in paragraph 4 refers to
   Ⓐ the surface
   Ⓑ the rock
   Ⓒ a crack
   Ⓓ pressure

9. Look at the four squares [■] that indicate where the following sentence could be added to paragraph 5.

   This process, called exfoliation, works something like peeling off the layers of an onion.

   Where would the sentence best fit into the paragraph? Circle the square **9A**, **9B**, **9C**, or **9D** where the sentence should be added to the paragraph.

(Note: On the actual TOEFL iBT Test, the directions would ask you to "Click on a square to add the sentence to the passage." On the computer, you will then **click on** the correct square [■] and the sentence will appear in that location.)

10. The word exposed in paragraph 7 could best be replaced by
Ⓐ broken up
Ⓑ revealed
Ⓒ deposited
Ⓓ hidden

11. According to paragraph 7, it is probable that
Ⓐ domes will not be formed for the next hundred years
Ⓑ Yosemite will be destroyed as the Earth's plates move
Ⓒ the domes will become flat on top over a long period of time
Ⓓ the process of dome formation will continue in the future

12. **Directions:** *An introductory sentence for a brief summary of the passage is provided below. Complete the summary by selecting THREE answer choices that express the most important ideas in the passage. Some sentences do not belong in the summary because they express ideas that are not presented in the passage or are minor ideas in the passage.* **This question is worth 2 points** (2 points for 3 correct answers, 1 point for 2 correct answers, and 0 points for 1 or 0 correct answers).

The domes in Yosemite National Park tell an ancient geological story.

-
-
-

Answer choices: (choose 3)
1. Rock must release the pressure of uplift caused by the movement of Earth's plates.
2. Granite formed under ancient layers of rock and eventually surfaced due to erosion.
3. Yosemite granite is cracked into thin layers that lie at sharp angles to the surface.
4. Domes are formed by the sheeting of rock in long, smooth, and curving layers.
5. The Royal Arches demonstrate how sheets are formed.
6. Dome granite has unique qualities that lead to a specific type of cracking.

Reading Passage 2

Read the following passage and mark the correct answers.

Questions 13–26

The Harpsichord and the Piano

1 Pianos and harpsichords look so similar that many people who are not early music aficionados don't realize how different they actually are. In fact, the two are not even classified as the same type of instrument: a harpsichord is grouped with the stringed instruments, such as guitars and harps, whereas a piano is technically a percussion instrument, like a xylophone or a drum. However, due to the similarity in the design of the instruments, musicians who play one instrument are able to play the other. As pianos are more common, many harpsichordists in fact start their musical study on the piano.

2 The harpsichord is the earlier instrument. Mostly likely invented during the Middle Ages, it reached the height of its popularity in the Renaissance (1400–1600) and the Baroque (1600–1750) periods. During the Classical period (1750–1830) composers wrote music for both harpsichord and piano, with some prominent composers such as Haydn and Mozart writing first for the earlier instrument before changing to the newer one. Composers of the late Classical period, such as Beethoven, wrote only for the piano. However, the harpsichord never died out entirely, with even some twentieth-century composers such as Poulenc, Martinu, and Carter writing new music for the harpsichord. Some musicians who perform music of the Renaissance and Baroque still prefer to use the original instrument, though others substitute the piano.

3 19A The piano was invented in the late 1700s, although different types and versions were created and used simultaneously for a while until finally an instrument that resembles our modern-day piano won out around the mid-1800s. 19B Liszt, Beethoven, Mendelssohn, and Brahms were among the first to try out the new pianos and to compose music for them. 19C While the pianos of the 1800s differed in various ways from the modern piano, they were certainly similar, and music of that period is always played on the piano today. 19D

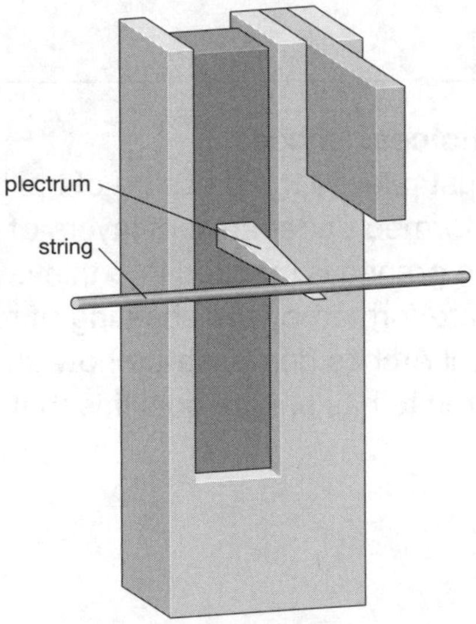

4 The most important difference between the two instruments is in how they create sound. When a harpsichord player depresses a key on the keyboard, it causes the jack to rise, which in turn causes the plectrum to lift and pluck the string (see Figure 1). Whether the player hits the keys hard or soft makes no difference—the resulting sound will be equally loud. The player also cannot control the speed at which the sound decays—the sound only stops when the string completely stops vibrating. In order to create different types of sounds, then, many harpsichords were built with two or even three different keyboards, one behind the other, for the player to choose between.

plectrum
string

Figure 1: harpsichord jack

continued . . .

5 A piano works somewhat differently. When a player presses a key, a mechanism is activated that strikes the piano wires (see Figure 2). Pressing the key gently will make a softer sound; pressing it harder will make a louder sound. In fact, the name "piano" comes from the early Italian name for the instrument, *pianoforte*, which means "soft-loud" in Italian. When the player releases the key, a felted hammer, called a "damper," falls on the strings and stops the sound. Thus, a player can stop the sound by lifting his or her fingers. A player who wishes the vibrations to continue even after the fingers have been lifted (to play other notes, for example) creates this effect by pressing a sustaining pedal with the foot, which keeps the damper from falling.

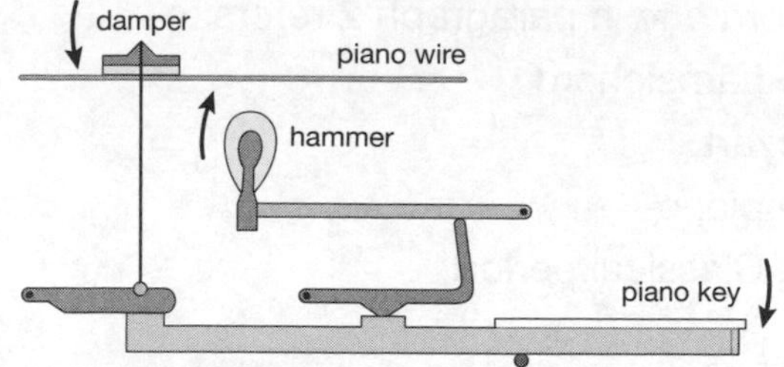

Figure 2: piano action

6 A further key difference is in the tuning of the instruments. Harpsichords, with their shorter, thinner wires, can be tuned by the player. They go out of tune quickly and easily, responding to even subtle changes like the temperature of the room and whether it is a rainy or a dry day. Players tune their instruments weekly or daily, and tune before concerts, in the same way that violinists and other string players do in orchestras. In the Baroque era, the A string was tuned to 415 Hz (hertz; a unit that measures sound cycles per second), or about a half-tone lower than today's standard of A = 440 Hz. Many harpsichord players today still tune at the lower frequency. Piano wires, in contrast, are longer, thicker, and heavier, and require a professional tuner. They hold their tuning longer, and most pianos only need to be tuned once or twice a year, or after having been moved. Pianos are always tuned to the modern A440.

---

13. The word aficionados in paragraph 1 is closest in meaning to
    - Ⓐ fans
    - Ⓑ instruments
    - Ⓒ composers
    - Ⓓ technicians

14. A xylophone is the same type of instrument as a
    - Ⓐ harpsichord
    - Ⓑ guitar
    - Ⓒ harp
    - Ⓓ piano

15. The word prominent in paragraph 2 could best be replaced by
    - Ⓐ unknown
    - Ⓑ middle-aged
    - Ⓒ modern
    - Ⓓ famous

16. The word one in paragraph 2 refers to
   Ⓐ the harpsichord
   Ⓑ Mozart
   Ⓒ the piano
   Ⓓ the Classical period

17. What does the author imply about composers in paragraph 2?
   Ⓐ There are more composers of piano music than harpsichord music.
   Ⓑ There are more composers of harpsichord music today than in the past.
   Ⓒ There are more composers of harpsichord music than musicians who can play it.
   Ⓓ There are more composers of harpsichord music than piano music.

18. All of these composers are mentioned as writing for the piano EXCEPT
   Ⓐ Mozart
   Ⓑ Beethoven
   Ⓒ Brahms
   Ⓓ Carter

19. Look at the four squares [■] that indicate where the following sentence could be added to paragraph 3.

   Chopin, the "poet of the piano," composed almost exclusively for that instrument.

   Where would the sentence best fit into the paragraph? Circle the square 19A, 19B, 19C, or 19D where the sentence should be added to the paragraph.

20. What is the main purpose of paragraph 4?
   Ⓐ To teach a piano player how to play a harpsichord
   Ⓑ To explain why the harpsichord is considered a stringed instrument
   Ⓒ To contrast the sound of the harpsichord and the piano
   Ⓓ To show why composers preferred the harpsichord

21. The word decays in paragraph 4 could best be replaced by
   Ⓐ fades away
   Ⓑ moves
   Ⓒ halts
   Ⓓ increases

22. The piano took its name because
   Ⓐ it could produce loud and soft sounds
   Ⓑ its sounds were softer than a harpsichord's
   Ⓒ it was invented in Italy
   Ⓓ it was easier to play than the harpsichord

23. A piano player who wanted a sound to remain for a long time would
   Ⓐ hit the key softly
   Ⓑ use a second keyboard
   Ⓒ lift the finger quickly
   Ⓓ use a pedal

24. The word subtle in paragraph 6 is closest in meaning to
   Ⓐ quick
   Ⓑ small
   Ⓒ rare
   Ⓓ invisible

25. Why does the writer give the figures of 415 and 440 Hz?
   Ⓐ To explain why a piano is more difficult to tune
   Ⓑ To describe the thickness of harpsichord and piano wires
   Ⓒ To show a difference in the harpsichord's and the piano's sound
   Ⓓ To explain why a piano sounds louder than a harpsichord

26. **Directions:** *Select the appropriate phrases from the answer choices, and match them to the instrument to which they relate. TWO of the answers will not be used.* **This question is worth 3 points** (3 points for 5 correct answers, 2 points for 4 correct answers, 1 point for 3 correct answers, and 0 points for 2, 1, or 0 correct answers).

piano	• • •
harpsichord	• •

Answer choices: (choose 5)
1. Is a percussion instrument
2. Is no longer played today
3. Was played in the 1600s
4. Cannot be played loudly or softly
5. Includes a sustaining pedal
6. Is not used in orchestras
7. Must be tuned by a professional

Reading Passage 3

Read the following passage and mark the correct answers.

Questions 27–39

Food Preservation Techniques

1 Food preservation is a vitally important part of food storage. From the moment that plants are picked or animals die, they begin to break down chemically. Tiny disease-causing organisms called pathogens can form as this process of spoiling continues. The food will eventually taste bad and may also become unsafe to eat. Therefore, long before the invention of modern refrigerators and freezers, it was essential that the earliest humans learned ways to preserve foods. The ability to do so helped our ancestors survive in difficult times when fresh food was not always readily available. Food preservation techniques, including drying, salting, and freezing, stopped food from spoiling and causing sickness, and allowed people to safely keep and eat food for longer periods of time.

2 Among the most ancient of the preservation techniques is drying. Because the presence of water in food invites harmful pathogens to grow, drying is an excellent and simple way to remove the water. **29A** In order to dehydrate food, early humans first most likely learned to put it out to air-dry in the sun or wind. **29B** When food was slowly dried over low heat in this way, they probably discovered by accident that the smoke also helped make it last longer. **29C** The reason is that compounds in smoke have special properties which prevent the growth of the organisms that lead to spoilage. **29D**

3 Dried meat and fish became particularly important foods for hunters far from home or for other groups of people who moved from place to place. Native North Americans created their own particularly healthy food, pemmican, made by grinding together dried meat, dried fruit, and fat. Incidentally, fat is also thought to act as a preservative because it seals out air that can make food spoil more quickly in an open environment. Other settled agricultural societies, such as those in ancient Egypt, stored grains that they had harvested and dried.

4 Salting is another age-old method used to preserve or "cure" food. Because adding salt to food acts to dehydrate food by drawing out the water, it can also help to inhibit the growth of pathogens. Due to its unique chemical composition, high levels of salt also create conditions unfriendly to such organisms. Curing with salt can be accomplished by either rubbing it on the surface of the food or by mixing it with water and soaking food in this brine. As long ago as 3500 B.C., salting was the most common method of preserving fish in the Mediterranean region. It was also used in ancient China around 2700 B.C., where enhanced preservation was achieved by adding special spices to the salt. Finally, salting and drying outdoors or over smoking fires were effectively used in combination.

continued . . .

5 Early northern peoples learned that cool temperatures and freezing were also effective in preserving foods. At low temperatures the growth of unwanted organisms slows down and can sometimes be completely eliminated when food is frozen; however, timing is important because the faster the drop in temperature, the more successfully this happens. Many cultures stored ice or snow in underground houses or caves for cooling food. Early Japanese and Korean peoples learned to freeze-dry fish. Ancient South American cultures in Peru and Bolivia, living in cold, mountainous areas, also freeze-dried potatoes. They were successful in using this technique because the dry, high altitudes, combined with cold temperatures, caused the food to quickly freeze and dehydrate.

6 Today, traditional methods of food preservation are not as widely practiced as they were in past times, when many people grew crops and raised animals on their own land. Modern industrial methods, using artificial chemicals and new technologies, have quickly replaced the more natural and simpler methods of preservation for the majority of people. However, some, such as salting or drying and smoking over fire, are still used with little change from ancient times because they add special and familiar flavors to foods.

---

27. All of the following are mentioned in paragraph 1 about early humans EXCEPT
    Ⓐ They were not always able to find fresh food to eat.
    Ⓑ They learned how to preserve food so it was not harmful to eat.
    Ⓒ They frequently ate spoiled food that had been kept too long.
    Ⓓ They used three methods for preserving food.

28. The word readily in paragraph 1 is closest in meaning to
    Ⓐ easily
    Ⓑ willingly
    Ⓒ simply
    Ⓓ clearly

29. Look at the four squares [■] that indicate where the following sentence could be added to paragraph 2.

    Once fire was discovered, prehistoric peoples then also began to dry raw food over it.

    Where would the sentence best fit into the paragraph? Circle the square 29A, 29B, 29C, or 29D where the sentence should be added to the paragraph.

30. Why does the author mention pemmican in paragraph 3?
    Ⓐ To indicate how early cultures preserved meat
    Ⓑ To explain the healthy diet of Native North Americans
    Ⓒ To illustrate how fat is used to keep food from spoiling
    Ⓓ To provide a specific example of preserved food

31. The word inhibit in paragraph 4 could best be replaced by
Ⓐ begin
Ⓑ advance
Ⓒ prevent
Ⓓ support

32. It is stated in paragraph 4 that
Ⓐ salt contains special elements that help preserve food
Ⓑ pathogens pull water from food when salt is added
Ⓒ water is applied to the outside of salted foods to preserve them
Ⓓ salting was the most regularly used preservation method

33. The word enhanced in paragraph 4 is closest in meaning to
Ⓐ limited
Ⓑ rapid
Ⓒ complete
Ⓓ improved

34. According to the passage, both air-drying and salting
Ⓐ produce disease-fighting chemicals
Ⓑ eliminate water in the food
Ⓒ require heating or cooling
Ⓓ seal the food rapidly

35. Which of the sentences below best expresses the essential information in the highlighted sentence in paragraph 5?
Ⓐ Cold temperatures eventually cause unwelcome organisms in food to die.
Ⓑ Very cold or frozen food was safely eaten by ancient people living in northern climates.
Ⓒ Food must be kept in cold or freezing temperatures for a long time in order to effectively protect against sickness.
Ⓓ Chilling or freezing food quickly reduces or stops the spread of harmful organisms.

36. Why does the author include information in paragraph 5 about where the ancient South Americans lived?
Ⓐ To give examples of the countries where freeze-dried foods were eaten
Ⓑ To relate how the climate and landscape affected their preservation methods
Ⓒ To illustrate the difficulty the people had preserving food in the mountains
Ⓓ To compare the geographical features required for freezing different kinds of food

37. The word some in paragraph 6 refers to
Ⓐ methods of preservation
Ⓑ artificial chemicals
Ⓒ the majority of people
Ⓓ natural techniques

38. The author implies in paragraph 6 that most people no longer use the ancient methods of preservation because

Ⓐ industry has created healthier and better ways to preserve food
Ⓑ they are not considered safe enough now
Ⓒ there isn't a great need to preserve their own food at home
Ⓓ it takes too much time in a busy modern world to use them

39. **Directions:** *Select the appropriate phrases from the answer choices, and match them to techniques of preservation to which they relate. TWO of the answers will not be used.* **This question is worth 4 points** (4 points for 7 correct answers, 3 points for 6 correct answers, 2 points for 5 correct answers, 1 point for 4 correct answers, 0 points for 3, 2, 1, or 0 correct answers).

drying	• •
salting	• • •
cooling/freezing	• •

Answer choices: (choose 7)
1. Achieved by working the preservative into the outside of foods
2. Requires high heat from the sun or from fire
3. Involves placing food outdoors in the wind or sun
4. Uses snow and ice stored below the ground
5. Accomplished by putting food in a brine
6. Requires high elevations and low temperatures
7. Includes using fire and smoke
8. Achieved by grinding the preservative with grains or fruit
9. Includes adding spices to aid preservation

THIS IS THE END OF THE READING POST-TEST.

Record your score: _______

LISTENING OVERVIEW

The Listening section tests your ability to understand spoken English that is common on North American college and university campuses. You will hear two main types of talks:

- academic lectures
- conversations

Academic lectures feature either a professor talking alone or a professor and a few students asking and answering questions. Topics include general information from subject areas such as the arts, general sciences (biology, chemistry, geology, etc.), and social sciences (economics, history, international relations, etc.). You do not need any specialized knowledge to answer the questions.

Conversations feature an interaction between a student and someone else. There are two main types: *office hours*, where a student talks to a professor in his or her office (these can be about classroom policies, questions about a course, or academic content), and *service encounters*, where a student talks to someone on campus such as a housing advisor, a campus safety staff member, or office clerks in various departments.

On the actual test, you will hear six to nine separate talks: four to six lectures, and two to three conversations. The lectures will be approximately 5 minutes long and the conversations will be approximately 2 to 3 minutes long. Each lecture will be followed by 6 questions and each conversation by 5 questions. The entire section takes 60–90 minutes.

During the Listening section, you may take notes. You will be given a pencil and paper to use. The notes are not scored or seen by anyone else, but you may not take them with you after the test. They will be collected by the test center. You may use your notes when you answer the questions. (See pages 87–91 for Note-Taking Skills.)

Most questions on the Listening section are multiple-choice; however, there are some chart-type questions as well. Some questions, called "replay" questions, will repeat a short portion of the talk for you to focus on. There is also a question type that asks you to select two out of four answers. These question types will be covered in more detail in the Skills units in this section.

Here are the different types of questions:

- Main idea
- Detail
- Function (understanding why something was said)
- Stance (understanding a speaker's feeling or opinion)
- Organization and Connecting Content
- Inference

You will only hear the lectures and conversations once, so it is important to listen carefully and take good notes. You cannot skip questions, and you cannot go back to questions once you have submitted your answers.

Tool Bar for the Listening Section

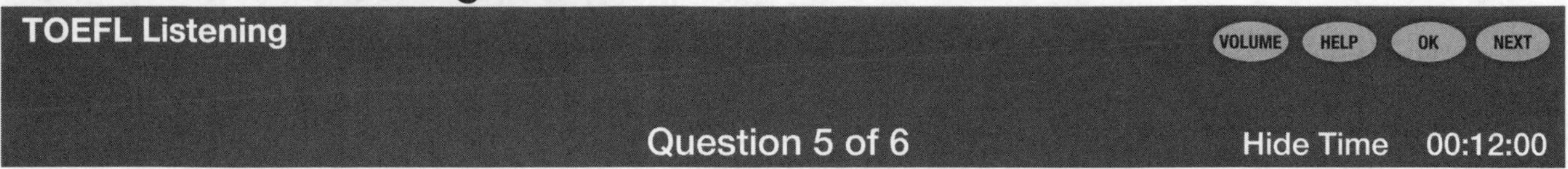

The section you are in and the question you are answering will always be displayed on the tool bar at the top of the computer screen.

Help—Offers the help you need when you click on this button. However, we recommend that you learn the features of the test in advance during this course so that you don't need to use it. In the event that your equipment itself doesn't work, raise your hand and a testing center worker will assist you.
Next—Allows you to go to the next question.
OK—After clicking on "Next," you can confirm your answer by clicking on "OK." You must answer the question before you click on "OK" or "Next"—you cannot skip a question. In addition, you cannot go back to a previous question after you click on "OK."
Volume—Enables you to change the volume during the test.
Hide Time—Hides the clock any time during the test when you click on this button. However, we recommend that you do *not* use it; you need to pay attention to how much time you have left on the clock.

The Listening section of the TOEFL iBT® Test is administered as follows:

1. You will have a chance to adjust your headset and the volume.
2. You will see general directions for the Listening section on the computer screen.
3. When you are ready, you will click on a button that says "Next" to move to the first question.
4. You will see and hear short instructions for the first question.
5. You will hear (but not see!) the first lecture or conversation. You *will* see a photo of the lecture or the service encounter. You *might* see special terms or the names of people or places spelled on a whiteboard.
6. When the talk is finished, you will hear and see the questions, and you will see the answer choices.
7. After you answer the question, you will click to confirm your answer, and then click to move to the next question.

Steps 4–7 will repeat for each question until the Listening section is complete. In the individual Skills units of this section, you will see examples of the computer screens used for each type of question.

IMPROVING YOUR LISTENING ABILITY

Listening can be a challenging skill to practice on your own, especially if you are not living in a country where English is commonly spoken. However, there are still ways to practice. Try some or all of these, and remember that listening is not a skill that you can learn a few days before the test. Practice a little bit every day as far in advance as you can!

- Listen to English podcasts.
- Listen to English radio stations, either locally or online.
- Watch DVDs of English movies and television shows (this will help with following conversations).
- Watch DVDs of English documentaries (this will help with following lectures).
- Listen to DVDs on a wide variety of topics and subjects, to get used to hearing different vocabulary and speaking styles.
- Listen to English songs on CDs or online. Sing along!
- Have conversations with other people in English. It doesn't matter if they are native or non-native speakers. Any practice helps!
- Speak as much English as you can, even if you speak to yourself, alone. Speaking practice helps with listening skills.
- Practice taking notes as you listen to radio and watch movies or television shows. You can use the "subtitle" option on DVDs of movies and television to check the accuracy of your notes.
- If you live in an English-speaking country, (1) call information numbers on the telephone and follow the direction to press specific buttons; (2) call businesses that have recorded information about hours and services. Take notes on the information you hear.

Note-Taking Skills

It is essential that you learn to take quick notes during the Listening and the Integrated Speaking and Writing sections of the TOEFL iBT Test.

Organizing Your Notes

There are two basic formats you can use effectively to organize your notes: an outline or column format.

1. Outline Format—This format works well for lectures, talks, or discussions that follow a series of events or steps chronologically (for example, a history lecture or the steps in the process of preserving food). In addition, it is also useful when specific parts or features of a topic are presented (for example, "The Life Cycle of the Honey Bee").

For the outline format:

- Write the main ideas on the left.
- Indent a few spaces, and then write the supporting ideas to the right.
- Keep indenting every time you hear a detail or more specific point.

EXAMPLE

(Topic) *Elephants = social animals*

Group
6–12, leader of herd, oldest, most experience female + children, sisters
males—travel alone / with other males

Social interaction
separated—stay in contact over long distance
make noise = travel 10 kilometers
specific sounds when danger / to find other members

together— express happiness; see new babies / relatives after long time
spin around, flap ears, loud "happy" noises

express sadness, one dies in group
stay with dead member long time / stop & stand quietly at place where group member died in past

visit old graveyards of relatives & hold bones in sensitive trunks & look at them

2. Column Format—This format is quite useful for lectures, talks, or discussions that follow a cause/effect, comparison/contrast, or problem/solution type of organization.

For the column format:

A.

- Write the main ideas in a column on the left.
- Write the supporting ideas and details in a column on the right.
- Label the columns with the specific points in the lecture, talk, or discussion.

B.

- Write the cause, one item or idea being compared/contrasted, or the problem in the column on the left.
- Write the effects, the other items or ideas being compared/contrasted, or the solutions in the column on the right.
- Label the columns with the specific organizational categories (for example, cause or effect) in the lecture, talk, or discussion.

EXAMPLE: Comparison/Contrast

(Topic) *Hawks & Falcons: "predatory" birds—hunt, kill, eat other animals*

Hawks	**Falcons**
Wings	*Wings*
separated (slotted) finger-like feathers	*not slotted*
wider than falcon with rounded edges	*longer than hawk & curve toward back, pointed not round*
use for soaring & moving between branches of trees while search for / follow prey	*use for high-speed chase in more open areas, not soar as much as hawks*
Tails	*Tails*
short, rounded; easy to move for soaring	*narrow, longer tails than hawks; better for speed*
Beak	*Beak*
not notched, kill prey by crushing	*notched, upper beak (looks like small tooth), kill prey with speed, smash in flight, bite throat*

EXPRESS TIP

You will not have enough time during the lectures and conversations on the TOEFL iBT Test to write down more than a few quick notes. To take good notes:

- Do not write down every word you hear; focus on content words that contain the most important information, such as nouns and verbs or sometimes adjectives and adverbs.
- Do not use full sentences; omit smaller function words that do not contain important information, such as:

Forms of the verb *be*	*am / is / are / was / were*
Auxiliary verbs	*be / have / do*
Articles	*a / an / the*
Personal pronouns	*he / she / they / it / them*
Relative pronouns	*which / that / who / whom*
Demonstratives	*this / that / these / those*
Some prepositions	*at / from / of*

What you hear: *However, even if separated, elephants keep in contact with each other over long distances. As they move from place to place, elephants communicate with each other by making noises that can travel almost 10 kilometers. These specific sounds help elephants warn each other when there is danger, and help them find other herd members.*

How it looks in note form: *elphs separated—stay in contact over long dist.*
make noise = travel 10 km
specif. sounds when danger / to find other membs

Using Abbreviations and Symbols

1. Abbreviations—If you use a cell phone to send text messages, you might already understand how to abbreviate words and expressions. For example, *LOL* means "laugh out loud." Abbreviations are used to make words shorter. Shorten words by:
   - using only the first few letters or the first syllable

     astro = astronomy   info = information   gym = gymnasium
   - omitting the vowels or the middle of a word

     glss = glass   rd = road   Assn = Association
   - using initials for the names of people, places, or organizations

     PP = Pablo Picasso   LA = Los Angeles   WHO = World Health Organization

Here is a list of some commonly used abbreviations:

Abbreviation	Meaning	Abbreviation	Meaning
w/	with	max.	maximum; the greatest possible amount, degree, or number
w/o	without		
b/4	before		
b/c	because		
i.e.	in other words	p/pp	page/pages
e.g. or ex	for example/example/such as	ft	feet
etc.	and so on; and other things	kg	kilogram
re	regarding; about; concerning	lb	pound
esp	especially	m	meter
min.	minimum; the least possible amount, degree, or number	yr	year
		pro	for; agree with; in favor of
		con	against; disagree with; opposed to

2. Symbols – It is important to spend some time learning the most common symbols because using them will really help you to take notes much more quickly.

Here is a list of some standard symbols:

Abbreviation	Meaning	Abbreviation	Meaning
+ or &	and; plus; in addition; also; more	>	is greater than
		<	is less than
@	at	∴	therefore; so
→	leads to; produces; causes; makes	%	percent
		″	inches
←	comes from; is the result of	′	minute (also min)
↑	increases; goes up; rises	°	degree
↓	decreases; goes down; lowers	~ or ±	about; approximately; more or less
/	per; or		
=	is; means; equal to; same as	" "	ditto; repeated words
≠	is not; doesn't mean; different	♀	woman; female
#	number	♂	man; male

EXPRESS TIP

- Do not worry about spelling; your notes aren't rated or scored, so it isn't important.
- Put a star next to or circle a specific term or item if you realize that information is important.
- Watch for and write down in your notes any words or expressions that appear on the computer screen "whiteboard" during a lecture or discussion.

Note-Taking Practice

Rewrite the notes on pages 88 and 89, using information from the *Express Tip* box on page 89 to omit unnecessary information. Use abbreviations and symbols from the charts on page 90 to shorten or replace words. Feel free to make up your own symbols or abbreviations.

LISTENING SKILLS 1 AND 2

UNDERSTANDING THE MAIN IDEA; UNDERSTANDING DETAILS

Listening Skill 1: Understanding the Main Idea

Questions about a listening passage's *main idea* ask about the general topic or situation. It is the passage's most important idea. This information might be stated directly by one of the speakers, or you might need to infer it from a few different pieces of information.

You should be able to determine the main idea close to the beginning of the talk. Ask yourself, "What is the point of this talk/conversation?" Your answer will be the main idea.

EXPRESS TIP

You are more likely to hear a main idea announced directly in a lecture than in a conversation. Near the beginning of a lecture, the professor might say, *Today we're going to look at some economic causes of the Civil War,* or *Last week, we examined political causes of the Civil War, and then today we'll look at some of the economic causes.*

If you hear a statement like this, be sure to include it in your notes.

Questions that ask about a passage's main idea look like this:

- *What is the topic of the lecture?*
- *Why is the student talking to the professor?*
- *What is the purpose of the meeting?*
- *What does the student want to do?*
- *What is the talk mainly about?*

Most incorrect answers will have information that is either not true or not given in the talk. However, some incorrect answers might have specific details that, while true, do not summarize the main idea of the talk.

In order to answer these questions correctly, you must identify the central topic of the listening passage. Incorrect answers will either contain false information or will mention specific ideas.

Look at this example of a main idea question on a computer screen.

First you will hear a lecture, a discussion, or a conversation:

EXAMPLE: Main Idea Question

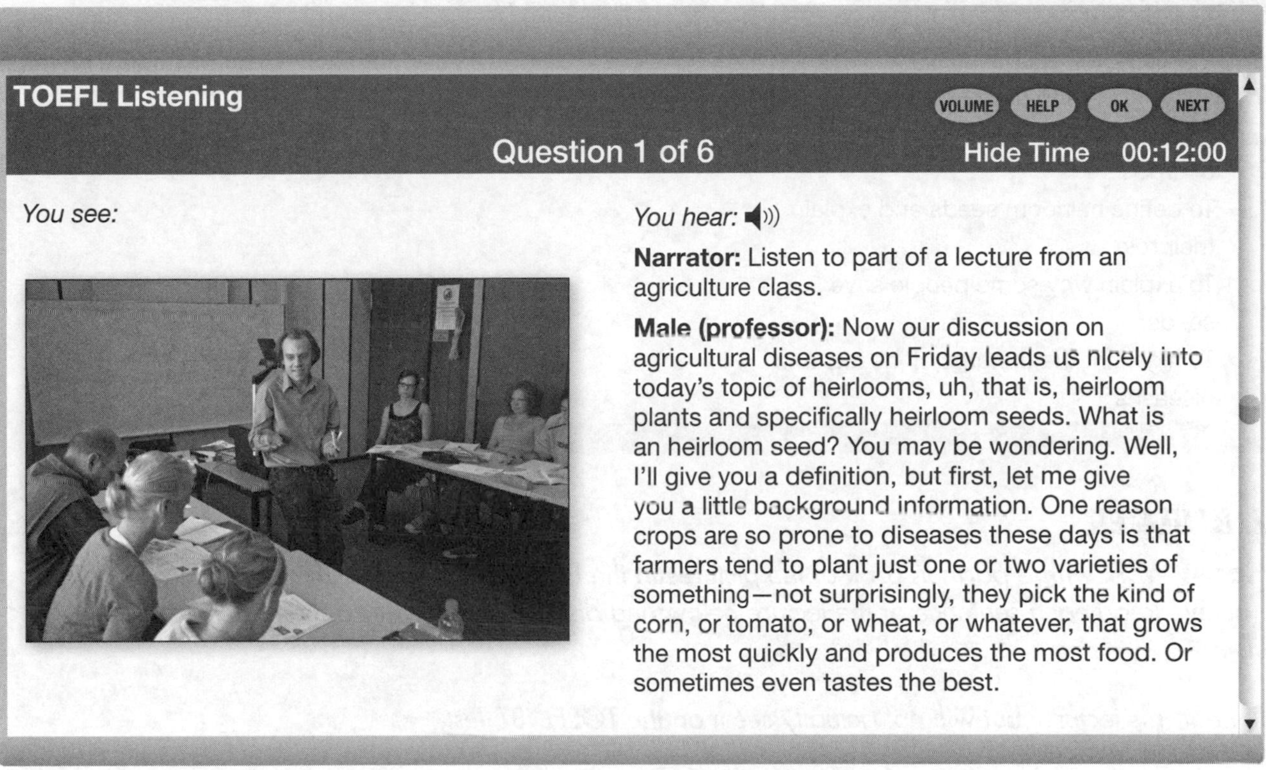

Sometimes you will see some information presented on a whiteboard, such as names of people or places, or specialized terms, especially ones that would be difficult to spell or pronounce. These screens do not stay up during the entire talk, however.

Then you will see the question and answer choices, and you will hear the question.

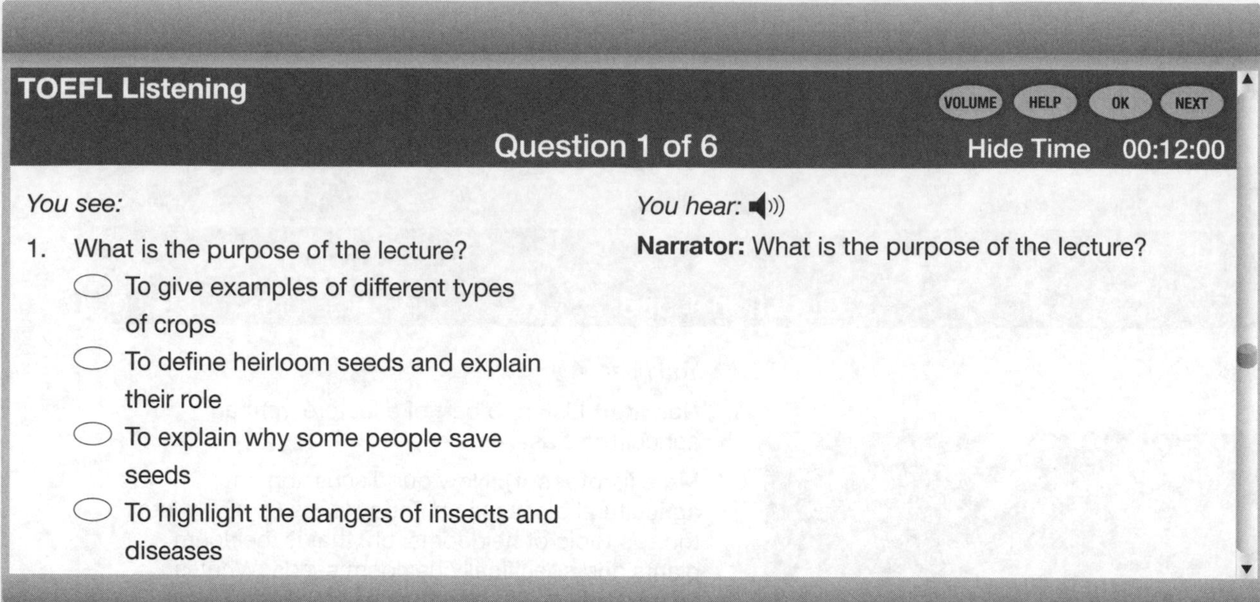

SKILL BUILDER

Directions: *Work with a partner. Look at the pictures in the Example again, which go with the lecture below. Read each sentence of the lecture below and discuss whether it is a main idea or a detail.*

You will hear this lecture, but will not actually see it on the TOEFL iBT Test.

Narrator: Listen to part of a lecture from an agriculture class.

Male (professor): Now our discussion on agricultural diseases on Friday leads us nicely into today's topic of heirlooms, uh, that is, heirloom plants and specifically heirloom seeds. What is an heirloom seed? You may be wondering. Well, I'll give you a definition, but first, let me give you a little background information. One reason crops are so prone to diseases these days is that farmers tend to plant just one or two varieties of something—not surprisingly, they pick the kind of corn, or tomato, or wheat, or whatever, that grows the most quickly and produces the most food. Or sometimes even tastes the best. But, insects that feed on crops, as well as plant diseases—I'm talking funguses, root rot, that sort of thing—develop more quickly and they're stronger when they have just one type of plant to feed on. So the long-term health of crops depends on having a variety of tomatoes, or corn, and so on. Does that make sense? You need a lot of different types all at once because they're more disease-resistant. That's where heirloom seeds come in. You already know the word *heirloom*, of course—something valuable that's passed down from generation to generation. But an heirloom doesn't have to be a piece of jewelry or furniture. Seeds are valuable, too, for the reasons I just mentioned. And there are people, hobby gardeners or in farming communities, who save seeds from different varieties of plants, and whose parents and even grandparents also saved these seeds and passed them down—like heirlooms. And now we're finding that these people, I mean, these seeds, they have the very real potential to help our agricultural industry. Now let's take a look at some specific examples.

Now listen to the lecture and mark the correct answers. 1-2

1. What is the purpose of the lecture?
   Ⓐ To give examples of different types of crops
   Ⓑ To define heirloom seeds and explain their role
   Ⓒ To explain why some people save seeds
   Ⓓ To highlight the dangers of insects and diseases

2. What is the lecture's main point about heirloom seeds?
   Ⓐ They are not as common today as they were in the past.
   Ⓑ They can help protect crops from damage.
   Ⓒ They are passed down in certain families.
   Ⓓ Insects and diseases don't affect them.

EXPRESS TIP

As soon as you have a feeling for what the main idea might be, write it in your notes. You can add an abbreviation such as MI (for "main idea") to help you remember. It's OK to write down more than one guess. Not every listening passage will have a question about the main idea, but writing down the main idea will prepare you for such a question if it occurs, and will also help focus your listening.

MI: *robots in medicine? advances in robotics?*

Skill Builder Answers:

1. **Answer B is correct.** The professor says at the beginning "What is an heirloom seed? You may be wondering. Well, I'll give you a definition . . ." and then explains what heirloom seeds are used for: keeping the agricultural industry healthy by having more plants that are resistant to insects and diseases. Answer A is incorrect because while the professor does list a few different types of crops, it is not the main purpose of the lecture to talk about crops; types of crops is a detail. Answer C is incorrect because it is a detail: The professor does say that some people save seeds, but people who save seeds are only an example of how heirloom seeds can be saved and passed on. Answer D is incorrect because the dangers of insects and diseases are a reason why heirloom seeds are important; explaining the dangers themselves is not the main purpose of the passage.

2. **Answer B is correct.** The importance of heirloom seeds is that they protect crops: "You need a lot of different types [of crops] all at once because they're more disease-resistant. That's where heirloom seeds come in." Answer A is incorrect because the professor does not give any information about how common heirloom seeds are now and were in the past. Answer C is not correct because, although it is true, it is a detail, not the main idea. Answer D is incorrect because the information is false. The lecturer doesn't say that insects and diseases cannot affect heirloom plants, only that when just one type of plant is common, then insects and diseases develop more quickly and are stronger.

PRACTICE

Directions: *Listen to the passages and the* ***main idea*** *questions that follow them. Then mark the correct answers to the questions.*

Passage 1 (Questions 1–2)

Now get ready to listen. You may take notes.

Listen to a conversation between a student and the registrar. 1-3

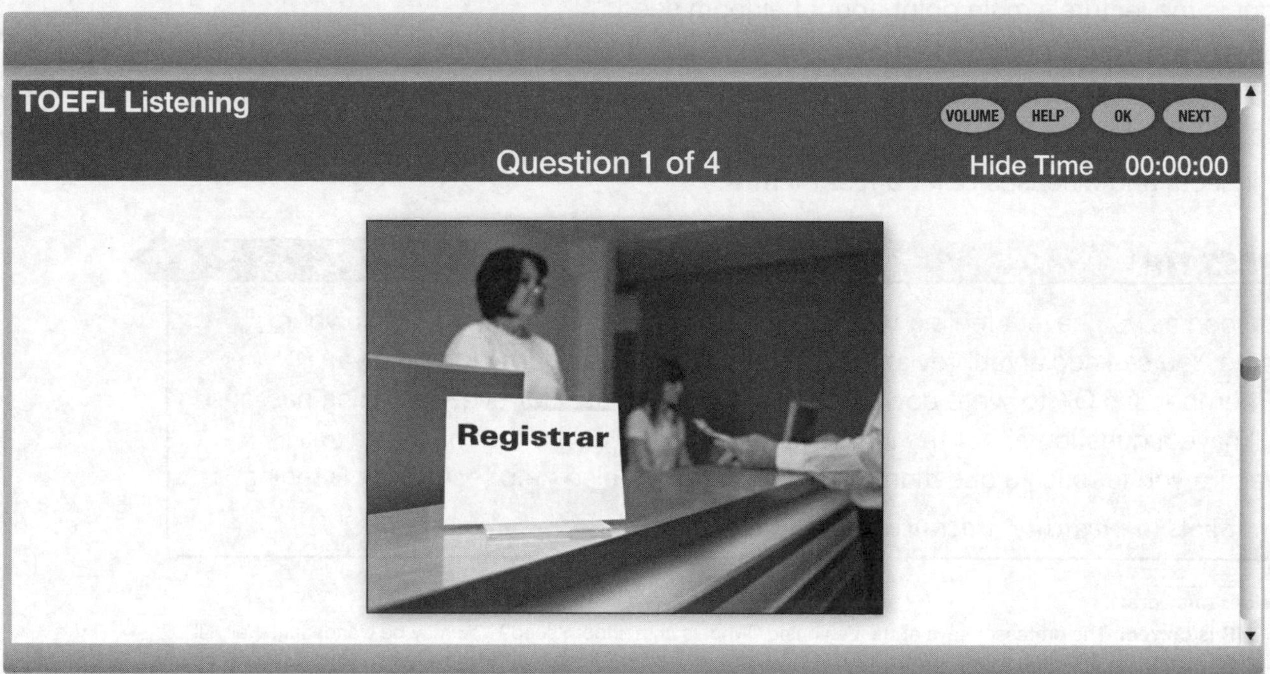

Now get ready to answer the questions. You may use your notes to help you answer the questions.

1. Why does the man go to talk to the registrar?
   - Ⓐ He made a mistake with his class registration.
   - Ⓑ He needs help registering online.
   - Ⓒ He can't register for a class he wants.
   - Ⓓ He can't decide which class to choose.

2. What is the problem with the Business Writing class?
   - Ⓐ It isn't offered on Mondays and Wednesdays.
   - Ⓑ There isn't a waiting list.
   - Ⓒ It's not available until spring.
   - Ⓓ It is currently full.

Passage 2 (Questions 3–4)

Now get ready to listen. You may take notes.

Listen to part of a lecture from an entomology class. 1-4

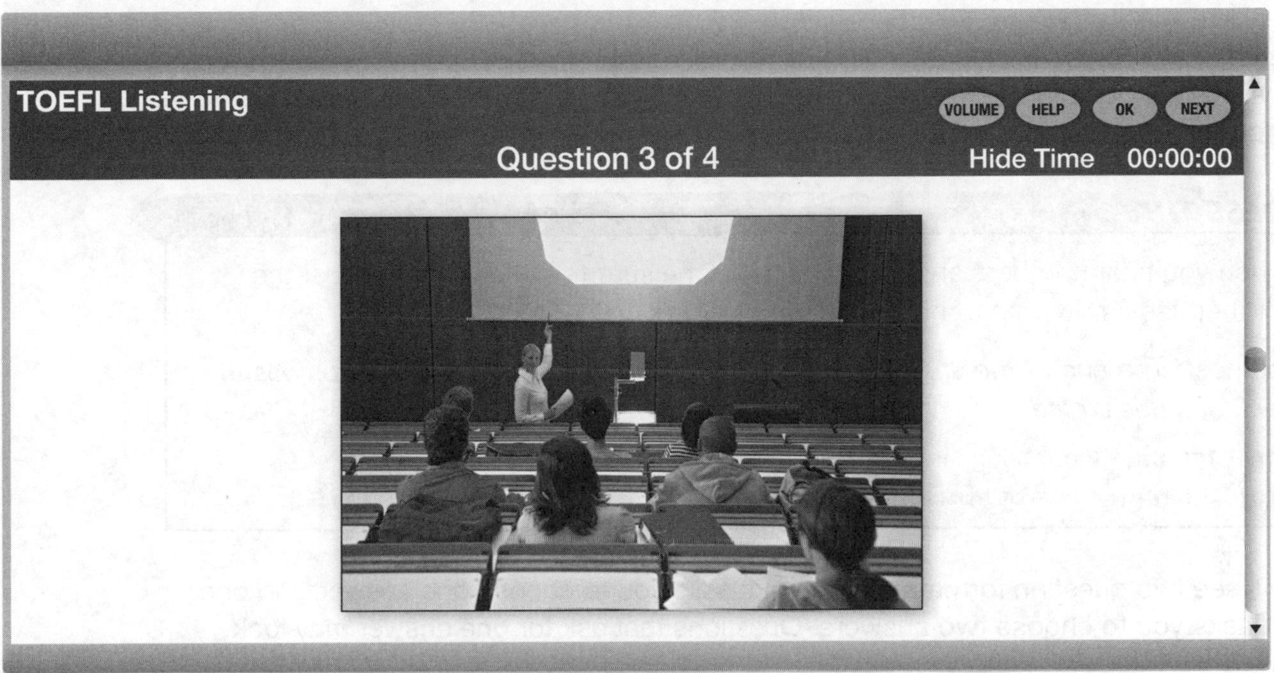

Now get ready to answer the questions. You may use your notes to help you answer the questions.

3. What is the lecture mainly about?
   (A) The appearance of spider webs
   (B) Types of spider webs
   (C) How spider webs are made
   (D) Features of spider webs

4. What is the professor's main point about spider webs?
   (A) They are remarkable.
   (B) They are strong.
   (C) They are used for catching insects.
   (D) They are delicate.

Listening Skill 2: Understanding Details

Questions about a passage's details ask for specific information: dates and times; names of people, places, and specialized terms; statistics or other numbers; and other facts. It can be difficult to remember all of the details from a listening passage, so it is important to take good notes.

Remember that the questions are in the same order as information in the passage. Therefore, the answer to a question at the beginning will be at the top of your notes, and an answer at the end will be toward the bottom of your notes.

EXPRESS TIP

When you hear numbers and specific figures, be sure to write down not just the number itself, but what it means.

You hear: *The end of the Jurassic period, from 161 to 146 million years ago, was the peak of dinosaur life.*

X 161–146 *mya* (not enough information)
√ 161–146 *mya = end of Jurassic, peak of dinosaurs*

You will see two question formats: One format asks you to choose one answer, and one format asks you to choose two answers. Questions that ask for one answer may look like this:

- *How many different species of flamingos are there?*
- *What color are flamingos when they are young?*
- *How many birds live in each flamingo colony?*

Questions that ask for two answers look like this:

What do flamingos eat?

Click on 2 answers.

Like the Reading section (see pages 30–41), a detail question might be in the form of a negative question. Questions of this type will include the word NOT or EXCEPT:

- *The James's Flamingo is found in all of these countries EXCEPT*
- *Which of these factors is NOT thought to be a cause for declining flamingo populations?*

Look at this example of a detail question on a computer screen.

First you will hear a lecture, a discussion, or a conversation:

EXAMPLE: Detail Question

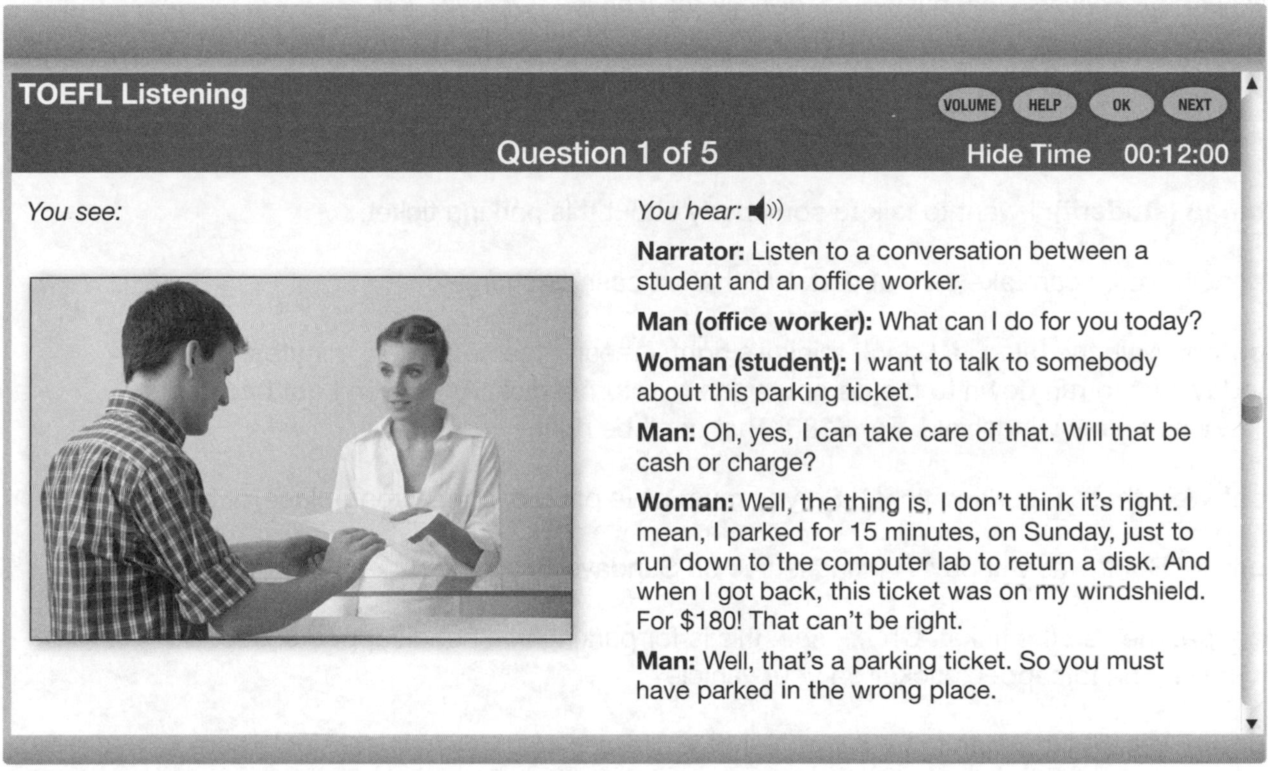

Then you will see the question and answer choices, and you will hear the question.

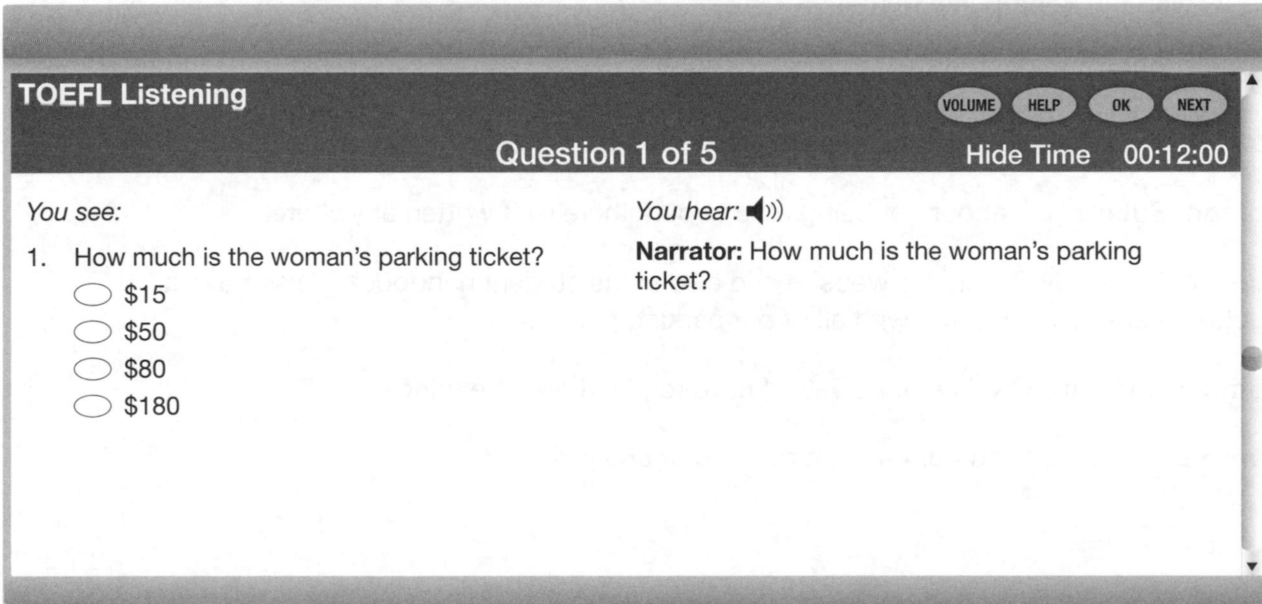

SKILL BUILDER

Directions: *Work with a partner. Look at the pictures in the Example again, which go with the conversation. Read the conversation together, and discuss which details you think are important to include in your notes.*

You will hear this conversation, but will not actually see it on the TOEFL iBT Test.

Narrator: Listen to a conversation between a student and an office worker.

Man (office worker): What can I do for you today?

Woman (student): I want to talk to somebody about this parking ticket.

Man: Oh, yes, I can take care of that. Will that be cash or charge?

Woman: Well, the thing is, I don't think it's right. I mean, I parked for 15 minutes, on Sunday, just to run down to the computer lab to return a disk. And when I got back, this ticket was on my windshield. For $180! That can't be right.

Man: Well, that's a parking ticket. So you must have parked in the wrong place.

Woman: But it was Sunday! Parking is free on Sundays!

Man: Let me see the ticket. Oh . . . see, this is for parking in a handicapped space. Do you have a handicapped sticker on your vehicle?

Woman: What? No, I don't, but it was Sunday. Classes aren't even in session! There weren't any other cars there! And I was only there for 15 minutes.

Man: That doesn't make any difference. Those spots are reserved all day, every day for people with the appropriate permit.

Woman: But how was I supposed to know that? It doesn't say so anywhere.

Man: All of the handicapped places are marked both on the pavement and with a sign.

Woman: But the rule about not being able to park there isn't written anywhere.

Man: Well, actually, it's on our website and also in the student handbook. I also have a brochure here I can give you with all of our parking policies.

Woman: No, that's OK. I get it now. So I have to pay the whole thing?

Man: Yes, I'm afraid you do. Will that be cash or charge?

Now listen to the conversation and mark the correct answers. 1-5

1. How much is the woman's parking ticket?
   - Ⓐ $15
   - Ⓑ $50
   - Ⓒ $80
   - Ⓓ $180

2. The rules for parking in a handicapped place are published in all of the following places EXCEPT
   - Ⓐ on the university website
   - Ⓑ on a sign near the parking places
   - Ⓒ in a brochure
   - Ⓓ in the student handbook

EXPRESS TIP

Many detail questions are answers to questions about *where*, *when*, or *how* something happens or occurred. The answers to these questions are often found in prepositional phrases. Therefore, be alert to these while you are taking notes.

Where . . . ? = *at the observatory, in the laboratory, in Spain*
When . . . ? = *in 1872, after the water boils, in his late 30s*
How . . . ? = *by candlelight, with a thermometer, by removing the bark*

Skill Builder Answers:

1. **Answer D is correct.** The woman says, "And when I got back, this ticket was on my windshield. For $180!" Answer A is incorrect because the woman says she parked for 15 minutes; 15 was not the ticket price. Answer B is incorrect because 50 (which sounds like 15) is not mentioned as the price of the ticket. Answer C is incorrect because the ticket price is $180, not $80.

2. **Answer B is correct.** "On a sign near the parking places" is not mentioned as a place where the rules are posted. Answers A, C, and D are incorrect because they are all mentioned: the rule is ". . . on our website and also in the student handbook. I also have a brochure here . . ."

PRACTICE

Directions: *Listen to the passages and the* ***detail*** *questions that follow them. Then mark the correct answers to the questions.*

Passage 1 (Questions 1–2)

Now get ready to listen. You may take notes.

Listen to part of a lecture from an economics class. 1-6

Now get ready to answer the questions. You may use your notes to help you answer the questions.

1. When was the term *supply-side economics* first used?

   Ⓐ 1970
   Ⓑ 1975
   Ⓒ 1981
   Ⓓ 1989

2. How can producers be encouraged to increase supplies?

   Choose 2 answers.

   [A] Increase taxes for consumers
   [B] Increase business regulations
   [C] Lower taxes for investors
   [D] Decrease tariffs on raw materials

Passage 2 (Questions 3–4)

Now get ready to listen. You may take notes.

Listen to part of a discussion from a literature class. 1-7

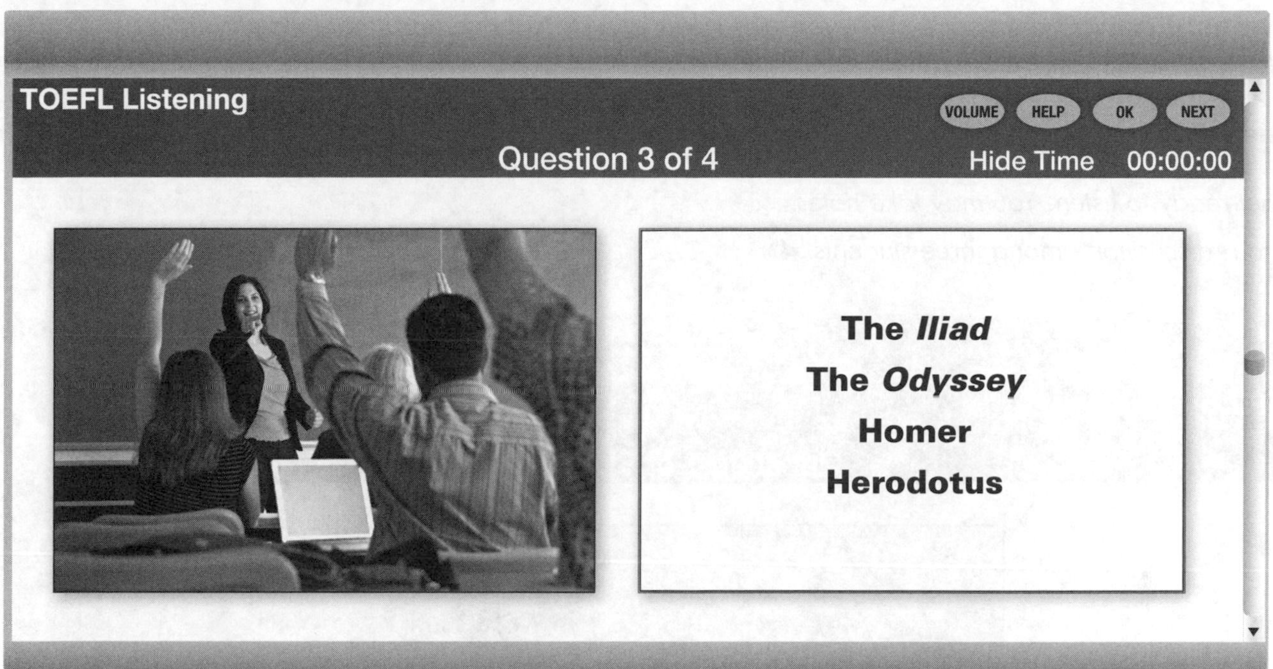

Now get ready to answer the questions. You may use your notes to help you answer the questions.

3. When was the Trojan War?
   Ⓐ The 12th century B.C.
   Ⓑ The 9th century B.C.
   Ⓒ The 7th century B.C.
   Ⓓ The 5th century B.C.

4. Which of the following is NOT given as a reason for believing that Homer didn't write the *Iliad* and the *Odyssey*?
   Ⓐ The books were written by several different authors.
   Ⓑ The books' styles are very different from each other.
   Ⓒ One of the books was probably written by Herodotus.
   Ⓓ There isn't much information about the life of Homer.

SKILLS REVIEW

Listening Skills 1 and 2: Understanding the Main Idea and Understanding Details

Directions: *Listen to the passage and the* ***main idea*** *and* ***detail*** *questions that follow it. Then mark the correct answers to the questions.*

Questions 1–5

Now get ready to listen. You may take notes.

Listen to a discussion among three students. 1-8

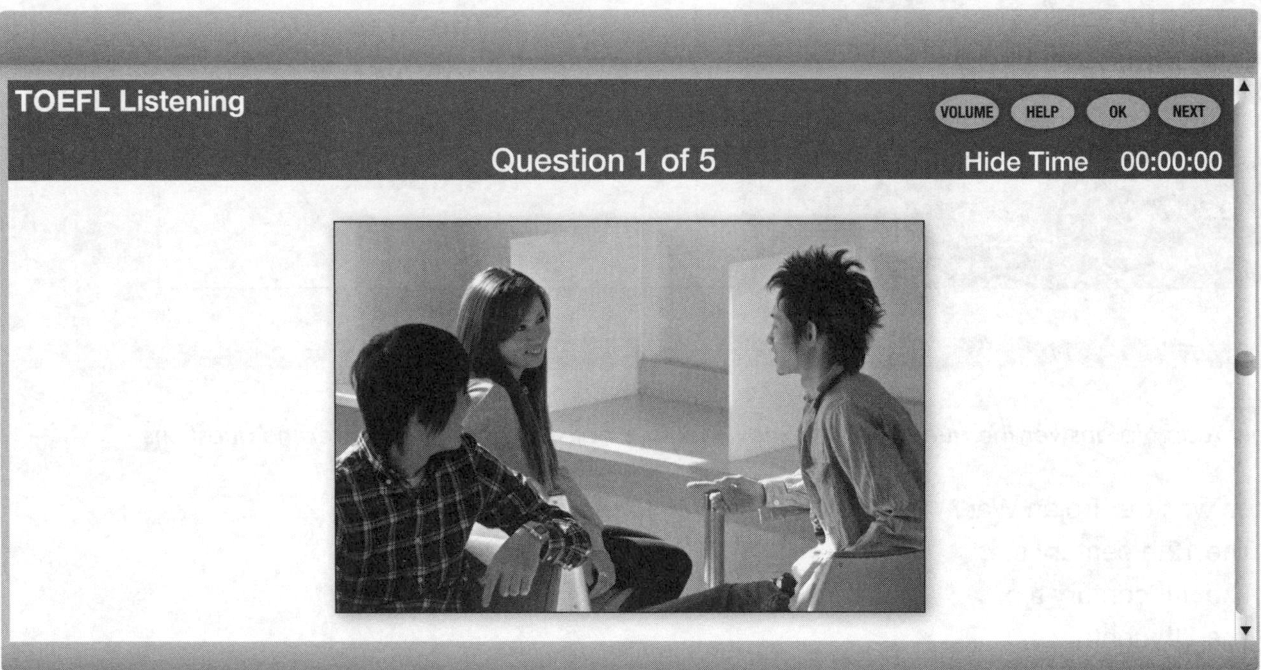

Now get ready to answer the questions. You may use your notes to help you answer the questions.

1. What is the purpose of this discussion?
   - Ⓐ To plan a video script
   - Ⓑ To figure out when a project is due
   - Ⓒ To divide an assignment's workload
   - Ⓓ To learn how to make a film

2. When is the video presentation due?
   - Ⓐ On the 27th
   - Ⓑ On the 28th
   - Ⓒ On the 29th
   - Ⓓ On the 30th

3. What is Kate's main responsibility?

Ⓐ To organize the project

Ⓑ To write the report

Ⓒ To film the video

Ⓓ To write the script

4. What does the written report need to include?

Choose 2 answers.

[A] A copy of the video script

[B] A summary of what was learned

[C] Citations of all sources used

[D] Some interviews with experts

5. Which of the following is NOT mentioned as part of editing the video?

Ⓐ Cutting out any sections that weren't good enough

Ⓑ Putting in some special effects

Ⓒ Adding music tracks

Ⓓ Re-filming any scenes that didn't work well

LISTENING SKILLS 3 AND 4

UNDERSTANDING THE FUNCTION; UNDERSTANDING THE SPEAKER'S STANCE

Listening Skill 3: Understanding the Function

Function questions require you to listen to part of a conversation or lecture from the passage again, and then you will be asked to determine the function or purpose of a smaller portion that is replayed. This type of question is not asking you for the general topic or main idea of what the speaker said, but rather is asking you *why* the speaker said something.

The *functions* of what is said in this type of replay question include the following:

- to apologize
- to ask for or add more information
- to change the subject
- to clarify or make a previous statement clearer
- to complain
- to interrupt
- to make a suggestion or a recommendation

In addition, some of the questions will ask you what was *implied* when the speaker used a certain expression or answered a question in a specific way. In other words, you will need to understand the speaker's purpose when it is *not* directly stated.

The following are examples of this type of question:

Listen again to part of the conversation. Then answer the question. 🔊

- *Why does the speaker say this?* 🔊
- *What does the speaker mean?* 🔊
- *What does the speaker imply when he says this?* 🔊
- *What is the purpose of the speaker's response?* 🔊

Note that the [🔊] icon indicates that part of the conversation or lecture will be replayed. You will not see this part of the conversation or lecture on the computer screen.

In order to answer the question correctly, you must listen closely and understand who the speakers are, where they are, and what is happening in the context of the conversation or lecture. You must then figure out the speaker's purpose or reason based on the context.

EXPRESS TIP

It is common for people to say something that sounds like a statement of fact when actually they have another purpose for saying it. For example, a woman says this to her roommate:

Woman: *Hey, Susan, I think the people in the next apartment can probably hear your music.*

It is likely that the woman is not saying this to inform Susan that the neighbors can hear her music. The real purpose is to get Susan to turn down the volume because it is too loud. Therefore, you must learn to listen not just to the words that are spoken, but to what they actually **mean** in any particular situation. Tone of voice can provide addition clues.

Look at this example of a function question on a computer screen.

First, you will see some images and hear a lecture, discussion, or conversation.

EXAMPLE: Function Question

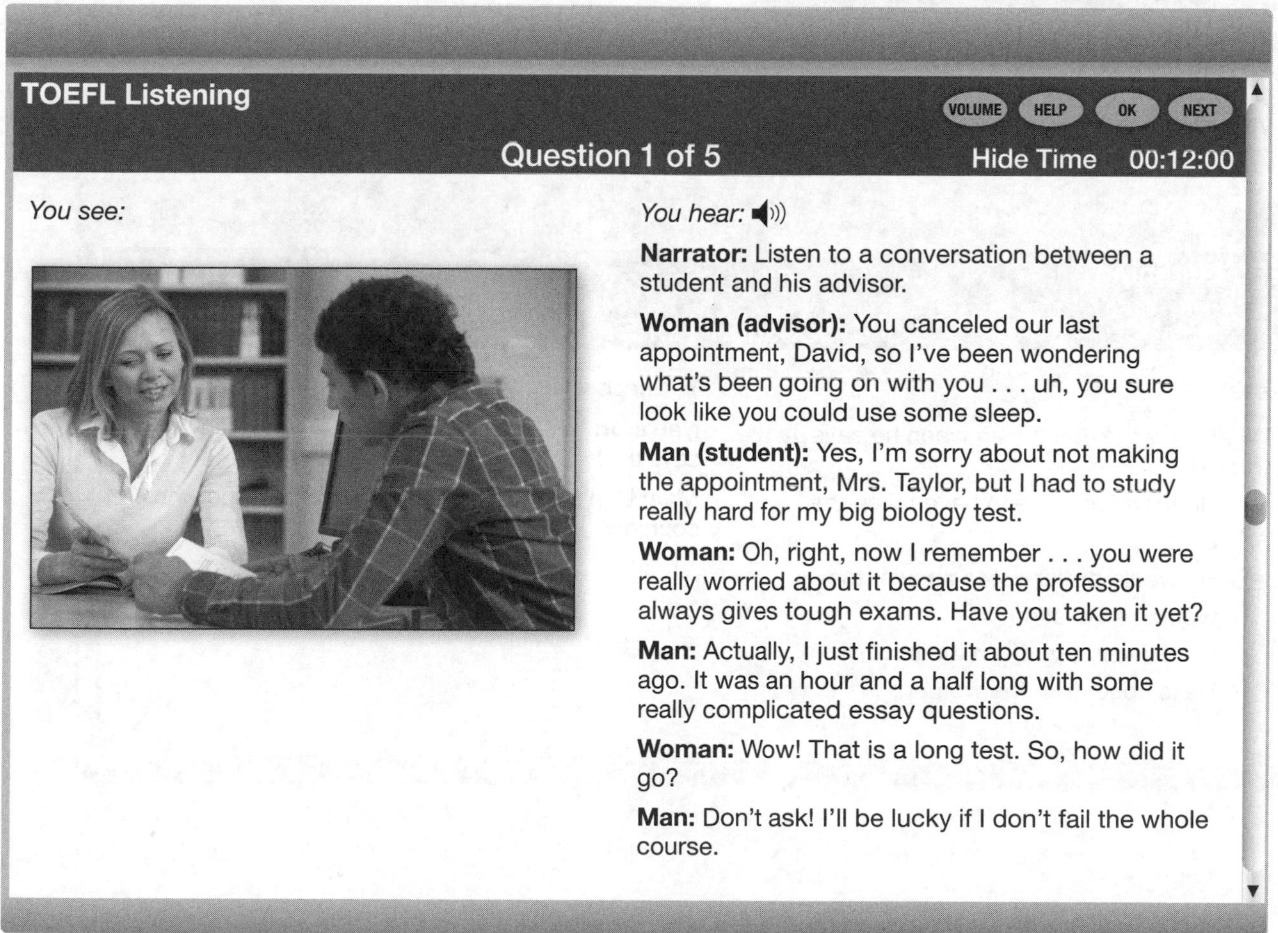

Then you will see a picture and hear part of the conversation replayed:

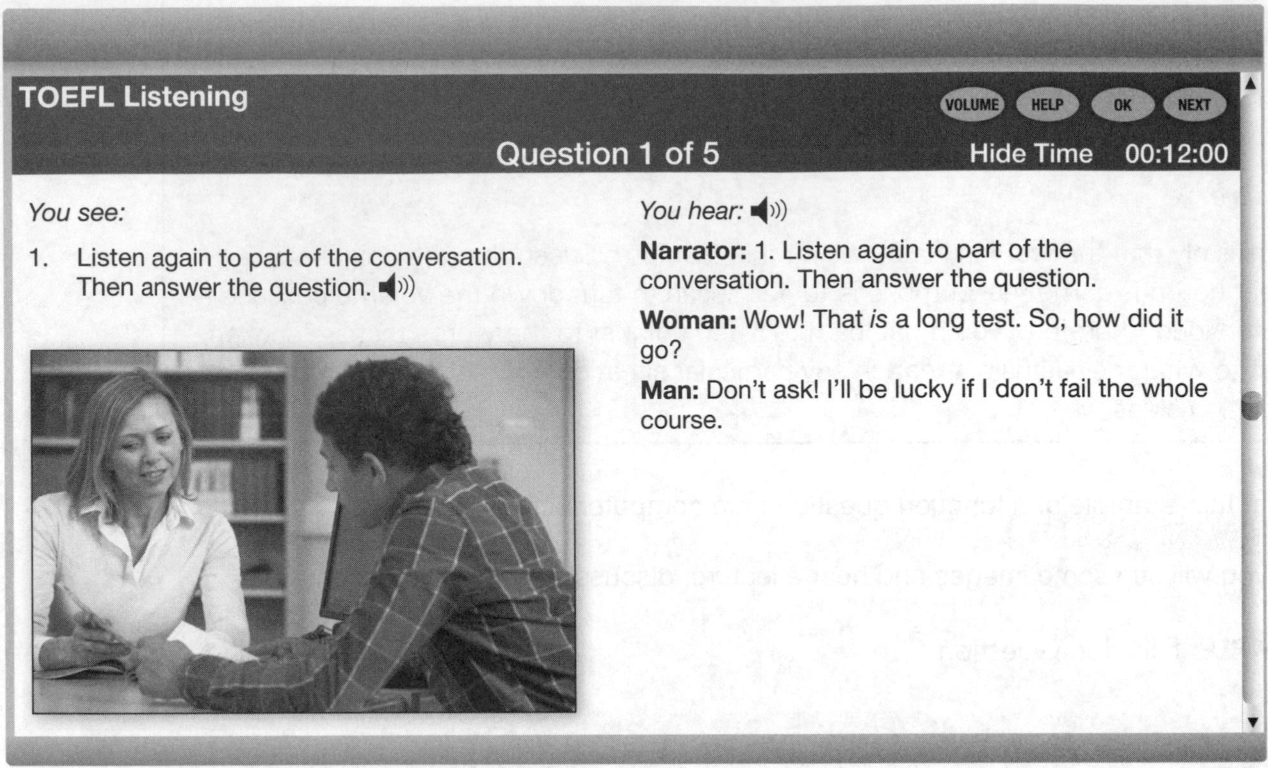

Then you will see and hear the questions:

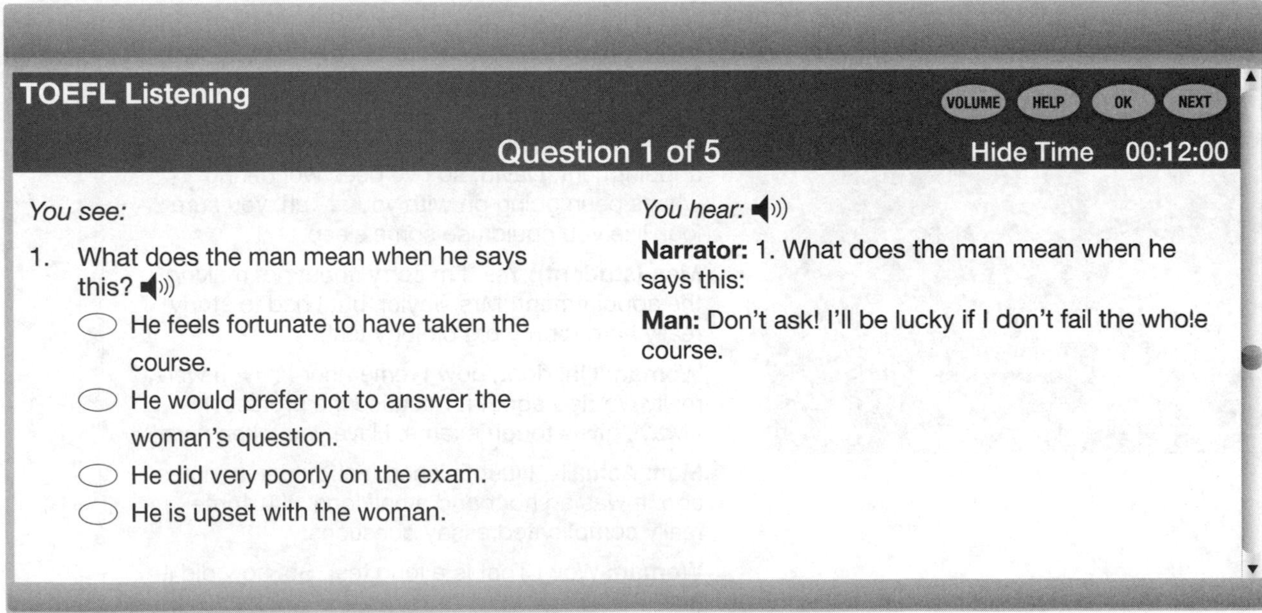

SKILL BUILDER

Directions: *Work with a partner. Look at the pictures in the Example again, which go with the conversation below. Read the conversation aloud.*

You will hear this conversation, but will not actually see it on the TOEFL iBT Test.

Narrator: Listen to a conversation between a student and his advisor.

Woman (advisor): You canceled our last appointment, David, so I've been wondering what's been going on with you . . . uh, you sure look like you could use some sleep.

Man (student): Yes, I'm sorry about not making the appointment, Mrs. Taylor, but I had to study really hard for my big biology test.

Woman: Oh, right, now I remember . . . you were really worried about it because the professor always gives tough exams. Have you taken it yet?

Man: Actually, I just finished it about ten minutes ago. It was an hour and a half long with some really complicated essay questions.

Woman: Wow! That *is* a long test. So, how did it go?

Man: Don't ask! I'll be lucky if I don't fail the whole course.

Woman: Oh, come on. You're probably just tired right now. I'm sure you did better than you think you did.

Man: Well, I guess I'll just have to wait and see. I missed a few lectures because I spent too much time practicing for the tennis championship matches.

Woman: That probably wasn't such a great idea. You need to keep on top of your academic studies.

Man: That's true, but it's the tennis scholarship that's paying my way through school, so what I am supposed to do?

Woman: I think you need to find a better way to balance both your coursework and your sports.

Working with your partner, take turns answering the questions below.

1. Why has the woman been wondering about the man?
2. What has the man just finished doing?
3. What is the man's reaction to what he has just finished doing?
4. How does the woman react to what the man says about this?
5. How well does the man think he did?
6. What does the woman say to him about his feelings?
7. Why does the man think he performed the way he did?
8. What does the woman say to him about his studies and his other activities?

Now listen to the conversation and mark the correct answers. 1-9

1. Listen again to part of the conversation. Then answer the question. 1-10
   What does the man mean when he says this?
   Ⓐ He feels fortunate to have taken the course.
   Ⓑ He would prefer not to answer the woman's question.
   Ⓒ He did very poorly on the exam.
   Ⓓ He is upset with the woman.

2. Listen again to part of the conversation. Then answer the question. 1-11
   Why does the woman say this?
   Ⓐ To explain how to play tennis better
   Ⓑ To disagree with the man's alternative plan
   Ⓒ To encourage the man to stop playing sports
   Ⓓ To advise the man about his coursework

EXPRESS TIP

Listen very carefully to the short, replay part of the question and take a few, quick notes. Remember the speaker may not directly state the purpose. Therefore, avoid choosing an answer that repeats the exact, same words you heard in the replay.

Skill Builder Answers:

1. **Answer C is correct.** The man says, "I'll be lucky if I don't fail the whole course." He means that he might fail the course because he did so *poorly on the exam*. Answer A is incorrect because the man does not say is *fortunate to have taken the course*; his tone of voice indicates that he is upset and not feeling fortunate. Answer B is incorrect because he does not mean that he *would prefer not to answer the woman's question* when he says, "Don't ask!" This phrase is used when someone is upset about something and it means that the answer to a question about it will not be positive. It doesn't literally really mean someone shouldn't ask. Answer D is incorrect because the man is not upset with the woman; he is upset with himself for doing poorly on the exam.

2. **Answer D is correct.** The woman is offering the man advice by suggesting, "I think you need to find a better way to balance both your coursework and your sports." Answer A is incorrect because she is not explaining how to *play tennis better*, but is explaining a better way to be a good student. Answer B is incorrect because there is no information in the conversation that indicates an alternative plan is being offered. Answer C is incorrect because the woman does not say he should *stop playing sports*, but that he should balance his sports and coursework.

PRACTICE

Directions: *Listen to the passages and the* **function** *(replay) questions that follow them. Then mark the correct answers to the questions.*

Passage 1 (Questions 1–3)

Now get ready to listen. You may take notes.

Listen to part of a discussion between some students and a university official during a new-student orientation. 1-12

Now get ready to answer the questions. You may use your notes to help you answer the questions.

1. Listen again to part of the discussion. Then answer the question. 1-13
   What is the purpose of the female student's response?
   Ⓐ To ask for clarification
   Ⓑ To apologize for interrupting
   Ⓒ To indicate that she disagrees
   Ⓓ To complain about the policy

2. Listen again to part of the discussion. Then answer the question. 1-14
   Why does the male student say this?
   Ⓐ He doesn't believe the university official.
   Ⓑ He is surprised by the information.
   Ⓒ He is impressed by the student.
   Ⓓ He doesn't understand what was said.

3. Listen again to part of the discussion. Then answer the question. 1-15
What does the university official imply when he says this?
Ⓐ The students are likely to have similar problems.
Ⓑ The students have not given him the correct response.
Ⓒ The students have never had anything like this happen to them.
Ⓓ The students should take what he is saying seriously.

Passage 2 (Questions 4 –7)

Now get ready to listen. You may take notes.

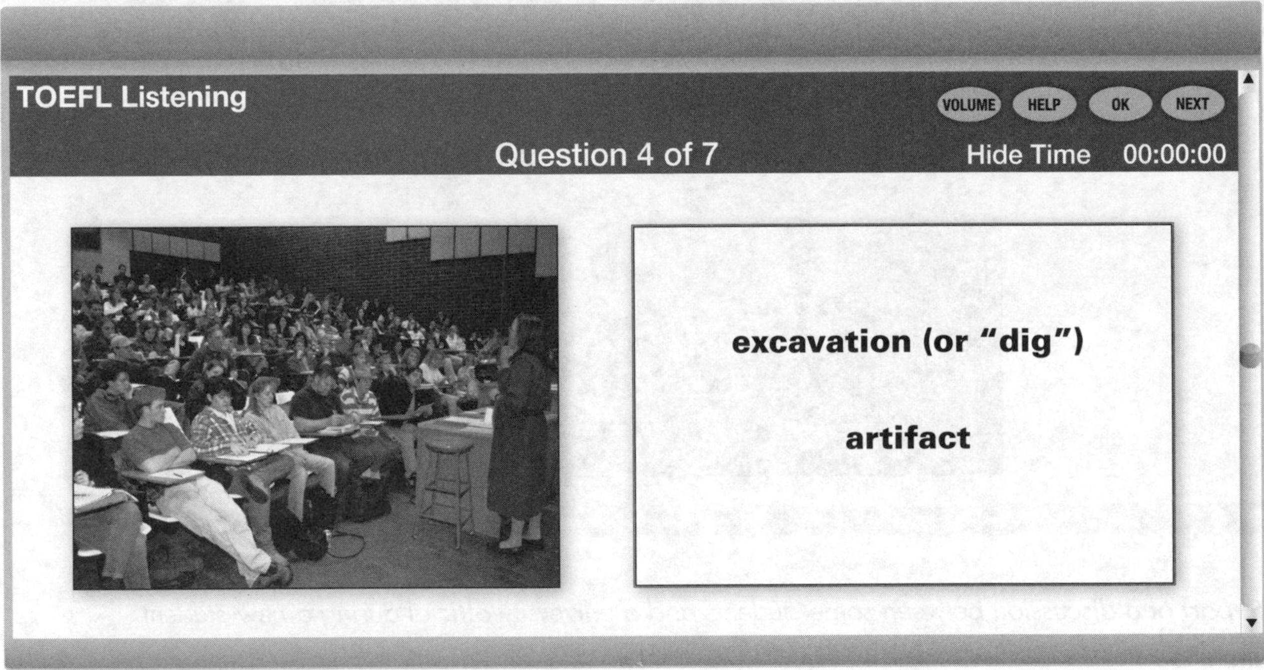

Listen to part of a lecture in an archaeology class. 1-16

Now get ready to answer the questions. You may use your notes to help you answer the questions.

4. Listen again to part of the discussion. Then answer the question. 1-17
What does the professor mean when she says this?
Ⓐ There are many possible approaches.
Ⓑ Traveling great distances is required.
Ⓒ The task is difficult and takes a long time.
Ⓓ Taking dangerous roads is part of the job.

5. Listen again to part of the discussion. Then answer the question. 1-18
Why does the professor say this?
Ⓐ She is introducing a new topic.
Ⓑ She is adding some information.
Ⓒ She is correcting a mistake.
Ⓓ She is emphasizing an important point.

6. Listen again to part of the discussion. Then answer the question. 1-19

   Why does the professor say this?

   Ⓐ She wants to make sure the students understand.

   Ⓑ She is going to tell a story related to the topic.

   Ⓒ She is asking the students for help.

   Ⓓ She moved away from the main topic and is returning to it.

7. Listen again to part of the discussion. Then answer the question. 1-20

   Why does the professor say this?

   Ⓐ She is apologizing in case she was unclear.

   Ⓑ She is pausing in order to remember a point.

   Ⓒ She forgot to mention something important.

   Ⓓ She wants to explain her opinion.

Listening Skill 4: Understanding the Speaker's Stance

Stance questions require you to listen to a part of a conversation or lecture from the passage that will be replayed; you will be asked to determine what the stance or the attitude of the speaker is in the portion that is replayed. This type of question is asking you to listen for the speaker's feelings or opinions about a person, thing, or an event, which include:

- agreement or disagreement
- enjoyment or amusement
- enthusiasm or indifference
- excitement or boredom
- happiness or sadness
- irritation or anger
- likes or dislikes
- satisfaction or disappointment
- worry or anxiety

In addition, some of the questions will ask you how *certain* a speaker is about his or her opinion. You will need to understand if the speaker is expressing a personal opinion or is stating an accepted fact.

The following are examples of this type of question:

Listen again to part of the conversation. Then answer the question.

- *How does the speaker feel about X?*
- *Which of the following best expresses the speaker's attitude toward X?*
- *What is the speaker's opinion of X?*
- *What can be inferred about the speaker when she says this?*
- *What does the speaker imply when he says this?*
- *What does the speaker mean when she says this?*

Note that the [ ] icon indicates that part of the conversation or lecture will be replayed. You will not see this part of the conversation or lecture on the computer screen.

In order to answer the question correctly, you must listen carefully and understand how the speaker is feeling and how certain the speaker is about what he or she is saying. This information may *not* be *directly* stated, so you must infer the speaker's feeling or degree of certainty by paying close attention to the context and the emotional tone the speaker uses.

EXPRESS TIP

Listen to the way the speakers talk. The tone of voice, intonation (the rise and fall in the voice), and stress (words that are louder than others) can give you important information about how the speaker is feeling and how certain the speaker is.

For example: 1-21

That's a great idea! (The speaker likes the idea and agrees it's a good one.)

Great. I guess we'll have to use his idea. (The speaker is unhappy or disappointed and does not really think the idea is a good one.)

*It **looks** safe enough to climb.* (The speaker emphasizes *looks* to mean that it might not be safe.)

It looks safe enough to climb. (The speaker is stating the fact that it seems safe.)

Remember to pay attention to tone of voice.

Look at this example of a stance question on a computer screen.

First, you will see some images and hear a lecture, discussion, or conversation.

EXAMPLE: Stance Question

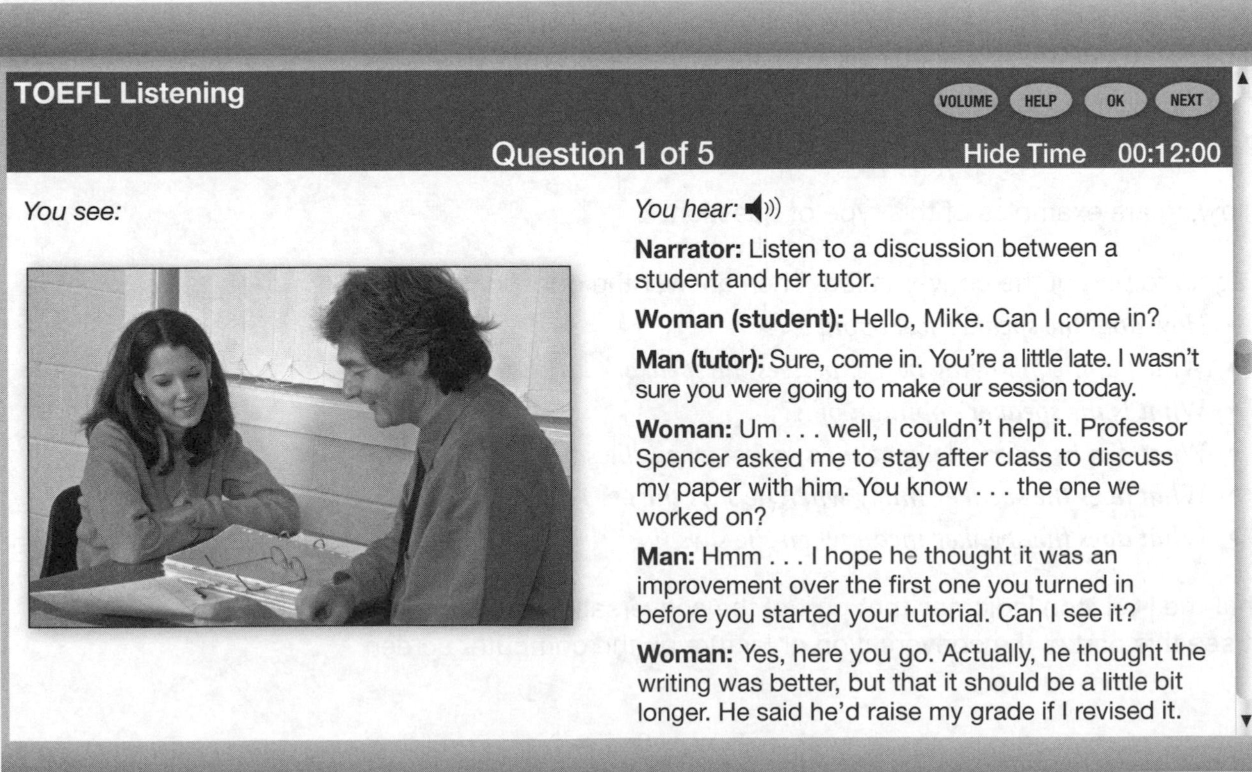

TOEFL Listening
VOLUME
HELP
OK
NEXT
Question 1 of 5
Hide Time 00:12:00
You see:
You hear:
Narrator: Listen to a discussion between a student and her tutor.
Woman (student): Hello, Mike. Can I come in?
Man (tutor): Sure, come in. You're a little late. I wasn't sure you were going to make our session today.
Woman: Um . . . well, I couldn't help it. Professor Spencer asked me to stay after class to discuss my paper with him. You know . . . the one we worked on?
Man: Hmm . . . I hope he thought it was an improvement over the first one you turned in before you started your tutorial. Can I see it?
Woman: Yes, here you go. Actually, he thought the writing was better, but that it should be a little bit longer. He said he'd raise my grade if I revised it.

Then you will see a picture and hear part of the conversation replayed:

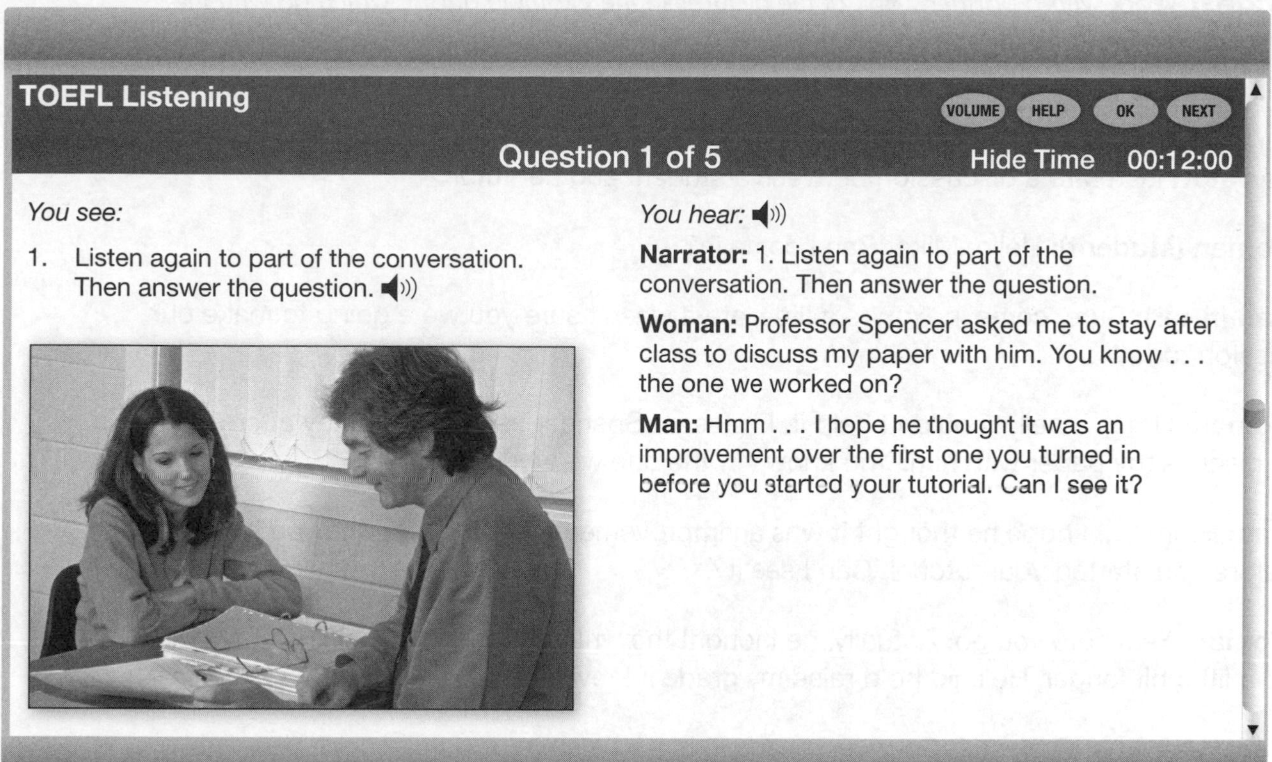

Then you will see and hear the questions:

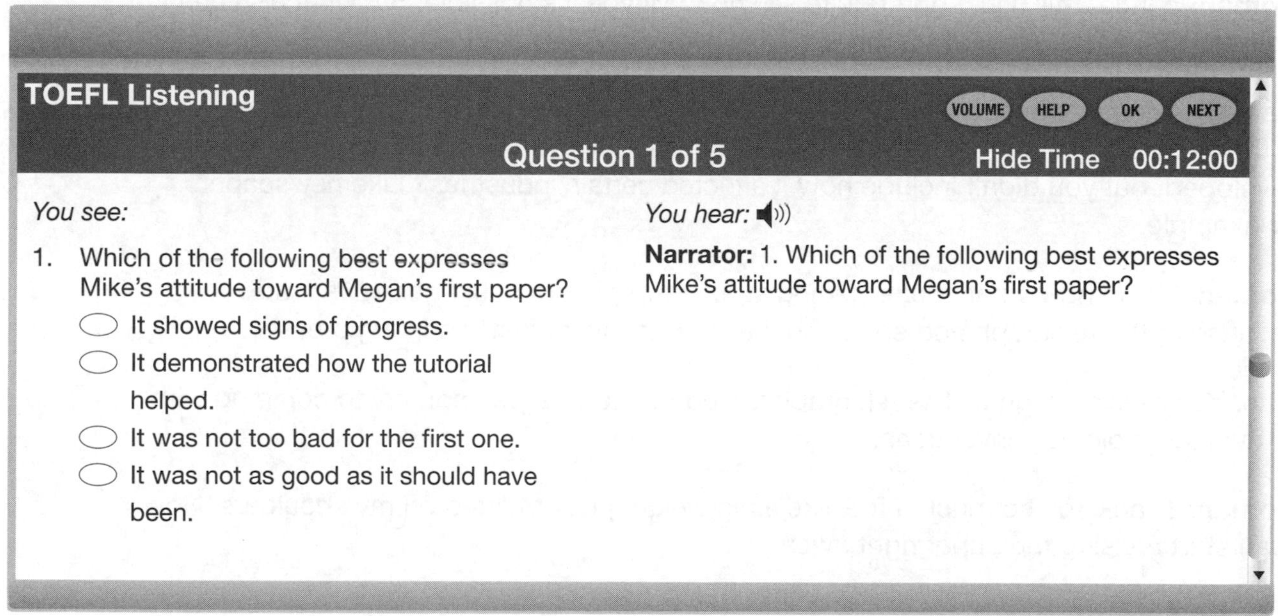

SKILL BUILDER

Directions: *Work with a partner. Look at the pictures in the Example again, which go with the conversation below. Read the conversation aloud.*

You will hear this conversation, but will not actually see it on the TOEFL iBT Test.

Narrator: Listen to a discussion between a student and her tutor.

Woman (student): Hello, Mike. Can I come in?

Man (tutor): Sure, come in. You're a little late. I wasn't sure you were going to make our session today.

Woman: Um . . . well, I couldn't help it. Professor Spencer asked me to stay after class to discuss my paper with him. You know . . . the one we worked on?

Man: Hmm . . . I hope he thought it was an improvement over the first one you turned in before you started your tutorial. Can I see it?

Woman: Yes, here you go. Actually, he thought the writing was better, but that it should be a little bit longer. He said he'd raise my grade if I revised it.

Man: I see what Professor Spencer means; it is a little short. I wish I'd seen your final draft before you turned it in. Anyway, have you thought about how you might expand the topic?

Woman: A little. Still, I just don't quite see how. Maybe it's possible, but what else can I include? Oh, this is so hard for me.

Man: Oh, Megan, cheer up! Let's take a look at your topic again . . . "The Invention of the Telegraph." Hmm . . . I see that you discussed who invented it and how it was developed, but you didn't include how it affected certain industries? Like newspapers, for example.

Woman: Uh, I know what you're getting at . . . newspapers could get news faster because of the telegraph and so . . . so they had to invent faster printing presses.

Man: You're exactly right! The telegraph forced the newspaper industry to come up with its own technological inventions.

Woman: Thank you so much. I feel like a big weight just got lifted off my shoulders. Now I can start revising the paper right away!

Working with your partner, take turns answering the questions below.

1. How does Mike, Megan's tutor, respond when she shows up? What does he say that reveals what he is feeling?
2. What was Megan doing before she came to see Mike? Can you guess how she felt?
3. What is Mike's opinion of Megan's writing skills before he started tutoring her?
4. What is Mike's attitude about Megan's final draft? What does he say to her about it?
5. Does Mike agree or disagree with Professor Spencer's recommendation? What phrase tells you he agreed or disagreed?
6. How does Megan feel about what Professor Spencer asked her to do? What does she say that helps you to understand her emotions?
7. Why does Mike say "Cheer up!" to Megan?
8. How does Megan feel at the end of the conversation? Do you understand the phrase she uses to express her feelings? Does the context help you?

Now listen to the conversation and mark the correct answers. 1-22

1. Listen again to part of the conversation. Then answer the question. 1-23
   Which of the following best expresses Mike's attitude toward Megan's first paper?
   Ⓐ It showed signs of progress.
   Ⓑ It demonstrated how the tutorial helped.
   Ⓒ It was not too bad for the first one.
   Ⓓ It was not as good as it should have been.

2. Listen again to part of the conversation. Then answer the question. 1-24
   How does Megan feel about what Professor Spencer has recommended?
   Ⓐ She is sure that it cannot be done.
   Ⓑ She is uncertain about how difficult it will be.
   Ⓒ She is unsure about being able to do it.
   Ⓓ She is certain that she included everything.

3. Listen again to part of the conversation. Then answer the question. 1-25
   What does Megan mean when she says this?
   Ⓐ Mike's suggestion has made her feel relieved.
   Ⓑ She is grateful to Mike for his help, but is still worried.
   Ⓒ She will feel better after she does some exercises.
   Ⓓ Mike doesn't understand how much stress she is experiencing.

EXPRESS TIP

Stance questions usually require you to make an inference about information that is not directly stated. For more information on the skills necessary for answering inference questions, please see Listening Skill 6, "Making Inferences," pages 130–137.

Skill Builder Answers:

1. **Answer D is correct.** The tutor, Mike, says, "I hope he thought it was an improvement over the first one you turned in . . . ," which means if he thought Megan's paper needed *improvement*, it was *not as good as it should have been*. Answer A is incorrect because it states the opposite of Mike's attitude. Answer B is incorrect because she turned in her first paper *before* she started her tutorial; therefore, the tutorial couldn't have helped her. Answer C is incorrect because the paper isn't good (*not so bad* means it's OK) and because Mike compares the paper they are now discussing with the first paper, so this cannot be her first one.

2. **Answer C is correct.** Megan says, "Still, I just don't quite see how. Maybe it's possible, but what else can I include? Oh, this is so hard for me." This means that if she doesn't quite understand how to expand the topic then she is *unsure about being able to do it*. Her tone of voice also indicates that she is unsure. Answer A is incorrect because Megan is not indicating she is sure that she *can't* do, but rather is unsure about *how* to do it. Answer B is incorrect because Megan *is* sure about how difficult it is; "Oh, this is so hard for me." Answer D is incorrect because there is no information in the conversation to indicate Megan feels this way.

3. **Answer A is correct.** The expression, "a big weight lifted off someone's shoulders" means that someone feels thankful or relieved that a problem is solved. Mike's suggestion has helped Megan solve the problem. Answer B is incorrect because there is no indication that Megan is still worried. Answer C is incorrect because there is no indication that Megan is going to exercise; this is an incorrect meaning of the expression "a big weight lifted off someone's shoulders." Answer D is incorrect because it is clear Megan is feeling less stress by the expression she uses and her tone of voice.

PRACTICE

Directions: *Listen to the passages and the* ***stance*** *(replay) questions that follow them. Then mark the correct answers to the questions.*

Passage 1 (Questions 1–3)

Now get ready to listen. You may take notes.

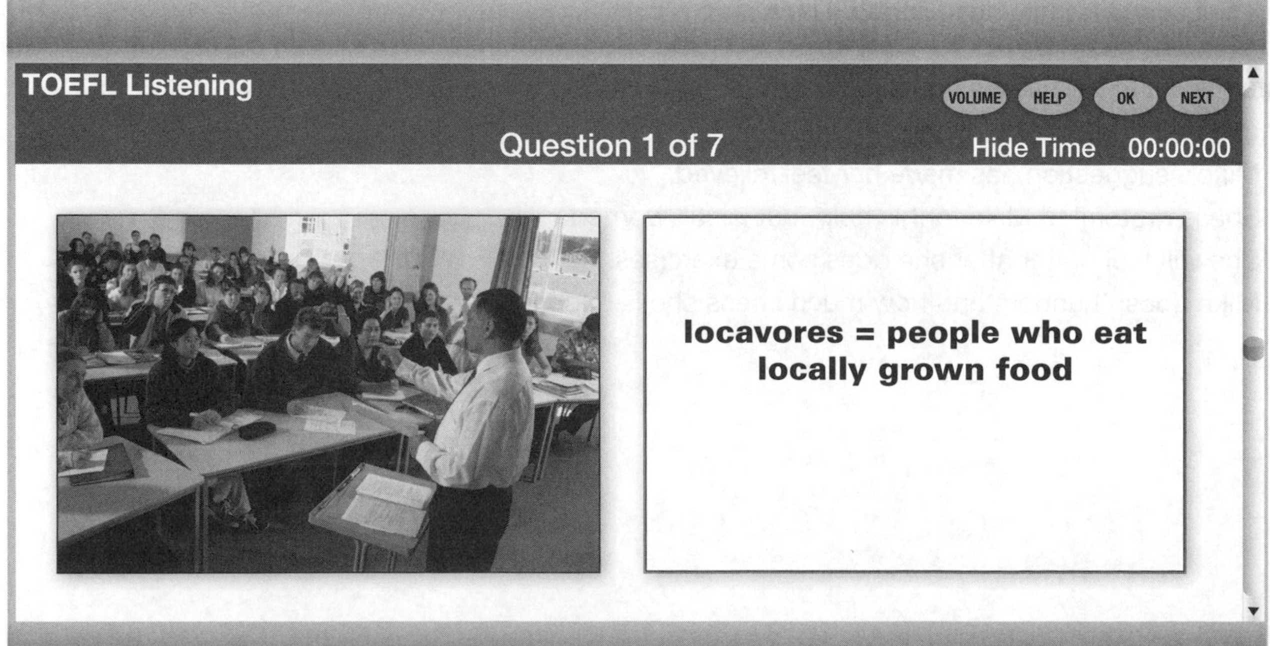

Listen to part of a lecture in an environmental studies class. 1-26

Now get ready to answer the questions. You may use your notes to help you answer the questions.

1. Listen again to part of the lecture. Then answer the question. 1-27
   What is the professor's attitude about the "eat locally" food movement?
   Ⓐ He doesn't support it.
   Ⓑ He doesn't care about its goals.
   Ⓒ He has mixed feelings about it.
   Ⓓ He feels it offers great benefits.

2. Listen again to part of the lecture. Then answer the question. 1-28
   How does the professor feel about serious "locavores"?
   Ⓐ They should be admired for their dedication.
   Ⓑ They provide truly innovative suggestions.
   Ⓒ They are practical about what can be done.
   Ⓓ They are extreme in some of their ideas.

3. Listen again to part of the lecture. Then answer the question. 1-29
   What is the professor's opinion of shipping food?
   Ⓐ It is not the best solution, but it is sometimes necessary.
   Ⓑ It is the only way to avoid dangerous crop failures.
   Ⓒ It is not essential because there is enough food.
   Ⓓ It should be done, but not by the current means of transportation.

Passage 2 (Questions 4–7)

Now get ready to listen. You may take notes.

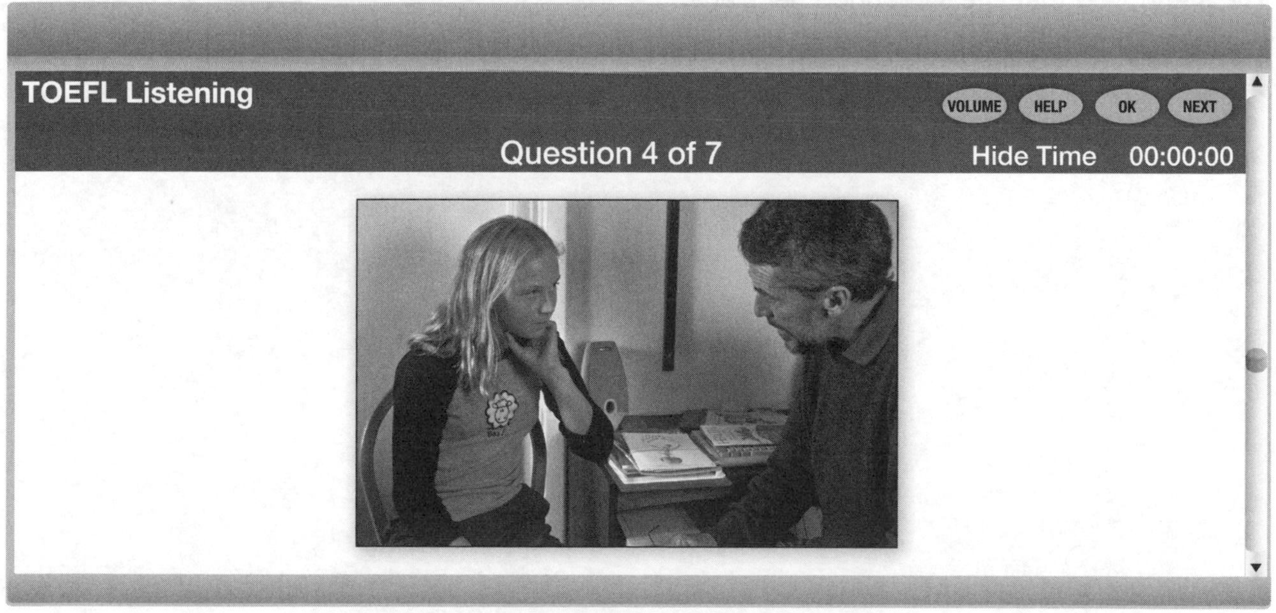

Listen to a conversation between a student and her professor. 1-30

Now get ready to answer the questions. You may use your notes to help you answer the questions.

4. Listen again to part of the conversation. Then answer the question. 1-31
   What does the man mean when he says this?
   Ⓐ He wants the woman to pay more attention to her drawings.
   Ⓑ He thinks the woman's pictures were the best ones.
   Ⓒ He is surprised that some of the woman's pictures were missing.
   Ⓓ He is certain that the woman has many different talents.

5. Listen again to part of the conversation. Then answer the question. 1-32
   Which of the following best expresses the woman's attitude toward photography?
   Ⓐ She feels that she is not as good at it as her father.
   Ⓑ She has always been passionate about it.
   Ⓒ She is bored by having done it for so long.
   Ⓓ She doesn't remember why she liked it.

6. Listen again to part of the conversation. Then answer the question. 1-33
   What does the woman imply when she says this?
   Ⓐ She thinks the museum will not like her pictures.
   Ⓑ She is worried about finding the pictures.
   Ⓒ She wants the professor to make a decision for her.
   Ⓓ She is doubtful about which picture to choose for the contest.

7. Listen again to part of the conversation. Then answer the question. 1-34
   How does the man feel about what the woman said?
   Ⓐ He agrees with what she's proposed.
   Ⓑ He is annoyed that she's changed her plans.
   Ⓒ He feels she isn't taking the contest seriously.
   Ⓓ He thinks she should have other options.

SKILLS REVIEW

Listening Skills 3 and 4: Understanding the Function and Understanding the Speaker's Stance

Directions: *Listen to the passage and the replay* **function** *and* **stance** *questions that follow it. Then mark the correct answers to the questions.*

Questions 1–6

Now get ready to listen. You may take notes.

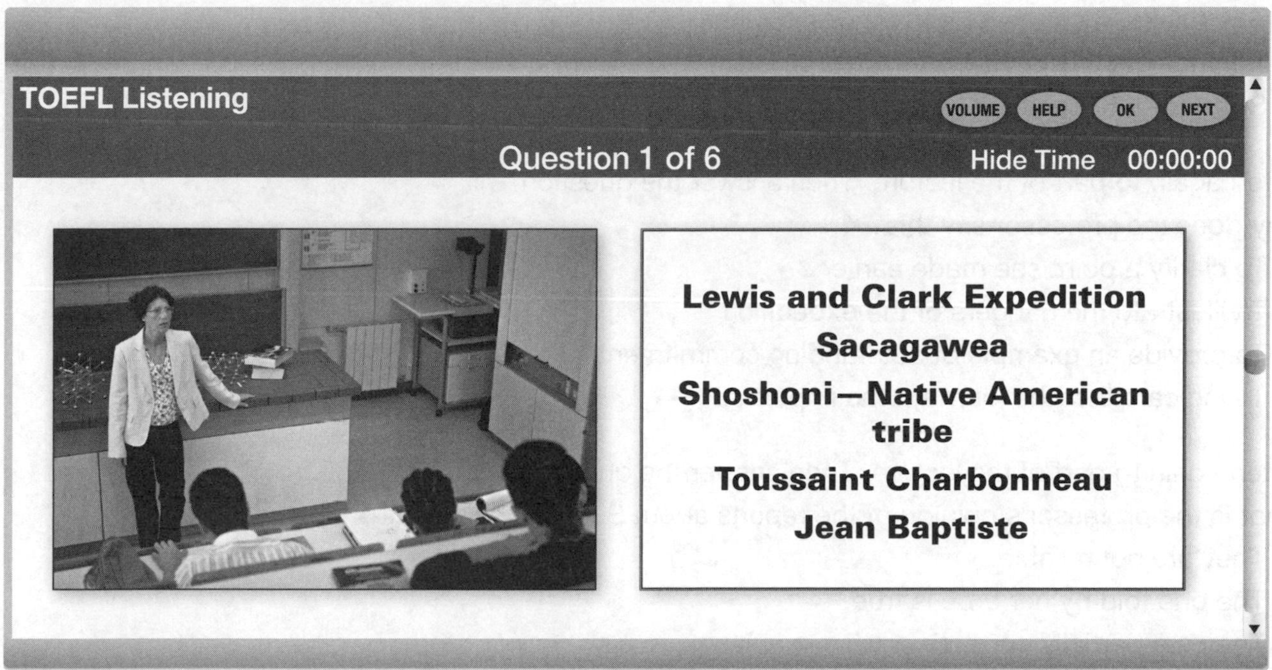

Listen to part of a lecture in an American history class. 1-35

Now get ready to answer the questions. You may use your notes to help you answer the questions.

1. Listen again to part of the lecture. Then answer the question. 1-36
   Why does the professor say this?
   Ⓐ She wants the students to pay careful attention.
   Ⓑ She forgot to add some important information.
   Ⓒ She is summarizing certain aspects of a person.
   Ⓓ She is introducing the main topic.

2. Listen again to part of the lecture. Then answer the question. 1-37
   What does the professor imply when she says this?
   Ⓐ Sacagawea was treated unkindly by the men in the expedition.
   Ⓑ Sacagawea went beyond everything that was expected from her.
   Ⓒ Sacagawea discovered she was more helpful than she anticipated.
   Ⓓ Sacagawea was not a successful guide during the journey.

3. Listen again to part of the lecture. Then answer the question. 1-38
Why does the professor say this?
   Ⓐ She is hurrying to conclude the lecture.
   Ⓑ She is reviewing the topic from the first part of the lecture.
   Ⓒ She is introducing a new idea.
   Ⓓ She is signaling that more examples will be discussed.

4. Listen again to part of the lecture. Then answer the question. 1-39
Which of the following best expresses the professor's attitude toward Sacagawea?
   Ⓐ She doesn't believe Sacagawea was so strong.
   Ⓑ She thinks Sacagawea was a good mother.
   Ⓒ She has great admiration for Sacagawea.
   Ⓓ She thinks Sacagawea was foolish.

5. Listen again to part of the lecture. Then answer the question. 1-40
Why does the professor say this?
   Ⓐ To clarify a point she made earlier
   Ⓑ To illustrate the dangers of the expedition
   Ⓒ To provide an example of outstanding commitment
   Ⓓ To indicate that the journey was important

6. Listen again to part of the lecture. Then answer the question. 1-41
What is the professor's opinion of the reports about Sacagawea's death?
   Ⓐ They are not reliable.
   Ⓑ The one told by her tribe is true.
   Ⓒ They are partially correct.
   Ⓓ They are historically valuable.

LISTENING SKILLS 5 AND 6

UNDERSTANDING ORGANIZATION AND CONNECTING CONTENT; MAKING INFERENCES

Listening Skill 5: Understanding Organization and Connecting Content

Questions about organization ask about the structure of the passage—how ideas are arranged—or about relationships among ideas in the passage, such as the function of a particular piece of information. Answers are not given directly in the passage because the questions are about how the ideas are presented.

Questions that ask about a passage's organization are of two types. One type is multiple choice, and some questions can be phrased like this:

- *How is the lecture organized?*
- *How is the information in the presentation organized?*

Answers will name the organizational pattern: *In chronological order*; *As a definition with examples*; *As a narrative*.

Other multiple-choice questions would be phrased like this:

- *Why does the professor list types of cloud formations?*
- *Why does the professor tell a story about going camping?*

Answers will relate to the overall organization of the passage: *To provide an example*; *To explain the second stage*.

EXPRESS TIP

A lecture is more likely to include a direct reference to its overall organization, such as *Today we're going to examine three results of planned obsolescence* or *I'm going to trace the history of the spice trade.* However, conversations or student discussions might also include a reference such as *Let's figure out which of these events was the most significant.*

References like this will occur near the beginning of the passage.

Here are some common patterns for lecture organizations, and some signal words that sometimes mark these patterns:

- Chronological order (dates; times)
- Sequence or process (*first*, *next*, *then*, *finally*)
- Ranking; for example, by level of importance or popularity (*the most*, *the next most*, *the least*)
- Cause/effect and problem/solution (*because of*; *due to*; *therefore*, *as a consequence*)
- Main idea and examples (*another aspect of*; *is also an example of*)
- Comparison or contrast, or both (*similar to*, *like*, *in the same way*; *on the other hand*, *in contrast*, *unlike*)

These are not the only possible organizational patterns.

EXPRESS TIP

> As soon as you hear signal words that might indicate an organizational pattern (such as *first, next, then*; *will cover three main points*; etc.), write them down in your notes. Then you will have those clues in case there is a question about organization.

A second type of organizational question asks about specific information included in the talk. Unlike other detail questions, however, this information could come from more than one sentence or section of the talk. You will need to check all of your notes and think about the entire talk to answer these questions.

In addition, these questions sometimes feature YES/NO charts. You will see a chart with two columns, labeled YES and NO, and four answer choices. You must choose either YES or NO for each answer choice listed.

Is each of these points about pandas included in the lecture?
This question is worth 2 points (2 points for 4 correct answers, 1 point for 3 correct answers, and 0 points for 2, 1, or 0 correct answers).
For each answer, click in the YES or NO column.

For each answer, click in the **YES** or **NO** column.		
	YES	**NO**
Panda's habitat		
Panda's diet		
Panda's predators		
Panda's behavior		

Look at these examples of organization questions on a computer screen.

First, you will see some images and hear a lecture, discussion, or conversation.

EXAMPLE: Organization Question

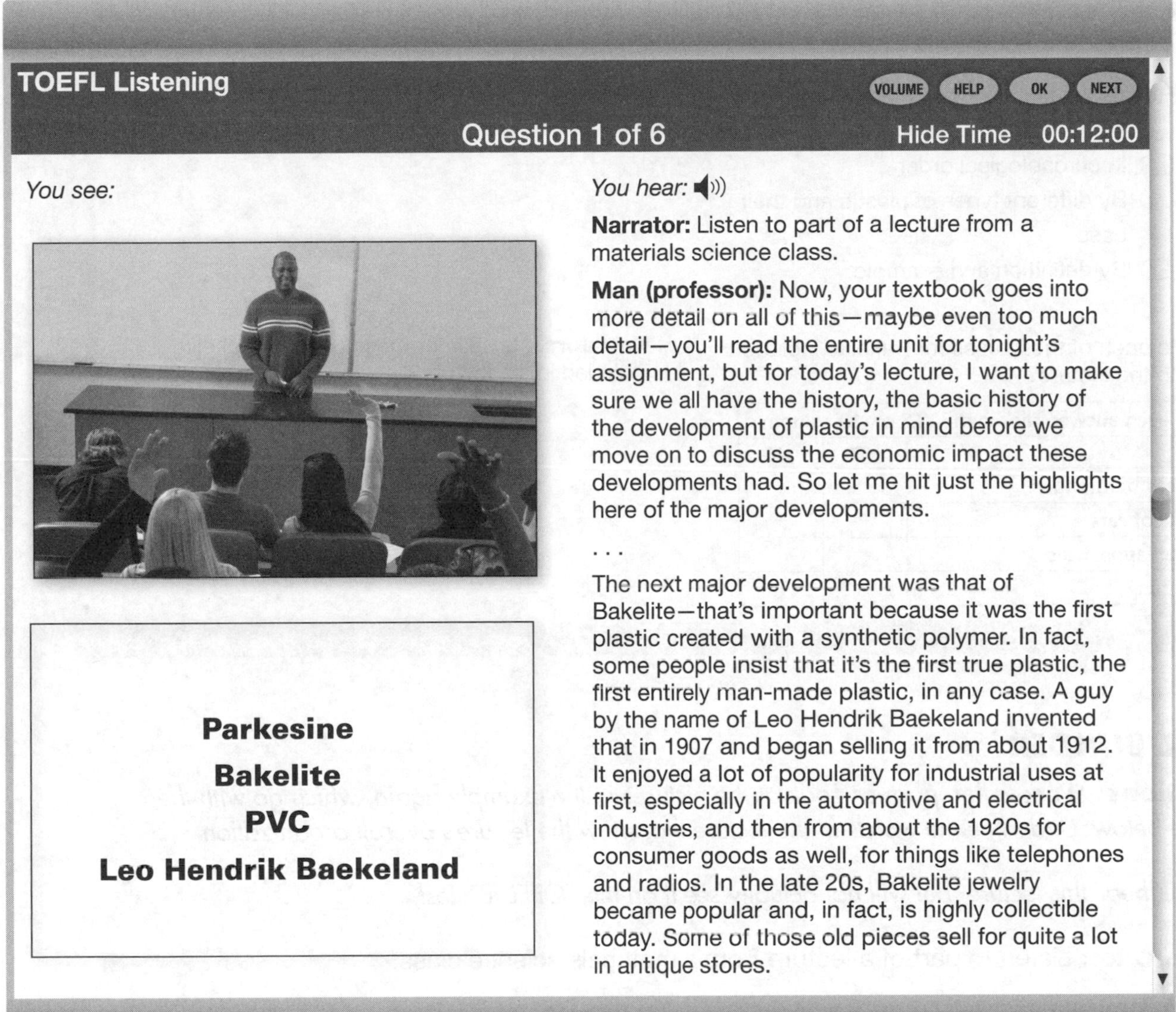

TOEFL Listening
VOLUME
HELP
OK
NEXT
Question 1 of 6
Hide Time 00:12:00
You see:
Parkesine
Bakelite
PVC
Leo Hendrik Baekeland
You hear:
Narrator: Listen to part of a lecture from a materials science class.
Man (professor): Now, your textbook goes into more detail on all of this—maybe even too much detail—you'll read the entire unit for tonight's assignment, but for today's lecture, I want to make sure we all have the history, the basic history of the development of plastic in mind before we move on to discuss the economic impact these developments had. So let me hit just the highlights here of the major developments.
. . .
The next major development was that of Bakelite—that's important because it was the first plastic created with a synthetic polymer. In fact, some people insist that it's the first true plastic, the first entirely man-made plastic, in any case. A guy by the name of Leo Hendrik Baekeland invented that in 1907 and began selling it from about 1912. It enjoyed a lot of popularity for industrial uses at first, especially in the automotive and electrical industries, and then from about the 1920s for consumer goods as well, for things like telephones and radios. In the late 20s, Bakelite jewelry became popular and, in fact, is highly collectible today. Some of those old pieces sell for quite a lot in antique stores.

Then you will see and hear the questions:

TOEFL Listening

VOLUME HELP OK NEXT

Question 1 of 6 Hide Time 00:12:00

You see:

1. How is the lecture's information organized?
   - From most important to least important
   - In chronological order
   - By different types of plastic and their uses
   - By definition and example

You hear:

Narrator: 1. How is the lecture's information organized?

You see:

3. Is each of these uses for Bakelite included in the lecture?

For each answer, click in the **YES** or **NO** column.		
	YES	**NO**
Pieces of furniture		
Parts of cars		
Small appliances		
Clothing		

You hear:

Narrator: 3. Is each of these uses for Bakelite included in the lecture?

SKILL BUILDER

Directions: *Work with a partner. Look at the pictures in the Example again, which go with the lecture below. Underline the words in the lecture that show the lecture's overall organization.*

You will hear this lecture, but will not actually see it on the TOEFL iBT Test.

Narrator: Listen to part of a lecture from a materials science class.

Man (professor): Now, your textbook goes into more detail on all of this—maybe even too much detail—you'll read the entire unit for tonight's assignment, but for today's lecture, I want to make sure we all have the history, the basic history of the development of plastic in mind before we move on to discuss the economic impact these developments had. So let me hit just the highlights here of the major developments.

The first substance that meets our definition of the word *plastic*—you remember that from last week—was a substance called Parkesine, developed in 1856. Earlier than we often associate with plastic, I know. Now, the fellow who invented it, Alexander Parkes, didn't get anywhere with it commercially, and his company was out of business by 1868. But it was the first, and that's important.

continued . . .

The next major development was that of Bakelite—that's important because it was the first plastic created with a synthetic polymer. In fact, some people insist that it's the first true plastic, the first entirely man-made plastic, in any case. A guy by the name of Leo Hendrik Baekeland invented that in 1907 and began selling it from about 1912. It enjoyed a lot of popularity for industrial uses at first, especially in the automotive and electrical industries, and then from about the 1920s for consumer goods as well, for things like telephones and radios. In the late 20s, Bakelite jewelry became popular and, in fact, is highly collectible today. Some of those old pieces sell for quite a lot in antique stores.

The next significant development was polyvinyl chloride, or PVC—never mind about writing down the full names now, they're in your book—which was refined in 1926. Earlier versions did exist, but they had flaws that made the product unsuitable for widespread use. So it was really in the 1930s and after that it took off. It's cheap, strong, and easy to work with—its flexibility is a key attribute.

But the most important development of the 1930s, and we're going to spend some time on this today, was nylon. That's right, nylon is a plastic, even though, as you know, it's often used for clothing. Stockings, for example, used to be called "nylons" because they were made from, of course, nylon.

Now listen to the lecture and mark the correct answers. 1-42

1. How is the lecture's information organized?
   Ⓐ From most important to least important
   Ⓑ In chronological order
   Ⓒ By different types of plastic and their uses
   Ⓓ By definition and example

2. Why does the professor mention PVC?
   Ⓐ As an example of a type of plastic students are familiar with
   Ⓑ Because it was an important type of plastic
   Ⓒ To illustrate an unusual type of plastic
   Ⓓ As a contrast with traditional types of plastic

3. Is each of these uses for Bakelite included in the lecture?

For each answer, click in the **YES** or **NO** column.		
	YES	**NO**
Pieces of furniture		
Parts of cars		
Small appliances		
Clothing		

EXPRESS TIP

If you hear a signal phrase such as *several examples* or *three different types of*, make sure to list all of those in your notes. This will help you answer the YES/NO chart questions accurately.

Skill Builder Answers:

1. **Answer B is correct.** The passage mentions the earliest date (1856) first, and moves in time order through to the most recent dates mentioned (the 1930s). Answer A is incorrect because each of the events mentioned is called important, although for different reasons. But one is not called more important than another. Answer C is incorrect because the lecture does not classify all of the different types of plastics; it talks about only a few important ones, and lists them in chronological order, not by use. Answer D is incorrect because the professor only refers to a definition of plastic he has given some time in the past; this lecture does not define plastic.

2. **Answer B is correct.** The professor says "The next significant development was polyvinyl chloride, or PVC . . . "; "significant" is a synonym for "important." Answer A is incorrect because the professor explains what PVC is, so it is likely that the students are not familiar with it yet. Answer C is incorrect because the professor does not say it was unusual. He refers to the fact that it "took off"—became popular—which implies that it is now common. Answer D is incorrect because the professor does not divide plastics into "traditional" and "modern," but rather explains how new types were continually being developed.

3. **Parts of cars** and **small appliances** are mentioned. The professor says, "It [Bakelite] enjoyed a lot of popularity for industrial uses at first, especially in the automotive and electrical industries, and then from about the 1920s for consumer goods as well, for things like telephones and radios. *Pieces of furniture* and *clothing* are not mentioned, so they are incorrect.

PRACTICE

Directions: *Listen to the passages and the* **organization** *questions that follow them. Then mark the correct answers to the questions.*

Passage 1 (Questions 1–2)

Now get ready to listen. You may take notes.

Listen to a discussion among students in an ophthalmology class. 1-43

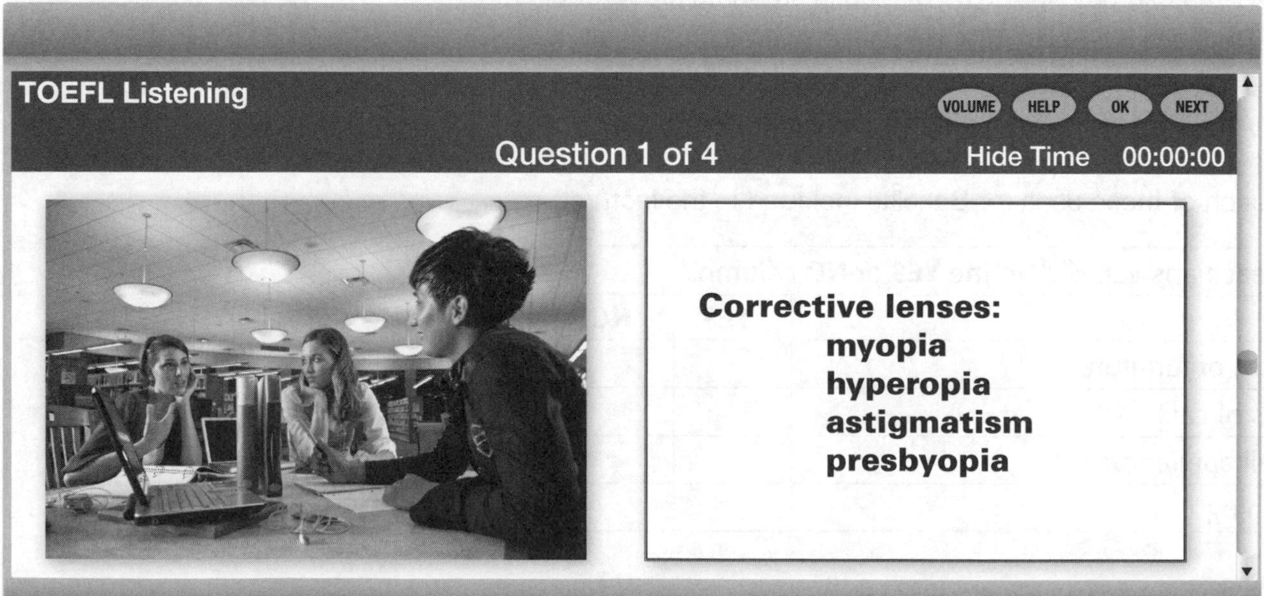

Now get ready to answer the questions. You may use your notes to help you answer the questions.

1. How did the professor classify the types of glasses?
   Ⓐ By how much they cost
   Ⓑ By how common they are
   Ⓒ By when they were invented
   Ⓓ By their purpose

2. Is each of these types of eyeglasses mentioned in the discussion?
   This question is worth 2 points (2 points for 4 correct answers, 1 point for 3 correct answers, and 0 points for 2, 1, or 0 correct answers).

For each answer, click in the **YES** or **NO** column.		
	YES	**NO**
Safety goggles		
Sunglasses		
Swimming goggles		
Bifocals		

Passage 2 (Questions 3–4)

Now get ready to listen. You may take notes.

Listen to part of a discussion from a fire science class. 1-44

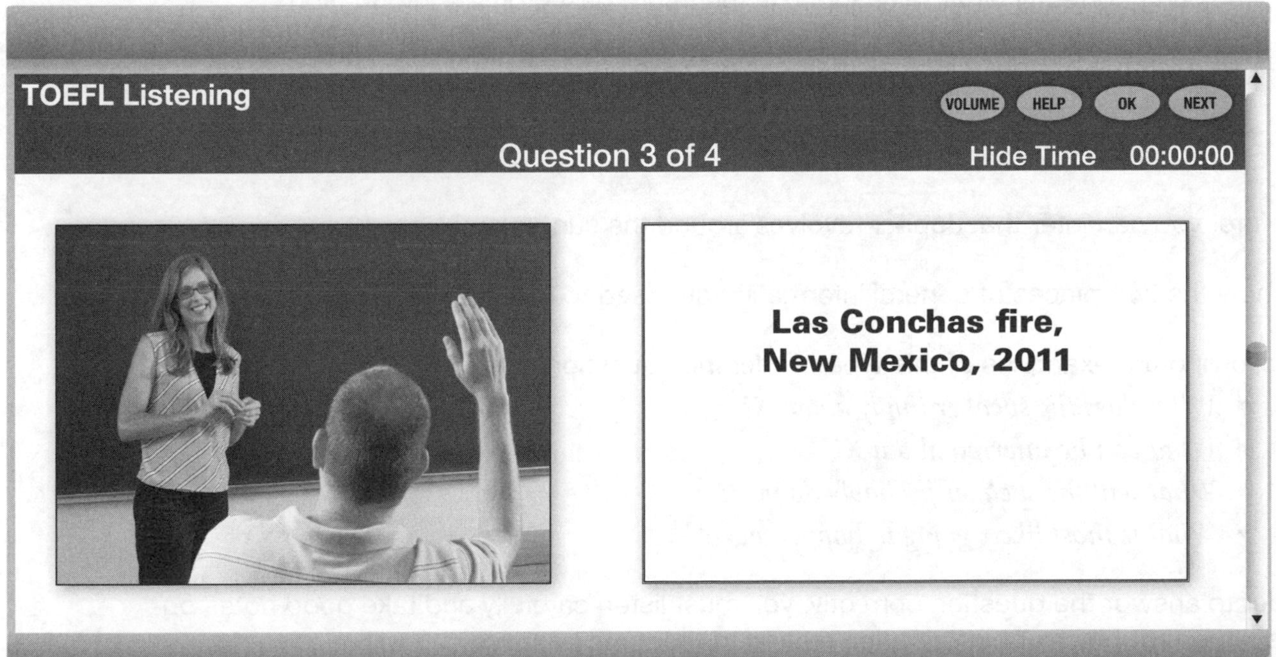

Now get ready to answer the questions. You may use your notes to help you answer the questions.

3. How is the information in the lecture organized?
   Ⓐ The professor discusses some causes of forest fires and then their effects.
   Ⓑ The professor compares and contrasts different techniques for fighting forest fires.
   Ⓒ The professor gives some definitions of firebreaks and explains them with examples.
   Ⓓ The professor explains why some types of firebreaks are more effective than others.

4. What does the Las Conchas fire illustrate?
   Ⓐ A created firebreak
   Ⓑ An unsuccessful firebreak
   Ⓒ A natural firebreak
   Ⓓ A preventative firebreak

Listening Skill 6: Making Inferences

An *inference* question is commonly used to test your understanding of how information is connected. An inference is a conclusion or prediction which requires the following steps:

- listening for the most important information
- making a connection between or among two or more pieces of information
- drawing the proper conclusion based on the information

  OR

  predicting correctly what will happen in the future based on the information

Here is an example of how a typical inference is made:

1. Jupiter is a planet.
2. All planets revolve around the sun.

Therefore, you can infer that Jupiter revolves around the sun.

Note how the two pieces of general information are used to make a specific conclusion.

The following are examples of this type of inference question:

- *What does the speaker imply about X?*
- *What can be inferred about X?*
- *What will the speaker probably do next?*
- *What is most likely going to happen next?*

In order to answer the question correctly, you must listen carefully and take good notes on all the important pieces of information related to the topic because you will need to draw an inference from different pieces of information heard throughout the lecture. Use your powers of reasoning, your critical thinking skills, to make logical and reasonable connections between important ideas and points. Eliminate any answers which do not provide a logical inference. Be sure there is accurate and complete evidence or proof to support the conclusion or prediction in the answer you choose.

EXPRESS TIP

The information may be stated *indirectly* and you will need to make a conclusion based on what is implied. However, sometimes the information is *directly* stated and you may be asked to understand how certain details are related in order to:

- connect the steps in a process
- establish cause or effect
- compare or contrast

Whether the information is stated indirectly or directly, the pieces of information you need to answer the question **will *not* have come from one single place** in the passage. In both cases, you will be required to bring together various ideas or details from throughout the entire listening passage. Obviously, to do this well, you must learn to take thorough and accurate notes while listening to the passage.

Look at this example of an inference question on a computer screen.

EXAMPLE: Inference Question

First, you will see some images and hear a lecture, discussion, or conversation.

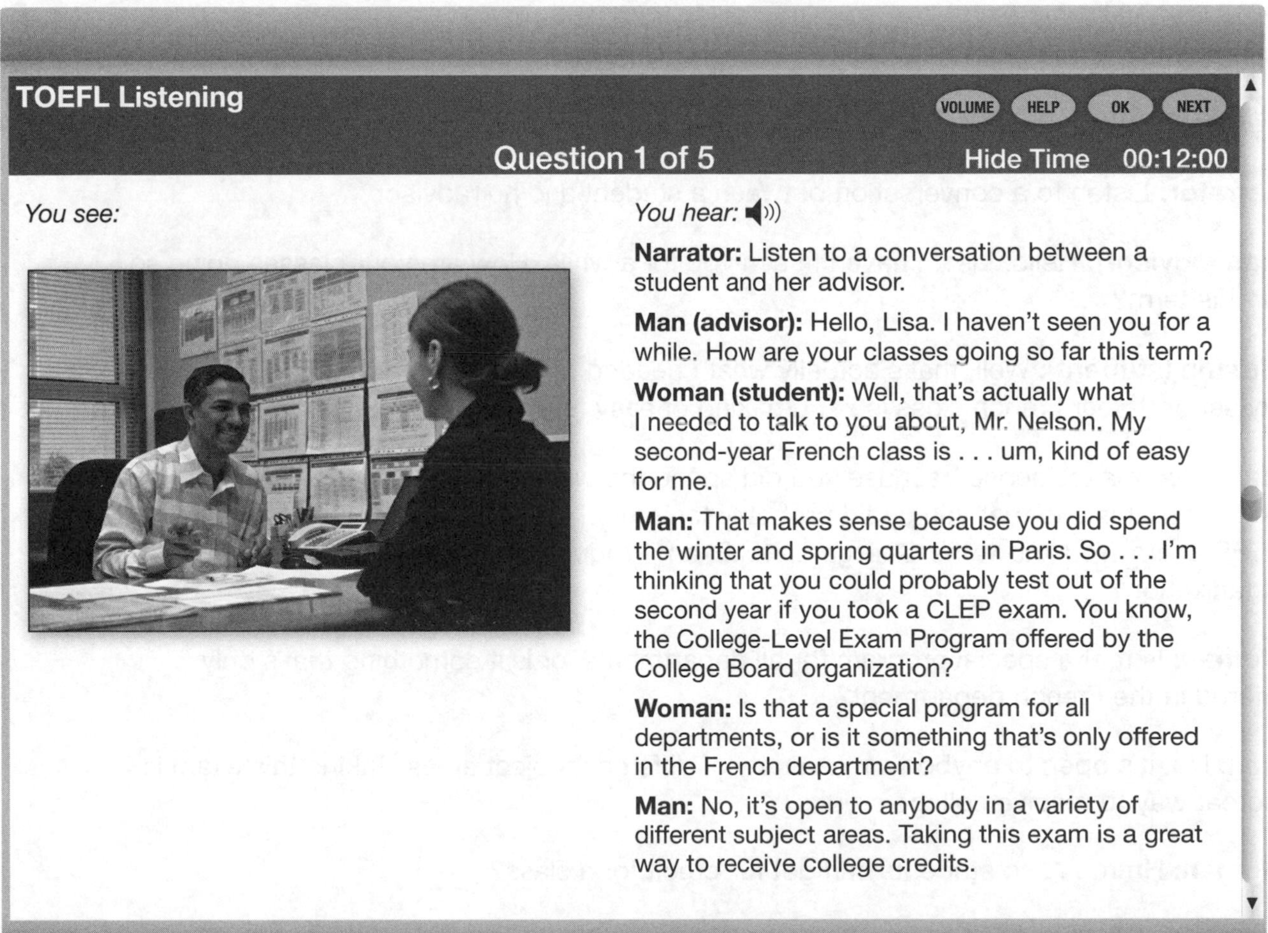
TOEFL Listening
VOLUME
HELP
OK
NEXT
Question 1 of 5
Hide Time 00:12:00
You see:
You hear:
Narrator: Listen to a conversation between a student and her advisor.
Man (advisor): Hello, Lisa. I haven't seen you for a while. How are your classes going so far this term?
Woman (student): Well, that's actually what I needed to talk to you about, Mr. Nelson. My second-year French class is . . . um, kind of easy for me.
Man: That makes sense because you did spend the winter and spring quarters in Paris. So . . . I'm thinking that you could probably test out of the second year if you took a CLEP exam. You know, the College-Level Exam Program offered by the College Board organization?
Woman: Is that a special program for all departments, or is it something that's only offered in the French department?
Man: No, it's open to anybody in a variety of different subject areas. Taking this exam is a great way to receive college credits.

Then you will see and hear the questions:

TOEFL Listening

VOLUME HELP OK NEXT

Question 1 of 5

Hide Time 00:12:00

You see:

1. What can be inferred about Lisa?
   - ◯ She doesn't speak French well enough to pass the CLEP exam.
   - ◯ She thinks that the CLEP exam is too expensive.
   - ◯ She doesn't know much about the CLEP exam.
   - ◯ She will take the CLEP exam in France.

You hear:

Narrator: 1. What can be inferred about Lisa?

SKILL BUILDER

Directions: *Work with a partner. Read the conversation aloud.*

You will hear this conversation, but will not actually see it on the TOEFL iBT Test.

Narrator: Listen to a conversation between a student and her advisor.

Man (advisor): Hello, Lisa. I haven't seen you for a while. How are your classes going so far this term?

Woman (student): Well, that's actually what I needed to talk to you about, Mr. Nelson. My second-year French class is . . . um, kind of easy for me.

Man: That makes sense because you did spend the winter and spring quarters in Paris. So . . . I'm thinking that you could probably test out of the second year if you took a CLEP exam. You know, the College-Level Exam Program offered by the College Board organization?

Woman: Is that a special program for all departments, or is it something that's only offered in the French department?

Man: No, it's open to anybody in a variety of different subject areas. Taking this exam is a great way to receive college credits.

Woman: Hmm . . . so students can get full credit for a class?

continued . . .

Man: That's right. If you pass, you'll get four full credits for second-year French.

Woman: Ah . . . I'm a little worried. I *did* take language classes in Paris, but I'm not sure my French is good enough . . . I didn't use it that much over the summer after I got home.

Man: Oh, come on, you got excellent grades in your first-year French class. And the exam would take care of your last Arts and Languages requirement.

Woman: I can't say that wouldn't be a relief, and there are so many other classes I'd like to take.

Man: And, since it only costs around $60, compared to what you pay in tuition for the class, if you pass it . . . which I'm betting you will, then it will be worth every penny.

Woman: So, you really think I should take it?

Man: Well, it can't hurt to try. Why not go to the College Board website and see the sample questions? And you can even get practice materials.

Now listen to the conversation. 1-45

Take turns answering the questions by circling True or False after the statements. Then mark the correct answers to the questions.

A. Lisa has signed up to take an exam for her French class.	True	False
B. The advisor understands Lisa's problem.	True	False
C. The CLEP exam is available to all students.	True	False
D. Lisa has lived and studied overseas.	True	False
E. Lisa did not do well in her first year of French class.	True	False
F. The advisor explains that the CLEP exam is expensive.	True	False

1. What can be inferred about Lisa?
   A) She doesn't speak French well enough to pass the CLEP exam.
   B) She thinks that the CLEP exam is too expensive.
   C) She doesn't know much about the CLEP exam.
   D) She will take the CLEP exam in France.

2. What does the advisor imply about the CLEP (College-Level Exam Program)?
   A) It is only available to students in Lisa's department.
   B) It is a good value for the price.
   C) It will provide Lisa with enough credits to graduate.
   D) It is difficult and so it is a big risk for Lisa.

EXPRESS TIP

The correct answer choices for inference questions will usually not repeat exactly the same words or phrases that you heard in the passage. It is more likely that the correct answers will use synonyms or paraphrases of the information in the passage. For example, look at the following lines taken from a compare/contrast lecture:

You hear: *In the popular imagination, sharks are considered to be one of the most dangerous creatures on the Earth. . . . Statistics indicate that there were about forty shark attacks in the United States. . . . In reality, only two lead to death. . . . On the other hand, the number of humans killed by bee stings is around fifty-three per year . . .*

Question: What does the speaker imply about shark attacks?

The correct answer is paraphrased as: B) They are not as deadly as bee stings.

Skill Builder Answers:

A. False B. True C. True D. True E. False F. False

1. **Answer C is correct.** It can be inferred that Lisa doesn't know much about the CLEP because she asks her advisor several questions about it: "Is that a special program for all departments, or is it something that's only offered in the French department?" and "Hmm . . . so students can get full credit for a class?" Answer A is incorrect because we don't know if Lisa's French is good enough or not. While Lisa is worried about her French, her advisor definitely thinks she could pass the exam; he says, "if you pass it . . . which I'm betting you will . . ." Answer B is incorrect because Lisa does not indicate she thinks the CLEP is too expensive. However, the advisor says that the CLEP "only costs around $60," which indicates that the exam is not so expensive. Answer D is incorrect because it is there is no information that indicates Lisa will take the CLEP in France. In fact, it is likely, since she is already taking classes at the university, that she will take the CLEP on her campus.

2. **Answer B is correct.** The advisor tells Lisa that taking the CLEP ". . . will be worth every penny." The expression "worth every penny" means something is a good value. Therefore, because the CLEP is only about $60 and cheaper than paying tuition for the French class, the advisor implies it's a good value for the price. Answer A is incorrect because the advisor clearly states that the CLEP exam is ". . . open to anybody in a variety of different subject areas." Answer C is incorrect. The advisor does says she will get four credits if she passes the exam, but he does not indicate that this enough for her to graduate; it will only take care of her last Arts and Language requirement. Answer D is incorrect because the advisor says the opposite about the CLEP; he thinks she will pass it and that ". . . it will be worth every penny." This means it's not a big risk for Lisa because she could benefit if she passes it.

PRACTICE

Directions: *Listen to the passages and* ***inference*** *questions that follow them. Then mark the answers to the questions.*

Passage 1 (Questions 1–3)

Now get ready to listen. You may take notes.

Listen to part of a conversation between a student and a doctor at a university health center. 

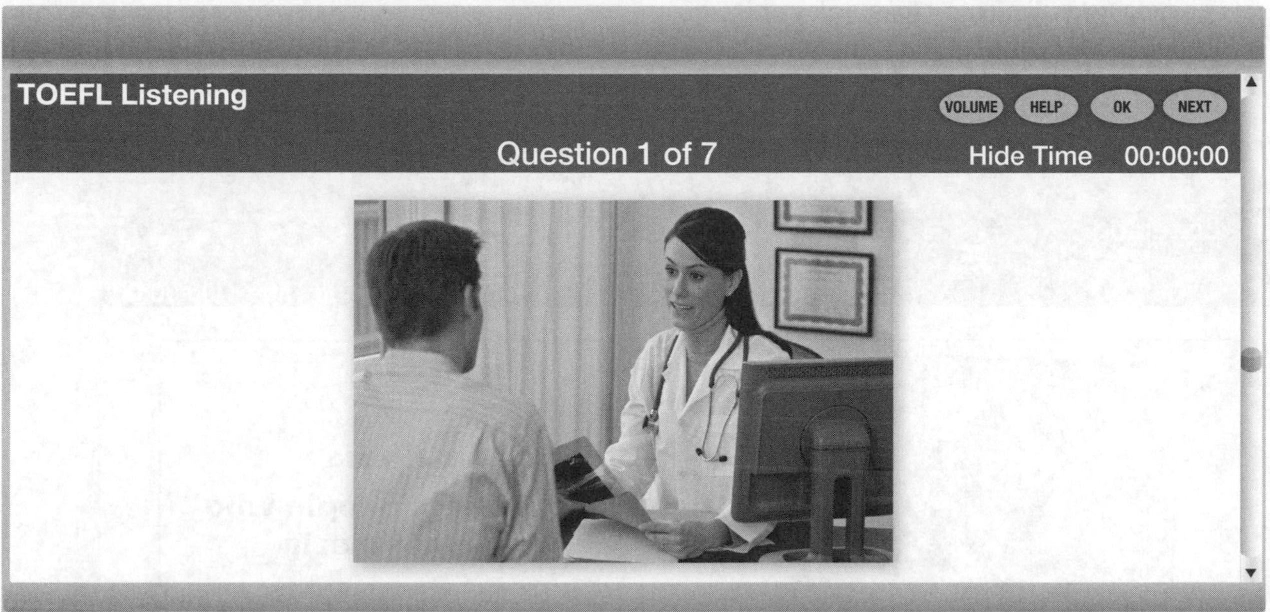

Now get ready to answer the questions. You may use your notes to help you answer the questions.

1. What does Doctor Cline imply about Brian's problems?
   (A) They are typical among the students on campus.
   (B) They can be avoided if he uses a locker.
   (C) They can't be treated if he continues to carry books.
   (D) They are unusual for the members in his group.

2. What can be inferred about Brian?
   (A) He spends too much time using his computer in the library.
   (B) He doesn't like the idea of using a backpack with wheels.
   (C) He can't make a decision about which backpack to buy.
   (D) He is using the wrong shoulder for carrying his backpack.

3. What is most likely going to happen next?
   (A) The doctor will demonstrate how to carry a backpack.
   (B) They will end the appointment.
   (C) Brian will start doing some exercises.
   (D) They will review some solutions to the problem.

Passage 2 (Questions 4–7)

Now get ready to listen. You may take notes.

Listen to part of a lecture in a neurology class. 2-1

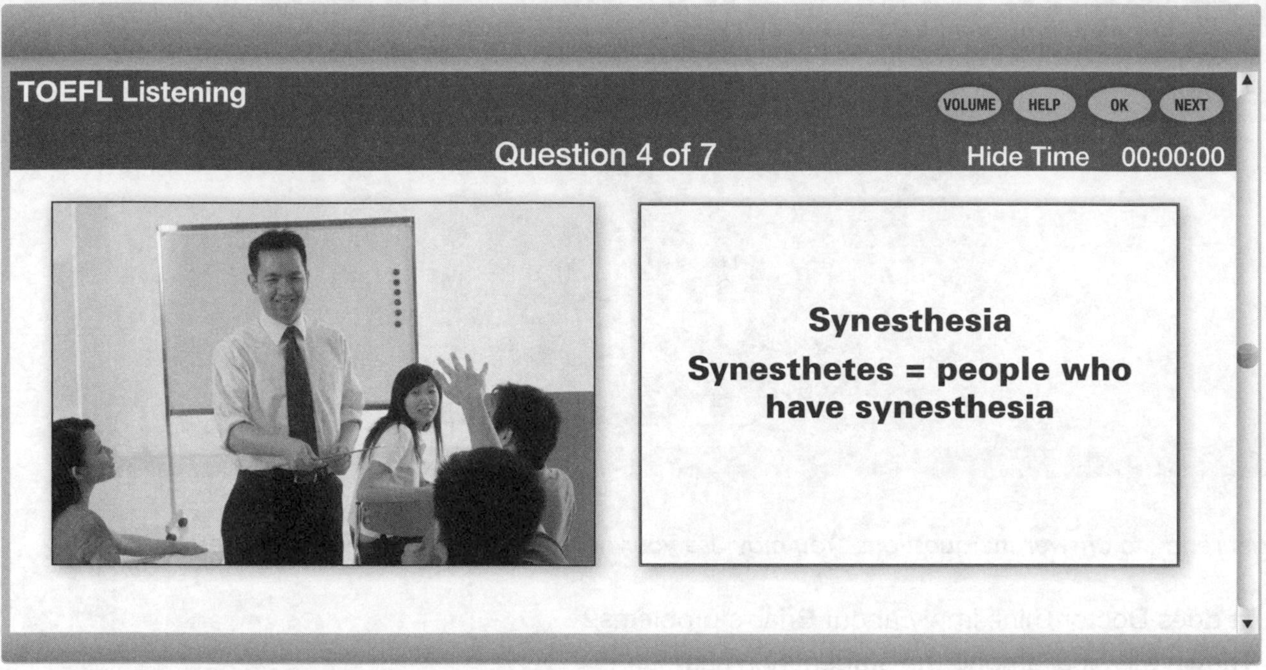

Now get ready to answer the questions. You may use your notes to help you answer the questions.

4. What can be inferred about synesthesia?
   Ⓐ It is easily controlled by those who have it.
   Ⓑ It occurs when the brain can't make connections.
   Ⓒ It can be experienced by members in the same family.
   Ⓓ It causes an inability to understand written language.

5. What does the professor imply about synesthetes?
   Ⓐ They are musically and mathematically talented.
   Ⓑ They have a combination of different diseases.
   Ⓒ They don't always have positive experiences.
   Ⓓ They have a strong ability to imagine objects.

6. What will scientists studying synesthesia probably do in the future?
   Ⓐ Agree on the correct method for studying the condition
   Ⓑ Find a cure in order to eliminate the suffering of synesthetes
   Ⓒ Create connections between different parts of the brain
   Ⓓ Continue to study the causes of the condition

7. What is most likely going to happen next in the classroom?
   Ⓐ The professor will read some stories about synesthetes.
   Ⓑ The students will hear from some young people.
   Ⓒ The professor will review the students' questions.
   Ⓓ The students will be discussing the lecture.

SKILLS REVIEW

Listening Skills 5 and 6: Understanding Organization, Connecting Content, and Making Inferences

Directions: *Listen to the passage and the* ***organization***, ***connecting content****, and* ***inference*** *questions that follow it. Then mark the correct answers to the questions.*

Questions 1–6

Now get ready to listen. You may take notes.

Listen to part of a lecture in a fashion design class. 2-2

Now get ready to answer the questions. You may use your notes to help you answer the questions.

1. How is this lecture organized?
   Ⓐ The design features of a garment are ranked from least important to most important.
   Ⓑ The steps of creating a piece of clothing are listed in chronological order.
   Ⓒ The history of fashion design is explained through examples.
   Ⓓ The different types of fashion design are contrasted.

2. What does the professor imply about many fashion designers?
   Ⓐ They may attend more than two fashion shows a year.
   Ⓑ They create specific types of fabrics for their designs.
   Ⓒ They have a long time to decide on their design ideas.
   Ⓓ They report on trends for trade research groups.

3. What can be inferred about pattern makers?
   Ⓐ They choose unattractive styles.
   Ⓑ They draw designs on paper copies.
   Ⓒ They must be extremely accurate.
   Ⓓ They cut and arrange the designer's garments.

4. Why does the professor discuss various types of work environments?
   Ⓐ To illustrate how fashion design companies are organized
   Ⓑ To explain why fashion design is complicated
   Ⓒ To describe how teams of designers work
   Ⓓ To clarify information about a specific stage of design

5. Is each of these areas of fashion design included in the lecture?
   This question is worth 2 points (2 points for 4 correct answers, 1 point for 3 correct answers, and 0 points for 2, 1, or 0 correct answers).

For each answer, click in the **YES** or **NO** column.		
	YES	**NO**
Information about current trends in fashion		
Research techniques for initial design ideas		
How garments are made		
Listing of colors and shapes used in design		

6. What will the students probably do next?
   Ⓐ Watch a movie about the most recent fashion designs
   Ⓑ See what other students have created
   Ⓒ Take notes and make some quick drawings
   Ⓓ Prepare a variety of questions for the professor

Note: Scoring information for this Listening Post-Test is available on page 326. Keep track of your score on this Listening Post-Test and add it to your scores for the Reading, Speaking, and Writing Post-Tests. The Listening Post-Test can also be taken on the CD-ROM, where it is combined with the other Post-Tests into one full test. It can be taken on the CD-ROM in either the "Practice Mode" (not timed; you can work at your own pace) or the "Timed Mode" (TOEFL iBT® Test timing; you will not be able to pause). On the CD-ROM, the Listening Post-Test will automatically be scored for you. If you want to see how you would score on an authentic TOEFL iBT® Test, take the test on the CD-ROM in the "Timed Mode."

LISTENING POST-TEST

Directions:

The Listening Section of the TOEFL iBT® Test measures your understanding of English conversations and lectures and your ability to answer questions about them. It contains six passages and a set of five or six questions about each passage. You have 60 minutes in which to complete the Listening Section.

You will hear each conversation and lecture **only one time**.

You can take notes as you listen. You can use your notes to help you answer the questions.

When you see the icon 🔊 in the replay questions, it indicates that you will hear part of the talk again, but on the actual TOEFL iBT Test the conversation or lecture will not be shown on the computer screen.

The majority of questions are worth 1 point; however, some questions are worth more than 1 point. If the question is worth more than 1 point, it will have additional directions that indicate how many points are possible.

When you have finished reading these directions, go on to the first listening passage.

Listening Passage 1

Questions 1–5

Now get ready to listen. You may take notes. 2-3

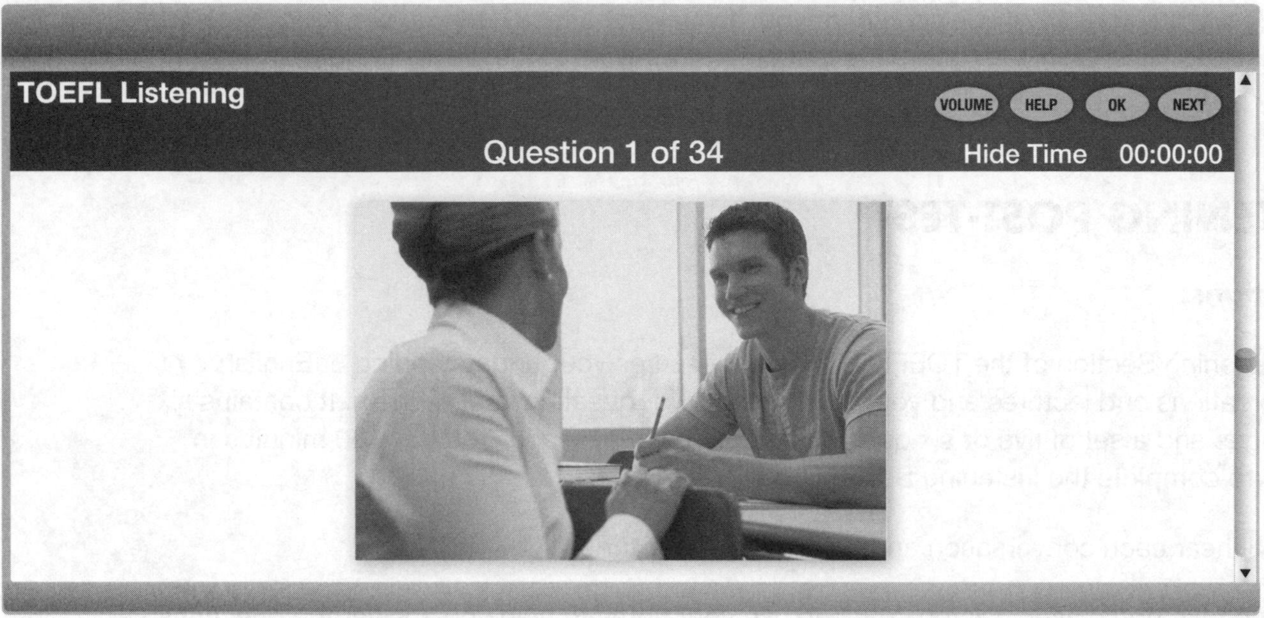

Now get ready to answer the questions. You may use your notes to help you answer the questions.

1. What is true about the Algebra 201 course? 2-4
   Ⓐ It doesn't meet on Thursdays.
   Ⓑ There is more than one section of the class.
   Ⓒ There is no textbook for the class.
   Ⓓ It is only offered in the mornings.

2. What does the professor think the student's problem is at first? 2-5
   Ⓐ That he has missed an important class
   Ⓑ That he is worried about the final exam
   Ⓒ That he is having a medical emergency
   Ⓓ That he is having difficulty with an assignment

3. Listen again to part of the conversation. Then answer the question. 2-6
   What does the professor imply when she says this?
   Ⓐ The student is exaggerating the importance of his appointment.
   Ⓑ The family commitment is more important than the midterm.
   Ⓒ Missing the test will be a big problem.
   Ⓓ The student wasn't speaking loudly enough.

4. When is the student going to take the midterm? 2-7
   Ⓐ Monday at 9:00
   Ⓑ Tuesday during class
   Ⓒ Wednesday during office hours
   Ⓓ Thursday at 2:00

5. The student says all of these will help him study for the test EXCEPT 2-8
   Ⓐ talking to his roommate
   Ⓑ going over his notes
   Ⓒ visiting the professor during office hours
   Ⓓ his performance so far in the class

Listening Passage 2

Questions 6–12

Now get ready to listen. You may take notes. 2-9

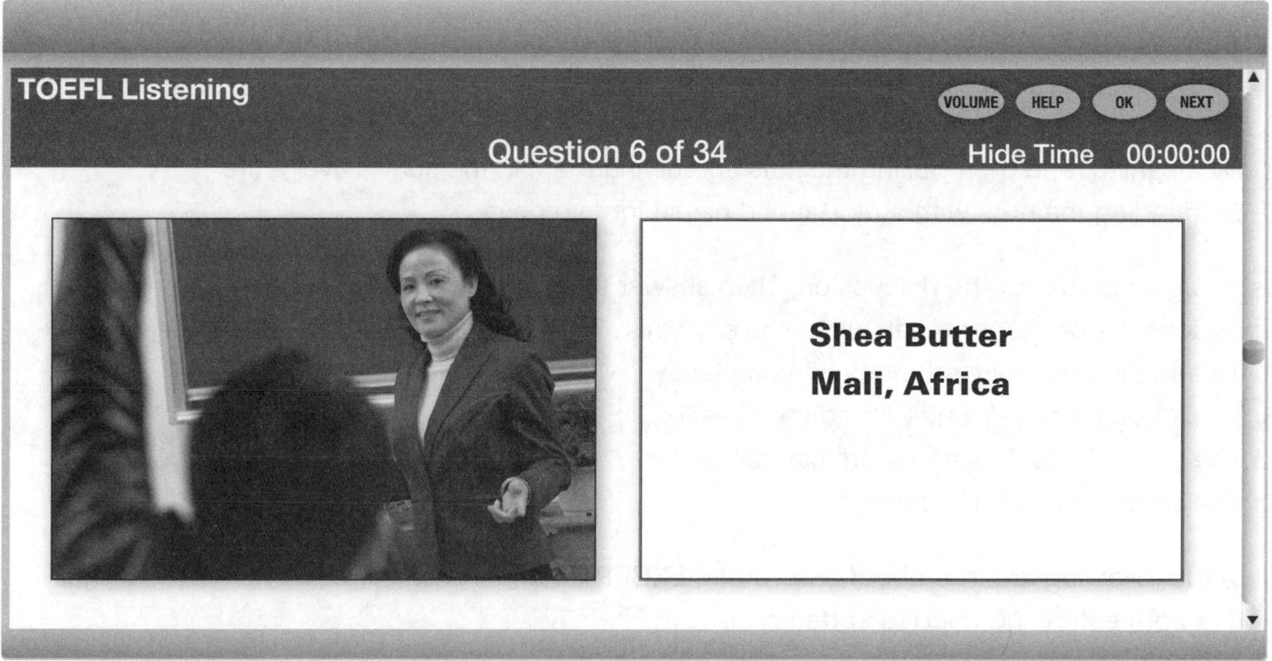

Now get ready to answer the questions. You may use your notes to help you answer the questions.

6. How is the information in the discussion organized? 2-10

Ⓐ By presenting problems and their solutions
Ⓑ By definitions and examples
Ⓒ By advantages and disadvantages
Ⓓ By sequential steps in a process

7. What can be inferred about the professor? 2-11

Ⓐ She has spent time in Mali with shea producers.
Ⓑ She has written various articles about international development.
Ⓒ She wants to encourage the students to pay more attention to the issue.
Ⓓ She is involved in the sale and distribution of shea butter.

8. Listen again to part of the discussion. Then answer the question. 2-12

What does Linda mean when she says this?

Ⓐ She feels a little uncertain about the process.
Ⓑ She is bored by the subject and doesn't want to study it.
Ⓒ She understands how hard the women work.
Ⓓ She is surprised by what she read about Malians.

9. According to the professor, how is the white paste produced? 2-13

Ⓐ By boiling a reddish-brown paste to remove the water from it
Ⓑ By adding hot water to the ground nuts and mixing it by hand for a long time
Ⓒ By cleaning, and then boiling the nuts and drying them in the sun or over a fire
Ⓓ By grinding the nuts with a mortar and pestle for two days

10. Listen again to part of the discussion. Then answer the question. 2-14

What does the professor mean when she says this?

Ⓐ The student has missed the point completely.
Ⓑ The student doesn't understand the question.
Ⓒ The student should listen more carefully.
Ⓓ The student is partially correct.

11. All of the following are true about shea butter EXCEPT 2-15

Ⓐ It is both eaten and used to soften skin.
Ⓑ It is only produced in Mali.
Ⓒ It is produced mainly by Malian women.
Ⓓ The nuts come from a fruit.

Listing Passage 3

Questions 12–17

Now get ready to listen. You may take notes. 2-16

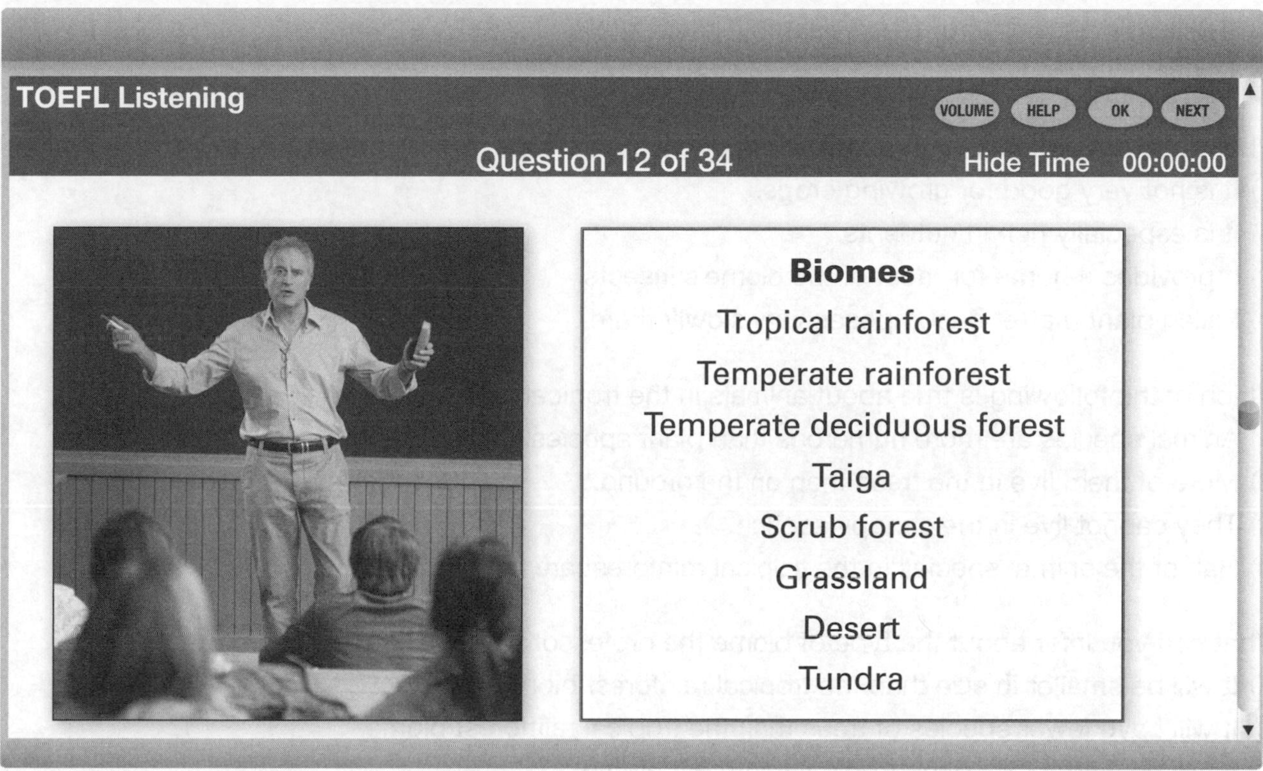

Now get ready to answer the questions. You may use your notes to help you answer the questions.

12. How is the discussion of biomes organized? 2-17
    Ⓐ From the most common to the least common
    Ⓑ From the hottest to the coldest
    Ⓒ From the wettest to the driest
    Ⓓ From the most important to the least important

13. What types of biomes is the professor going to talk about today? 2-18
    Ⓐ The major land biomes
    Ⓑ Both land and water biomes
    Ⓒ Different types of forest biomes
    Ⓓ Only the wet types

14. What factors determine how hot or cold a biome is? **This question is only worth 1 point** (1 point for 2 correct answers and 0 points for 1 or 0 correct answers). 2-19

Choose 2 answers.

A How much precipitation falls in a year
B The diversity of the plant and animal life
C The land's distance from the equator
D The land's elevation

15. What does the professor say about soil in the rainforest? 2-20
Ⓐ It is not very good for growing crops.
Ⓑ It is especially rich in nutrients.
Ⓒ It provides a home for most of the biome's insects.
Ⓓ Fallen plant matter decomposes very slowly there.

16. Which of the following is true about animals in the tropical rainforest biome? 2-21
Ⓐ Animal species are more numerous than plant species.
Ⓑ More of them live in the trees than on the ground.
Ⓒ They cannot live in the canopy section.
Ⓓ Half of the animal species in the tropical rainforest are now extinct.

17. What can you infer about the type of biome the professor will talk about next? 2-22
Ⓐ It will be smaller in size than the tropical rainforest biome.
Ⓑ It will have fewer species of trees than the tropical rainforest biome.
Ⓒ It will be warmer than the tropical rainforest biome.
Ⓓ It will have less diversity of animal species than the tropical rainforest biome.

Listing Passage 4

Questions 18–22

Now get ready to listen. You may take notes. 2-23

Now get ready to answer the questions. You may use your notes to help you answer the questions.

18. Why does the woman want to rent an apartment? 2-24
    Ⓐ First-year students aren't allowed in the dorms.
    Ⓑ She doesn't like the university dorms.
    Ⓒ The dorms don't allow pets.
    Ⓓ She wants a large study space.

19. What is NOT true about the apartment? 2-25
    Ⓐ It has a huge front yard.
    Ⓑ The kitchen is very small.
    Ⓒ It comes with furniture.
    Ⓓ It's close to the university.

20. Listen again to part of the conversation. Then answer the question. 2-26
    What does the man mean when he says this?
    Ⓐ Cats are usually easy to keep in apartments.
    Ⓑ He thinks the woman's pet might damage the apartment.
    Ⓒ People agree that the woman's cat is well-behaved.
    Ⓓ Some people don't tell the truth about their pets.

21. What does the man say about the deposit? 2-27
   Ⓐ It is equal to the first and last month's rent.
   Ⓑ She should pay it when she moves out.
   Ⓒ It is required for dogs, but not for cats.
   Ⓓ She has to pay it before she moves in.

22. What is the woman probably going to do next? 2-28
   Ⓐ Pay the damage deposit.
   Ⓑ Choose a different apartment.
   Ⓒ Arrange to visit the apartment.
   Ⓓ Sign a lease for the apartment.

Listening Passage 5

Questions 23–28

Now get ready to listen. You may take notes. 2-29

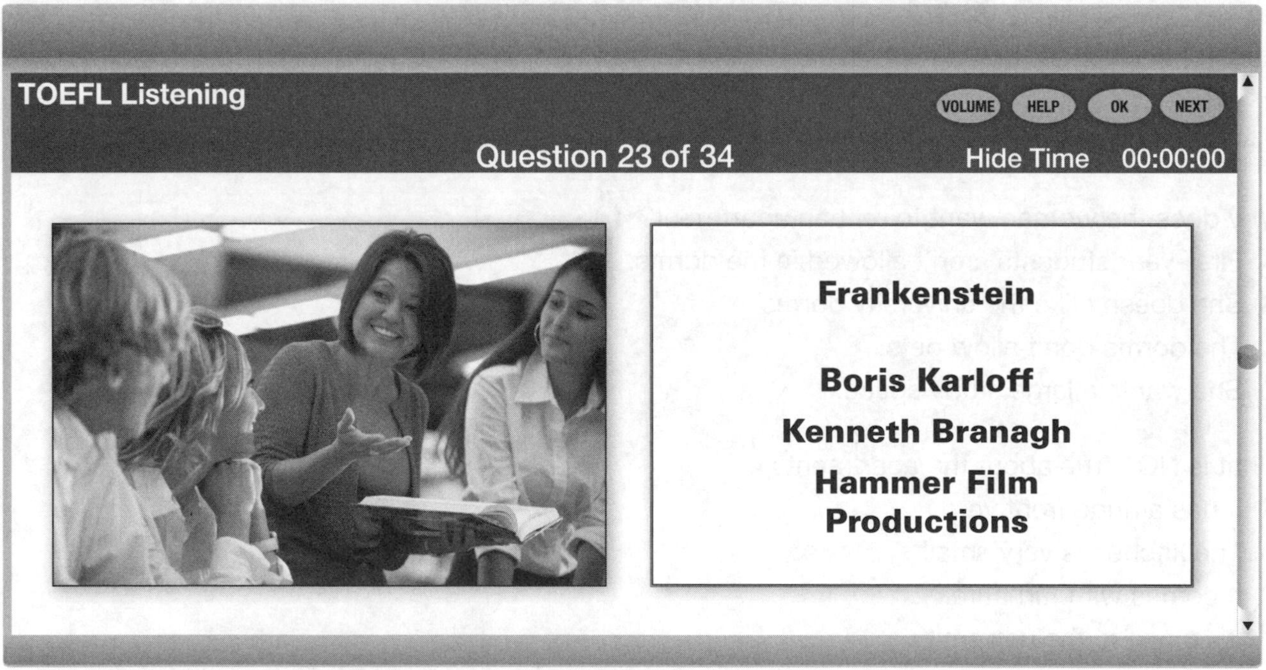

Now get ready to answer the questions. You may use your notes to help you answer the questions.

23. What is the discussion mainly about? 2-30

Ⓐ How the movie versions of Frankenstein are related to the novel
Ⓑ How many different movies about Frankenstein there have been
Ⓒ Popular misunderstandings about the monster in the films
Ⓓ How the movie versions of Frankenstein are different from each other

24. When was the first movie about Frankenstein made? 2-31

Ⓐ 1910
Ⓑ 1921
Ⓒ 1930
Ⓓ 1931

25. Are these features of the 1931 version of Frankenstein? **This question is worth 2 points** (2 points for 4 correct answers, 1 point for 3 correct answers, and 0 points for 2, 1, or 0 correct answers). 2-32

For each answer, put a check mark (✓) in the **YES** or **NO** column.		
	YES	**NO**
A monster that can't talk		
The actor Boris Karloff		
Color film		
The actor Kenneth Branagh		

26. Listen again to part of the conversation. Then answer the question. 2-33
What does the woman mean when she says this?

Ⓐ The monster was still mostly a bad character.
Ⓑ The monster wasn't able to feel sorry for people.
Ⓒ She can't think of an accurate way to describe the monster.
Ⓓ The monster's looks were worse than its personality.

27. What does the professor say about the 1957 film from Hammer Film Productions? 2-34

Ⓐ It was a comedy.
Ⓑ It presented the monster's point of view.
Ⓒ It was a true horror movie.
Ⓓ It featured a monster that could talk.

28. What does the professor imply about the comedy movies? 2-35

Ⓐ They aren't really about Frankenstein.
Ⓑ The students won't watch any of them in class.
Ⓒ They cannot be used for the final project.
Ⓓ They were made after the horror movies were produced.

Listening Passage 6

Questions 29–34

Now get ready to listen. You may take notes. 2-36

Now get ready to answer the questions. You may use your notes to help you answer the questions.

29. How is the information in the lecture organized? 2-37
    - Ⓐ By comparison of several expeditions
    - Ⓑ In the order in which the events occurred
    - Ⓒ From the least dangerous to the most dangerous journeys
    - Ⓓ By causes of the events and their effects

30. Why does the professor mention cloves and cinnamon? 2-38
    - Ⓐ To provide an example of crops grown on the Maluku Islands
    - Ⓑ To illustrate how expensive various spices were
    - Ⓒ To emphasize that Spain had control of the market for them
    - Ⓓ To explain the reason for Magellan's expedition

31. Listen again to part of the lecture. Then answer the question. 2-39
    Why does the professor say this?
    - Ⓐ To indicate that he's said something out of sequence
    - Ⓑ To offer a prediction of future events
    - Ⓒ To strongly state his opinion of the facts
    - Ⓓ To avoid saying something he doesn't want to mention

32. What can be inferred about Magellan's knowledge of the Pacific Ocean? 2-40

Ⓐ He knew where the Pacific islands were located.

Ⓑ He was unable to predict the number of ships needed to cross it.

Ⓒ He didn't understand how big it was.

Ⓓ He had accurate maps of it from a previous expedition.

33. According to the passage, what happened to the ships in Magellan's expedition? **This question is only worth 1 point** (1 point for 2 correct answers and 0 points for 1 or 0 correct answers). 2-41

Choose 2 answers.

[A] The *Santiago* and *San Antonio* were destroyed during a fight.

[B] The *Trinidad* was taken by a competing country.

[C] The *Victoria* left the expedition in South American to return to Spain.

[D] The *Concepción* was set on fire because they lacked a crew to sail it.

34. Listen again to part of the conversation. Then answer the question. 2-42
Which of the following best expresses the professor's attitude toward Juan Sebastian del Cano?

Ⓐ He feels sorry for what happened to him in the end.

Ⓑ He believes del Cano deserves more credit for his achievement.

Ⓒ He thinks that historians don't pay enough attention to what the man said.

Ⓓ He feels that Magellan treated del Cano unfairly.

THIS IS THE END OF THE LISTENING POST-TEST.

Record your score: _______

SPEAKING OVERVIEW

The Speaking section tests your ability to speak English fluently and accurately when responding to a variety of topics.

There are six questions covering two types of tasks:

- Independent (a response based on your own knowledge, experience, or opinions)
- Integrated (a response based on both a reading passage and a lecture/conversation or a response based on a lecture/conversation)

You will be asked to respond to a question or a prompt for six tasks: two independent tasks and four integrated tasks. The entire section takes approximately 20 minutes.

INDEPENDENT TASKS

Task 1—Free-Choice: You will respond to a question or a prompt about a topic that is familiar to you, such a person, place, or event. You will be asked to include specific examples and details in your response. You will have 15 seconds to prepare your response and 45 seconds to respond.

Task 2—Paired-Choice: You will respond to a question or a prompt that asks you to choose one of two possible actions, situations, or opinions. You will be asked to provide detailed support for your preference by explaining the reasons for your choice and by using specific examples. You will have 15 seconds to prepare your response and 45 seconds to respond.

INTEGRATED TASKS

Task 3—Announcement or Notice (Reading + Conversation): You will first read an announcement or notice related to life on a university campus. Then you will hear a conversation between two students discussing the announcement or notice. Then you will answer a question that asks you to use information from *both the reading passage and the conversation*. You will have 45 seconds to read the passage of 75–100 words, which will be followed by a 60- to 80-second conversation. You will then have 30 seconds to prepare your response and 60 seconds to respond.

Task 4—General/Specific (Reading + Lecture): You will first read a passage based on an academic subject (for example, science, history, literature). The reading passage will provide general information. After the reading passage, you will hear a short lecture on the same subject, but the lecture will provide examples and specific information about the subject. Then you will answer a question that asks you to summarize and connect the information from *both the reading and the lecture*. You will have 45 seconds to read the passage of 75–100 words, which will be followed by a 60- to 80-second lecture. You will then have 30 seconds to prepare your response and 60 seconds to respond.

Task 5—Problem/Solutions (Conversation): *You will not be asked to read a passage for this task.* You will hear a conversation between a student and another student, a professor, or a campus official. The conversation will be about a typical, campus-related problem. Then you will answer a question that asks you to summarize the problem, discuss the solutions, and *state your opinion* about which solution you prefer and why. You will listen to a 60- to 90-second conversation. You will then have 20 seconds to prepare your response and 60 seconds to respond.

Task 6—Summary (Lecture): *You will not be asked to read a passage for this task.* You will listen to an academic lecture. Then you will answer a question that asks you to summarize the main points of the lecture or a question about the main topic that you must support with examples or reasons from the lecture. *You will not be asked to give your own opinion.* You will listen to a 60- to 90-second lecture. You will then have 20 seconds to prepare your response and 60 seconds to respond.

During the Speaking section, you may take notes. You will be given a pencil and paper to use. The notes are not scored or seen by anyone else, but you may not take them with you after the test. They will be collected by the test center. You may use your notes when you answer the questions. (See pages 87–91 for Note-Taking Skills.)

For Integrated Tasks 4 and 5, you will see the reading passage on the screen for only 45 seconds. In addition, for the all the Integrated tasks, you will not see the lectures and conversations printed on the screen. Therefore, it is important to quickly take good notes on both the reading and listening passages. *You cannot skip questions, and you cannot go back to questions once you have submitted your answers.*

EXPRESS TIP

For the Speaking section of the TOEFL iBT® Test, you will need to wear headphones and speak into a microphone attached to them. Be sure to adjust your headphones, microphone, and the volume before you begin this portion of the test.

Tool Bar for the Speaking Section

TOEFL Speaking	VOLUME	NEXT
Question 3 of 6		

The section you are in and the question you are answering will always be displayed on the tool bar at the top of the computer screen.

Volume—Enables you to change the volume during the test.
Next—Allows you to go to the next question.

Note: Each of the tasks will appear with their own clocks, which will count down the preparation time and response time.

Independent Tasks 1 and 2 on the Speaking portion of the TOEFL iBT Test are administered as follows:

1. The general directions for the Speaking section will appear on the computer screen. However, you should already be familiar with the directions, so don't waste time reading them; immediately click on "Continue" to move to the first speaking task.
2. You will see and hear short instructions for the first question.
3. You will hear and see the question or prompt.
4. There will be a clock on the screen that counts down the seconds for preparation and response time.
5. You will hear, "Begin to prepare your response after the beep," and then a "beep" sound. The clock will count down 15 seconds while you prepare your response.
6. You will then hear, "Begin speaking after the beep" followed by a "beep" sound. The clock will count down 45 seconds while you respond to the question.
7. After 45 seconds, you will hear a "beep" sound followed by "Now, stop speaking." Your response will be saved and sent to a scoring center.

EXPRESS TIP

You may run out of time before you can say everything that you want in your response. However, the raters understand that this happens sometimes. It is important to organize your response in a clear way, as well as to include a lot of information. That is, the quality of your response is equally as important as the quantity. So, don't start speaking too quickly when you see you are running out of time.

Integrated Tasks 3 and 4 on the Speaking portion of the TOEFL iBT Test are administered as follows:

1. You will see and hear short instructions for the first question.
2. You will hear and see the question or prompt.
3. There will be a clock on the screen that counts down the seconds for reading, preparation, and response time.
4. You will hear, "You will now have 45 seconds to read the passage. Begin reading now," and then a "beep" sound. The clock will count down 45 seconds while you read the passage.
5. You will hear a "beep" sound after 45 seconds, followed by "Now, stop reading."
6. The reading passage will be replaced by a photograph of people talking or a professor giving a lecture. You will hear, "Now listen to a conversation on this topic between two students" or "Now listen to part of a lecture on this topic in a [academic field] class."
7. After the listening passage is finished, the photograph will be replaced on the screen with "Now get ready to answer the question."
8. You will then hear and see the question on the screen.

9. You will hear, "Begin to prepare your response after the beep," and then a "beep" sound. The clock will count down 30 seconds while you prepare your response.
10. Next, you will hear, "Begin speaking after the beep," followed by a "beep" sound. The clock will count down 60 seconds while you respond to the question.
11. After 60 seconds, you will hear a "beep" sound followed by "Now, stop speaking." Your response will be saved and sent to a scoring center.

Integrated Tasks 5 and 6 on the Speaking portion of the TOEFL iBT Test are administered in the same way as Integrated Tasks 3 and 4, EXCEPT that steps 4 and 5 for reading the passage are not included, and the preparation time is **20 seconds**.

In the individual Skills units of this section, you will see examples of the computer screens used for each type of question.

The spoken responses are listened to and scored by trained ETS staff. Responses that receive a high score:

- use comprehensible speech that flows without too many pauses or hesitations
- use good pronunciation
- use natural pacing and intonation
- use appropriate vocabulary
- are mostly grammatically accurate
- use a variety of sentence structures, from basic to complex
- directly address the prompt
- completely answer the question
- coherently develop the topic by clearly connecting ideas and progressing logically from one point to the next
- use all or most of the time allowed

EXPRESS TIP

If you finish before time runs out, don't just repeat what you've already said. Instead, think of another example to support one of your points.

Improving Your Speaking Ability

The Speaking section can be challenging for students who don't have many opportunities to practice speaking in English. However, there are still ways that you *can* practice. Try some or all of these, and remember that you can't improve your speaking ability unless you spend time *actually* talking.

- Record yourself speaking. Listen to see if your pronunciation is clear and if you speak without a lot of hesitations. If possible, play your recording for your English teachers or for native English speakers. Ask them to evaluate your speaking ability and give you feedback for improvement.
- Work with a partner. Brainstorm a list of topics that require you to state an opinion or a preference. However, do *not* show your partner the list. Then take turns speaking about the topics while your partner times your response with a watch or clock. Try to give your response in a minute or less. The preparation time for the Speaking section of the TOEFL iBT Test is very, very short, so you need to learn to think and speak quickly, without much preparation.
- Read an interesting short article and make an outline of it. Use the outline to give an oral summary of the main points in the article.
- Practice taking notes by listening to science shows on television, news programs/interviews on the radio, or DVDs of English-language documentaries. Use your notes to create an outline. Then give an oral summary from your notes. Report what you heard in your own words (paraphrase). Practice your summary response a few times, record it, and self-evaluate, or ask your English teacher or a native English speaker to evaluate your recorded response.
- Exchange interesting stories about your life or your country with other people in English.
- Read a local or international news story that interests you and then tell it to someone else.
- Read a story or article aloud to practice fluency and pronunciation. Record yourself if you can.
- Sing along with English songs on CDs or online. Singing can help promote fluency. If you don't know the words to the songs (lyrics), you may be able to find them online or in song books.

INDEPENDENT TASK 1

FREE-CHOICE

Skills 1, 2, and 3: Giving Detailed Descriptions; Using Narrative; Providing Examples

The first task in the Independent Speaking section, the free-choice task, requires you to speak for 45 seconds on a topic that is familiar to you, usually about your life or your opinions. The topics are broad enough that you should always have something to say. Your recorded response will be evaluated on fluency, organization, vocabulary, and grammar. You will have 15 seconds to think about the topic and take notes before you begin speaking.

The following are examples of free-choice questions:

- *What do you like to do on rainy days? Use details in your response.*
- *What was the most useful class that you took in high school? Give reasons for your response.*
- *Talk about the type of transportation you prefer to take while traveling and why.*

You will both hear the questions and see them on the computer screen.

To answer these types of questions:

- Pay attention to all parts of the prompt so that you can give a complete answer.
- Make very brief notes in outline form to plan your response. Include the reasons and details you plan to mention. Remember, though, that 15 seconds is not much time! Use abbreviations where possible.
- Try to give at least two reasons, details, or examples in your response, or relate a short anecdote or narrative.
- When you speak, indicate details and examples with clear signposts, such as *for instance*, *for example*, *another reason*, *furthermore*, and so on.
- Speak at a natural pace, at a good volume.

EXPRESS TIP

There is no way for a rater to judge your response on "truthfulness." While your response should sound reasonable, it is all right to add details and support even if they are not strictly true. Remember that you are trying to demonstrate your knowledge of and proficiency *in English*.

The rater will be listening for a clear, well-spoken response that includes a complete answer to the question with the requested supporting ideas such as examples or reasons.

Look at this example of a free-choice question on a computer screen.

EXAMPLE: Free-Choice Question

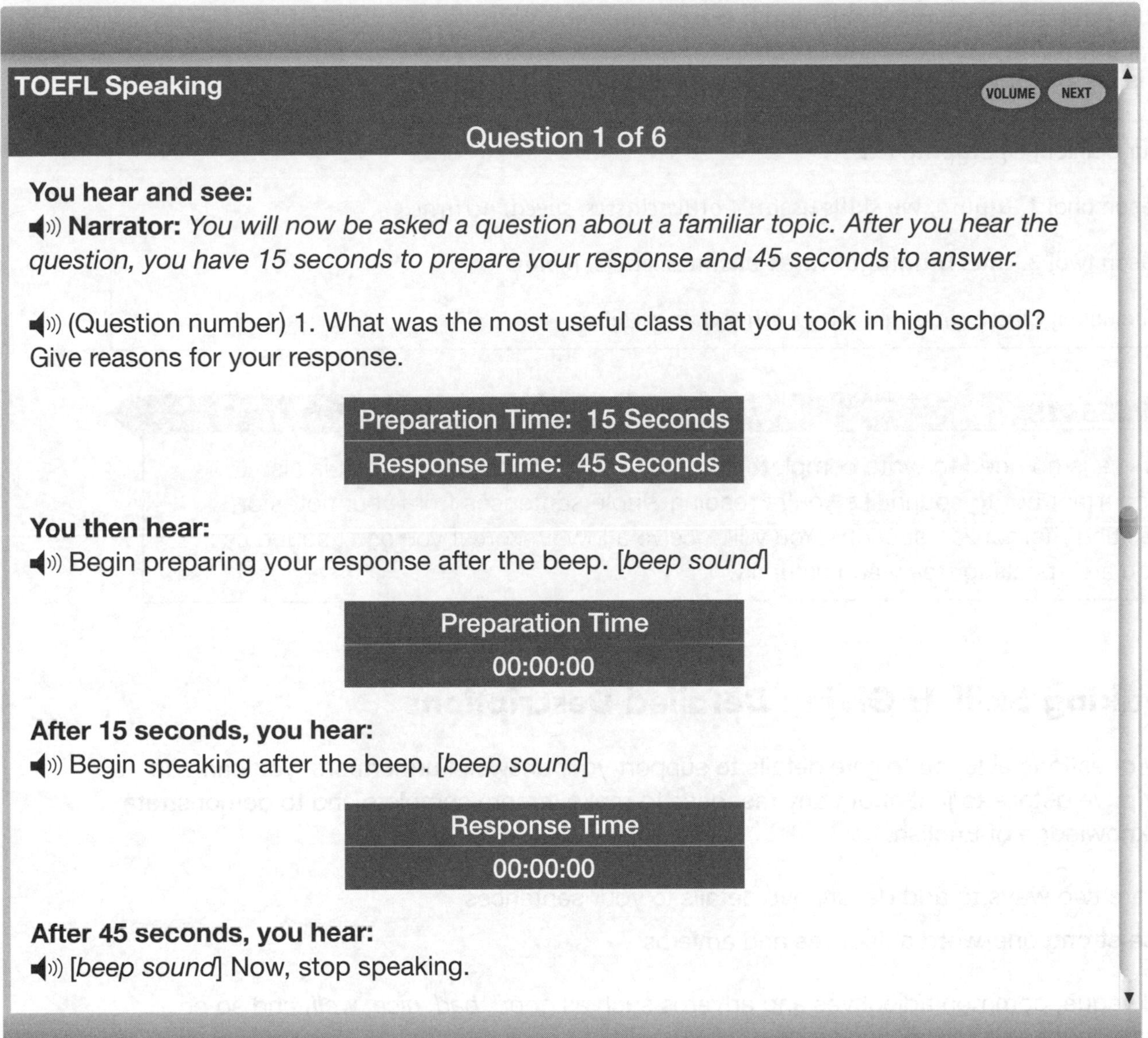
TOEFL Speaking
VOLUME
NEXT
Question 1 of 6
You hear and see:
Narrator: *You will now be asked a question about a familiar topic. After you hear the question, you have 15 seconds to prepare your response and 45 seconds to answer.*
(Question number) 1. What was the most useful class that you took in high school? Give reasons for your response.
Preparation Time: 15 Seconds
Response Time: 45 Seconds
You then hear:
Begin preparing your response after the beep. [*beep sound*]
Preparation Time
00:00:00
After 15 seconds, you hear:
Begin speaking after the beep. [*beep sound*]
Response Time
00:00:00
After 45 seconds, you hear:
[*beep sound*] Now, stop speaking.

NOTE-TAKING AND RATING PRACTICE

Directions: *Read the following prompt and make notes for your response. Then compare your notes to the note-taking model below.*

1. What was the most useful class that you took in high school? Give reasons for your response.

Note-Taking Model

Your notes for the free-choice task should include these things: your answer to the question, two or three details or examples to support your answer, any special vocabulary or ideas you want to remember as you speak, and a concluding thought.

Here is an example of notes from the prompt above.

[your opinion] *Op: typing class*

[reason one] *1. typing, wp skills useful 4 other classes; speed, accuracy*

[reason two] *2. class taught format 4 business letters, reports*

[conclusion] *Concl: class helped w/ other classes & job*

EXPRESS TIP

There is no need to write complete sentences when you take notes. It is also important not to sound like you're reading whole sentences from your notes or reciting memorized sections. You will receive a lower score if you don't sound as if you are speaking freely and naturally.

Speaking Skill 1: Giving Detailed Descriptions

Many questions ask you to give details to support your answer. Furthermore, you can add descriptive details to just about any response to make it more complete and to demonstrate your knowledge of English.

Here are two ways to add descriptive details to your sentences.

1. Use strong one-word adjectives and adverbs.

Avoid vague, common adjectives and adverbs such as *good*, *bad*, *nice*, *well*, and so on. Instead, choose more precise words.

As you study and practice for the TOEFL iBT Test, use a notebook to keep a chart such as the one below and use it to record and learn vocabulary.

Common Word	More Precise Synonyms
good	valuable, practical, talented, inspiring
bad	frightening, difficult, unpleasant, depressing
nice (for a person)	kind, helpful, encouraging, generous
well (adverb)	skillfully, quickly, efficiently
poorly	unwillingly, carelessly

2. Use prepositional phrases as adjectives or adverbs.

A prepositional phrase (preposition + noun, such as *around the corner* or *with a smile*) functions as an adjective or an adverb. Phrases like these can sometimes offer a more detailed explanation than a single word. Note that prepositional phrases are far more likely to function as adverbs; this is useful because one-word adverbs are less common than one-word adjectives. Adverb phrases give more information in a sentence about time, place, reason, and manner, and often come at the very end of sentences (the most common position) or at the beginning of sentences (the second most common position).

EXAMPLE:

- *I learned a lot of useful skills for work in my typing class.*
- *In my typing class, I learned a lot of useful skills for work.*

Common Word	Prepositional Phrase
time	at night, in the summer, on weekends, during class, in the long run
place	in the mountains, at home, under the canopy, along the riverbank
reason / purpose	for money, against orders, by law
manner	by bicycle, with a lever, by moving forward, with a friend

SKILL BUILDER

Directions: *Work with a partner. Look at the following questions and excerpts from answers. Add more information to each answer by using single words and phrases (use your imagination!). Write the improved sentences on a separate sheet of paper, and take turns reading the new answers aloud with your partner. Then take turns giving answers of about the same length, using your own ideas. The first one has been done for you.*

1. What was the most useful class that you took in high school? Give reasons for your response.

   Typing was a good class because I learned a lot. It was hard, but I'm glad that I worked hard and made progress. Now I can type well without looking at my hands.

   EXAMPLE: *Typing was a practical class because I learned a lot of word-processing skills. It was a difficult class with daily homework assignments, but I'm glad that I worked hard and made significant progress. Now I can type quickly, easily, and accurately without looking down at my hands.*

2. What is your favorite activity to do by yourself? Give reasons to explain your answer.

   I like to surf the Internet when I am alone. I can find a lot of news stories and other good websites. It doesn't cost much. It isn't difficult.

3. Talk about a relative who taught you something important. Explain what you learned.

   I learned how to be patient from my uncle. He's a patient man. He doesn't get angry. He rarely feels stressed.

4. Talk about an interesting place that you have visited. Use details in your response.

   I went to Paris. It was nice. It was large. I saw a lot of things. I ate some good food, and I met some nice people.

EXPRESS TIP

Don't use exactly the same wording of the question in your response. Answer the question in your own words.

Skill Builder Sample Answers:

Answers will vary, but should include detailed descriptions with precise vocabulary and prepositional phrases.

Possible notes:

2. *I like to surf the Internet* ***for hours*** *when I am alone. I can find a lot of interesting* ***local and international*** *news stories and other good websites* ***about my hobbies and interests****. It doesn't cost much,* ***which is convenient, and I also enjoy it because*** *it isn't difficult.*

3. *I learned how to be patient from my uncle. He's* ***an excellent example of*** *a patient man. He doesn't get* ***upset or*** *angry* ***when plans change or things go wrong****. He rarely feels stressed.*

4. *I went to Paris* ***for two weeks when I was in high school****. It was* ***a wonderful experience****. It* ***was the largest city I had ever visited****. I saw a lot of* ***famous monuments and museums****. I ate some* ***fancy French*** *food, and I met some* ***friendly French*** *people* ***my*** *age.*

PRACTICE

A. *Read the prompt.*

B. *Take quick notes on a separate piece of paper. Then write an answer to the question in the prompt that uses* ***descriptive words and phrases****.*

Which holiday from your country do you enjoy the most? Use details to support your answer.

C. *Work with a partner. Read your written answer aloud. If possible, time your response.*

D. *Then, without using your written response, give your response aloud again and record it. Try to speak for no more than 45 seconds.*

E. *Listen to the recording of your response to the Practice for Skill 1 and complete the self-evaluation chart below. How well do you feel you did these things? Rank questions 1–7 from 1 to 5. Then answer questions 8–10.*

Self-Evaluation: Skill 1

	1 = low, 5 = high
1. Understand the prompt	
2. Take notes to help you speak	
3. Answer the question completely in the time allowed	
4. Use interesting and appropriate single-word adjectives and adverbs	
5. Use prepositional phrases to give more information	
6. Speak fluently, without too many pauses and repetitions	
7. Speak accurately, with correct grammar and vocabulary	
8. What is something you did especially well?	
9. What one or two things would you like to improve on?	
10. How do you plan to improve those things?	

Speaking Skill 2: Using Narrative

Some answers for the free-choice questions can best be explained or illustrated through the use of a short narrative, or story. For example, if a prompt asks you about an influential relative, you can tell about a time that he or she did something brave or selfless.

Narratives are generally told in chronological order; that is, events are related from the earliest to the most recent. Begin the story with a time marker that explains when the story begins; for example, *When I was seven years old*, *At the beginning of my first year in high school*, *During my last summer vacation*.

Use time markers and transitions to order the events in the story, such as *first*, *next*, *then*, *while*, *during*, *after that*, *a few days later*, *after having ~ed*, *at the end of the day*, *finally*.

EXPRESS TIP

Remember that you only have 45 seconds to speak, so be sure to mention only the most important part of the story and two or three supporting details to highlight it and answer the question.

Narratives relate events that have already taken place. Make sure you use past tense verb forms to relate these events.

Use . . .

Verb Tense	Purpose
The simple past	to describe events that are completed: *He gave me some advice; I took an overnight train*
The past continuous	to show an action in progress in the past, usually interrupted by another action: *I was running toward the goal posts when I tripped and fell.*
The past perfect	to show an action in the past that was completed before another action in the past: *The scholarship deadline had already passed before I read the announcement.*

EXPRESS TIP

To work on your spoken grammar to prepare for the TOEFL iBT Test, work through exercises from another book or website and read the examples and exercises out loud as you do them, so that you become used to speaking correctly.

SKILL BUILDER

Directions: *Work with a partner. Look at the following questions. Take quick notes on a separate piece of paper that include a short narrative to illustrate your answer to the question.*

Write your responses down and then take turns reading them aloud with your partner.

1. Talk about a skill that you taught yourself. What was it, and how did you learn it?
2. Describe a vacation that you enjoyed.
3. Talk about a time that you were misunderstood. Were you able to correct the misunderstanding?
4. Describe a time when you were pleasantly surprised. Use details in your response.

Skill Builder Sample Answers:

Answers will vary, but should include a narrative with verb tenses used correctly, as well as detailed descriptions as practiced with Skill 1.

Possible notes:

1. *how to juggle: bought set of juggling balls, then watched YouTube vid. many times = good juggler*
2. *camping trip w/ HS friends: 1st trip no parents, camped in woods, trouble w/ tent, rained, slept in car, best time because w/ good friends*
3. *friend thought didn't invite her to party, but she didn't check e-mail. v. upset, didn't tell me why, another friend told, talked, solved prob.*
4. *nat. history test: thought did badly, but got special award, decided to become hist. major*

PRACTICE

A. *Read the prompt.*

B. *Take quick notes on a separate piece of paper. Then write an answer to the question in the prompt that includes a* ***narrative****.*

Describe a treasured possession that you own. Why is it important? Give reasons to explain your answer.

C. *Work with a partner. Read your written answer aloud. If possible, time your response.*

D. *Then, without using your written response, give your response aloud again and record it. Try to speak for no more than 45 seconds.*

E. *Listen to the recording of your response to the Practice for Skill 2 and complete the self-evaluation chart below. How well do you feel you did these things? Rank questions 1–7 from 1 to 5. Then answer questions 8–10.*

Self-Evaluation: Skill 2

	1 = low, 5 = high
1. Understand the prompt	
2. Take notes to help you speak	
3. Answer the question completely in the time allowed	
4. Tell a narrative with a time phrase to begin the story and sequencing words and transitions to order the events	
5. Use past tense verbs, pronounced clearly, to relate the narrative	
6. Speak fluently, without too many pauses and repetitions	
7. Speak accurately, with correct grammar and vocabulary	
8. What is something you did especially well?	
9. What one or two things would you like to improve on?	
10. How do you plan to improve those things?	

If you gave yourself any low rankings, discuss some study strategies with a partner, a group, or your instructor, or make your own plan to work on the areas that need improvement. Remember that improvement comes with continued practice.

Speaking Skill 3: Providing Examples

As you have noticed, many of the free-choice questions ask you to provide examples, reasons, or details. Details can be as simple as descriptive words (see Skill 1), or they can be ideas, facts, or incidents.

If a prompt asks you to provide details and examples, be sure to signal them clearly with phrases such as *For instance*, *For example*, *Another example of (x) is . . .* Since you will know from your notes how many examples you are going to talk about, you can signal this with phrases such as *There are two reasons I especially enjoy . . .*; *I learned three important things from. . . .*

Remember that you will have 15 seconds to plan your response and 45 seconds to record it. Don't try to include too many examples. Two or three is enough. It is better to explain two examples completely than to mention four and only have time to talk about two, or to talk about three without much description or detail.

If you cannot think of more than one example, either use your imagination to add to your own experience, or choose a different answer that you can talk about more easily.

EXPRESS TIP

Correct mistakes that you know you've made. Don't be afraid to go back and start the sentence again.

SKILL BUILDER

Directions: *Work with a partner. Look at the following questions and take quick notes on a separate sheet of paper that include two to three examples. Then take turns listing your examples to your partner.*

1. What qualities do you have that make you a good friend? Give examples to explain your answer.
2. What do you do to keep yourself healthy? Give examples to support your answer.
3. What is your favorite type of food to prepare? Give reasons to explain your answer.
4. What animal do you think best represents your personality? Give reasons to explain your answer.

Skill Builder Sample Answers:

Answers will vary, but should include examples clearly marked with phrases such as *for example* and *for instance*.

Possible notes:

1. *patient / loyal / kind*
2. *eat breakfast / exercise / don't drink coffee, tea, or soda*
3. *pasta: spaghetti w/ meatballs, veg. noodle soup, lasagna*
4. *fox: smart & clever, strong family connections*

PRACTICE

A. *Read the prompt.*

B. *Take quick notes on a separate piece of paper. Then write an answer to the question in the prompt that includes a* ***narrative****.*

Talk about a challenge you have faced in your life. How did you meet that challenge?

C. *Work with a partner. Read your written answer aloud. If possible, time your response.*

D. *Then, without using your written response, give your response aloud again and record it. Try to speak for no more than 45 seconds.*

E. *Listen to the recording of your response to the Practice for Skill 3 and complete the self-evaluation chart below. How well do you feel you did these things? Rank questions 1–7 from 1 to 5. Write N/A if the skill didn't apply to the type of answer you gave. Then answer questions 8–10.*

Self-Evaluation: Skill 3

	1 = low, 5 = high
1. Understand the prompt	
2. Take notes to help you speak	
3. Answer the question completely in the time allowed	
4. Include two or three examples	
5. Signal the examples with signal words or phrases	
6. Speak fluently, without too many pauses and repetitions	
7. Speak accurately, with correct grammar and vocabulary	
8. What is something you did especially well?	
9. What one or two things would you like to improve on?	
10. How do you plan to improve those things?	

SKILLS REVIEW

Independent Speaking Skills 1–3 for the Free-Choice Task: Giving Detailed Descriptions, Using Narrative, and Providing Examples

Directions: *Record your responses to the following prompts.*

1. *You will now be asked a question about a familiar topic. After you hear the question, you have 15 seconds to prepare your response and 45 seconds to answer.* 2-43

1. Talk about a time that you did something you were proud of. What did you do, and why did you feel proud? Use reasons to support your response.
Preparation Time: 15 Seconds
Response Time: 45 Seconds

2. *You will now be asked a question about a familiar topic. After you hear the question, you have 15 seconds to prepare your response and 45 seconds to answer.* 2-44

2. What skill or ability that you don't currently have would you like to develop, and why?
Preparation Time: 15 Seconds
Response Time: 45 Seconds

Self-Evaluation: Skills Review

Listen to the recordings of your responses to the Skills Review for Skills 1–3 and complete the self-evaluation chart below. How well do you feel you did these things? Rank questions 1–11 from 1 to 5. Write N/A if the skill didn't apply to the type of answer you gave. Then answer questions 12–14.

	1 = low, 5 = high
1. Understand the prompt	
2. Take notes to help you speak	
3. Answer the question completely in the time allowed	
4. Use interesting and appropriate single-word adjectives and adverbs	
5. Use prepositional phrases to give more information	
6. Tell a narrative with a time phrase to begin the story and sequencing words and transitions to order the events	
7. Use past tense verbs, pronounced clearly, to relate the narrative	
8. Include two or three examples	
9. Signal the examples with signal words or phrases	
10. Speak fluently, without too many pauses and repetitions	
11. Speak accurately, with correct grammar and vocabulary	
12. What is something you did especially well?	
13. What one or two things would you like to improve on?	
14. How do you plan to improve those things?	

INDEPENDENT TASK 2

PAIRED-CHOICE

Skills 4, 5, and 6: Expressing Opinions; Supporting Your Choice or Preference with Reasons; Using Comparison and Contrast in Your Response

The second task in the Independent Speaking section, the paired-choice task, requires you to respond for 45 seconds to a question based on your *own personal* ideas, experiences, or opinions. This type of question will present you with a prompt or a question that asks you to choose one of two possible actions, situations, or opinions. You will be asked to provide detailed support for your preference by explaining the reasons for your choice and by using specific examples. You will have 15 seconds to think about the topic and take notes before you begin speaking.

The questions are about topics with which you will usually be familiar. Some of these topics are college- or university-related issues, while others are more general.

The following are examples of this type of question:

- *Some college students prefer to take night classes. Others prefer to take classes only in the daytime. Which class schedule do you think is best for students and why?*
- *Some people believe that employees should be rewarded according to their ability. Others believe rewards and promotions should be given according to age and experience. Which opinion do you agree with and why?*

You will both hear the questions and see them on the computer screen.

In order to answer the question correctly, you must:

- Listen to and read the prompt carefully; make sure you completely understand the question.
- Decide on your choice or preference, and then make some quick notes about the specific reasons for it. You only have 15 seconds to prepare, so just write down words or short phrases about the most important points that support the action, situation, or opinion you have chosen. See the example notes on page 170.
- In addition, because your response is based on your own experience, try to think of relevant examples from your personal life that support your preference.
- When you begin recording your response, it is important to first state your choice or preference.
- Support your choice or preference with at least two reasons.
- Develop a logical flow of information by using transitions (*the first reason*, *the second reason*, *in addition*, *however*, *on the other hand*, *because*, and *for example*).
- Speak at a natural pace and at a good volume.
- Conclude your response by restating your choice, preference, or opinion.

EXPRESS TIP

You don't have to choose one side of the issue or the other; you can actually support both of the two choices or preferences. However, be very sure that you give specific reasons that support *both* of them in terms of their positive points and their negative points.

I think both approaches have advantages. I think X is a good approach because . . . However, while Y doesn't offer all of the same advantages as X, it can also be a useful approach because . . .

Look at this example of a paired-choice question on a computer screen.

EXAMPLE: Paired-Choice Question

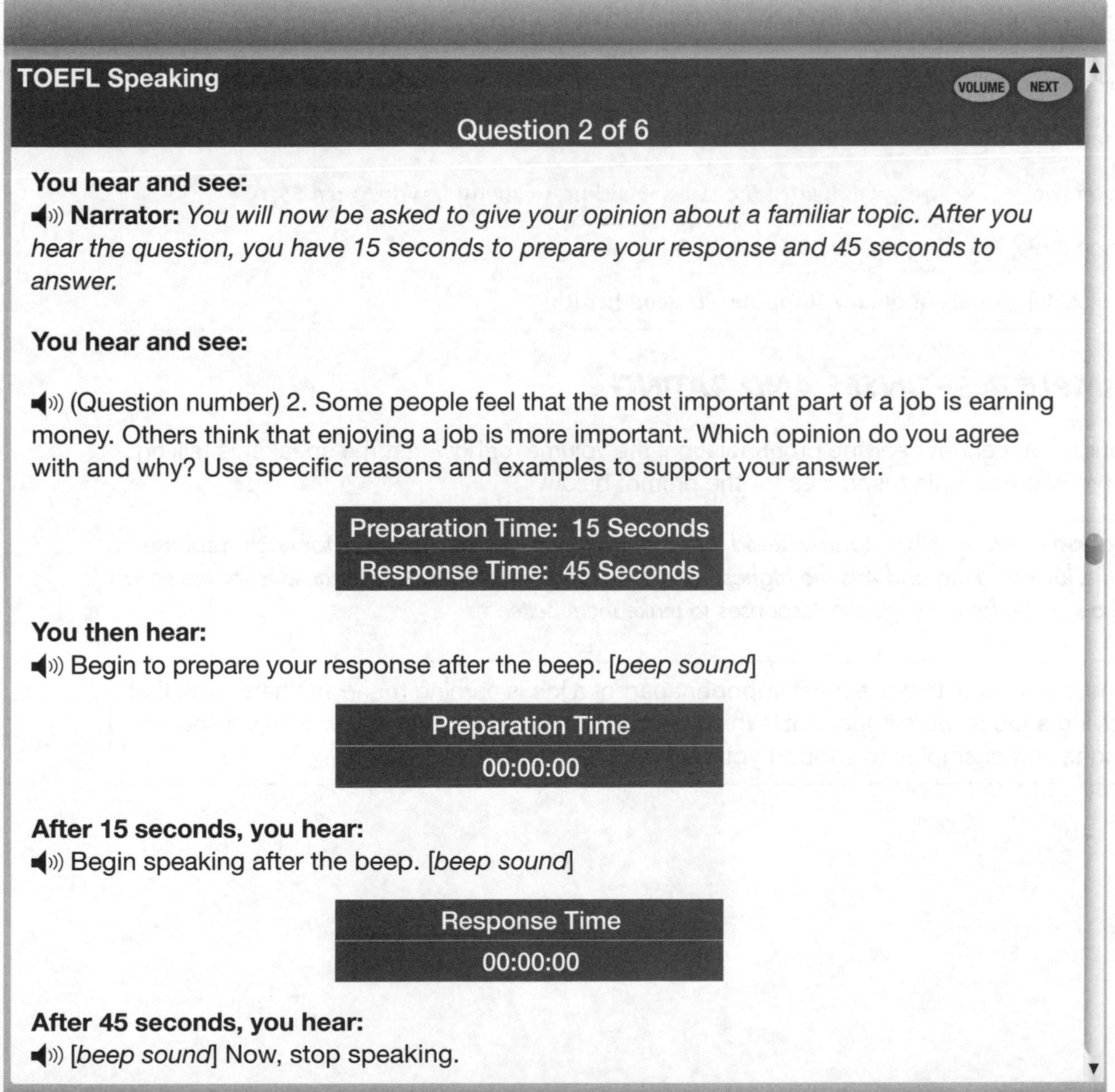

TOEFL Speaking
VOLUME
NEXT
Question 2 of 6
You hear and see:
Narrator: You will now be asked to give your opinion about a familiar topic. After you hear the question, you have 15 seconds to prepare your response and 45 seconds to answer.
You hear and see:
(Question number) 2. Some people feel that the most important part of a job is earning money. Others think that enjoying a job is more important. Which opinion do you agree with and why? Use specific reasons and examples to support your answer.
Preparation Time: 15 Seconds
Response Time: 45 Seconds
You then hear:
Begin to prepare your response after the beep. [beep sound]
Preparation Time
00:00:00
After 15 seconds, you hear:
Begin speaking after the beep. [beep sound]
Response Time
00:00:00
After 45 seconds, you hear:
[beep sound] Now, stop speaking.

NOTE-TAKING AND RATING PRACTICE

Directions: *Read the following prompt and make notes for your response. Then compare your notes to the note-taking model below.*

> Some people feel that the most important part of a job is earning money. Others think that enjoying a job is more important. Which opinion do you agree with and why? Use specific reasons and examples to support your answer.

Note-Taking Model:

Your notes for the paired-choice task should include these things: your opinion, two or more reasons that support your opinion, and any examples that are relevant to the topic.

Here is an example of notes from the prompt above.

[your opinion]	*Op: enjoy job*
[reason one]	*1. no excite → no gd wrkr = ↓ $$*
[reason two]	*2. ↓ stress = ↑ health (ex: stress → sickness = away fr wrk / med $$)*
[reason three]	*3. unhappy = bad 4 family & friends*
[conclusion]	*Concl: money ≠ happiness & good health*

EXAMPLE RESPONSES AND RATING

Although you cannot hear the pronunciation, the volume, or how fast the speaker is talking, here are some sample responses for the prompt below.

Directions: *Work with a partner. Read the responses and look at the scores for each response (1 is the lowest rating and 4 is the highest) and the explanations. Discuss the reasons for the scores and how you might change the responses to make them better.*

> Some people feel that the most important part of a job is earning money. Others think that enjoying a job is more important. Which opinion do you agree with and why? Use specific reasons and examples to support your answer.

Responses, Scores, and Score Explanations:

Answer A Uh . . . money is good thing. So I agree with . . . um . . . um . . . opinion on that. I need a job with good money first . . . and . . . it's . . . it's not important that I enjoy . . . uh . . . later with lots of money from earned at job, I can have a family and and . . . uh, maybe . . . house . . . uh . . . nice car and that is enjoy for me. Enjoy job would be nice, but not happy without money. Money makes me more happy in life, I think.	**Answer B** I feel that it is most important to enjoy a job . . . uh . . . because life is short and we have little time for happiness. For example, my older brother have a job with lots of money, but he . . . um . . . does not like any more and he is very unhappy. It makes me sad to see how hard he works and how tired he . . . um . . . is sometimes. He is in bad mood a lot and this is not good for us . . . as um . . . I believe brothers should be having fun together. In my opinion, money isn't the most important thing about a job . . . uh, I want to be happy and not so tired . . . and to enjoy my life at work and after it.	**Answer C** I . . . uh . . . I definitely agree with the opinion that it is better to enjoy your job. If I'm not excited about a job, I won't be such a good worker and . . . um . . . I think my job performance would slowly get worse and . . . probably that means less money, too. In addition, when I like my job, I don't feel as much stress and my health is better. For example, if you feel stress, it causes you to . . . uh, get sick and lose works days and have to pay for expensive medicine. Finally, if my job makes me unhappy, I believe it could affect my friends and family and make them unhappy, too. So, from my point of view, money does not equal happiness and health, but enjoying your job can give you both.
Score: 2	Score: 3	Score: 4
This response would get a score of 2 because there are too many pauses, which disrupt the flow of natural speech and make comprehension more difficult. In addition, the student's vocabulary is very limited, and there are basic vocabulary and grammatical mistakes. The sentence structures are not varied, and many are incomplete. Further, while the student did manage to state an opinion and support it with a few reasons, the development of ideas is very limited. The response lacks coherence; one idea does not relate smoothly to another because there is little or no use of transitional signals. The student did not make good use of the time allowed for the response.	**This response would get a score of 3** because the student makes some grammatical and vocabulary mistakes and generally uses simple sentence structures. The student starts off well, but the flow of speech is choppy and there are a fair number of pauses. In addition, the response lacks some coherence due to lack of appropriate transitions. However, the student stated a definite opinion and attempted to use a personal example and some reasons to support the opinion. The student did not use all of the time available for the response, and so could possibility have further developed the opinion.	**This response would get a score of 4** because the student paused very little and made very few grammatical or vocabulary mistakes. The sentence structures are complex and varied. While the response is not perfect in every way, it is coherent and progresses smoothly with very good use of transitions. The student provides many detailed reason for the opinion clearly stated at the beginning of the response. The response ends with a good conclusion that sums up the student's reasons for the opinion. The student made good use of the time allowed for the response.

Speaking Skill 4: Expressing Opinions

It is essential to know how to express your opinion for the paired-choice task so that the people rating your response (the raters) can hear and clearly identify it. Here are some specific phrases that will signal to the raters what your opinion is:

- *In my opinion . . .*
- *From my point of view/In my view . . .*
- *I agree/disagree with . . .*
- *I prefer . . .*
- *I believe . . .*
- *I think . . .*
- *I feel that . . .*

Note that the superlative forms of adjectives can be used to indicate which choice you prefer:

In my opinion, X is *the adjective + ~est* (*best, worst*) choice because . . .

I believe that X is *the most adjective* (*important, intelligent*) choice because . . .

SKILL BUILDER

Work with a partner. Look at the following questions. Take quick notes on a separate piece of paper that include: your opinion, two or more reasons to support your opinion, and any examples that are relevant to the topic. Use phrases from the list above to state your opinion and at least one reason why you have this opinion. Write your responses down. Then take turns saying them aloud with your partner. The first one has been done for you.

1. Some people feel that the most important part of a job is earning money. Others think that enjoying a job is more important. Which opinion do you agree with and why?

EXAMPLE: ***In my opinion****, it's much more important to earn enough money at your job than to enjoy it. The reason* ***I think*** *this is that if you don't have enough money to buy a house or support your family or even take vacations, for example, you will be unhappy at home. This means you might be happy at work, but will feel worried all the time about your personal life.* ***I prefer*** *to enjoy time away from work with my friends and family. And another reason is that* ***I believe****, even though you might not like your job so much now, you will be able to work hard while you are young and save money for a better future when you are older.*

2. Many high schools require students to take art classes. Do you think this is a good idea or not? Why?
3. Do you think living in a place that is sunny and warm all year long is better than living in a place that has a variety of different seasons and weather during the year? Why?
4. Some people prefer to eat small amounts of food frequently throughout the day. Other people prefer to eat three larger meals at breakfast, lunch, and dinner. Which do you think is better and why?
5. Which do you think is better for university students, attending large classes with fifty to a hundred students or attending small classes with ten to fifteen students? Why?

EXPRESS TIP

Remember to respond to all parts of the question, and be clear and certain about your opinion or preference throughout your response.

Skill Builder Sample Answers:

Answers will vary, but should include phrases for stating an opinion, relevant examples, and one or two reasons for the stated opinion.

PRACTICE

A. *Read the prompt.*

B. *Take quick notes on a separate piece of paper. Then write an answer to the question in the prompt using expressions for* ***giving an opinion****.*

Some universities require students to take physical education classes, such as swimming, dance, golf, or basketball. Others do not have this requirement. Which do you agree with and why? Use specific reasons and examples to support your answer.

C. *Work with a partner. Read your written answer aloud. If possible, time your response.*

D. *Then, without using your written response, give your response aloud again and record it. Try to speak for no more than 45 seconds.*

E. *Listen to the recording of your response to the Practice for Skill 4 and complete the self-evaluation chart below. How well do you feel you did these things? Rank questions 1–8 from 1 to 5. Then answer questions 9–11.*

EXPRESS TIP

When you listen to your recorded responses, pay attention to any grammar mistakes you hear and write them down. You may notice that you make the same mistakes repeatedly. Learn how to correct these mistakes and focus on using the correct grammar in your responses.

Self-Evaluation: Skill 4

	1 = low, 5 = high
1. Understand the prompt	
2. Take notes to help you speak	
3. Answer the question completely in the time allowed	
4. State your opinion first	
5. Use the appropriate expressions for stating your opinion, preference, or choice	
6. Provide at least two detailed reasons and some examples for your opinion, preference, or choice	
7. Speak fluently, without too many pauses and repetitions	
8. Speak accurately, with correct grammar and vocabulary	
9. What is something you did especially well?	
10. What one or two things would you like to improve on?	
11. How do you plan to improve those things?	

Speaking Skill 5: Supporting Your Choice or Preference with Reasons

After you have expressed your opinion, you must support it with reasons and examples. Again, it is important to use phrases and transitions that will make your response flow smoothly and that will provide clear signals to the raters about what your reasons are. Here are some specific phrases that you can use to state you reasons for having a specific opinion or preference:

- That's *why* I think . . .
- I agree/disagree with X *for the reason that* . . .
- *The reason* is . . . *because*
- *One reason/The first reason* I think X is a better choice is *because* . . .
- *Another reason/The second reason* I think X is the best idea is *because* . . .
- *For example* . . .

EXPRESS TIP

It is not sufficient to simply state what you *feel* about a topic: *I think homework is bad* or *Living in a warm climate is good idea.* You must give a logical reason for *why* something is positive or negative.

SKILL BUILDER

Directions: *Work with a partner. Look at the following questions. Take quick notes on a separate piece of paper that include: your opinion, two or more reasons to support your opinion, and any examples that are relevant to the topic. Give your opinion, then use phrases from the list above to state your reasons for your preference. Write your responses down, and then take turns saying them aloud with your partner. The first one has been done for you.*

1. Some people think that it is better not to eat meat. Others feel that a vegetarian diet is not the best choice. Which do you agree with and why?

EXAMPLE: *I agree with those people who think that not being a vegetarian is better.* ***The reason*** *is that I enjoy eating a variety of food, and I feel that eating only vegetables might get . . . um . . . a little boring for me.* ***Another reason*** *I prefer to eat meat is that I know I am getting enough protein in my diet without having to think about it. My friend Joe, for example, who is a vegetarian, started feeling tired all the time. The doctor told him that he needed to get more protein in his diet. Now, he has to worry about what he eats all the time.*

2. Should students be given homework by their teachers every day or not? Why?
3. Some restaurants allow their customers to use their cell phones while dining. Others do not. Which restaurant policy do you agree with and why?
4. Do you think that large tour buses should be allowed inside national parks or at other famous outdoor landmarks or not? Why?
5. Should lawyers be paid more for doing their job than doctors? Why or why not?

EXPRESS TIP

There is no right or wrong answer to the paired-choice questions. The best response depends *not* on the opinion you have, but on how well you *support* it with detailed reasons and examples.

Skill Builder Sample Answers:
Answers will vary, but should include phrases for stating an opinion and phrases and transitions for stating the reasons for having a specific opinion or preference.

PRACTICE

A. *Read the prompt.*

B. *Take quick notes on a separate piece of paper. Then write an answer to the question in the prompt using the expressions for* ***stating your reasons****.*

Some people think that it is better to use mass transportation, such as buses, trains, and subways. Others feel that driving a car is a better means of transportation. Which do you agree with and why? Use specific reasons and examples to support your answer.

C. *Work with a partner. Read your written answer aloud. If possible, time your response.*

D. *Then, without using your written response, give your response aloud again and record it. Try to speak for no more than 45 seconds.*

E. *Listen to the recording of your response to the Practice for Skill 5 and complete the self-evaluation chart below. How well do you feel you did these things? Rank questions 1–8 from 1 to 5. Then answer questions 9–11.*

EXPRESS TIP

When you listen to your recorded responses, note any repetition of vocabulary. It is important to use a variety of vocabulary in your responses. However, don't use "big" vocabulary words that you don't know the exact of meaning of just to sound impressive. It is not the right time to try using new words when you are recording your responses on the TOEFL iBT Test.

Self-Evaluation: Skill 5

	1 = low, 5 = high
1. Understand the prompt	
2. Take notes to help you speak	
3. Answer the question completely in the time allowed	
4. State your opinion first, using the appropriate expressions	
5. Provide at least two detailed reasons and some examples for your opinion, preference, or choice	
6. Use the appropriate phrases and transitions for stating your reasons for having a specific opinion or preference	
7. Speak fluently, without too many pauses and repetitions	
8. Speak accurately, with correct grammar and vocabulary	
9. What is something you did especially well?	
10. What one or two things would you like to improve on?	
11. How do you plan to improve those things?	

Speaking Skill 6: Using Comparison and Contrast in Your Response

Because you are choosing between two ideas for the paired-choice question, it is useful to be able to compare and contrast them in your response. Using specific comparison and contrast words and phrases can help to connect your ideas in an organized and logical way. It also signals to the raters that you are able to communicate your opinions using more sophisticated language structures. Here are some specific words and phrases that you can use to compare and contrast the choices or preferences in the prompts:

Comparison	Contrast
Compared to Y, X is . . . Like X, Y is also . . . X is like Y because . . . X is similar to Y because . . . X is the same as Y because . . . On the one hand, . . .	In contrast to Y, X is . . . Unlike X, Y is not . . . X is unlike Y because . . . X differs from Y because . . . While/Although/Even though X is . . ., Y is . . . Despite the fact that X is . . ., Y is . . . On the other hand, . . . X is . . . However, Y is . . . X is . . ., but Y . . .

Note that the comparative forms of adjectives can also be used:

X is *adjective +~er (better, worse, safer) than* Y because . . .

X is *more adjective (difficult, modern, interesting) than* Y because . . .

EXPRESS TIP

Avoid listing a series of comparisons and contrasts all together in one sentence: *I prefer hiking in the mountains because, unlike running on city streets, the air is cleaner, it is less crowded on the trails, and climbing builds more muscles.* Your response will flow more smoothly if you address each point separately and give details and examples for each one.

SKILL BUILDER

Directions: *Work with a partner. Look at the following questions. Take quick notes on a separate piece of paper that include: your opinion, two or more reasons to support your opinion, and any examples that are relevant to the topic. Give your opinion and then use the words and phrases from the list above to state your reasons by providing comparisons or contrasts between the two choices. Write your responses down, and then take turns saying them aloud with your partner. The first one has been done for you.*

1. Which kind of exercise is better, running or swimming? Why?

EXAMPLE:

In my opinion, swimming is the best form of exercise. ***Compared to*** *running, I think swimming is better because it isn't as hard on your body. For example,* ***unlike*** *running, swimming doesn't put as much stress on your legs and knees. It seems like everyone I know that runs has had some kind of injury to their knees or their ankles* ***in contrast to*** *my friends who swim and don't have any injuries. In addition, swimming builds muscles in both the upper and lower body.* ***On the other hand****, running mostly builds muscles in the lower body.* ***Although both*** *swimming and running make the heart stronger and build muscles, I think swimming is better exercise for the whole body.*

2. Some students believe that being in an all-male or an all-female classroom leads to better learning. Others disagree with this and prefer a mixed classroom with both male and female students. Which type of classroom do you think is better and why?
3. Is watching television helpful or harmful for children?
4. Do you think that students should evaluate their teachers? Why or why not?
5. Which do you think is better, living in a rural area (the countryside) or living in an urban area (a city)? Why?

Skill Builder Sample Answers:

Answers will vary, but should include phrases for stating an opinion, phrases and transitions for stating the reasons for having a specific opinion or preference, and words and expressions for providing comparisons and contrasts between the two choices offered in the prompt.

EXPRESS TIP

It is OK to mention that both of the choices in the paired-choice task may be similar in some ways. However, if your opinion in the response is that one choice is *better than the other*, make sure you clearly state that and follow it directly with the reasons for your opinion. For example:

Both e-mail and the telephone are excellent ways to stay in touch with your friends and family because they are more convenient and faster than writing a letter. However, I think e-mail is the best way to communicate because you don't have to worry about whether or not you are bothering someone when they are busy. The person you e-mail can choose to read your e-mail whenever they have time. In addition, e-mailing is better than talking on the telephone since it allows you to send short messages without feeling rude when you don't have a lot to say or don't have much time. When you call on the telephone, on the other hand, it's sort of expected that you have to spend more time making polite small talk like "How are you?" It just seems less polite to just say one or two things and then end a telephone call, so e-mailing is, in my opinion, the best way to stay in touch with people.

PRACTICE

A. *Read the prompt.*

B. *Take quick notes on a separate piece of paper. Then write an answer to the question in the prompt using the* ***comparison and contrast words and expressions****.*

Some people believe that telecommuting, or doing their job from home, is the best way to work. Others think that working in an office is better. Which do you agree with and why? Use specific reasons and examples to support your answer.

C. *Work with a partner. Read your written answer aloud. If possible, time your response.*

D. *Then, without using your written response, give your response aloud again and record it. Try to speak for no more than 45 seconds.*

E. *Listen to the recording of your response to the Practice for Skill 6 and complete the self-evaluation chart below. How well do you feel you did these things? Rank questions 1–9 from 1 to 5. Then answer questions 10–12.*

Self-Evaluation: Skill 6

	1 = low, 5 = high
1. Understand the prompt	
2. Take notes to help you speak	
3. Answer the question completely in the time allowed	
4. State your opinion first, using the appropriate expressions	
5. Provide at least two detailed reasons and some examples for your opinion, preference, or choice using the appropriate phrases and transitions	
6. Compare and contrast the two choices in the prompt	
7. Use comparison and contrast words and phrases to connect ideas in an organized and logical way	
8. Speak fluently, without too many pauses and repetitions	
9. Speak accurately, with correct grammar and vocabulary	
10. What is something you did especially well?	
11. What one or two things would you like to improve on?	
12. How do you plan to improve those things?	

SKILLS REVIEW

Independent Speaking Skills 4–6 for the Paired-Choice Task: Expressing Opinions, Supporting Your Choice or Preference with Reasons, and Using Comparison and Contrast in Your Response

Directions: *Record your responses to the following prompts.*

1. *You will now be asked a question about a familiar topic. After you hear the question, you have 15 seconds to prepare your response and 45 seconds to answer.* 2-45

1. Most universities offer a note-taking service for specific classes. Students can buy the notes for a reasonable fee. Some students feel this is a good service. Others think students should take their own notes in class. Which do you think is best for students and why?

Preparation Time: 15 Seconds
Response Time: 45 Seconds

2. *You will now be asked a question about a familiar topic. After you hear the question, you have 15 seconds to prepare your response and 45 seconds to answer.* 2-46

> 2. Many movies use books as the basis for their stories. Some people think it is better to read the book before going to such a movie. Others believe that it is better to see the movie first and read the book after. Which opinion do you agree with and why?
>
> Preparation Time: 15 Seconds
>
> Response Time: 45 Seconds

Self-Evaluation: Skills Review

Listen to the recordings of your responses to the Skills Review for Skills 4–6 and complete the self-evaluation chart below. How well do you feel you did these things? Rank questions 1–9 from 1 to 5. Write N/A if the skill didn't apply to the type of answer you gave. Then answer questions 10–12.

	1 = low, 5 = high
1. Understand the prompt	
2. Take notes to help you speak	
3. Answer the question completely in the time allowed	
4. State your opinion first, using the appropriate expressions	
5. Provide at least two detailed reasons and some examples for your opinion, preference, or choice using the appropriate phrases and transitions	
6. Compare and contrast the two choices in the prompt	
7. Use comparison and contrast words and phrases to connect ideas in an organized and logical way	
8. Speak fluently, without too many pauses and repetitions	
9. Speak accurately, with correct grammar and vocabulary	
10. What is something you did especially well?	
11. What one or two things would you like to improve on?	
12. How do you plan to improve those things?	

INTEGRATED TASK 3

ANNOUNCEMENT OR NOTICE (READING + CONVERSATION)

Skills 7 and 8: Summarizing; Paraphrasing

The first task in the Integrated Response section requires you first to read a short text and then to listen to a conversation about the text. You will not see the conversation printed. You will take notes on both the printed reading passage (which you will see on the screen for 45 seconds only) and the listening passage. Then you will use your notes to answer a question that asks you to apply what you heard to what you read. After you hear the question, you will have 30 seconds to plan an answer and then 60 seconds to record your answer.

The reading texts are related to some aspect of life on a North American university campus, such as announcements of classes and events; explanations of university rules and policies; and information for people who live, work, and study on campus. The reading texts could be letters, articles, or notices. However, you do *not* need any specific knowledge of North American university life or culture to understand this section.

EXPRESS TIP

> Sometimes the reading text will propose a policy or course of action, and give one or two reasons to support the proposal. Include the proposal and supporting reasons in your notes.

The listening passage will usually be a conversation between two students discussing the information in the reading text. Often the two speakers will give different opinions about the topic—one might support a proposal while the other disagrees with it, for example. If the students give such opinions, they will also state reasons for those opinions.

EXPRESS TIP

> Be sure to include both speakers' opinions and reasons for those opinions in your notes. You won't know which speaker you will be asked about until you hear the prompt.

Your recorded response will be evaluated on content and organization, fluency, vocabulary, and grammar, as well as how directly and completely it answers the question.

You will both hear the questions and see them on the computer screen. Here are some examples of integrated response questions for Task 3:

- *The man expresses his opinion about the information in the professor's syllabus. State his opinion and explain his reasons for that opinion.*
- *The professor expresses her opinion about the policy described in the university's e-mail. State her opinion and explain the reasons she gives for holding that opinion.*

To answer these types of questions, you must:

- Take brief notes to plan your response. Include the main ideas from both the reading and the listening passage, and supporting ideas for the speakers' opinions.
- Briefly summarize the main idea of the reading passage. Then state the speaker's opinions and supporting reasons directly. Add more detail if you have time.
- Make sure that you answer the question directly, and specifically label the required information with signal words and phrases.
- Speak at a natural pace and at a good volume.

EXPRESS TIP

Do not give your own opinion about the topic. You will only be asked to relate the opinion of someone you heard to the information contained in the reading text.

Look at this example of a Task 3 integrated response question on a computer screen.

EXAMPLE: Integrated Task 3: Announcement or Notice (Reading + Conversation) Question

TOEFL Speaking

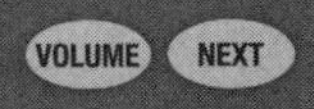

Question 3 of 6

You hear and see:

In this question you will read a short passage about a campus situation and then listen to a talk on the same topic. You will then answer a question using information from both the reading passage and the talk. After you hear the question, you will have 30 seconds to prepare your response and 60 seconds to speak.

You see:

Read the announcement about construction on the City University campus.

You will have 45 seconds to read the announcement. Begin reading now.

Reading Time: 45 Seconds

Notice of Construction

Please be advised that construction on the walkways between Johnson and Harold Halls, as well as the parking lots for both Halls and the undergraduate library, will commence on May 17. Construction is . . .

Then the reading passage will be replaced with a photograph and you will see:

Then you hear and see: 🔊 *Now listen to a conversation between two students about this notice.*

While you look at the photograph, you will hear but not see the conversation:
🔊 **Man:** Oh, hey, look at this. They're finally going to fix those walkways.
Woman: Between Johnson and Harold? Oh, great! Those are in terrible condition. And I have two classes in Johnson this term.
Man: Yeah, and the parking lot as well. That's what I'm really happy about.
Woman: Wait, the parking lot? But . . . wait a minute, where am I supposed to park? The nearest lot is . . . I guess by the sports center, but that's a fifteen-minute walk away.
. . .

The photograph is replaced with this screen on the computer:

Now get ready to answer the question.

You hear and see:
🔊 3. The woman gives her opinion about the best way for her to travel to campus during the time period mentioned in the announcement. State her opinion and explain the reasons she gives for holding that opinion.

Preparation Time: 30 Seconds
Response Time: 60 Seconds

You hear:
🔊 Begin to prepare your response after the beep. [*beep sound*]

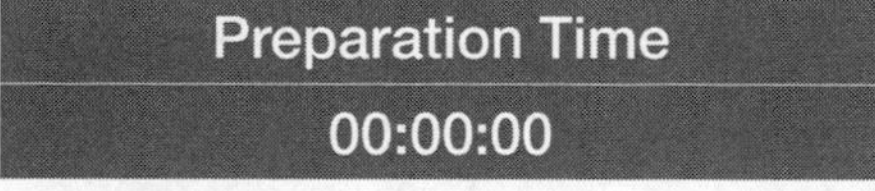

After 30 seconds, you hear:
🔊 Begin speaking after the beep. [*beep sound*]

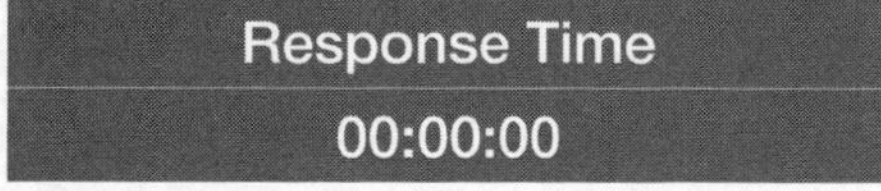

After 60 seconds, you hear:
🔊 [*beep sound*] Now, stop speaking.

Note-Taking Model

Your notes for Integrated Task 3 should include (1) the main idea of the reading and as much supporting information as you have time to note and (2) the opinions of each speaker in a conversation and reasons to support their opinions. Remember to use abbreviations wherever possible so that you can write more quickly.

Here is an example of notes from the prompt above. Notice how the note-taker underlined parts that seemed to be main ideas.

1. The woman gives her opinion about the best way for her to travel to campus during the time period mentioned in the announcement. State her opinion and explain the reasons she gives for holding that opinion.

Reading: Constr. – walkways betw. Johnson & Harold Halls, + parking lots for Halls & undergrad libr. June & July.

No parking 4 studs, fac, visitors in 23B, only constr & emergnc.

ticketed & towed.

Bus route diff., stps front of bkstore, check posted sched.

Conv.: Man = take bus, convenient, bus pass, can study on bus.

Woman = early class, other parking lot far, ~~bus~~ = more than 1 hr, ~~bike~~ = traffic, carpool share driving only park 1 time

Speaking Skill 7: Summarizing

To answer the question for Task 3, you need to summarize at least two things: the information in the reading and a speaker's response to it. Because the speaker is giving a reaction to information in the reading, a logical way to organize your response is to summarize the reading first and then summarize the speaker's response. However, be careful to leave yourself enough time to give both the speaker's opinion and his or her supporting reasons.

Since you will be evaluated on your ability to identify and report the main ideas and supporting details of the reading and the conversation, you should use signal phrases to show that you are doing this.

Purpose	Words and Expressions to Use in Your Response
To signal a main idea	*The main idea of the notice is that . . .* *The most important point of the announcement is . . .* *The woman's opinion is that . . .* *The man's position is that . . .* *The woman states that she is going to . . .* *According to the man, . . .*
To show supporting information	*The woman gives two reasons for her opinion: . . . and . . .* *To support his opinion, the man states that . . .* *There are two reasons the woman disapproves of the change: . . .*
To combine a main idea and supporting information in the same sentence	*The man disagrees with the woman because . . . and . . .* *The woman supports the university's proposal to raise fees because . . .*

EXPRESS TIP

It is better to speak slowly and clearly and say a little less than to include more information but at a rate that makes it hard for you to be understood.

SKILL BUILDER

A. *Work with a partner. Read the text and take notes. Then close your book and summarize the information aloud to each other, using your notes.*

Notice of Construction

Construction on the sidewalks between Johnson and Harold Halls, and the parking lots for both Halls and the undergraduate library, will commence on May 17 and last through July. During this time, no student, faculty, or visitor parking is permitted in Lot 23B outside Johnson Hall. Parking is reserved for construction and emergency vehicles only. Violators will be ticketed and towed. Bus service will be rerouted during this time. The #27 bus will stop in front of the campus bookstore, and then detour along West 23rd Avenue. For bus schedules during the construction period, please consult the posted information at each bus stop. We regret any inconvenience during this time.

B. *Now listen to and read the conversation about the same topic and take notes. Then close your books. Student A, summarize the man's position and reasons. Student B, summarize the woman's position and reasons. Then read the conversation again and switch roles.* 2-47

Man: Oh, hey, look at this. They're finally going to fix those walkways.

Woman: Between Johnson and Harold? Oh, great! Those are in terrible condition. And I have two classes in Johnson this term.

Man: Yeah, and the parking lot as well. That's what I'm really happy about.

Woman: Wait, the parking lot? But . . . where am I supposed to park then? The nearest lot is . . . I guess by the sports center, but that's a fifteen-minute walk away.

Man: So why don't you take the bus?

Woman: Because I'd have to change buses downtown, and it would take me over an hour. And my first class is at 8:00 A.M.

Man: Oh, sorry. For me, the bus is really easy—it takes me ten minutes from my apartment to campus. I usually come in the mornings, but all my classes are in the afternoon, so I can just study for a while or talk with friends.

Woman: I wish I didn't have this morning class! But I'd have to wake up at something like 5:00 A.M. to take the bus. That's just crazy.

Man: Why don't you ride your bike?

Woman: Well, traffic is really bad near my apartment, especially in the morning.

Man: What are other people in your class going to do?

Woman: Hey, that's right—we'll all have the same problem. I know a bunch of people who drive. We can carpool and take turns driving.

Man: Someone will still have to park . . .

Woman: Yeah, but the driver can let everyone off near Johnson Hall, just before the construction zone, and then go park. And if we take turns, then each person will only have to park once a week. I can manage that, I guess. The exercise will be good for me.

C. *Read the sample prompt and responses. Write the letter of the response in front of the evaluation that describes it. Some statements may describe more than one response.*

The woman gives her opinion about the best way for her to travel to campus during the time period mentioned in the announcement. State her opinion and explain the reasons she gives for holding that opinion.

Answer A	**Answer B**	**Answer C**
The reading says there is a construction uh . . . between two halls, so . . . uh . . . you must take a construction or emergency vehicle. And, uh, . . . Violators will be ticketed and towed . . . The woman she say, bus is easy, she can has ten-minute ride. She can comes to school early and talks with friends. Exercise, she can get some exercise . . . I think . . . yes, bus is good for her. I like bus, too.	According to reading, there is summer construction, so you, so students has to not park there. Only some other kinds of cars can park there at that time. There are, there is a bus still comes. In front of bookstore and detour on another street. Yes, so . . . For the woman, yes, the woman's position is she can't take the bus because it is inconvenience for her . . . because of time. Um . . . It takes her more than one hour, her class is too early for that. And then . . . In addition, riding a bike is not good because of traffic. It maybe, I think it is very danger for her to take a bicycle. . . . So she likes to share a ride with her class's other students. It is (*end of time*)	The main idea of the announcement is that because of construction on campus, a parking lot will be closed. However, bus service was, will still be available, though the bus stop will be temporarily moved. The woman says that the best way for her to travel to campus during the construction period will be to share rides with other students. The driver will parks in a different parking lot, and the passengers will get out near the building. The driver will have to walk a little way, but only once a week. The bus isn't convenient for the woman because she has to wait to transfer lines, and to ride her bike isn't safe because traffic is bad near her house. So sharing rides is best for her.
Score: 2	Score: 3	Score: 4

_________ There aren't many grammatical mistakes.

_________ Too much information from the reading is included, so there isn't enough time to include all of the necessary information about the conversation.

_________ The speaker didn't give his or her own opinion.

_________ The reading is not summarized correctly.

_________ There are only a few hesitations.

_________ The response didn't use enough time.

_________ Both short and long sentences are used.

_________ The answer summarizes the wrong person's position.

_________ Both the reading and the woman's position are summarized.

_________ A sentence copied word-for-word from the reading makes it seem as if the speaker didn't understand it.

_________ Contractions make the speaking sound more natural.

_________ The response wasn't finished.

_________ Transition words help link ideas.

Skill Builder Answers:

A: The reading is not summarized correctly; The response didn't use enough time; Both the reading and the woman's position are summarized; A sentence copied word-for-word from the reading makes it seem as if the speaker didn't understand it.

B: Too much information from the reading is included, so there isn't enough time to include all of the necessary information about the conversation; The speaker didn't give his or her own opinion; The response wasn't finished; Transition words help link ideas.

C: There aren't many grammatical mistakes; There are only a few hesitations; Both the reading and the woman's position are summarized; Contractions make the speaking sound more natural; Transition words help link ideas. The speaker didn't give his or her own opinion.

PRACTICE

1.

A. *Read the passage and take quick notes on a separate piece of paper. Save your notes to use for your response.*

Teamwork Study Participants Needed

Are you a member of an undergraduate organization such as a sports team or student organization? Would you like to assist us with our research? Two graduate students in the Psychology Department are seeking participants in a study on teamwork and decision making. If you are interested, we will ask three members of your organization to come to Room 243 of the Psychology Department on March 12 to complete a short questionnaire and carry out some short interactive tasks, which will be videotaped. Each person will undergo a separate interview. The entire process will take approximately two hours, and each participant will be paid $50. (Participants must be currently enrolled as full-time students.) For further information and to sign up for the study, e-mail ptamsin@ibtx.edu.

B. *Work with a partner. Using your notes, write a* ***short summary of the main ideas of the reading passage****.*

C. *Read your written summary aloud to your partner.*

D. *Now listen to the conversation about the same topic. Take notes on a separate piece of paper. Save your notes to use in your response.*

Now get ready to listen: 2-48

E. *Work with a partner. Student A,* ***summarize the man's opinion and supporting reasons****. Student B,* ***summarize the woman's opinion and supporting reasons****.*

F. *Read your written summary aloud to your partner.*

G. *Then, without using your written summaries but with your notes, record a response where you summarize the reading and the opinion of the person you did not write about in E; that is, Student A now summarizes the woman's opinion and Student B summarizes the man's opinion. Time yourself to see how long it took.*

2.

A. *Read the passage and take quick notes on a separate piece of paper. Save your notes to use for your response.*

Engineering Home Study Kit

Engineering students: Do you need help studying for final year exams, or do you just want that extra edge? Sign up now for a 30-day free trial of the Home Study Kit in electrical engineering, structural engineering, mechanical engineering, or any of 12 additional branches. This comprehensive online study program not only coaches you through the standard university curriculum but also supplements the material with practical, easy-to-understand, real-life examples and applications. A special exam practice section with fully solved answers helps you hone your test-taking skills in a timed situation. 24/7 online support is available if you have questions or problems. Don't wait until your grades slip—start supplementing your classes today with our proven Study Kit.

B. *Work with a partner. Using your notes, write a* ***short summary of the main ideas of the reading passage****.*

C. *Read your written summary aloud to your partner.*

D. *Now listen to a conversation about the same topic. Take notes on a separate piece of paper. Save your notes to use in your response.*

Now get ready to listen: 2-49

E. *Work with a partner. Student A,* ***summarize the man's opinion and supporting reasons****. Student B,* ***summarize the woman's opinion and supporting reasons****.*

F. *Read your written summary aloud to your partner.*

G. *Then, without using your written summaries but with your notes, record a response where you summarize the reading and the opinion of the person you did not write about in E; that is, Student A now summarizes the woman's opinion and Student B summarizes the man's opinion. Time yourself to see how long it took.*

H. *Listen to the recording of your response to the Practice for Skill 7 and complete the self-evaluation chart below. How well do you feel you did these things? Rank questions 1–7 from 1 to 5. Then answer questions 8–10.*

Self-Evaluation: Skill 7

	1 = low, 5 = high
1. Understand the reading and the conversation	
2. Take notes on the reading and conversation to help you speak	
3. Answer the question completely in the time allowed	
4. Summarize the main points of the reading	
5. Summarize the main position and supporting reasons of the person in the conversation	
6. Speak fluently, without too many pauses and repetitions	
7. Speak accurately, with correct grammar and vocabulary	
8. What is something you did especially well?	
9. What one or two things would you like to improve on?	
10. How do you plan to improve those things?	

Speaking Skill 8: Paraphrasing

When you give your answer, it is important to not sound as if you are repeating exactly the same sentences or phrases that are used in the reading text or that you heard in the talk. Of course, it is fine (and probably necessary) to use some of the same words. However, if you repeat longer phrases or whole sentences, then you are not demonstrating your own ability in English. It is also possible that the rater will think you didn't understand what you are repeating.

To demonstrate your understanding of the passages, both written and spoken, and your own ability to speak English, it is important to paraphrase—to give the same information, but expressed in a different way.

For example, you read these sentences in the Skill Builder for Skill 7:

> *Construction is expected to last through the months of June and July. During this time, no student, faculty, or visitor parking is permitted in Lot 23B outside Johnson Hall.*

You can say the same information in a number of different ways:

- *Students and staff can't park outside Johnson Hall in June and July because of construction.*
- *Parking Lot 23B by Johnson Hall will be closed during construction in June and July.*

To paraphrase, you can use one or more of these techniques:

- Use synonyms (words that mean almost the same thing) or explain a term (*Violators will be ticketed.* = *People who break the law will receive a ticket.*)
- Change the part of speech (*Violators will be ticketed.* = *People who break the law will receive a ticket.*)
- Use opposites (*The parking lot will be closed.* = *The parking lot won't be open.*)
- Change the order of the ideas in the sentence (*Parking is reserved for construction and emergency vehicles only.* = *Only emergency and construction vehicles will be allowed to park there.*)

A paraphrase can be either longer or shorter than the original sentence.

EXPRESS TIP

When you take notes, don't write verbs such as *is*, *are*, and *have*; instead, write nouns and verbs that represent the main ideas. That will make it easier for you to paraphrase. You probably won't repeat a sentence directly if you haven't copied it directly.

Paraphrasing takes a lot of practice. To build this skill, do short bits of practice frequently. For example, when you read the newspaper or check some information online, practice paraphrasing just the first few sentences in your head. If you practice this every day, you will improve.

EXPRESS TIP

Not everything can be paraphrased—it's OK to quote directly when you refer to names, dates, times, and other numerical amounts.

SKILL BUILDER

A. *Work with a partner. Read the sentences and circle the letter of the most effective paraphrase.*

1. Tuition fees for the following year will be increasing by an estimated 2.3 percent.
   Ⓐ The cost of attending the university is going up by about 2.3 percent next year.
   Ⓑ We estimate that 2.3 percent of students will not be continuing their studies.

2. The Museum of Natural History will be closed during final exams week.
   Ⓐ During final exams week, the Museum of Natural History won't be open.
   Ⓑ The building dedicated to the display of the scientific study of plants and animals will not be open during the seven-day period devoted to end-of-term testing.

3. **Man:** "I won't be able to take Marketing 202 next spring because I haven't taken Marketing 201 yet."
   Ⓐ The man explains that you have to take Marketing 201 before you can take Marketing 202.
   Ⓑ The man states that he will have to take Marketing 201 in the spring term.

4. **Woman:** "It's cheaper for me to live in an apartment and cook my own meals than it is to live in the dorms and pay for their meal plan."
   Ⓐ In the woman's opinion, the university would save money by letting her live off-campus.
   Ⓑ The woman states that living independently costs less than staying and eating on campus.

B. *Work with a partner. Take turns reading and paraphrasing excerpts 1–4 below like this:*

- Read the information silently, no more than twice. Then close your book and paraphrase the information to your partner, who will check the book to make sure your paraphrase is accurate.
- Then change roles.
- Repeat the exercise so that you each paraphrase every item; remember that there is more than one way to paraphrase information.

1. To check out materials from the Reserved Room, please see the Reference Librarian in Room L21.
2. Please finish Chapter 8 in your textbook and come to class on Thursday prepared to discuss the material.
3. **Woman:** "I don't think the university should charge students to attend athletic events on campus."
4. **Man:** "Making it less difficult for students to recycle on campus is one important thing this university can do to become greener."

Skill Builder Answers:

A: 1. a is the correct answer; b gives information that is not correct ("tuition going up" is not the same as "students won't be continuing") 2. a is the correct answer; b attempts to paraphrase set terms that cannot be changed, such as "Museum of Natural History"; 3. a is the correct answer; b makes an assumption (that the man will take Marketing 201 the next semester) that is not justified by the sentence (for example, that class might not be offered in the spring) 4. b is the correct answer; a gives incorrect information because the sentence says that the woman could save money by living off campus, not that the university would save money. B: Answers will vary.

PRACTICE

1.

A. *Read the passage and take quick notes on a separate piece of paper. Save your notes to use for your response.*

University Announces Early-Bird Discount Plan

Looking for a way to save some money on college tuition? It might involve setting your alarm a little earlier. On Wednesday, Provost Jack Kingman announced a new policy designed to help the university cope with overcrowded classrooms: classes that start before 8:00 A.M. will cost students 15% less. Originally offered to help those students who also held part-time jobs, these classes have traditionally been under-enrolled. The more popular 10:00–2:00 time slots, on the other hand, typically carry long waiting lists. It remains to be seen whether students would rather save money—or sleep in.

B. *Work with a partner. Using your notes, write a* ***short summary of the main ideas of the reading passage****.*

C. *Read your written summary aloud to your partner.*

D. *Now listen to the conversation about the same topic. Take notes on a separate piece of paper. Save your notes to use in your response.*

Now get ready to listen: 2-50

E. *Work with a partner. Student A,* ***summarize the man's opinion and supporting reasons****. Student B,* ***summarize the woman's opinion and supporting reasons****.*

F. *Read your written summary aloud to your partner.*

G. *Then, without using your written summaries but with your notes, record a response where you summarize the reading and the opinion of the person you did not write about in E; that is, Student A now summarizes the woman's opinion and Student B summarizes the man's opinion. Time yourself to see how long it took.*

2.

A. *Read the passage and take quick notes on a separate piece of paper. Save your notes to use for your response.*

Open Auditions for Off Pitch

Want to join what the *Town Crier* called "the campus's most vibrant and well-known club"? Off Pitch, founded in 1945, is the University's premier co-ed singing group. We perform traditional and contemporary songs and even write our own music. Off Pitch has received musical awards in 8 out of the last 10 years. We practice three times a week, with rehearsals open to the public on Friday afternoons, and perform a minimum of four concerts a year. Some travel is involved. Interested applicants should sign up for an audition time at our next open rehearsal, Friday at 5:00, in front of the Student Union. Auditions will begin the week of August 12. Please prepare one solo of no more than four minutes.

B. *Work with a partner. Using your notes, write a* ***short summary of the main ideas of the reading passage****.*

C. *Read your written summary aloud to your partner.*

D. *Now listen to the conversation about the same topic. Take notes on a separate piece of paper. Save your notes to use in your response.*

Now get ready to listen: 2-51

E. *Work with a partner. Student A,* ***summarize the man's opinion and supporting reasons****. Student B,* ***summarize the woman's opinion and supporting reasons****.*

F. *Read your written summary aloud to your partner.*

G. *Then, without using your written summaries but with your notes, record a response where you summarize the reading and the opinion of the person you did not write about in E; that is, Student A now summarizes the woman's opinion and Student B summarizes the man's opinion. Time yourself to see how long it took.*

H. *Listen to the recording of your response to the Practice for Skill 1 and complete the self-evaluation chart below. How well do you feel you did these things? Rank questions 1–7 from 1 to 5. Then answer questions 8–10.*

Self-Evaluation: Skill 8

	1 = low, 5 = high
1. Understand the reading and the conversation	
2. Take notes to help you speak	
3. Answer the question completely in the time allowed	
4. Summarize the main points of the reading	
5. Summarize the main position and supporting reasons of the person in the conversation	
6. Speak fluently, without too many pauses and repetitions	
7. Speak accurately, with correct grammar and vocabulary	
8. What is something you did especially well?	
9. What one or two things would you like to improve on?	
10. How do you plan to improve those things?	

SKILLS REVIEW

Integrated Speaking Skills 7 and 8 for Task 3, Announcement or Notice: Summarizing and Paraphrasing

1. *You will now read a short passage and then listen to a conversation on the same topic. After you hear the question about them, you have 30 seconds to prepare your response and 60 seconds to answer.*

Reading Time: 45 Seconds

SPORTS AND RECREATION CENTER MEMBERSHIP ELIGIBILITY

All students who are enrolled for one or more credits, faculty/staff and their partners, and university alumni are eligible for membership to the Student Recreation Center, Student Tennis Center, and outdoor fields and swimming pool.

Current student membership fees are included in university tuition fees. All other memberships are sold per term or on an annual basis according to the academic calendar.

MEMBERSHIP RATES

MEMBERSHIP	RATE	RATE
Currently enrolled students	$45 per term	$180 annual
Off-term students	$65 per term	–
Faculty and staff	$70 per term	$230 annual
Faculty and staff partners	$70 per term	$230 annual
Alumni	$120 per term	$400 annual

1. *Now listen to a conversation on this topic.* 2-52

Directions: *Record your response to the following prompt.*

1. The woman gives her opinion about the pricing policy for the university sports center explained on the website. State her opinion and explain the reasons she gives for holding that opinion.

Preparation Time: 30 Seconds

Response Time: 60 Seconds

2. *You will now read a short passage and then listen to a conversation on the same topic. After you hear the question about them, you have 30 seconds to prepare your response and 60 seconds to answer.*

Reading Time: 45 Seconds

Write for *The Collegian*

Calling all aspiring reporters! Here is your chance to see your name in print. *The Collegian* is now accepting freelance articles for our "Features" section. "Features" articles are generally about 1000–1500 words long and highlight some aspect of campus community life—club or organization activity, special events and presentations, or even profiles of interesting students. Check past issues of *The Collegian* for examples of the types of "Features" articles we publish. All published articles must adhere to *The Collegian* and Central University guidelines. A copy of the guidelines is available at *The Collegian* office in the Student Union. Articles may be edited for length and content. Gain experience and share your views with your fellow students. E-mail infocollegian@ibtx.edu or check our website http://www.ibtx.edu/thecollegian for more information.

2. *Now listen to a conversation on this topic.* 2-53

Directions: *Record your response to the following prompt.*

2. The man gives his opinion about writing articles for the student newspaper described in the notice. State his opinion and explain the reasons he gives for holding that opinion.

Preparation Time: 30 Seconds

Response Time: 60 Seconds

Self-Evaluation: Skills Review

Listen to the recordings of your responses to the Skills Review for Skills 7 and 8 and complete the self-evaluation chart below. How well do you feel you did these things? Rank questions 1–8 from 1 to 5. Then answer questions 9–11.

	1 = low, 5 = high
1. Understand the readings and the conversations	
2. Take notes to help you speak	
3. Answer the questions completely in the time allowed	
4. Summarize the main points of the readings	
5. Summarize the main position and supporting reasons of the person in the conversations	
6. Paraphrase ideas from the original readings and conversations	
7. Speak fluently, without too many pauses and repetitions	
8. Speak accurately, with correct grammar and vocabulary	
9. What is something you did especially well?	
10. What one or two things would you like to improve on?	
11. How do you plan to improve those things?	

INTEGRATED TASK 4

GENERAL/SPECIFIC (READING + LECTURE)

Skills 9 and 10: Organizing and Addressing the Main Points in the Reading and the Lecture; Integrating General Information from the Reading with Specific Information from the Lecture

For the Integrated Task 4, the general/specific task, you will first be given 45 seconds to read a short passage of 75–100 words, and then you will listen to a short lecture for 60–90 seconds. After the reading and the lecture, you will be required to respond for 60 seconds to a question based on both what you read in the passage and heard in the lecture. This type of question will present you with a prompt or a question that asks you to summarize and connect the information from *both the reading and the lecture*. You will have 30 seconds to think about the topic and take notes before you begin speaking.

The reading and lecture topics are based on academic fields of study, such as the sciences, literature, history, or language.

The reading passage will provide *general* information, such as a definition, a theory, a process, or a problem.

The lecture, on the other hand, will give *specific* examples that will:

- expand on or support the topic of the reading passage
- contradict or disagree with the reading topic
- illustrate how the general reading topic can be specifically applied
- explain how a problem was successfully or unsuccessfully solved or how a solution produced an unexpected result

For example:
General Reading Topic: a popular architectural style: *Prairie School*
Specific Lecture Topic: a library constructed in the Prairie School style, such as Isabel Roberts' *Veterans Memorial Library* in St. Cloud, Florida

You will both hear the questions and see them on the computer screen. The following are examples of the question in Task 4:

- *The professor describes the Veterans Memorial Library. Explain how its design relates to the Prairie School style of architecture.*
- *Explain how the two evaluation techniques discussed by the professor can be applied in different academic settings.*

In the example questions above, be aware that the first part of the question refers to the specific information in the lecture, while the second half of the question is related to the general information in the reading passage:

The professor describes the Veterans Memorial Library . . . [specific information from the lecture]
. . . the Prairie School style of architecture . . . [general information from the reading passage]
. . . the two evaluation techniques discussed by the professor. . . [specific information from lecture passage]
. . . different academic settings . . . [general information from the reading passage]

In order to answer the question correctly, you must:

- Read the passage quickly and take brief notes on the main ideas or points. Ask yourself what the general information in the passage is: A definition? A theory? A process? A problem?
- Listen carefully to the lecture and take brief notes on the main ideas or points about the specific information. Ask yourself how the lecture relates to the reading: Does it give further information about the reading? Contradict it? Apply it in some way? Offer a solution?
- When you record your response, first summarize the main ideas or points in the reading.
- Next, summarize the main ideas of the specific information in the *lecture*. How does the lecture relate to the reading? Does the lecture expand on the reading, contradict it, apply it, or offer a solution to a problem?
- Then, connect (integrate) the information in the lecture with the information in the reading.
- Be sure you include a reasonable amount of information from both the reading and lecture in your response.
- Always clearly indicate which source, the reading or the lecture, the information you are giving is coming from.
- Develop a logical flow of information by using the appropriate transitions.
- Don't repeat the information in the reading and lecture by using the same wording. Paraphrase what you have read and heard by using different words and grammatical structures in your response.

EXPRESS TIP

It is very important to take notes on the reading passage because it will not be displayed on the computer screen during the time you are giving your response.

Look at this example of a Task 4 general/specific question on a computer screen.

EXAMPLE: Integrated Task 4: General/Specific Question

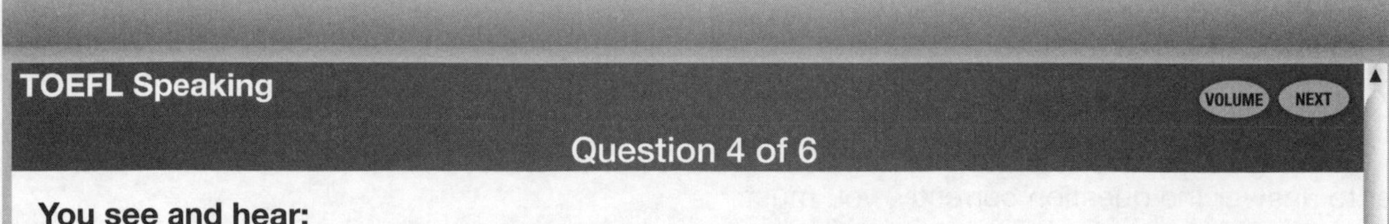

You see and hear:
🔊 **Narrator:** *You will now read a short passage and then listen to a lecture on the same academic subject. After you hear the question about them, you have 30 seconds to prepare your response and 60 seconds to answer. You will have 45 seconds to read the passage. Begin reading now.*

You see:

Reading Time: 45 Seconds

The International Style of Architecture

The International Style of architecture first arose in the 1920s and 1930s. This style was a reaction to earlier, more decorative styles, such as Art Nouveau which included highly artistic, handcrafted elements. The International Style was distinctly modern: It included new types of materials such as glass, steel, and concrete created by mass-production techniques . . .

The reading passage is replaced with a photograph and you see:

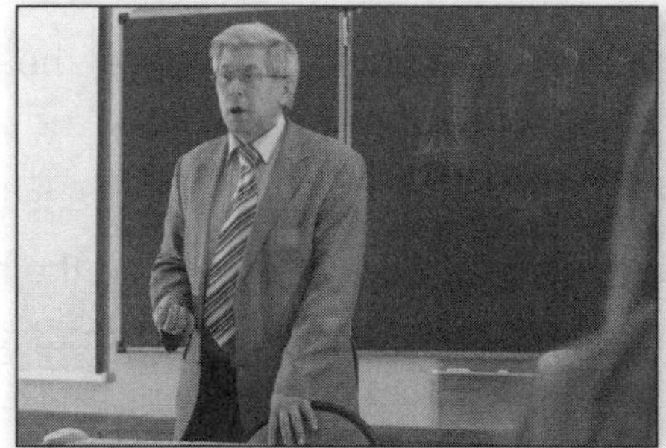

You then hear:
🔊 **Now listen to a lecture on this topic in an architecture class.**

Professor: The Lever Building in New York City was completed in 1952 and is considered one of the great successes of the International Style. It is a 24-story building whose exterior consists of a lightweight "skin" of blue-green glass and stainless steel. Beyond the repetitive, square series of windows, there are no additional exterior design elements . . .

continued . . .

The photograph is replaced with this screen on the computer:

Now get ready to answer the question.

You hear and see:

4. The professor describes the architectural design of the Lever Building. Explain how its design relates to the International Style.

Preparation Time: 30 Seconds

Response Time: 60 Seconds

You hear:
Begin to prepare your response after the beep. [*beep sound*]

Preparation Time
00:00:00

After 30 seconds, you hear:
Begin speaking after the beep. [*beep sound*]

Response Time
00:00:00

After 60 seconds, you hear:
[*beep sound*] Now, stop speaking.

NOTE-TAKING AND RATING PRACTICE

A. *Read the following passage and make notes for your response.*

The International Style of Architecture

The International Style of architecture first arose in the 1920s and 1930s. This style was a reaction to earlier, more decorative styles, such as Art Nouveau, which included highly artistic, handcrafted elements. The International Style was distinctly modern: It included new types of materials such as glass, steel, and concrete created by mass-production techniques. Buildings still constructed in this style purposely lack ornamentation and strive for simplicity of design; the surfaces are smooth and geometrical. The roofs are flat, and large portions of the walls are constructed of floor-to-ceiling glass, or the entire building is covered in a thin, lightweight curtain of glass.

B. *Read and listen to the following lecture and make notes for your response.* 2-54

Professor: The Lever Building in New York City was completed in 1952 and is considered one of the great successes of the International Style. It is a 24-story building whose exterior consists of a lightweight "skin" of blue-green glass and stainless steel. Beyond the repetitive, square series of windows, there are no additional exterior design elements; it is simply composed of two smooth "glass boxes." The two narrow, rectangular blocks that make up the skyscraper's distinctive geometric profile are set in the shape of the letter L. There is a vertical tower which sits at a right angle on top of a small area of a horizontal block. The lowest floor of the tower is set back from the tower, which further emphasizes the geometric relationship of the two flat-topped blocks.

C. *Compare your notes for the reading and the lecture to the note-taking model below.*

Note-Taking Model

Your notes for the general/specific task should include (1) the main ideas from the reading and what the general information is (a definition? a theory? a process? a problem?) and (2) the main ideas from the lecture, including how it specifically relates to the reading (expands? contradicts? applies? offers a solution?).

Here is an example of notes for the reading and lecture above:

Reading – purpose *Purp: define: Intrnl style = 1920–30s*
[main idea] *1. react 2 arty, hndcrft style; no décor*
[main idea] *2. modern: new matrl- glss, steel, concrete, mass-producd*
[main idea] *3. no ornament; simple; smooth; geometric*
[main idea] *4. roof = flat , walls = flr 2 ceil. glss or bldg cover thin, lght-wgt glss curtain*

Lecture – connection to reading: *example = success intrnl style =24-story, Lever Building -1952 ≠ early Art Nouv style*
[main idea] *1. exter = lght-wgt, blu-grn glass "skin"+ steel, repeat sq. windows = no add design*
[main idea] *2. 2 smooth, rectang, glss box, "L" shape = verti tower blk on horiz. blk at rght angle*
[main idea] *3. lowst flr set back = geomet. relation betw/ flat-top blcks*

D. *Example responses and rating*

Although you cannot hear the pronunciation, the volume, or how fast the speaker is talking, here are some sample responses for the prompt below based on the reading and lecture. Work with a partner. Read the responses and look at the scores for each response (1 is the lowest rating and 4 is the highest) and the explanations. Discuss the reasons for the scores and how you might change the responses to make them better.

The professor describes the architectural design of the Lever Building. Explain how its design relates to the International Style.

Responses, Scores, and Score Explanations

Answer A	**Answer B**	**Answer C**
Uh . . .there is a building . . . in . . . um New York City that is the Lever Building. It's a International Style building. This style has no decorate, but it's made of stuff like glass . . . um . . . steel...and other stuff. It's a simple shape. The Lever Building the professor talks about is made of glass too, and doesn't have anythings on it and . . . um . . . um . . . it's two glass boxes. And there is a lot of floors of windows, So, the Lever Building is like the International Style.	The reading talks about the International Style of architecture . . . it's a simple and modern style . . . with mass materials of glass and steel and it's . . . um . . . it's geometric. In the lecture, the Lever Building is like an International Style building because it has colored glass walls and steel. It is smooth without any other design except lots of glass windows. It is two boxes at . . . uh . . . a right angle on top of each other and it looks geometric in the way International Style building are supposed to look. Oh, and the professor says there is tower and another block are geometric, which is what the reading says is an International building style.	According to the reading, the International Style is not like fancier, early styles. This style uses modern materials . . . uh, like glass, steel, and concrete. The professor describes the Lever Building in New York City as a great example of the International Style because the outside "skin" is made of modern materials like blue-green glass and steel. In addition, the reading explains that the International Style buildings has smooth surfaces, flat roofs, and are geometric. The description of the Lever Building in the lecture shows how it is the International Style because the outside is smooth with no extra design. And, um . . . the Lever Building is an interesting geometrical shape of two glass boxes with flat roofs, that are placed in an L shape . . . um . . . a vertical tower on top of another horizontal block. The professor also says that one floor of the tower is built in a way that shows the geometric shape of the building.
Score: 2	Score: 3	Score: 4
This response would a get score of 2 because there are too many pauses, which disrupt the flow of natural speech and make comprehension more difficult. In addition, the student's vocabulary is very limited, there are basic vocabulary and grammatical mistakes, and the sentence structures are not varied and too simple. Further, while the student did understand a few main points, the student did not fully answer the question with enough details and actually misunderstood one of the main points. There is very little connection made between the general ideas in the reading and the specific ideas in the lecture. In fact, the student rarely indicates whether the information is coming from the reading or the lecture. The response lacks coherence; one idea does not relate smoothly to another because there is little or no use of transitional signals. The student did not make good use of the time allowed for the response.	**This response would get a score of 3** because the student makes some grammatical and vocabulary mistakes and does not use very complex sentence structures or necessary transitions. The student did not use all of the time available for the response, and so could possibility have added more information. Further, there is not quite enough detail, and the organization is a bit confused in places and lacks some coherence. However, the student attempted to use appropriate vocabulary and generally understood and covered most of the important points from the reading and lecture. In addition, the student generally did a good job of indicating from which source the information was being taken.	**This response would get a score of 4** because the student paused very little and made very few grammatical or vocabulary mistakes. The sentence structures are complex and varied. While the response is not perfect in every way, it is coherent and progresses smoothly, with good use of transitions. It is clear from the amount of detail that the student had a good grasp of the information from both the reading and the lecture. The student also did a good job of integrating the information and indicating from which source the information was taken. The student made good use of the time allowed for the response.

EXPRESS TIP

Responses that use all or most of the time given for recording generally receive higher scores.

Speaking Skill 9: Organizing and Addressing the Main Points in the Reading and the Lecture

When you record your response for Task 4, it is important to organize your response in a logical way. Your response will be easier to understand and will flow more smoothly if you provide signal words and expressions for the raters that indicate the main ideas or points you are responding to from the reading and the lecture. Look at the chart below for ways in which to organize and use signal words and expressions:

READING

Purpose	Words and Expressions to Use in Your Response
To introduce and summarize the main points	*The reading **discusses / presents** two theories of language learning, whole language learning theory and multiple intelligence theory.* *The **main point(s) / idea(s)** of the reading **is / are** that Agatha Christie wrote in many different genres, including romance stories and a travel autobiography.* ***According to** the reading, there are two well-known theories of language learning, whole language learning theory and multiple intelligence theory.*
To say what the general information is presenting: a definition, a theory, or a problem	*The reading **defines / explains** the tectonic processes of mountain formation. The first process is . . .* ***In addition**, the reading **states** / the reading **adds** that Agatha Christie is most famous for her mystery and detective novels.* *The general information in the reading **is about a problem** that the scientist Alexander Fleming had when he was . . . The problem was that he . . .*

LECTURE

Purpose	Words and Expressions to Use in Your Response
To introduce and summarize the specific points	*In the lecture, the professor* ***specifically discusses / talks about / gives detailed examples of*** *how whole language and multiple intelligence theory are effectively used for different kinds of students.* ***One kind / type of*** *student . . .* *The lecture* ***discusses the specific process of*** *volcanism in forming mountains.* ***According to*** *the lecture, this process is . . .* *The professor* ***goes on to say that / adds that*** *Agatha Christie's detective novel,* Poirot, *was made into a British television series.* *The professor* ***specifically explains*** *in the lecture the unexpected discovery that Fleming made which lead to a solution to . . .*

EXPRESS TIP

Do not use the exact same language as used in the reading; try to paraphrase.
Please see Speaking Skill 8, pages 190–191, for additional information on paraphrasing.

SKILL BUILDER

A. *Read the passage and take notes on a separate piece of paper. Save your notes because you will need them later to complete the Skill Builder for Skill 10. Then, in the example response, fill in the words and expressions for introducing and summarizing the main ideas and saying what the general information is presenting: definition, a theory, a problem, and so on. More than one answer is possible for each blank.*

Volcanic Islands

The geological processes responsible for the formation of some volcanic islands begin with the movement of tectonic plates that make up the Earth's crust. These plates are always in motion; where two plates begin to pull apart or collide with each other, boiling hot rock called lava erupts from deep in the Earth. When this volcanic explosion occurs at the boundaries or edges of the plates, lava is forced up from the bottom of the sea. Over tens of thousands of years, enough layers of lava from the volcano build up and cool, eventually rising above the surface of the water. The main opening or vent from which the lava erupted cools down, but smaller vents can remain hot and active. Over time, soil forms from the broken-down lava rock, allowing plants to grow and animals to inhabit the island.

EXAMPLE READING RESPONSE

The reading ______(1)______ the geological processes of some volcanic island formation. ______(2)______ the reading, when two tectonic plates come apart or run into each other, hot lava explodes from down in the Earth. The reading ______(3)______ that when this happens at the edge of a tectonic plate, the lava is pushed up from the sea bottom. ______(4)______, the reading ______(5)______ that over a long time, layers of the lava from the volcano build up and cool and finally, the layers rise above the water. The reading ______(6)______ that the main vent cools down, although smaller openings can still be active. In the end, soil is created from the broken lava rocks, and plants and animals can then live on the island.

B. *Work with a partner. Compare your responses to the reading and then read your introduction/ summary aloud to your partner.*

C. *Read along as you listen to the lecture and take notes on a separate piece of paper. Save your notes because you will need them later to complete the Skill Builder for Skill 10. Then, in the example response, fill in the words and expressions for introducing and summarizing the specific points. More than one answer is possible for each blank.*

Now read and listen to a lecture on this topic in a geology class. 3-1

Professor: Now that you've had a chance to read some general information about volcanic islands, I'd like to discuss another idea about their formation. So, OK, in 1963, there was this geophysicist, J. Tuzo Wilson, who challenged the accepted tectonic plate theories at this time by hypothesizing that volcanic islands were formed over "hot spots." Wilson theorized that islands, which are *not* near the boundaries of tectonic plates, must have formed in a relatively small, long-lasting, and *unusually* hot region called a hot spot. He believed that a hot spot is fixed in one place, very deep within the Earth's interior. Lava erupts from these spots and forms volcanoes as a tectonic plate slowly moves over the hot spots. Wilson's idea was that after many eruptions an island emerges, but then plate movement carries it to a new location and another volcano forms in the hot spot where the old island once was. The Hawaiian Island chain was seen as proof of his theory because the farther away from the original hot spot each island in the chain is, the progressively older and more eroded its rock is. Uh . . . the original hot spot . . . is thought to be under the *youngest* island of Hawaii. And, in fact, new volcanic rock is *still* being formed on the big island of Hawaii.

EXAMPLE LECTURE RESPONSE

The lecture ___1___ J. Tuzo Wilson's theory about how volcanic islands are formed. ___2___ the professor, some islands are not formed at the edges of tectonic plates. The professor ___3___ in the lecture that Wilson believed these islands develop over small, long-lived, and extremely hot regions called hot spots. The lecture ___4___ Wilson believed lava bursts out from a hot spot and a volcano appears as the tectonic plate slowly passes over it. After the volcano erupts for a long time, an island is created; however, the plate movement carries the island to another place and it is replaced with a new hot spot. The professor ___5___ the Hawaiian Islands as ___6___ of evidence for Wilson's theory because the older and more broken-down islands in the chain are far away from the first hot spot. The professor ___7___ that the original hot spot is probably under the island of Hawaii, which is the youngest island in the chain and is still creating new volcanic rock.

D. *Work with a partner. Compare your responses to the lecture and then read your introduction / summary aloud to your partner.*

EXPRESS TIP

Be sure to provide supporting details for the main points in both the reading passage and the lecture.

Skill Builder Sample Answers:

Suggested answers are in bold below, but student answers may vary.

A. Example Reading Response: 1. **discusses/presents/explains** 2. **According to** 3. **explains** 4. **In addition,** 5. **states** 6. **adds**

C. Example Lecture Response: 1. **specifically discusses** 2. **According to** 3. **specifically explains** 4. **goes on to say that** 5. **gives** 6. **specific examples** 7. **adds**

PRACTICE

A. *Try to read the passage in no more than 45 seconds and take quick notes on a separate piece of paper. Save your notes because you will need them later to create a summary of the reading.*

Animal Defenses

Survival in the animal world is a constant and daily challenge. There is always some predator actively hunting or hiding and waiting for its next meal. Fortunately, many animals have developed ingenious ways to defend themselves. A common defense mechanism used by animals is camouflage, which is the ability to blend in with the colors in the environment in order to become nearly invisible.

Other animals use various parts of their body as methods of defense. Some animals, for example, have tails that are so strong that they can knock out or severely damage any predator that tries to attack them. Another very interesting defense is the process known as autotomy. Autotomy means that various species drop off or detach a body part that an attacker has grabbed onto, allowing them to escape. The animal is able to grow the lost body part back eventually.

B. *Work with a partner. Using your notes, write a short summary of the reading passage* ***using words and expressions for introducing and summarizing the main idea*** *of the general information in the reading. Be sure to include what the purpose of the reading is.*

C. *Read your written summary aloud to your partner.*

D. *Now listen to part of a lecture on a related topic. Take quick notes on a separate piece of paper. Save your notes as you will need them later to create a summary of the lecture.*

Now listen to part of a lecture on this topic in a zoology class. 3-2

E. *Work with a partner. Using your notes, write a short summary of the lecture* ***using words and expressions for introducing and summarizing the main idea of the specific information in the lecture.***

F. *Read your written summary aloud to your partner.*

G. *Then, without using your written summaries, say both your reading and lecture summaries aloud again and record them. Time yourself to see how long it took.*

H. *Listen to the recording of your response to the Practice for Skill 9 and complete the self-evaluation chart below. How well do you feel you did these things? Rank questions 1–9 from 1 to 5. Then answer questions 10–12.*

Self-Evaluation: Skill 9

	1 = low, 5 = high
1. Take notes on both the reading and the lecture	
2. Introduce and summarize the main ideas in the reading passage using the appropriate words and expressions	
3. Introduce and summarize the main ideas in the lecture using the appropriate words and expressions	
4. Indicate which source, the reading or the lecture, the information you are giving is coming from	
5. Use transitions to develop a logical flow	
6. Paraphrase the ideas from the reading and the lecture	
7. Avoid stating your opinion or adding information that was not included in the reading and lecture	
8. Speak fluently, without too many pauses and repetitions	
9. Speak accurately, with correct grammar and vocabulary	
10. What is something you did especially well?	
11. What one or two things would you like to improve on?	
12. How do you plan to improve those things?	

Speaking Skill 10: Integrating General Information from the Reading with Specific Information from the Lecture

Perhaps the most essential skill needed for your Task 4 response is the ability to relate (integrate) the general information from reading to the specific information in the lecture by (1) indicating which source the information you are giving is coming from and (2) explaining the *reasons* the information is related.

If your notes include the purpose of the reading (definition, process, problem), then you should be able to show how the examples and main points in the lecture connect to the general ideas in the reading.

Look at the chart below for ways in which to integrate the information using signal words and expressions (see page 176, Speaking Skill 6, for a list of comparison and contrast words and expressions).

LECTURE AND READING

Purpose	Words and Expressions to Use in Your Response
To state the points in the lecture that are specific examples of general points in the reading **To explain the reasons that the lecture points relate to the reading**	***The author mentions*** *that rattlesnakes do not strike unless they are surprised.* ***However, the lecture says*** *that during a certain season, rattlesnakes are blind and will strike at any movement even if they are not provoked.* *The* ***professor talks*** *about a* ***specific example*** *of students who can best benefit from the multiple intelligence theory* ***discussed in the reading.***
To use comparison or contrast words and expressions where appropriate	***Like / Similar*** *to the types of mountain formation* ***discussed in the reading, the lecture states*** *that volcanism* ***is also . . . because . . .*** ***Unlike / In contrast to*** *the types of mountain formation* ***mentioned in the reading****, the* ***professor says that*** *volcanism* ***isn't . . . because . . .*** ***According to the lecture****, the* ***solution to*** *Fleming's problem* ***explained in the reading*** *was . . .* ***because . . .***

EXPRESS TIP

Remember to include a reasonable amount of information from both the reading and lecture in your response.

SKILL BUILDER

A. *Use your notes and the summaries for the Skill Builder in Skill 9 to fill in the integrated response to the prompt below. Be sure to indicate which source (the reading or the lecture) the information you are giving is coming from and explain the reasons the information is related. Use the appropriate signal words and expressions. More than one answer is possible for each blank.* ***[Please note that the fill-in response below is longer than the actual response you would record on the TOEFL iBT Test.]***

EXAMPLE INTEGRATED READING AND LECTURE RESPONSE TO PROMPT

Narrator: The professor discusses J. Tuzo Wilson's theory of volcanic island formation. Explain how his theory relates to the geological processes of island formation.

Prompt:

The professor discusses J. Tuzo Wilson's theory of volcanic island formation. Explain how his theory relates to the geological processes of island formation.

In the ____1____, the author ____2____ one geological ____3____ that makes volcanic islands. ____4____ the reading, some volcanic islands are formed when two tectonic plates come apart or run into each other, and then lava is pushed up from deep in the Earth. The reading ____5____ that when lots of it from an underwater volcano builds up and gets cool, it becomes an island. ____6____, according to the ____7____, Wilson's theory is ____8____ the volcanic formation mentioned in the ____9____. ____10____ says that Wilson thought that another process must be happening ____11____ some islands form that are not on the edges of the plates. ____12____ the information in the ____13____, Wilson believed that hot spots, small and extremely hot places, cause volcanic islands to form. ____14____ the professor, lava from the hot spots creates volcanoes, ____15____ the reading, which says they form because of plate movement. The professor ____16____ the tectonic plate moves over the hot spots; after the island rises out of the water, the plate moves it to a new location and another hot spot forms where it was. The lecture ____17____ the Hawaiian Islands are proof of Wilson's theory ____18____ each island gets increasingly older and more broken down the farther away it gets from the original hot spot on the island of Hawaii. The professor ____19____ the youngest island of Hawaii, the original hot spot, is still producing new volcanic rock.

B. *Work with a partner. Compare your answers in the integrated response above and then read your response aloud to your partner.*

EXPRESS TIP

Remember to use a variety of grammatical structures, from simple to complex, in your response.

Skill Builder Sample Answers:

Suggested answers are in bold below, but student answers may vary.

A. Example Integrated Reading and Lecture Response to prompt: 1. **reading** 2. **discusses/explains/presents/talks about** 3. **process** 4. **According to** 5. **mentions/explains** 6. **However** 7. **lecture /professor** 8. **unlike /not the same as** 9. **reading** 10. **The professor/lecture** 11. **because** 12. **In contrast to** 13. **reading** 14. **According to** 15. **unlike/in contrast to/whereas/while** 16. **goes on to say/adds that** 17. **says/mentions/explains that** 18. **because** 19. **adds/explains that**

PRACTICE

A. *Try to read the passage in no more than 45 seconds and take quick notes on a separate piece of paper. Save your notes to use for your response.*

B. *Listen to a lecture on a related subject and take quick notes on a separate piece of paper. Save your notes to use for your response.*

The Stages of Sleep

Humans progress through five stages of sleep at night, and each one is associated with its own distinct patterns of brain waves and physical reactions. The first stage is a transition between wakefulness and sleep which lasts for only a few minutes and is marked by rapid, short brain waves. Stage 2, which makes up about one-half of our total sleeping time, is characterized by slower, more regular brain waves, and we go deeper into sleep as this stage progresses.

In Stages 3 and 4, the brain waves become even slower and people in these stages react increasing less to outside noise or movement. Finally, there is Stage 5, which is called REM or rapid eye movement sleep. This is the stage with the most intense period of physical activity; the heart rate, blood pressure, and rate of breathing increase.

Now listen to part of a lecture on this topic in a psychology class. 3-3

C. *Read the prompt. Then, using your notes, write a response that* ***integrates the information from both the reading and the lecture****. Be sure to indicate which source (the reading or the lecture) the information you are giving is coming from and explain the reasons the information is related.* ***Use the appropriate signal words and expressions.***

The professor discusses REM sleep. Explain how it relates to the stages of sleep.

D. *Work with a partner. Read your written response aloud to your partner.*

E. *Then, without using your written response, say it aloud again and record it. Time yourself to see how long it took.*

F. *Listen to the recording of your response to the Practice for Skill 10 and complete the self-evaluation chart below. How well do you feel you did these things? Rank questions 1–10 from 1 to 5. Then answer questions 11–13.*

Self-Evaluation: Skill 10

	1 = low, 5 = high
1. Take notes on both the reading and the lecture	
2. Integrate the information from both the reading passage and the lecture using appropriate signal words and expressions	
3. Compare or contrast the general purposes (definition, process, problem) of the reading passage to the specific examples, counter-examples, applications, or solutions in the lecture	
4. Indicate which source, the reading or the lecture, the information you are giving is coming from	
5. Include a reasonable amount of information from both the reading and the lecture in your response	
6. Use transitions to develop a logical flow	
7. Paraphrase the ideas from the reading and the lecture	
8. Avoid stating your opinion or adding information that was not included in the reading and lecture	
9. Speak fluently, without too many pauses and repetitions	
10. Speak accurately, with correct grammar and vocabulary	
11. What is something you did especially well?	
12. What one or two things would you like to improve on?	
13. How do you plan to improve those things?	

EXPRESS TIP

Keep in mind that the reading passage and the lecture may have the same points of view or they may have different points of view. This is important because the words and expressions you use to integrate the information from the reading and the lecture will be different depending on the views expressed in each.

SKILLS REVIEW

Integrated Speaking Skills 9 and 10 for Task 4, General/Specific: Organizing and Addressing the Main Points in the Reading and the Lecture, and Integrating General Information from the Reading with Specific Information from the Lecture

1. *You will now read a short passage and then listen to a lecture on the same academic subject. After you hear the question about them, you have 30 seconds to prepare your response and 60 seconds to answer.*

Reading Time: 45 Seconds

The Environmental Impact of Plastic Bags

Plastic bags represent a significant threat to the environment, humans, and animals. It is estimated that somewhere between 500 billion and a trillion plastic bags are used worldwide each year. It takes a great deal of precious non-renewable resources, such as oil and natural gas, to produce them. In addition, plastic bags are not biodegradable, meaning they do not readily break down. The result is an excessive build-up when they are dumped in landfills or harmful air pollution if they are burned. The bags contain toxic chemicals that can leak into the soil and water, creating serious health risks for both animals and humans. Likewise, animals can accidently eat the bags, making them sick or even killing them.

Now listen to part of a lecture on this topic in an environmental studies class. 3-4

Directions: *Record your response to the following prompt.*

1. Explain how the examples discussed by the professor relate to the environmental impact of plastic bags.

Preparation Time: 30 Seconds

Response Time: 60 Seconds

2. *You will now read a short passage and then listen to a lecture on the same academic subject. After you hear the question about them, you have 30 seconds to prepare your response and 60 seconds to answer.*

Reading Time: 45 Seconds

Steps in the Process of Invention

The process of invention involves specific steps for creatively solving a specific problem. The process begins when an inventor identifies and defines a problem and then asks: "How can I solve this?" The next step is to do all of the necessary background research; even if someone has already created the invention, the inventor's task is to find ways to improve it. After thoroughly researching the invention, the inventor usually creates a detailed drawing and then builds or has someone build an example model or a prototype. Then the inventor tests the prototype to see how it works and makes any needed changes. Finally, if the invention is successful, the inventor applies for a patent or copyright, which provides the exclusive rights to make and sell the invention.

Now listen to part of a lecture on this topic in an industrial science and technology class. 3-5 

Directions: *Record your response to the following prompt.*

2. The professor discusses the windshield wipers invented by Mary Anderson. Explain how her invention illustrates the steps in the process of invention.

Preparation Time: 30 Seconds

Response Time: 60 Seconds

Self-Evaluation: Skills Review

Listen to the recordings of your responses to the Skills Review for Skills 9 and 10 and complete the self-evaluation chart below. How well do you feel you did these things? Rank questions 1–11 from 1 to 5. Then answer questions 12–14.

	1 = low, 5 = high
1. Take notes on both the readings and the lectures	
2. Introduce and summarize the main ideas from both the reading passages and the lectures using the appropriate words and expressions	
3. Integrate the information from both the reading passages and the lectures using appropriate signal words and expressions	
4. Connect the general purposes (definition, process, problem) of the reading passages to the specific examples, counter-examples, applications, or solutions in the lectures	
5. Indicate which source, the readings or the lectures, the information you are giving is coming from	
6. Include a reasonable amount of information from both the readings and the lectures in your responses	
7. Use transitions to develop a logical flow	
8. Paraphrase the ideas from the readings and the lectures	
9. Avoid stating your opinion or adding information that was not included in the readings and lectures	
10. Speak fluently, without too many pauses and repetitions	
11. Speak accurately, with correct grammar and vocabulary	
12. What is something you did especially well?	
13. What one or two things would you like to improve on?	
14. How do you plan to improve those things?	

INTEGRATED TASK 5

PROBLEM/SOLUTIONS (CONVERSATION)

Skills 11 and 12: Listening for the Problems and Solutions; Responding to the Problem/Solutions and Stating Your Opinion

For the Integrated Task 5, the problem/solutions task, you will listen to a short conversation for 60–90 seconds. After the conversation, you will be required to respond for 60 seconds to a question based on what you heard in the conversation. *You will not be asked to read a passage for this task.*

This type of question will present you with a prompt or a question that asks you to summarize the problem, discuss the solutions, and state your opinion about which solution you prefer and why. You will have 20 seconds to think about your response and take notes before you begin speaking.

The Task 5 conversations are based on typical campus-related issues, such as scheduling or changing classes, transportation, housing, and other potential problems areas.

About the speakers:

- They will be two students; a student and a professor; or a student and some other campus official, such as a librarian, a sports coach, or an administrator.
- One of the speakers will discuss a problem (sometimes both speakers have the same problem).
- One or both of the speakers will present possible solutions to the problem. There will always be two solutions presented.

You will both hear the questions and see them on the computer screen. The following are examples of the question in Task 5:

- *The students discuss two possible solutions to the man's problem. Describe the problem and the two solutions. Then state which of the two solutions you prefer and why.*
- *The speakers discuss two possible solutions to the woman's problem. Briefly summarize the problem and the two solutions. Then explain what you think the woman should do and why.*

In order to answer the question correctly, you must:

- Listen carefully to the conversation and take brief notes on the problem that is discussed and the two solutions that are suggested.
- When you record your response, first briefly summarize the problem in the conversation (be sure to indicate if it is the man's or the woman's problem).
- Next, briefly summarize the two solutions offered (again, indicate who is offering the solutions).

- Then state clearly which of the two solutions you think is better and why you prefer that solution. You are being asked directly for your opinion in Task 5.
- Develop a logical flow of information by using the appropriate transitions (*in addition*, *also*, *then*, *another idea*, *the second solution*, *however*, *on the other hand*, *because*, and *for example*).
- Paraphrase what you have read and heard by using different words and grammatical structures in your response.

Look at this example of a Task 5, problem/solutions question on a computer screen.

EXAMPLE: Integrated Task 5: Problem/Solutions Question

You see and hear:

Narrator: *You will now listen to a conversation. You will then be asked a question about it. After you hear the question, you will have 20 seconds to prepare your response and 60 seconds to speak.*

Now listen to a conversation between two students.

You see:

You then hear a conversation:

Man: Wow! I can't believe how expensive the textbook is for my biology class. And it's only *one* of the books I have to buy. I'm really low on cash this semester, so I just don't know how I'm going to pay for all of them.

Woman: How about buying the used ones at the campus bookstore? They usually offer some pretty good discounts, and the lines aren't too bad in the afternoon.

Man: Well, I could do that, but sometimes the ones they have are in bad shape . . . um, falling apart or with lots of highlighting and notes. And the prices aren't always so great for the quality.

Woman: So, OK, why don't you do what I did last semester and try to find used textbooks online? A lot of websites . . .

continued . . .

When the conversation ends, the photograph will be replaced with this screen on the computer:

Now get ready to answer the question.

You hear and see:

The students discuss two possible solutions to the man's problem. Describe the problem and the two solutions. Then state which of the two solutions you prefer and why.

Preparation Time: 20 Seconds

Response Time: 60 Seconds

You hear:
Begin to prepare your response after the beep. [*beep sound*]

Preparation Time

00:00:00

After 20 seconds, you hear:
Begin speaking after the beep. [*beep sound*]

Response Time

00:00:00

After 60 seconds, you hear:
[*beep sound*] Now, stop speaking.

Speaking Skill 11: Listening for the Problems and Solutions

It is essential for your Task 5 response that you hear and understand the problem and both of the solutions that are discussed in the conversation. Look at the chart below for expressions that the speakers might use to state a problem and offer solutions:

Purpose	Expressions Used in the Conversation
To present the problem	***My problem is*** *that I just don't have enough time to finish the paper.* ***I've got a problem with*** *my roommate . . . she is always talking on her cell phone when I'm trying to study.* ***I just don't know how*** *I'm going to /* ***I can't*** *get to work on time now.* One speaker might ask the following questions, and then the other speaker will respond to the question by explaining the problem: **Man:** ***What's wrong / What's the matter? / What can I help you with? / What's on your mind?*** **Woman:** ***I can't decide whether*** *to drop the class* ***or not.***
To offer solutions	***Why don't you / Why not*** *ask the professor for more time?* ***If I were you, I'd*** *ask her to leave the room when she talks on her cell phone.* ***How about*** *asking someone to give you a ride?* ***I'd suggest / advise that*** *you drop the class.* ***My advice / My suggestion*** *is to drop the class.* ***Any chance / Is it possible you could*** *change your schedule?* ***I've been thinking about*** *getting a new roommate.* ***You could / should*** *ask someone to take notes for you.* ***Another thing you could do*** *is buy the notes from the note-taking service.*

EXPRESS TIP

If the speaker with the problem directly states reasons for liking or not liking the solutions offered, you may want to take brief notes on his or her reaction. This may help you to understand some of the advantages or disadvantages of each solution, which you can then use in your response. You should, however, try to state your *own reasons* for preferring one solution more than the other.

continued . . .

Woman: The problem is that it's almost impossible to find a parking space on campus.
Man: Well, you could take the bus instead of driving.
Woman: That's not a bad idea and it would save me some money on gas, but it does take a longer time to get to campus on the bus.

Example response: *Even though the woman says that taking the bus would make her trip to campus longer, I think it's a better solution to take the bus than to drive because she would not have to pay for gas. Also, it is better for the environment not to drive a car.*

SKILL BUILDER

A. *Listen for expressions in the following conversation that signal the problem and the solutions and quickly write them down in the notes below. While you are filling in the notes, be sure to use abbreviations and symbols* ***(see pages 87–91 for more information on note-taking)****.*

EXPRESS TIP

Write in your notes what each speaker is saying. For example, you can write "M" for the male speaker and "W" for the female speaker (see the notes below).

In addition, when you hear the problem, you may want to write "PR" in your notes and when you hear the solutions, you may want to write "SO 1" and "SO 2" in your notes as well. This will help you quickly find the problem and solutions you will need in order to summarize and discuss them in your response.

Listen to a conversation between two students. 3-6

[PR (problem)] M (man) – (expression: ______________________________)

[SO (solution) 1] W (woman) – (expression: ______________________________)

[SO (solution) 2] W (woman) – (expression: ______________________________)

B. *Work with a partner. Compare your notes. What was the problem? What were the two solutions? Were you able to hear and write down the expressions that helped you understand the problem and the solutions?*

EXPRESS TIP

The problem may not always be directly stated using any of the specific expressions listed above. However, you should listen for the tone of voice; the speaker with the problem will usually sound upset or stressed when explaining the problem.

Skill Builder Answers:

[PR] M – (expression: I can't (believe)) bio txtbk too much $; ♂ has little $

[SO 1] W – (expression: How about?) buy used @ campus bkstr b/c + discnt & lines OK

[SO 2] W – (expression: Why don't you?) find used bk on line b/c good price & cheaper than bkstr

PRACTICE

A. *Listen to the conversation and take quick notes on a separate piece of paper.* ***Be sure to listen for expressions from the list above that will tell you what the problem is and what the solutions are.***

Now listen to a conversation between a student and a Student Employment Assistant. 3-7

B. *Work with a partner. Using your notes, fill in the answers to the questions below. Then decide which solution you agree with.*

The person with the problem? ______________________________

Problem? ______________________________

Solution #1? ______________________________

Solution #2? ______________________________

I think Solution ___ is better.

C. *Complete the self-evaluation chart below for the Practice for Skill 11. How well do you feel you did these things? Rank questions 1–4 from 1 to 5. Then answer questions 5–7.*

Self-Evaluation: Skill 11

	1 = low, 5 = high
1. Hear the expressions or speaker's tone of voice that indicate what the problem is	
2. Take accurate and complete notes on the problem	
3. Hear the expressions that indicate what both of the solutions are	
4. Take accurate and complete notes on both of the solutions	
5. What is something you did especially well in your notes?	
6. What one or two things would you like to improve in your note-taking?	
7. How do you plan to improve those things?	

Speaking Skill 12: Responding to the Problem–Solutions and Stating Your Opinion

In Skill 11, you practiced listening for the problem and the solutions. In Skill 12, you will learn and practice using words and expressions for recording your summary of the problem and the solutions. Look at the chart below for words and expressions that you can use in your response.

Purpose	Expressions to Use in Your Response
To respond to the problem and include reasons for the problem	***The man's problem is*** *that he doesn't have enough time to finish the paper* ***because*** *he spent too much time practicing for a basketball game.* ***Susan has a problem with*** *her roommate, Claire,* ***because*** *Claire is always talking on her cell phone when Susan's trying to study.* ***The woman is having a lot of trouble*** *getting to work on time now* ***because*** *the bus route she was using was canceled.*
To respond to the first and second solutions	***The woman suggests that the man*** *ask the professor for more time.* ***She also suggests that the man*** *find a tutor to help him.* ***The man advises / encourages the woman to*** *ask her roommate to leave the room when she talks on her cell phone.* ***The man's second idea is for the woman to*** *try to find a new roommate.* ***The man thinks / says / feels that the woman should*** *ask someone to give her a ride to work.* ***Then the man says another thing the woman could do is*** *to find a job on campus.*
To state your opinion and the reasons for your opinion	***From my point of view / In my opinion,*** *the man should try to find a tutor to help him* ***because*** *the professor might not feel it's fair give him more time.* ***I feel / I think that the woman should*** *ask her roommate to go somewhere else to talk on her cell phone* ***because*** *Susan likes her roommate and doesn't want to find another one* ***and also because*** *her roommate, Claire, needs to understand that it's rude to talk on the phone when Susan is studying.* ***I agree with the first solution the man offers because*** *it might be really difficult for the woman to find a new job on campus.* ***I prefer the second solution the man suggests because*** *Susan's roommate sounds like a really difficult person to live with.*

EXPRESS TIP

Don't spend too much time summarizing the problem and the solutions. It is important that you have enough time to state your opinion and the reasons for it. Since you only have 60 seconds, you may want to plan to speak for 10 seconds about the problem, 15–20 seconds for the first solution and the second solution, and 30–35 seconds explaining which solution your prefer and why.

SKILL BUILDER

A. *Using your notes, write a summary of the problem and solutions from the conversation in the Skill Builder in Skill 11. Include the words and expressions from the list above for responding to the problem and the first and second solutions.*

B. *Work with a partner. Compare your summary and then read it aloud to your partner.*

C. *Then write a quick summary of the opinion you decided on in the Skill Builder for Skill 11 and your reasons for having that opinion* ***(for more information on giving your opinion, see Speaking Skill 4, pages 171–172)****.*

D. *Now, using your summaries of the problem and solutions and your opinion, read your complete written response aloud to your partner.*

Skill Builder Sample Answers (Student responses will vary):

A. (summary of problems and solutions) – **The man's problem is that** the biology textbook he needs to buy costs a lot and he doesn't have much money this semester to pay for this books. So, **the woman suggests that** the man buy a used textbook at the campus bookstore because it's cheaper and he probably won't have to wait in line for too long. **Then the woman says another thing the man could** do is shop online for used books, which are even less expensive than at the bookstore.

C. (summary of opinion) – **I agree with the second solution** the woman offers **because** I think the man can save more money if he tries to find a used textbook online. Even though it takes time to shop around at all the websites, the man can compare a bigger variety of prices and get the best deal. **Also, it's a good idea** to shop online **because** he can look for used books that are in good shape.

Improving the Response Activity

A. *Work with a partner. Read the prompt and the sample response below for the conversation from the Skill Builders for Skills 11 and 12. The sample response would only receive a low score rating of 2. Try to make the response better by adding words or expressions from Skills 11 and 12, providing additional information, correcting any grammatical mistakes, and adding appropriate transitions* (in addition, also, then, another idea, the second solution, however, on the other hand, because, the reason is, *and* for example).

Hints are provided for you inside the brackets ([ ]).

Prompt

> The students discuss two possible solutions to the man's problem. Describe the problem and the two solutions. Then state which of the two solutions you prefer and why.

Sample response [Score: 2]

> Full response: *Uh . . . the man . . . he . . . say his textbook is costing too much and . . . um, The woman think he should . . . go to bookstore for a discount. The woman tells him look online at websites for used books because it's easier. Uh . . . it would be better if the man buys the book at the bookstore . . . um, it takes less time.*

B. *Work with a partner. Fill in and improve the response.*

Uh . . . the man . . . [expression? ______________________] he . . . say his textbook is costing too much and . . . um, [reason? ______________________.]

The woman think he should . . . go to bookstore for a discount. [other reason? ______________________].

The woman [expression? ______________________] tells him look online at websites for used books because it's easier. [correct reason? ______________________.]

Uh . . . [expression? ______________________,] it would be better if the man buys the book at the bookstore . . . um, [transition word? ______________________] it takes less time. [more supporting reasons for the opinion? ______________________ ______________________].

C. *Compare your revised response with another pair of students.*

EXPRESS TIP

When you provide the reasons for your opinion in the response, remember that, in addition to using the information in the conversation, you can also use your own personal experience if it is related and helps support the solution you think is the best one. In other words, if you (or someone you know) have had a similar problem or have used similar solutions to solve a problem, your experience is a perfectly acceptable way to support your opinion. However, remember to stay focused on the problem the student in the conversation has, not on your own problem.

PRACTICE

A. *Listen to the conversation and take quick notes on a separate piece of paper.*

Listen to a conversation between two students. 3-8

B. *Work with a partner. Using your notes,* ***write a brief summary of the problem and solutions using words and expressions for responding to them****. Compare your summaries and then read them aloud to each other.*

C. *Then read the prompt below. Decide which solution you prefer and why. Write a quick summary of your opinion and your reasons for having that opinion.*

The students discuss two possible solutions to the woman's problem. Briefly summarize the problem and the two solutions. Then explain what you think the woman should do and why.

D. *Now, using your summary of the problem and solutions and your opinion, read your complete written response aloud to your partner.*

E. *Then, without using your written summaries, say your complete response aloud again and record it. Time yourself to see how long it took.*

F. *Listen to the recording of your response to the Practice for Skill 12 and complete the self-evaluation chart below. How well do you feel you did these things? Rank questions 1–5 from 1 to 5. Then answer questions 6–8.*

Self-Evaluation: Skill 12

	1 = low, 5 = high
1. State the problem clearly and include the appropriate words and expressions for responding to problem	
2. Provide the reason for the problem	
3. State the solutions clearly and include the appropriate words and expressions for responding to both the first solution and second solution	
4. Clearly state your opinion about which solution was better and why	
5. Use transition words to develop a logical flow	
6. What is something you did especially well?	
7. What one or two things would you like to improve on?	
8. How do you plan to improve those things?	

EXPRESS TIP

Remember that there is no right or wrong opinion. The important thing is to make sure that you clearly state the problem, the solutions, your opinion, and your reasons for having that opinion.

SKILLS REVIEW

Integrated Speaking Skills 11 and 12 for Task 5, Problem/ Solutions: Listening for the Problem and Solutions, and Responding to the Problem/Solutions and Stating Your Opinion

1. *You will now listen to a conversation. You will then be asked a question about it. After you hear the question, you will have 20 seconds to prepare your response and 60 seconds to speak.*

Listen to a conversation between a student and her advisor. 3-9

Directions: *Record your response to the following prompt.*

1. The speakers discuss two possible solutions to the woman's problem. Briefly summarize the problem and the two solutions. Then explain what you think the woman should do and why.

Preparation Time: 20 Seconds

Response Time: 60 Seconds

2. *You will now listen to a conversation. You will then be asked a question about it. After you hear the question, you will have 20 seconds to prepare your response and 60 seconds to speak.*

Listen to a conversation between two students. 3-10

Directions: *Record your response to the following prompt.*

2. The students discuss two possible solutions to the man's problem. Describe the problem and the two solutions. Then state which of the two solutions you prefer and why.

Preparation Time: 20 Seconds

Response Time: 60 Seconds

Self-Evaluation: Skills Review

Listen to the recordings of your responses to the Skills Review for Skills 11 and 12 and complete the self-evaluation chart below. How well do you feel you did these things? Rank questions 1–10 from 1 to 5. Then answer questions 11–13.

	1 = low, 5 = high
1. Listen for expressions or speaker's tone of voice that indicate what the problem is and take accurate and complete notes on the problem	
2. Listen for expressions that indicate what both of the solutions are and take accurate and complete notes on solutions	
3. State the problem clearly and include the appropriate words and expressions for responding to the problem along with specific reason(s) for the problem	
4. State the solutions clearly and include the appropriate words and expressions for responding to both the first and second solutions	
6. Clearly state your own opinion about which solution you prefer and give specific reasons for your choice	
7. Use transitions to develop a logical flow	
8. Paraphrase the ideas from the conversation	
9. Speak fluently, without too many pauses and repetitions	
10. Speak accurately, with correct grammar and vocabulary	
11. What is something you did especially well?	
12. What one or two things would you like to improve on?	
13. How do you plan to improve those things?	

INTEGRATED TASK 6

SUMMARY (LECTURE)

Skills 13 and 14: Identifying and Explaining the Main Idea; Identifying and Explaining Supporting Points

For Task 6 in the Integrated Speaking section, you will listen to an excerpt from an academic lecture for 60–90 seconds. You may take notes during the lecture. Then you will hear a question about the lecture, and you will have 20 seconds to prepare a response and 60 seconds to record your spoken response. You will not be asked to read a passage for this task.

You might be asked directly to summarize the main points of the lecture, or you might be asked a question about the main topic and be asked to support your answer with examples or reasons from the lecture. You will not be asked to give your own opinion.

The lectures will cover different academic areas, but no prior specialized knowledge is necessary to understand the lectures and answer the questions.

The following are examples of the question in Task 6:

- *Using points and examples from the lecture, describe how the element germanium affected the development of the personal computer.*
- *Using points and examples from the lecture, explain how elements from his personal life can be seen in Edvard Munch's painting* The Scream.
- *Using points and examples from the lecture, explain how animal camouflage helps both predators and prey.*

In order to answer the question correctly, you must do these things:

- Listen carefully to the lecture and take brief notes on the main idea as well as supporting points and examples.
- When you record your response, first briefly summarize the main idea of the lecture.
- Next, briefly list examples, reasons, points, and so on that illustrate or support the main idea.
- Do not give your personal opinion or reaction to the content of the lecture.
- Paraphrase what you have heard by using different words and grammatical structures in your response.
- Develop a logical flow of information by using the appropriate transitions.

Look at this example of a Task 6 summary question on a computer screen.

EXAMPLE: Integrated Task 6: Summary Question

TOEFL Speaking

VOLUME NEXT

Question 6 of 6

You see and hear:

Narrator: *In this question, you will listen to part of a lecture. You will then be asked to summarize important information from the lecture. After you hear the question, you will have 20 seconds to prepare your response and 60 seconds to speak.*

You see:

You hear:

Man: Zebra and tigers with their stripes, insects that look like sticks or leaves, fish whose color helps them blend in with the bottom of the river or ocean . . . these are all examples of animal camouflage. What do we mean by this? Simply put, camouflage means to hide or disguise the presence of something. Animals do this in three main ways: through color, through shape, and through motion or actions.

When the lecture ends, the photograph will be replaced with this screen on the computer:

Now get ready to answer the question.

You hear and see:

Using points and examples from the lecture, explain how animal camouflage helps both predators and prey.

Preparation Time: 20 Seconds

Response Time: 60 Seconds

continued . . .

You hear:

🔊 Begin to prepare your response after the beep. [*beep sound*]

Preparation Time
00:00:00

After 20 seconds, you hear:

🔊 Begin speaking after the beep. [*beep sound*]

Response Time
00:00:00

After 60 seconds, you hear:

🔊 [*beep sound*] Now, stop speaking.

Speaking Skill 13: Identifying and Explaining the Main Idea

It is essential for your Task 6 response that you be able to identify the main idea of the lecture. Not only will you have to mention this directly, but you need to know what the main idea is in order to figure out what points and examples support or illustrate it.

Sometimes the main idea will be stated very directly at the beginning of the lecture or after just a few introductory sentences. For example, here is a definition that is stated directly:

Today we're going to define existentialism and discuss its influence on the literature of nineteenth-century Russia.

Sometimes the main idea is implied, and you will need to use some inferencing skills to identify it. Here is a definition that is stated more indirectly:

Now what exactly do we mean by an integrated circuit?

Here are some methods you can use to identify main ideas:

- Listen for announcements at the beginning of the lecture that state the purpose of the talk, such as *Today I'll be examining*, *Let's look at the history of*, *Today's lecture focuses on*, *I'll define x*, and so on.
- Listen for words and phrases that signal importance, such as *main / mainly*, *principal*, *most important*, *key*, *chief*, *significant*.
- Listen for repeated words: If the main idea is about animal camouflage, it's likely that you'll hear the word *camouflage* several times during the lecture.
- Listen for concluding statements that summarize the main idea.

EXPRESS TIP

Even if you don't hear or you misunderstand a direct statement of the main idea, you can still infer it from the examples and supporting points. Taking good notes is especially important if you miss the main idea at the beginning.

As you remember from your work in previous Speaking tasks, you should not repeat what the lecturer says word for word. Instead, you should say the same idea in your own words (see Speaking Skill 8 on pages 190–191).

Here are some key expressions for stating the main idea:

- *The professor* ***defines*** *and* ***exemplifies*** *animal camouflage.*
- *The lecture* ***presents an overview*** *of the importance of the microchip.*
- *The professor* ***traces the discovery and the development of*** *the keystone.*
- *This lecture on autism* ***outlines the history of*** *treatments for the disease.*
- *The professor* ***gives a definition of*** *narcissism and* ***explains its importance.***
- *In the lecture, the professor* ***covers four main types of*** *cloud formations and* ***provides examples.***

Because the bold phrases can be used for many different topics, practice them until your delivery is smooth and your pronunciation is clear and accurate.

EXPRESS TIP

When you practice stating main ideas, try to say the same idea two or three different ways to become comfortable using a variety of different expressions.

SKILL BUILDER

A. *You will hear short excerpts from two lectures. Take notes on the main ideas.* 3-11

B. *Compare your notes with a partner. Did you each capture the main idea?*

C. *Look at the two main idea summaries below. Circle the best words or phrases to complete the sentences. Then practice reading them aloud.*

1. The lecturer (gives a definition of / traces the development of) a palomino horse. He (presents / explains) that palomino is a color, not a breed.
2. In her lecture, the professor (defines / outlines) the stages of language development in babies and (covers / traces) common features of the different stages.

EXPRESS TIP

When you take notes, mark the main idea by underlining or drawing a star.

Skill Builder Answers:
C: 1. gives a definition of; explains; 2. outlines; covers

PRACTICE

A. *Listen to the two lecture excerpts and take notes on a separate sheet of paper. Then* ***write your own summary of the main ideas of the lectures.*** 3-12

B. *Work with a partner. Read your summaries or say it again without looking at your notes.*

C. *Compare and discuss your notes. How were they similar? How were they different? Did you each capture the main idea?*

D. *Complete the self-evaluation chart below for the Practice for Skill 13. How well do you feel you did these things? Rank questions 1–6 from 1 to 5. Then answer questions 7–9.*

Self-Evaluation: Skill 13

	1 = low, 5 = high
1. Understand the main idea	
2. Hear words and phrases that expressed the main idea	
3. Take accurate and complete notes on the main idea	
4. Paraphrase the main idea when speaking	
5. Speak accurately, using key words and phrases for identifying a main idea	
6. Speak fluently, without hesitations and with natural intonation and good pronunciation	
7. What is something you did especially well?	
8. What one or two things would you like to improve on?	
9. How do you plan to improve those things?	

Speaking Skill 14: Identifying and Explaining Supporting Points

In addition to recognizing and restating the lecture's main idea, you must recognize and restate the supporting points, giving examples where you can.

Lecture topics may be subdivided in various ways:

- past, present, and future
- before, during, and after (a process)
- different types of
- examples or characteristics of
- advantages and disadvantages of
- causes and results / effects

Sometimes these will be specifically numbered in the lecture:

We'll be looking at four main types of cloud formations.

Sometimes the number of subdivisions will not be given:

We'll look at some major types of cloud formations.

When possible, give the number of supporting points in your spoken response. This shows that you heard and identified each of the supporting points.

Here are some phrases you can use to mention the supporting points of a talk. Notice how they follow the statement of the main idea:

Step 1: State the main idea/topic		Step 2: Add supporting points
The professor defines and exemplifies animal camouflage.	+	He explains that there are three types of animal camouflage: color, shape, and movement.
The lecture presents an overview of the importance of the microchip.	+	She covers four main uses: in computing, in home electronics, in appliances, and in transportation.
The professor traces the discovery and the development of the keystone.	+	He first talks about the earliest known appearances of the keystone and then discusses its use in civil engineering in different parts of the world.
This lecture on autism outlines the history of treatments for the disease.	+	The professor covers three types of treatments: behavior training, medicines, and alternative therapies, and explains when each type of treatment was most commonly used.
The professor gives a definition of narcissism and explains its importance.	+	He explains both positive and negative aspects of a narcissistic personality.
In the lecture, the professor covers four main types of cloud formations and provides examples.	+	She explains the characteristics of high-level, mid-level, low-level, and vertical development clouds.

EXPRESS TIP

Visually represent supporting points in your notes, and number them if you can. Leave room for examples.

*<u>4 major types cloud formations</u> explained

1. high-level clouds
   ex.: thin, white clouds, mostly ice; cirrus
2. mid-level
   ex: some water + some ice; altocumulus, altostratus
3. low-level
   ex. usually just water; nimbostratus
4. vertical development
   ex. tall clouds; cumulus

After you have listed the supporting points, explain each one and illustrate them with examples from the lecture. Use words such as

- *first, second, third*
- *first, next, then, finally*
- *one, the other*

and so on to clearly signal each supporting point. If you mention specific numbers instead of using words such as *another*, you clearly demonstrate that you heard all of the supporting points. Highlight examples with phrases such as *for example*, *for instance*, and *one example of this is*.

EXPRESS TIP

Remember not to add examples from your own knowledge or experience. Only use information that was presented in the lecture.

SKILL BUILDER

A. *Listen to the complete lecture excerpts from the Skill Builder for Skill 13. Take notes on a separate piece of paper.* 3-13

B. *Work with a partner. Compare your notes, both the content and formatting. Did you identify and note the same supporting points?*

C. *Look at the two summaries below. Circle the best words or phrases to complete the sentences. Cross out the sentence that doesn't belong. Then practice reading them aloud.*

1. The lecturer gives a definition of a palomino horse. He explains that palomino is a color, not a breed. He gives (some / three / four) characteristics of the palomino color: (first / for example), a palomino must have a golden coat. (Also / A second characteristic is that) the mane and tail must be (dark / light). A buckskin horse has the same colored body but a different mane and tail. (Next / Finally), a palomino's eyes must be (blue / brown). Different breeds of horse can be this special color. But in order to officially be a palomino horse, the animal must have (these three / some special) types of coloring.

2. In her lecture, the professor outlines the stages of language development in babies and (covers/ traces) common features of the different stages. The lecturer (lists / defines) (four / five) different ages of babies—three months of age, six months of age, (nine / twelve) months, eighteen months, and (twenty-four / thirty) months. By the time a baby is three months old, the baby will have different kinds of cries and knows how to coo. Most parents like their babies best at this stage. At (another / the next) stage of half a year old, the baby can babble, like da-da-da. The next stage is at one year old, and the baby can say simple (words / sentences). By eighteen months, the baby knows about (fifteen to twenty / twenty-five to fifty) vocabulary words. And (after that / finally), at two years of age, the baby can say short questions and sentences. These ages (are / aren't) the same for every baby, but they (are /aren't) true for most children.

D. *Work with a partner. Read and practice one of the responses from C until you can read it fluently.*

EXPRESS TIP

Don't worry if you are not sure how to spell a word. No one will check your notes. If it's an important word that you will need to say—for example, if you need that word to relate the main idea or a supporting point—just spell the word so that you will be able to pronounce it when you speak.

Skill Builder Answers

C. Students should have circled the bold words and expressions below. The irrelevant or incorrect sentence is crossed out.

1. The lecturer gives a definition of a palomino horse. He explains that palomino is a color, not a breed. He gives **three** characteristics of the palomino color: **first**, a palomino must have a golden coat. **A second characteristic is that** the mane and tail must be **light**. ~~A buckskin horse has the same colored body but a different mane and tail.~~ **Finally**, a palomino's eyes must be **brown**. Different breeds of horse can be this special color. But in order to officially be a palomino horse, the animal must have **these three** types of coloring.

2. In her lecture, the professor outlines the stages of language development in babies and **covers** common features of the different stages. The lecturer **lists five** different ages of babies—three months of age, six months of age, **twelve** months, eighteen months, and **twenty-four** months. By the time a baby is three months old, the baby will have different kinds of cries and knows how to coo. ~~Most parents like their babies best at this stage.~~ At **the next** stage of half a year old, the baby can babble, like da-da-da. The next stage is at one year old, and the baby can say simple **words**. By eighteen months, the baby knows about **fifteen to twenty** vocabulary words. And **finally**, at two years of age, the baby can say short questions and sentences. These ages **aren't** the same for every baby, but they **are** true for most children.

PRACTICE

A. *Listen to the complete lecture excerpts and take notes on a separate piece of paper.*

1. *Listen to part of a lecture from an Earth science class.* 3-14

B. *Using your notes, write a response to the question below.*

Using points and examples from the lecture, define a mirage and explain the different types.

C. *Now read your complete written summary aloud to your partner.*

D. *Then, without using your written summary, give your complete response aloud again and record it. Time yourself to see how long it took.*

2. *Listen to part of a lecture from a sports medicine class.* 3-15

E. *Using your notes, write a response to the question below.*

Using points and examples from the lecture, explain the causes and treatments for hamstring injuries.

F. *Now read your complete written summary aloud to your partner.*

G. *Then, without using your written summaries, give your complete responses aloud again and record it. Time yourself to see how long it took.*

H. *Listen to the recordings of your responses to the Practice for Skill 14 and complete the self-evaluation chart below. How well do you feel you did these things? Rank questions 1–6 from 1 to 5. Then answer questions 7–9.*

Self-Evaluation: Skill 14

	1 = low, 5 = high
1. Understand the main idea	
2. Identify all of the supporting points	
3. Take accurate and complete notes on the main ideas, supporting points, and examples	
4. Speak using appropriate words and expressions for stating the main idea	
5. Speak using appropriate words and expressions for stating the supporting points	
6. Speak fluently, without hesitations and with natural intonation and good pronunciation	
7. What is something you did especially well?	
8. What one or two things would you like to improve on?	
9. How do you plan to improve those things?	

SKILLS REVIEW

Integrated Speaking Skills 13 and 14 for Task 6, Summary (Lecture): Identifying and Explaining Main Ideas, and Identifying and Explaining Supporting Points

1. *You will now listen to part of a lecture. You will then be asked a question about it. After you hear the question, you will have 20 seconds to prepare your response and 60 seconds to speak.* 3-16

1. *Listen to part of a lecture from a cross-cultural communications class.*

Directions: *Record your response to the following prompt.*

1. Using points and examples from the lecture, explain the difference between high- and low-context cultures.

Preparation Time: 20 Seconds
Response Time: 60 Seconds

2. *You will now listen to part of a lecture. You will then be asked a question about it. After you hear the question, you will have 20 seconds to prepare your response and 60 seconds to speak.* 3-17

2. *Listen to part of a lecture from an agricultural science class.*

Directions: *Record your response to the following prompt.*

2. Using points and examples from the lecture, explain why invasive plants are a problem.

Preparation Time: 20 Seconds

Response Time: 60 Seconds

Self-Evaluation: Skills Review

Listen to the recording of your response to the Skills Review for Skills 13 and 14 and complete the self-evaluation chart below. How well do you feel you did these things? Rank questions 1–6 from 1 to 5. Then answer questions 7–9.

	1 = low, 5 = high
1. Understand the main idea	
2. Identify all of the supporting points	
3. Take accurate and complete notes on the main ideas, supporting points, and examples	
4. Speak using appropriate words and expressions for stating the main idea and for stating the supporting points	
5. Cover all of the important information within the 60-second time limit	
6. Speak fluently, without hesitations and with natural intonation and good pronunciation	
7. What is something you did especially well?	
8. What one or two things would you like to improve on?	
9. How do you plan to improve those things?	

Note: Scoring information for this Speaking Post-Test is available on page 327. If you are able to have a teacher or another English language speaker score the Speaking Post-Test for you, keep track of your score on this Speaking Post-Test and add it to your scores for the Reading, Listening, and Writing Post-Tests. The Speaking Post-Test can also be taken on the CD-ROM, where it is combined with the other Post-Tests into one full test. It can be taken on the CD-ROM in either the "Practice Mode" (not timed; you can work at your own pace) or the "Timed Mode" (TOEFL iBT® Test timing; you will not be able to pause). If you want to see how you would score on an authentic TOEFL iBT® Test, take the test on the CD-ROM in the "Timed Mode."

SPEAKING POST-TEST

Directions:

The Speaking section of the TOEFL iBT® Test measures your ability to speak about a variety of subjects. There are six tasks in this section. You may take notes while you listen and read, and use your notes to make your responses.

Tasks 1 and 2 are independent speaking tasks. After you hear and read the question, you will have 15 seconds to prepare a response. After you hear a beep, you will have 45 seconds to record your response.

Tasks 3 and 4 are integrated reading-listening-speaking tasks. You will first have 45 seconds to read a short passage. Then you will listen to a short conversation or lecture on the same topic. You will hear the passage only once. Then you will hear and read a question, after which you will have 30 seconds to prepare a response. After you hear a beep, you will have 60 seconds to record your response.

Tasks 5 and 6 are integrated listening-speaking tasks. You will first listen to a short conversation or lecture. You will hear it only once. Then you will hear and read a question, after which you will have 20 seconds to prepare a response. After you hear a beep, you will have 60 seconds to record your response.

Time your recorded responses or have your instructor time the responses for you. For Tasks 1 and 2, stop after 45 seconds. For Tasks 3, 4, 5, and 6, stop after 60 seconds.

When you take the actual TOEFL iBT Test, and if you take the Speaking section of the test on the CD-ROM, an on-screen clock will count down your preparation time and response time.

You may take notes on a separate piece of paper.

When you have finished reading these directions, go on to the first speaking task.

Speaking Task 1

1. You will now be asked to give your opinion about a familiar topic. After you hear the question, you have 15 seconds to prepare your response and 45 seconds to answer. 3-18

1. In what situations do you feel bored? How do you handle that feeling? Use examples to support your response.

Preparation Time: 15 Seconds

Response Time: 45 Seconds

Speaking Task 2

2. You will now be asked to give your opinion about a familiar topic. After you hear the question, you have 15 seconds to prepare your response and 45 seconds to answer. 3-19

2. Some university students feel it is important to join a club or student organization on campus. Other students believe that membership in a club or organization is not a necessary part of their university life. Which opinion do you agree with and why?

Preparation Time: 15 Seconds

Response Time: 45 Seconds

Speaking Task 3

3. You will now read a short passage and then listen to a conversation on the same subject. You will then hear a question about the topic. After you hear the question, you will have 30 seconds to prepare your response and 60 seconds to speak. 3-20

You will now have 45 seconds to read the passage.

Reading Time: 45 Seconds

VOLUNTEERS NEEDED For Dorm Welcome Program

Volunteers are needed on September 5 to help new students move into the residence halls. Assist with lifting, carrying, and unpacking. Meet and greet students and their families. Answer general questions about campus life and facilities. Now in its third year, the Dorm Welcome Program goes a long way in making new students feel accepted in the academic community. Drinks and light snacks provided.

Minimum 3-hour commitment; morning and afternoon shifts available. Please e-mail by Aug. 30 to schedule a shift time. Excellent volunteer opportunity for individual students and student organizations. dormwelcome@ibtxstat.edu

---

Now get ready to answer the question.

3. The man expresses his opinion about the opportunity described in the notice. State his opinion and explain his reasons for that opinion.

Preparation Time: 30 Seconds

Response Time: 60 Seconds

Speaking Task 4

4. You will now read a short passage and then listen to a lecture on the same academic subject. You will then hear a question about them. After you hear the question, you will have 30 seconds to prepare your response and 60 seconds to speak. 3-21

You will have 45 seconds to read the passage.

Reading Time: 45 Seconds

Teacher Evaluations

The evaluation of classroom teachers is an essential process for strengthening teaching practices and, thereby, improving the learning of all students. Teachers have traditionally been evaluated based on how well their students score on standard tests. However, many educators feel that this type of evaluation is limited. They feel that circumstances outside the classroom and not specifically related to a particular teacher's performance may have negative effects on student scores. For this reason, some educational institutions are combining student score evaluations with other types of assessment. For example, classroom observation by another qualified professional can provide teachers with direct and personalized assessment. Finally, student evaluations are also considered an informative mechanism for giving valuable feedback to the teacher.

Now get ready to answer the question.

4. The professor discusses student evaluations. Explain how these evaluations relate to other methods of teacher evaluation mentioned in the reading.

Preparation Time: 30 Seconds

Response Time: 60 Seconds

Speaking Task 5

5. You will now listen to a conversation. You will then be asked a question about it. After you hear the question, you will have 20 seconds to prepare your response and 60 seconds to speak. 3-22

Now get ready to answer the question.

5. The speakers discuss two possible solutions to the man's problem. Briefly summarize the problem and the two solutions. Then explain what you think the man should do and why.

Preparation Time: 20 Seconds

Response Time: 60 Seconds

Speaking Task 6

6. You will now listen to a lecture. You will then be asked a question about it. After you hear the question, you will have 20 seconds to prepare your response and 60 seconds to speak. 3-23

Now get ready to answer the question.

6. Using points and examples from the lecture, describe the different layers of fur that the professor explains.

Preparation Time: 20 Seconds
Response Time: 60 Seconds

THIS IS THE END OF THE SPEAKING POST-TEST.

Record your score: _______

WRITING OVERVIEW

The Writing section tests your ability to write coherent academic texts similar to those required in undergraduate college classes.

There are two different writing tasks:

- The Integrated Task: a response based on both a reading passage and a lecture
- The Independent Task: a free response

You will write one essay for each task. The entire section takes about an hour.

THE INTEGRATED TASK

This task combines a reading passage and a listening passage on an academic topic, followed by a question to which you will type a response. Topics include general information from subject areas such as the arts, general sciences (biology, chemistry, geology, etc.), and social sciences (economics, history, international relations, etc.). You do not need any specialized knowledge to understand the reading or the listening.

Tool Bar for the Writing Section

You will see this tool bar at the very top of your screen:

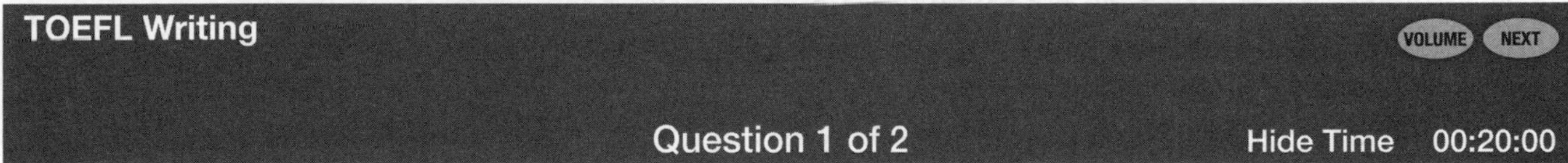

The section you are in and the question you are answering will always be displayed on the tool bar at the top of the computer screen.

Next—Allows you to go to the next question.
Volume—Enables you to change the volume during the listening portion of the Integrated Task.

Note: Each of the tasks will appear with their own clocks that will count down the preparation time and response time.

The Integrated Task is administered as follows:

1. You will have 3 minutes to read the passage; you may take notes while you read.
2. The reading passage will disappear, and then you will listen to an academic lecture on the same topic, but which treats it in a different way—for example, it may contradict or argue against points made in the reading, or it may support the information with additional examples or explanations. You may take notes during the lecture.

3. When the lecture is finished, the reading passage will be shown again on the screen, along with a question about how the lecture and reading are related. The screen is split in half, with the reading appearing on the left and space to type your response on the right.
4. You will then have 20 minutes to write and check your response.

When it is time for you to write your response, you will see this tool bar for the Integrated Task:

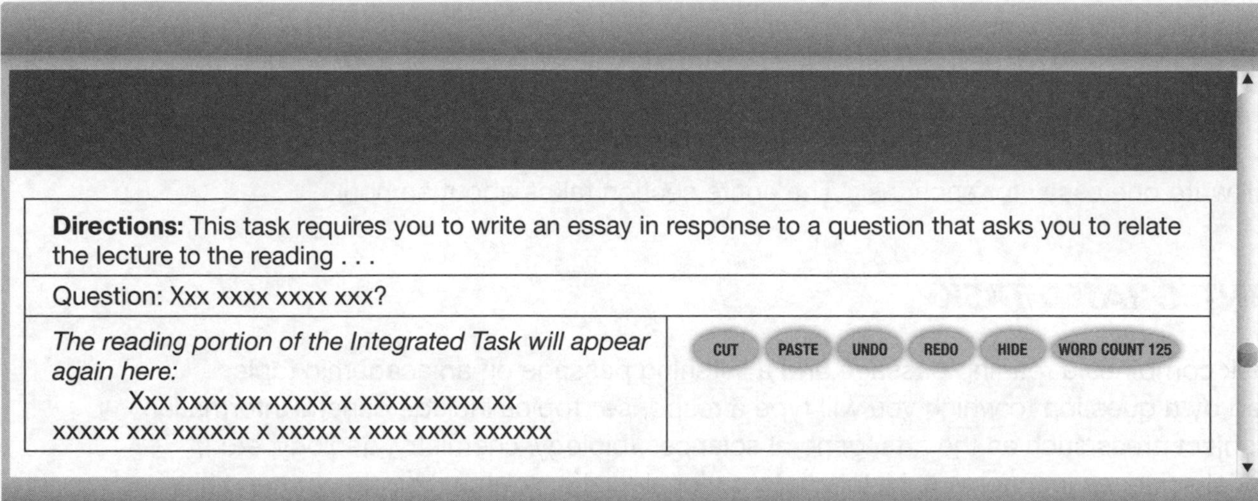
Directions: This task requires you to write an essay in response to a question that asks you to relate the lecture to the reading . . .
Question: Xxx xxxx xxxx xxx?
The reading portion of the Integrated Task will appear again here:
Xxx xxxx xx xxxxx x xxxxx xxxx xx
xxxxx xxx xxxxxx x xxxxx x xxx xxxx xxxxxx
CUT
PASTE
UNDO
REDO
HIDE
WORD COUNT 125

Cut—Allows you to remove a word or portion of text from where you typed it, but without erasing it completely.
Paste—Allows you to insert the cut text where you would like it to be placed.
Undo—Allows you to cancel the previous action you took, whether that was typing, cutting, pasting, and so on.
Redo—Allows you to repeat an action; for example, in the event that you hit "Undo" and then change your mind.
Hide—Allows you to hide the word count. We do not advise using this feature—you should be aware of how many words you have typed. It is unlikely that your answer will be too long, given the limited time, and if your answer is too short, you should know that.
Word count—Shows how many words you have typed.

EXPRESS TIP

For the Integrated Task, you will hear the listening only once, but you will be able to see the reading again while you type your response. For this reason, it is more important to take careful notes during the lecture than during the reading.

When you write the response, you should answer the prompt directly. The prompt will ask you to explain how the lecture is related to the reading—therefore, in your writing, you should follow the organization of the lecture (often the lecture and the reading cover points in the same order). Make sure to apply the information in the lecture to the points in the reading. Do not give your personal opinion about the information; do not mention any outside knowledge or points. Only report on information presented in the lecture and the reading.

The written responses are read and scored by trained ETS staff. Essays that receive a high score for the Integrated Task:

- include all of the main points mentioned in the lecture, in the same order as in the lecture
- clearly relate each main point in the lecture to information in the reading
- include a variety of sentence structures
- are mostly grammatically accurate
- use sophisticated but appropriate vocabulary
- are about 150–225 words long

THE INDEPENDENT TASK

This task requires you to write a personal essay on a given topic, usually by expressing a preference or giving your opinion about a question or issue. You do not need any specialized knowledge to answer the question.

The Independent Task is administered as follows:

1. After you have read the directions for the Independent Task, click on "Next."
2. A prompt (question) will appear on the screen with space for you to type your response. You will be able to see the prompt while you are writing.
3. You will have 30 minutes to write and check the essay.

Tool Bar for the Independent Task:

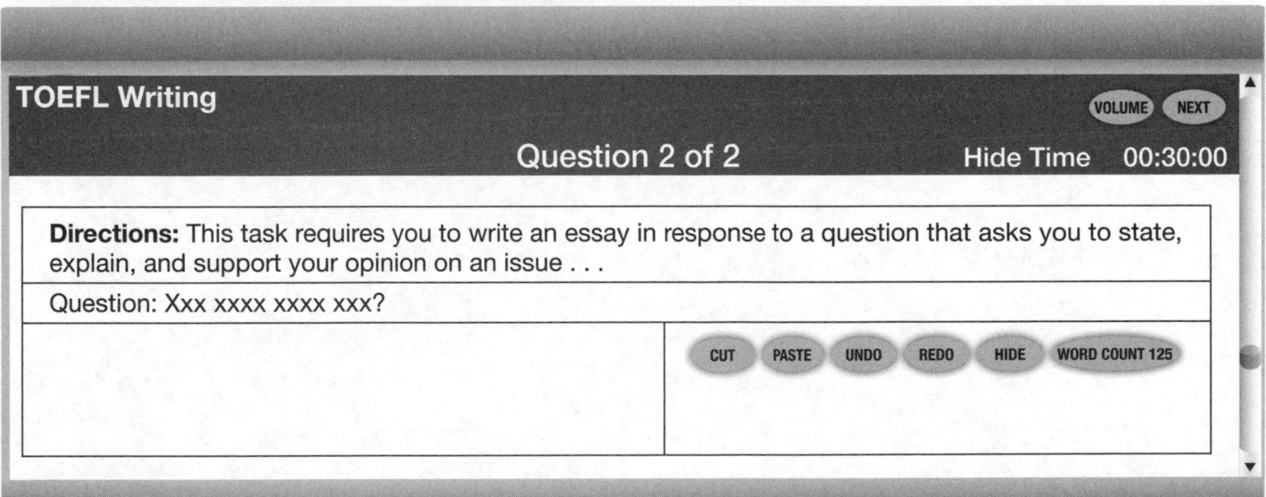
TOEFL Writing
VOLUME
NEXT
Question 2 of 2
Hide Time 00:30:00
Directions: This task requires you to write an essay in response to a question that asks you to state, explain, and support your opinion on an issue . . .
Question: Xxx xxxx xxxx xxx?
CUT
PASTE
UNDO
REDO
HIDE
WORD COUNT 125

The section you are in and the question you are answering will always be displayed on the tool bar at the top of the computer screen.

The buttons for the Independent Task function in the same way as the ones for the Integrated Task. Again, we do not recommend ever using the "hide" button to hide your word count.

Essays that receive a high score for the Independent Task:

- are well organized
- directly address the prompt
- include a variety of sentence structures
- are mostly grammatically accurate
- use sophisticated but appropriate vocabulary
- are about 300 words long

As you type your responses to the tasks, you will be able to see how many words you have typed. It is important to remember that you can NOT use spellcheck or a grammar checker on the TOEFL iBT® Test. You must proofread and edit yourself.

Remember to spend a few minutes planning your responses and to leave a few minutes at the end to check your work.

When the time is finished, your essay will be saved, and you will not be able to type any further. There is no "Save" button to press during the essay writing time, but your writing is still being saved.

Improving Your Writing Ability

There are actually two skills you must work on to improve your writing ability for the TOEFL iBT Test: writing and typing. Typing especially is not a skill that can be learned or much improved in a short amount of time before the test. Start practicing as soon as possible, and practice for a little bit each day or a few times each day.

- Write in English as often as you can. Keep a journal or diary on your computer where you write down the day's events and comment on them.
- Start a blog in English. Many free blog sites exist online; you can set your blog to "private" if you don't wish to have other people read what you write.
- Time yourself when you write to see how much you can write in 20 and then in 30 minutes. Get used to writing quickly within these time limits.
- Send e-mails to friends, acquaintances, and other students in English.
- Join social networking sites and post messages in English. If you typically post in your native language, write each post in both languages, so that you can practice your English at the same time.
- Search online for examples of essay questions. Of course questions in the style of the TOEFL iBT Test are useful, but any general essay questions will help you practice too.
- Search online for examples of student answers to essay questions. Study the model essays and note useful organizational patterns, phrases, and vocabulary.
- If you don't have constant access to a computer, practice writing by hand. You can still practice expressing yourself in writing.
- Because the Integrated Task also tests your reading and listening abilities, follow the suggestions in those sections to improve those skills at the same time; for example, you can read short articles and listen to short talks, and then write a short summary of them, including the major points.

All of the suggestions above will help with your typing. In addition, try these things:

- Find free online games and practices for improving your typing.
- Download or purchase a typing program for your computer, and use it for a short time every day.
- When you type, don't use spellcheck to correct your spelling. Instead, reread your own writing and try to find errors.
- When you can't think of anything to write, practice typing by copying reading passages from books, magazines, and newspapers.

INTEGRATED TASK 1

READING–LECTURE

Skills 1 and 2: Outlining the Integrated Response Essay; Integrating Ideas

The first task in the Writing section is the Integrated Task, which combines reading and listening for input, and then a written essay response.

First, you have 3 minutes to read a short text on an academic topic. After that, you will hear a short lecture for about 2 minutes on the same topic. Then you will have 20 minutes to write a response in which you

- summarize the points of the lecture
- relate or apply the information in the lecture to the reading

Essays that receive the highest scores are around 150–225 words long. You are not asked to give your personal opinion. You will type your answer directly on the computer screen.

EXPRESS TIP

If you are not already a proficient typist, spend some time *each day* practicing typing. There are free games and programs on the Internet that you can use to help you, or you can practice copying from books or just writing your own thoughts. It takes time to build typing speed and accuracy—you can't improve much in just a few days before the test.

You can take notes on both the reading passage and the listening passage.

For the **reading** passage, make notes about the main idea of the passage and the supporting points. Usually, the main idea will be supported by reasons, arguments, or examples. You can use these notes to help follow the organization of the lecture. You will not be able to see the reading text while you listen to the lecture.

However, when it is time to write, the reading passage will be shown to you again. For this reason, you should not try to copy every detail from the entire reading passage in your notes.

For the **listening** passage, take notes about information or arguments that contradict or refute points in the reading, or that answer questions or challenges brought up in the reading. You will hear the listening passage only once, so take detailed notes from the listening. Some students like to take notes from the reading and leave a lot of space, and then write the corresponding points from the listening into the same outline.

Before you write, quickly read the passage again and check your notes. Then write a quick outline of your response.

The following are examples of this type of question:

- *Summarize the points made in the lecture, being sure to explain how they answer questions raised in the reading passage.*
- *Summarize the points made in the lecture, being sure to explain how they support the points made in the reading passage.*
- *Summarize the points made in the lecture, being sure to explain how they challenge arguments made in the reading passage.*
- *Summarize the points made in the lecture, being sure to explain how they cast doubt on claims made in the reading passage.*

In order to answer the question correctly, you must:

- Directly answer the question.
- Identify the main idea and supporting points of the listening passage, and cover them in your written response.
- Understand the relationship between the points in the listening passage and the points in the reading passage, and make this clear in your response.
- Organize your response in a logical way, using transitions to explain relationships between paragraphs and sentences.
- Use a variety of sentence structures including simple, compound, and complex.
- Use correct sentence structures, appropriate vocabulary, and good grammar.

EXPRESS TIP

If you have time left, be sure to check your essay and revise if necessary. Never end the task early.

First, you will see a computer screen giving you the general directions for the task:

EXAMPLE: Integrated Task: Reading–Lecture Question

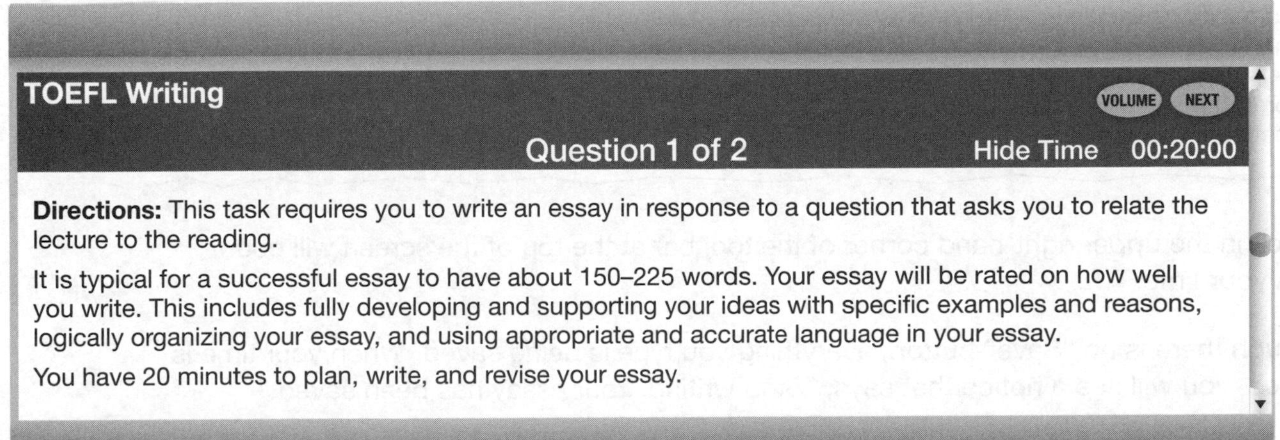

TOEFL Writing
VOLUME
NEXT
Question 1 of 2
Hide Time
00:20:00
Directions: This task requires you to write an essay in response to a question that asks you to relate the lecture to the reading.
It is typical for a successful essay to have about 150–225 words. Your essay will be rated on how well you write. This includes fully developing and supporting your ideas with specific examples and reasons, logically organizing your essay, and using appropriate and accurate language in your essay.
You have 20 minutes to plan, write, and revise your essay.

Then, when you have finished reading the directions, click "Continue." The next screen will show you the reading text:

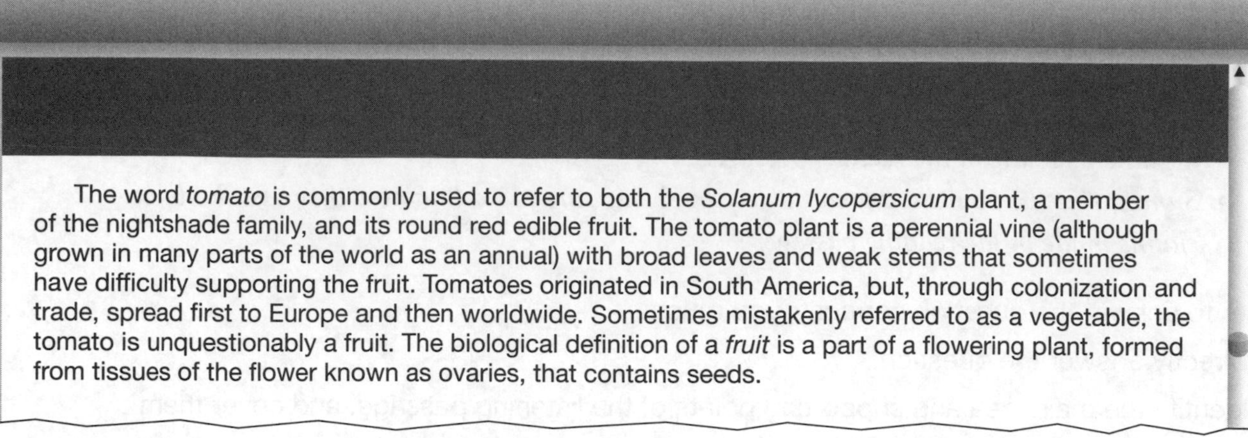
The word *tomato* is commonly used to refer to both the *Solanum lycopersicum* plant, a member of the nightshade family, and its round red edible fruit. The tomato plant is a perennial vine (although grown in many parts of the world as an annual) with broad leaves and weak stems that sometimes have difficulty supporting the fruit. Tomatoes originated in South America, but, through colonization and trade, spread first to Europe and then worldwide. Sometimes mistakenly referred to as a vegetable, the tomato is unquestionably a fruit. The biological definition of a *fruit* is a part of a flowering plant, formed from tissues of the flower known as ovaries, that contains seeds.

After 3 minutes, the reading passage will disappear. Then you will see a picture of a professor giving a lecture and hear a lecture on the same topic. You can take notes during the lecture. After the lecture is finished, you will see the reading again, on the left side of the screen. The right side of the screen is where you will write your response.

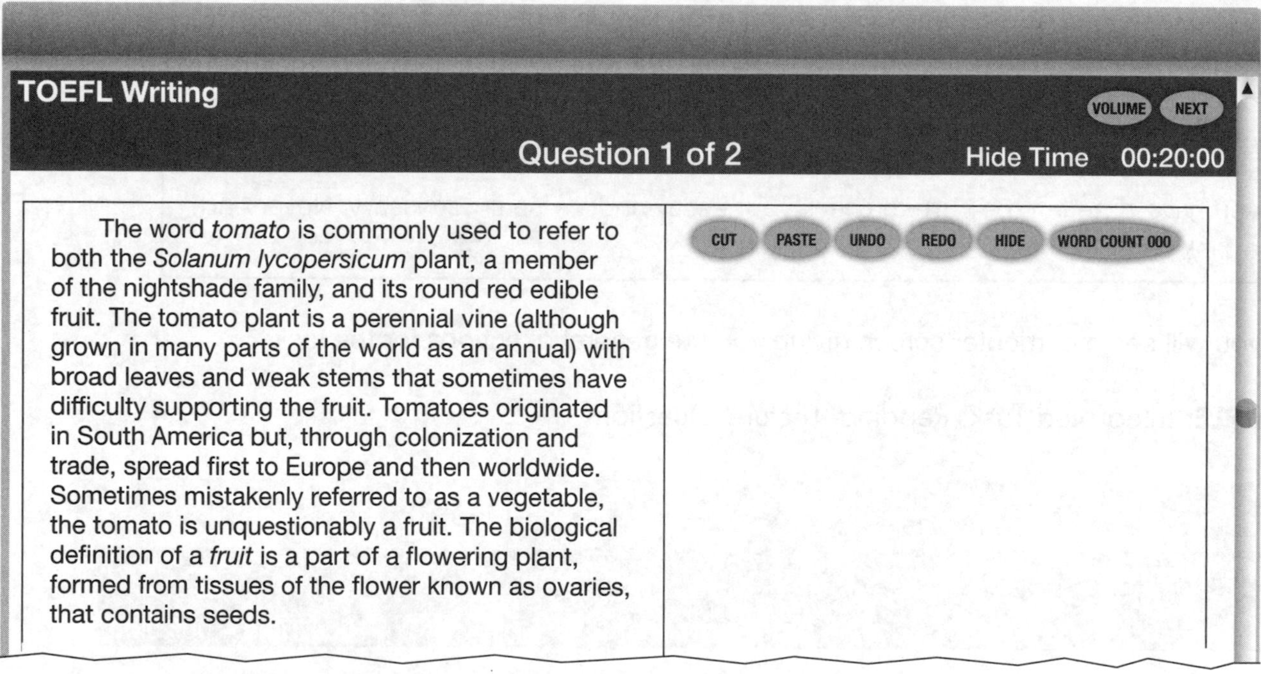

The word *tomato* is commonly used to refer to both the *Solanum lycopersicum* plant, a member of the nightshade family, and its round red edible fruit. The tomato plant is a perennial vine (although grown in many parts of the world as an annual) with broad leaves and weak stems that sometimes have difficulty supporting the fruit. Tomatoes originated in South America but, through colonization and trade, spread first to Europe and then worldwide. Sometimes mistakenly referred to as a vegetable, the tomato is unquestionably a fruit. The biological definition of a *fruit* is a part of a flowering plant, formed from tissues of the flower known as ovaries, that contains seeds.

A clock in the upper right-hand corner of the tool bar at the top of the screen will count down your time.

Although there is no "Save" button, everything you type is being saved. When your time is finished, you will see a notice that says, "Stop writing. Your essay has been saved."

Here are examples of:

1. A reading passage
2. A related lecture
3. A sample prompt
4. A sample response
5. A rater's comments

1. Reading passage:

The word *tomato* is commonly used to refer to both the *Solanum lycopersicum* plant, a member of the nightshade family, and its round red edible fruit. The tomato plant is a perennial vine (although grown in many parts of the world as an annual) with broad leaves and weak stems that sometimes have difficulty supporting the fruit. Tomatoes originated in South America but, through colonization and trade, spread first to Europe and then worldwide. Sometimes mistakenly referred to as a vegetable, the tomato is unquestionably a fruit. The biological definition of a *fruit* is a part of a flowering plant, formed from tissues of the flower known as ovaries, that contains seeds.

Several popular foods commonly considered vegetables, such as pumpkins, cucumbers, and eggplant, are likewise fruit: they develop from the flowers of plants, and they contain seeds. Tomatoes are not as sweet as the fruits typically served for desserts, such as apples or pears, but because they grow in the same way, they are scientifically classified as fruit.

---

2. Related lecture:

Professor: OK, I know it's almost a bit of a joke these days, is the tomato a fruit or a vegetable. But it's actually an interesting philosophical question, and here's why. Now, the textbook passage that you read is correct; we know that *biologically*, yes, it's a fruit—it grows on a plant, it develops from a flower, and it has seeds, all that. *Legally*, though—well, in the United States, that is—the tomato is a vegetable. The U.S. Supreme Court, in fact, ruled in 1893 that the tomato was a vegetable because, at that time, a lot of tomatoes were imported from Mexico, and there was a high tax on fruit imported from Mexico. The United States couldn't get cheap tomatoes unless they were a vegetable. So that legal definition, that had a huge impact on international trade between the two countries, not to mention the restaurant industry, and supermarkets, and what Americans ate. There's also the question of usage. For example . . . well, when you go to the store, where do you find the tomatoes? In the vegetable section. Where are recipes that include tomatoes? In the vegetable section of your cookbook. When do you serve tomatoes, and how? With other vegetables, or often in sauce—think pasta, think pizza—as part of the main course. Most people don't eat tomato ice cream or tomato cake for dessert. The real question, it seems to me, is a philosophical one—what defines an object? Is it biology? Is it the law? Is it usage? Does an object have only one definition? If you eat off a surface, it's a table; if you sit on it, it's a chair. Limiting our outlook to one definition limits the way in which we see, understand, and interact with the world. My answer is, yes, it's a fruit. And, yes, it's a vegetable. Its definition changes depending on the context.

---

3. Sample prompt:

Summarize the points made in the lecture you just heard, explaining how they challenge points made in the reading.

4. Sample response (score: 5):

The lecturer addresses the issue of whether a tomato is a fruit or vegetable by saying the biological definition given in the reading passage, which says the tomato is a fruit, is not sufficient.

The lecturer agrees with the reading by saying that the tomato is biologically a fruit. However, the professor then goes on to point out that the tomato is legally a vegetable in the U.S. because of a court ruling in the 1800s. This legal definition let Americans buy tomatoes from Mexico more cheaply, so it was an important definition.

Furthermore, the professor says that the tomato is treated as a vegetable: It is found in stores and cookbooks with other vegetables, and people cook, serve, and eat the tomato as a vegetable. While the reading does admit the tomato is unlike many other fruits, it doesn't treat this difference as significant, which the lecture does. The lecturer's philosophy is that an object can have more than one meaning.

In conclusion, the lecturer expands the definition of the tomato to include the biological definition presented in the reading and additional definitions from law and common use.

---

5. Rater's comments: The writer did a good job of including all of the lecturer's points, in the order mentioned, with one main point per paragraph. The writer related each point the lecturer made to information in the reading. In addition, the writer provided an excellent summary of the lecture's main point as an introduction, and restated the key differences between the lecture and the reading as a conclusion. Language use was accurate and varied.

EXPRESS TIP

Remember that when the lecturer does not agree with points raised in the reading, you should *not* give your own opinion about which is correct. Just explain the differences.

Writing Skill 1: Outlining the Integrated Response Essay

Because you are summarizing information that you read and that you heard, you do not need to choose your own way to organize the ideas. List them in the order they were presented. A typical outline for this type of essay looks like this:

I. One or two sentences that explain the topic and the main relationship between the lecture and the reading
II. Lecture's first point, and how it relates to the reading
III. Lecture's second point, and how it relates to the reading
(IV.) Lecture's third point, and how it relates to the reading
V. If time—one or two sentences of a conclusion

While it's possible to write your outline on your notepaper, for most people it's quicker and more efficient to type the outline directly onto the computer screen. Leave a few lines between the main points, and then go back and fill in the information. That way, even if you run out of time, your second point is at least written down, and the rater will know that you had the idea, although you may not have fully explained it.

For example, the initial typed outline to respond to the topic of whether the tomato is a fruit or a vegetable could have looked like this:

I. Lecturer addresses debate tomato: fruit or vegetable? by saying the biological definition is not sufficient.

II. Lecturer says tomato is technically a fruit (so reading is correct), but legally a veg. in US.

III. Professor says tomato used as vegetable: stores, cooking. Reading admits tomatoes not like many other fruits, but doesn't address importance.

IV. Lecturer says philosophical issue: objects have more than one kind of definition. Use or function is valid definition. Reading only addresses one type of definition.

V. Conclusion: Lecturer expands concept of tomato by adding more types of definitions to simple biology one presented in reading.

Do not organize your response as first a summary of the reading, and then a summary of the listening. Instead, follow the organization of the lecture, and relate each main point from the lecture to the corresponding point from the reading.

EXPRESS TIP

You will not have time to write long introductions and conclusions. The most important part of this type of essay is the body.

SKILL BUILDER

A. *Read the passage and complete the outline.*

Ask any schoolchild who invented the lightbulb and you'll probably hear "Thomas Edison." However, the truth is more complex. In fact, the first lightbulb was invented by Sir Humphry Davy, an English physician, in 1809—a good seventy years before Edison patented (licensed as intellectual property) his invention. Davy's invention, known at the time as the arc lamp, passed an electrical connection between two charcoal rods connected to a battery, which emitted a bright, though brief, light. Dozens of other inventors tried, with limited success, to improve both the power and the longevity of the lightbulb. Most people don't even remember their names—de la Rue, de Moleyns, Woodward, and Evans—but they all contributed to the development of the electric lightbulb.

The first patent for an incandescent lightbulb was given to Joseph Swan, an English scientist, in 1878—though he had been writing about and publicly demonstrating his inventions at least a decade before that. Edison, who was no doubt aware of Swan's work, patented a very similar bulb in 1879, just one year later. Swan sued Edison for copying his patented invention, and won. In the settlement, Edison was forced to form a partnership with Swan, which they eventually called Ediswan, to manufacture and market the invention in Great Britain.

I. Topic / main idea:
II. First inventor of the lightbulb:
III. Other people's results:
IV. First person to patent the lightbulb:
V. Edison's invention:

B. *Read and listen to the lecture excerpt and complete the outline of the lecture.* 3-24

Professor: So, did Edison invent the lightbulb? It depends on what you mean by "invent," but furthermore, it depends on what you mean by "lightbulb." Now the first person to create a lightbulb that worked was Humphry Davy, in Great Britain, as you read in the article. However, Davy's lightbulb, while it worked, didn't really light—its power output was small, and it didn't last long. So yes, technically it worked, but it wasn't practical; it couldn't be used. Subsequent adjustments by other inventors also had problems—the light wasn't strong enough, their inventions didn't work reliably, or the materials were too expensive. So you could get a glimmer in a lab, but you didn't have an invention anyone could use.

The real challenger to Edison's position as inventor of the lightbulb was Joseph Swan, who patented a very similar bulb a year before Edison patented his invention in 1879—he's the one the article credits as the true inventor. The bulbs were similar enough that Edison lost a lawsuit brought against him by Swan, and the two men went into business together for some years, until Edison bought out Swan's share.

continued . . .

But all this, I think, is missing the most important point—that what Edison really did was to develop and patent a system for the distribution of electrical power. I mean, think about it. If you hold a lightbulb in your hand, nothing happens. No light. You need a system, you need wires and infrastructure. It was Edison's development of the first electrical utility company, which delivered power to businesses and homes, that really earns him the title of the father of the electric light.

I. Edison's importance:

II. Problems with Davy's bulb:

III. Problems with other people's results:

IV. Comparison to Swan:

V. Edison's accomplishment:

Note: You will write an outline for the written response for Skill 2.

EXPRESS TIP

In your introduction, you might want to say that the lecturer agrees with (or disagrees with) some or all of the points in the reading. However, you won't know how the lecturer feels about all points in the reading until you have listened to the whole talk. For this reason, you might complete the first point of your outline—the Introduction—last.

Skill Builder Sample Answers:

A: I. Many contributed to invention of lightbulb.; II. Davy; III. short light; IV. Swan; V. electric lightbulb

B: I. electrical distribution; II. output small and didn't last; III. reliability and lighting poor; IV. similar invention but distribution lacking; V. first electrical utility co.

PRACTICE

A. *Begin reading now. Stop after 3 minutes. Then listen to the lecture.*

The practice of "block scheduling" was one of the principal educational reforms for high schools (and some middle schools) in the United States during the 1990s. Prior to that, a typical high school day was divided into six to eight periods, each lasting about 45 to 50 minutes. A student would have the same classes every day. Under block scheduling, a student has fewer, longer classes each day—for example, four periods of 90 minutes. The next day, the student has different classes, and then alternates every day.

Proponents of block scheduling cite the longer class period as the major advantage. With a 90-minute class, there is more time available to study a subject intensively, and there is also more time for group work, which can be slower and yet (claim some education specialists) more effective for learning. Less time is also lost in changing classrooms between periods. Furthermore, when classes meet every other day, longer homework assignments can be given because students have more time to complete them.

continued . . .

Whether block scheduling has been a successful reform is open to debate. Various studies have found both advantages and disadvantages, and several of the major studies seem to contradict one another. Clearly it is an area in which more research is needed.

B. *Now listen to part of a lecture on the same topic.* 3-25

C. *Now look at the reading again. Use your lecture notes and the reading to write a quick outline for the essay (3–5 minutes).*

D. *Now read the question. Then give yourself 20 minutes to write your response.*

> Summarize the points made in the lecture, being sure to explain how they contradict claims made in the reading passage.

E. *Complete the self-evaluation chart below. How well do you feel you did these things? Rank questions 1–5 from 1 to 5. Then answer questions 6–8.*

Self-Evaluation: Skill 1

	1 = low, 5 = high
1. Understand the reading and the lecture	
2. Take notes on the main ideas and important supporting points in the lecture	
3. Write a quick outline of the main points	
4. Cover each main point of the lecture and the reading	
5. Use correct sentences structures, appropriate vocabulary, good grammar, and a variety of sentence structures	
6. What is something you did especially well?	
7. What one or two things would you like to improve on?	
8. How do you plan to improve those things?	

Writing Skill 2: Integrating Ideas

The essential part of the Integrated Task is just that—the integration. You must show the relationship between the lecture and the reading passage. Make sure that you use clear transitions and signal words to show that you are doing this. Writing *The lecturer says A. The reading passage says B.* is not enough, because it doesn't show that you understand the relationship between the two ideas. This is a similar skill to the one you practiced in Skill 10 of the Speaking section, on pages 209–210.

Introduction: Often it is possible to write a summary sentence as your introduction that shows the comparison or contrast between the two texts, for example:

- *The lecturer* ***challenges the information*** *in the reading passage* ***by relating*** *examples that directly contradict it.*
- *The lecturer* ***supports the information*** *in the reading passage* ***by giving specific examples*** *of the general principles.*
- *In the lecture, the professor* ***responds to the problem*** *raised in the reading passage* ***by offering two solutions.***

Body: Then, in the body paragraphs of your essay, relate the lecture's points to the reading like this:

Purpose	Words and Expressions to Use in Your Response
Using two separate sentences	***The lecturer says that*** *more than one definition of a tomato is needed.* ***The reading refers*** *only to the biological definition.* ***In the reading passage****, only the biological definition of a tomato is given.* ***However, the lecture asserts that*** *more than one definition is important.*
Using one sentence	***The lecturer agrees with*** *the biological definition of the tomato as a fruit* ***as mentioned in the reading.*** ***The lecturer extends*** *the biological definition of the tomato as a fruit* ***by adding*** *definitions drawn from how people use tomatoes.* ***The lecturer challenges*** *the view that the tomato can only be a fruit* ***by arguing that*** *an object is defined by its use.* ***The lecturer contradicts*** *the definition given in the reading* ***by introducing*** *a different one.* ***The lecturer uses examples*** *from other fields* ***to show why he disagrees with*** *the definition in the reading.*

EXPRESS TIP

To make a quick conclusion, rephrase the idea that you used for your introduction.

SKILL BUILDER

A. *Read the text from the previous Skill Builder again.*

Ask any schoolchild who invented the lightbulb and you'll probably hear "Thomas Edison." However, the truth is more complex. In fact, the first lightbulb was invented by Sir Humphry Davy, an English physician, in 1809—a good seventy years before Edison patented (licensed as intellectual property) his invention. Davy's invention, known at the time as the arc lamp, passed an electrical connection between two charcoal rods connected to a battery, which emitted a bright, though brief, light. Dozens of other inventors tried, with limited success, to improve both the power and the longevity of the lightbulb. Most people don't even remember their names—de la Rue, de Moleyns, Woodward, and Evans—but they all contributed to the development of the electric lightbulb.

The first patent for an incandescent lightbulb was given to Joseph Swan, an English scientist, in 1878—though he had been writing about and publicly demonstrating his inventions at least a decade before that. Edison, who was no doubt aware of Swan's work, patented a very similar bulb in 1879, just one year later. Swan sued Edison for copying his patented invention, and won. In the settlement, Edison was forced to form a partnership with Swan, which they eventually called Ediswan, to manufacture and market the invention in Great Britain.

B. *Then listen to the lecture excerpt and take notes.* 3-26

C. *Work with a partner. Compare your lecture notes and your reading notes. Then complete the outline for a written response.*

I. Introduction: Edison's importance

II. Davy's bulb

A. Point from the reading:

B. Lecturer's response:

III. Other inventors

A. Point from the reading:

B. Lecturer's response:

IV. Swan

A. Point from the reading:

B. Lecturer's response:

V. Edison's most important contribution:

D. *Work with a partner. Write sentences using the language in the chart on page 261 to compare the lecture to reading for parts II, II, and IV of the outline.*

Skill Builder Sample Answers:

C: I. Introduction: Edison's importance

II. Davy's bulb
  - A. Point from the reading: Many inventors contributed
  - B. Lecturer's response: Yes, but it was all about distribution

III. Other inventors
  - A. Point from the reading: Good efforts though light wasn't bright
  - B. Lecturer's response: Tried, but products not reliable

IV. Swan
  - A. Point from the reading: First patent for lightbulb
  - B. Lecturer's response: Similar patent and won lawsuit

V. Edison's most important contribution: Created electric utility co.

PRACTICE

A. *Begin reading now. Stop after 3 minutes. Then listen to the lecture.*

The old adage "Drink eight glasses of water a day" may not, in fact, be true, in spite of being long recommended as a sound, healthful practice for just about every adult, with the understanding that certain types of people, such as athletes and those who spend time outdoors in hot climates, might need to take in even more water. Interestingly, the original source of this advice is not known. It may have started as folklore, or the original medical study that came to this conclusion may somehow have been lost or forgotten. But the phrase "eight of eight" (where one glass of water = eight ounces) lives on.

What is certain, however, is that many Americans are chronically dehydrated. An average adult loses about ten glasses of water a day; but then the equivalent of about four glasses of water are gained each day through the fluids found in food. Therefore, the actual shortage that a person must make up each day is closer to six glasses. Furthermore, overconsumption of beverages containing caffeine, such as coffee, tea, and sodas, leads to a loss of water. Exercising can cause a further loss of water through sweat. Dehydration in turn leads to poor skin tone, weak muscles, and even weight gain.

B. *Now listen to part of a lecture on the same topic.* 3-27

C. *Work with a partner. Compare your lecture notes and your reading notes. Discuss how the information in the lecture relates to the information in the reading.*

D. *Now look at the reading again. Use your lecture notes and the reading to write a quick outline for the essay (3–5 minutes).*

E. *Now read the question. Give yourself 20 minutes to write your response.*

Summarize the points made in the lecture, being sure to explain how they challenge information presented in the reading passage.

F. *Complete the self-evaluation chart below. How well do you feel you did these things? Rank questions 1–7 from 1 to 5. Then answer questions 8–10.*

Self-Evaluation: Skill 2

	1 = low, 5 = high
1. Understand the reading and the lecture	
2. Take notes on the main ideas and important supporting points in the lecture	
3. Write a quick outline of the main points	
4. Cover each main point of the lecture and the reading	
5. Connect the lecture points to the reading points with specific language to show the relationship	
6. Write a brief introduction and conclusion	
7. Use correct sentences structures, appropriate vocabulary, good grammar, and a variety of sentence structures	
8. What is something you did especially well?	
9. What one or two things would you like to improve on?	
10. How do you plan to improve those things?	

EXPRESS TIP

Remember that 20 minutes is a very short time. Your introduction and conclusion should be very brief—even one sentence is OK. Spend most of your time on the body of your essay.

SKILLS REVIEW

Independent Writing Skills 1 and 2 for Task 1, Integrated Skills Essay: Outlining the Integrated Response Essay and Integrating Ideas

A. *Begin reading now. Stop after 3 minutes. Then listen to the lecture.*

Predicting the future is not a perfect science. However, analyzing a set of data over a given period of time reveals trends; and the reasonable prediction to be made in journalism does not hold good news for the newspaper—that is, the actual paper newspaper. In fact, some industry analysts predict that the last physical newspapers will be delivered around the year 2040.

continued . . .

Circulation of daily newspapers has been declining for more than two decades. Small-town newspapers have run out of money and gone out of business. Larger newspapers are becoming smaller—fewer pages, and narrower pages, desperately trying to save money. Customers are turning instead to online news, which is not only cheaper, but free in many cases. With a choice of paying for a physical paper or not paying for the electronic version of the same paper, it's easy to see why customers are going online. Furthermore, electronic news is seen as easier to access, easier to customize, and more up-to-date. There's greater variety of reporting, too—not just traditional news sources, but a host of independent bloggers. With the increase in devices that deliver electronic content, such as smart phones, e-readers, and tablet computers, there is no evidence this downward trend will stop or even slow.

B. *Now listen to part of a lecture on the same topic.* 3-28

C. *Now read the question. Then give yourself 20 minutes to write your response.*

Summarize the points made in the lecture, being sure to explain how they challenge predictions made in the reading passage.

D. *Complete the self-evaluation chart below. How well do you feel you did these things? Rank questions 1–7 from 1 to 5. Then answer questions 8–10.*

Self-Evaluation: Review of Skills 1 and 2

	1 = low, 5 = high
1. Understand the reading and the lecture	
2. Take notes on the main ideas and important supporting points in the lecture	
3. Write a quick outline of the main points	
4. Cover each main point of the lecture and the reading	
5. Connect the lecture points to the reading points with specific language to show the relationship	
6. Write a brief introduction and conclusion	
7. Use correct sentences structures, appropriate vocabulary, good grammar, and a variety of sentence structures	
8. What is something you did especially well?	
9. What one or two things would you like to improve on?	
10. How do you plan to improve those things?	

INDEPENDENT TASK 2
OPINION–PREFERENCE

Skills 3, 4, and 5: Outlining the Independent Essay; Organizing the Introduction and Conclusion; Using Transitions to Connect Ideas in the Body of the Essay

The second task in the Writing section, the opinion–preference task, requires you to write an essay based on your *own personal* ideas, experiences, or opinions. It is similar to the Independent Speaking Task 2 (see pages 168–180). The essay question asks you to:

- give your opinion about a specific statement or choose **one** of two or more possible actions or situations
- provide detailed support for your opinion or preference by explaining the reasons for your choice and by using specific examples

The questions are about familiar topics. Some of these topics are about student or university-related issues, while others are more general. Sometimes the statement you are asked to write about will be a famous quote or a popular saying.

You will both hear the question and see it on the computer screen. The following are examples of this type of question:

- *Do you agree or disagree with the following statement? Teenagers should **not** be allowed to have a job while they are still students. Use specific reasons and examples to support your opinion.*
- *Some people prefer to take trains or subways when they commute to work. Other people like to take buses to get to their jobs. Which do you prefer? Use specific reasons and examples to support your choice.*
- *Is it better to work for a large company or is it better to work for a small company? Use specific reasons and examples to support your opinion.*
- *What do you think is the **most** important quality a person needs to work effectively in a group: open-mindedness, respect for others, or problem-solving abilities? Choose one quality and use specific reasons and examples to support your choice.*
- *It has recently been announced that a large shopping center will be built in your neighborhood. Do you support or oppose this plan? Why? Use specific reasons and examples to support your answer.*
- *"All life is an experiment. The more experiments you make, the better." Do you agree or disagree with this quotation from the American writer Ralph Waldo Emerson? Use specific reasons and examples to support your position.*
- *Many people today are concerned about the damage humans have done to the Earth. What do you think can be done to help create a better and cleaner environment? Use specific reasons and examples to support your answer.*

Note the following points for Task 2:

- You will have 30 minutes to plan, write, and revise your essay.
- You must type your essay directly on the computer screen.
- Essays that receive the highest scores are typically about 300 words long.

In order to answer the question correctly, you must:

- Read the prompt carefully; make sure you *completely* understand the question.
- Organize your essay well. Quickly make a short outline first, writing down only words or short phrases about the most important points that support the opinion or preference you have chosen. Simple outlines are taught in Writing Skill 3.
- Clearly state your opinion or preference at the beginning of your written response.
- Support your opinion or preference with at least two reasons, making sure they relate directly to the question.
- Include relevant examples from your personal life that support your opinion or preference.
- Develop a logical flow of information, from sentence to sentence and from paragraph to paragraph, by using transitions (*the first reason*, *the second reason*, *in addition*, *however*, *on the other hand*, *because*, *not only/but also*, and *for example*).
- Use a variety of sentence structures from simple to complex.
- Use correct sentence structures, appropriate vocabulary, and good grammar.
- Always check and revise your essay after you have finished.

EXPRESS TIP

It is important that you use the time given for writing the essay wisely. You have 30 minutes, so you may want to divide your time this way:

5 minutes = creating a brief outline for the essay
20 minutes = writing the essay
5 minutes = revising the essay

Look at this example of an opinion–preference question on a computer screen.

EXAMPLE: Independent Task: Opinion–Preference Question

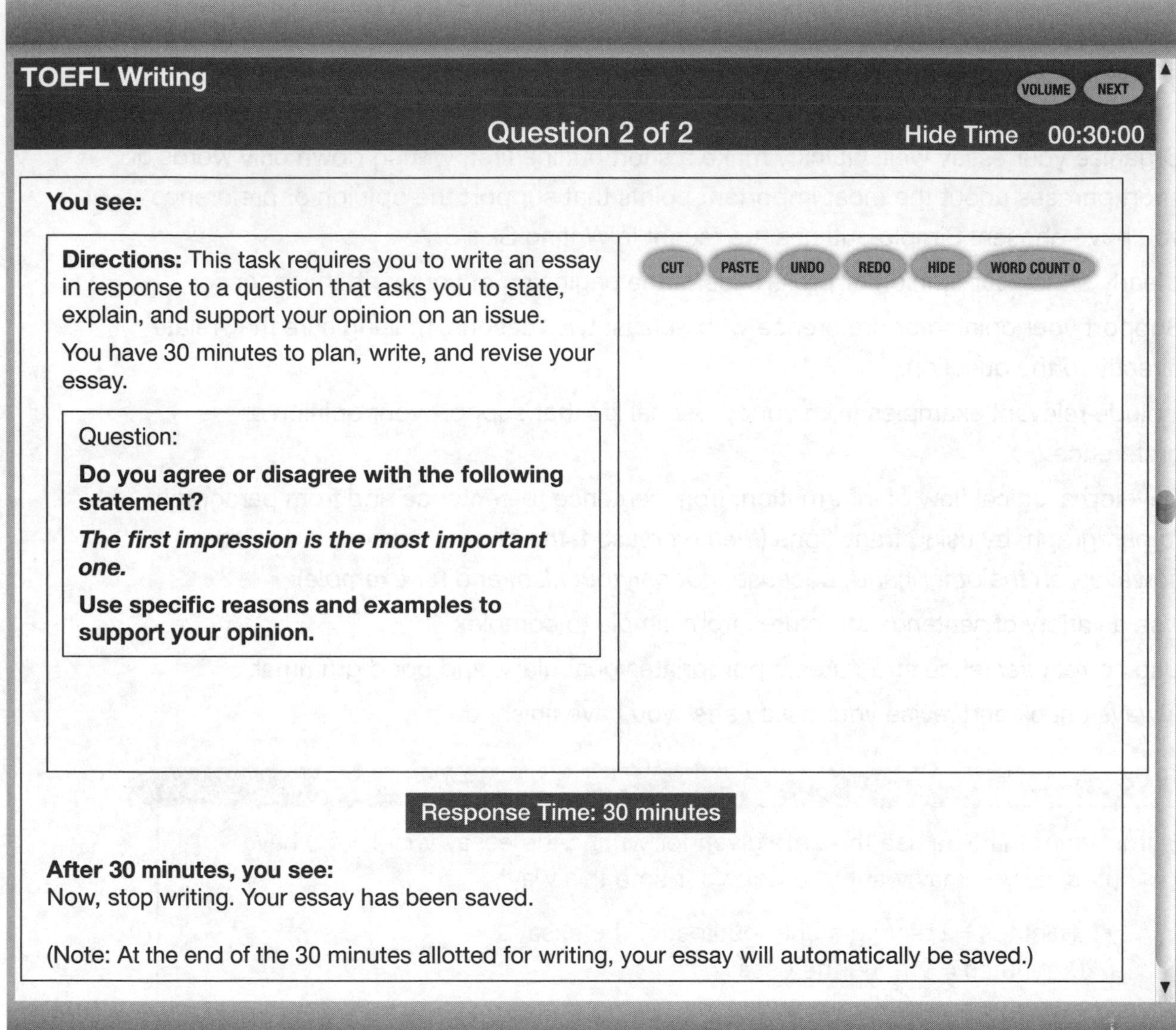

TOEFL Writing
VOLUME
NEXT
Question 2 of 2
Hide Time 00:30:00
You see:
CUT
PASTE
UNDO
REDO
HIDE
WORD COUNT 0
Directions: This task requires you to write an essay in response to a question that asks you to state, explain, and support your opinion on an issue.
You have 30 minutes to plan, write, and revise your essay.
Question:
Do you agree or disagree with the following statement?
The first impression is the most important one.
Use specific reasons and examples to support your opinion.
Response Time: 30 minutes
After 30 minutes, you see:
Now, stop writing. Your essay has been saved.
(Note: At the end of the 30 minutes allotted for writing, your essay will automatically be saved.)

EXAMPLE ESSAY RESPONSES, SCORES, AND SCORE EXPLANATIONS

Work with a partner. Read the essay responses to the question above and look at the scores for each response (1 is the lowest rating and 5 is the highest) and the explanations. Discuss the reasons for the scores and how you might change the responses.

EXPRESS TIP

Remember to indent 5 spaces when you start a new paragraph (see example essays on pages 269–270). This signals to the raters that you are moving to a new topic. You may also skip a line between paragraphs if you prefer.

Answer A = Score: 5

In my opinion, first impressions are extremely important because they establish the basis for whether or not we have successful relationships with people in many aspects of our lives. How we first perceive someone or how someone first feels about us affects us socially, academically, and professionally.

Many new and interesting people may come into our lives and we may only have one chance to create good impressions that lead to a lasting and positive relationship. Therefore, we should always try, no matter how bad we might be feeling or how unpleasant the situation is, to put our best foot forward. If we don't, we could miss the chance to have special and lifelong friendships.

Not only is making a good impression in our social life important personally, but it is also essential for educational success. In my own experience, I always try to be polite and respecting of my professors from the minute I join a class. I believe that this has resulted in professors giving me extra time to discuss my problems. And I also think it helped me to persuade a professor to let me into a class that was already full.

Finally, almost all people will have to interview for a job at some point in their lives. The interview is the only opportunity you have to impress a potential employer. During the interview, the employer will be asking himself, "What kind of a person is this guy? Would he be a good worker?" So, obviously, you need to make an excellent first impression by dressing up well and speaking intelligently if you want to get the job from the other competers.

Because I believe that making a good first impression has significant consequences in all aspects of your life—in social, academic, and workplace relationships—I always try to be on my best behavior the first time I meet or deal with other people.

This response would get a score of 5 because the student directly stated an opinion and provided the reasons for it in the introduction. This helps the rater anticipate the organization of the essay. The student made very few grammatical or vocabulary mistakes ("competers" should be "competitors"). The sentence structures are complex and varied, and the vocabulary is appropriate and sophisticated. Further, the use of questions ("What kind of person is this guy?") demonstrates high-level writing skill. While the essay is not perfect in every way, it is coherent and progresses smoothly with good use of transitions. It is clear from the amount of detail that the student had a good grasp of the question. The student also did a good job of using idiomatic language ("put our best foot forward"). The essay is longer than 300 words, which is quite acceptable because the student made excellent use of the time allowed for the essay response.

Answer B = Score: 3

It is human nature for judge other people from what we think about them when we meet them for the first time. That may not be fair, but it's true.

Firstly, most of us enjoys meeting new people and forming new friendships. When my best friend introduced me to his new girlfriend, she didn't join in the conversation at all. I thought she was with her nose in the air. I avoided seeing my best friend when he was with her for a long time. Later, I find out she is really shy and is actually a sweet person. My first impression wasn't true in this case, but this is how strongly we judge people the first time we meet them.

Secondly, teacher and other students make impressions of you on first site and this can make your school years wonderful or terrible. For example, there was this new guy that came to class dressed in punky clothes. The teacher didn't like him because he never asked questions to him. The other students thought he looked a little dangerous and he was not popular at the school.

Thirdly, first impressions can also effect your employee potentials. You might talk to new customers in an inappropriate way when you have a bad mood one day at work. It will hurt the business. And this will not make your boss very happy to lose new customers.

In conclusion, first impressions are important for many things we do. Therefore, you should always try to make a good first impression because if you don't, you will find that it can cause you less success and happiness.

This response would get a score of 3 because the student attempted to use some appropriate vocabulary and tried somewhat to develop the topic. However, the essay lacks coherence because the student does not clearly state an opinion in the introductory paragraph; the student begins by saying that judging by first impressions is unfair, but true. It isn't until later in the essay that it is clear the student agrees that a first impression is important. This is confusing to the rater. In addition, there are some basic transitions that connect ideas, but occasionally a necessary transitional signal is missing. The student is inconsistent in terms of proper grammatical and vocabulary usage (the present tense verb, "find out," should be in the past tense, "found out," and the noun "effect" should be the verb "affect"). There are minor structural errors and errors in the use of idiom (". . . she was with her nose in the air" should be "she had her nose in the air," meaning "thinks too highly of one's self"). Finally, the essay is nearly 300 words long; therefore, while there are problems with this essay, the student did try to make reasonable use of the time allowed for the essay response.

Answer C = Score: 2

Like the question say, first impression are important. I think peoples always like or don't like you quick when the first time you meet so impresion is very important. It's not so good that people are this way, but it is the true thing in our lives and we have to understand it.

If someone don't like you it's bad thing for you. And maybe you don't like someone because they just having a bad time that day, but that's not good too. The person might be really nice as useal, but not on one day or something. Friendships are important for us, so we should have good first impression to others too. I have friends I liked right away because they tried to make a good impression and they are my friends forever. They are good people you would like.

First impression is important is that it will help you in school with the teachers. Teachers want to give more help to student they think is good student that is trying hard to study well. Other student will not pick you for teams sometimes because they don't like you on the first day of school because maybe they got the wrong idea about you.

So, for all these reasons, I think the first impression is the most important.

This essay would get score of 2 because, while the student does make some points and provide examples about friendship and school, they are not well developed. The essay has many redundancies (the student repeats the same information again without adding new information). The student also digresses (gets away from the main topic: "I have friends I liked right away and they are my friends forever. *They are good people you would like.*"). In addition, the student's vocabulary is very limited, there are many basic vocabulary and grammatical mistakes, and the sentence structures are not varied and too simple. There are basic spelling mistakes: "impresion" (impression) and "useal" (usual). The response lacks coherence; one idea does not relate smoothly to another because there is little or no use of transitional signals. Both the introduction and conclusion are weak; the introduction is redundant and does little to grab the attention of the rater, and the conclusion is far too simple and does not properly summarize the student's main points. Finally, the essay is only about 200 words long; therefore, the student did not make good use of the time allowed for the essay response.

EXPRESS TIP

Unity is a key element that the raters will be looking for in your essay. Unity means that the main points you make in the essay must relate directly to the question and to your opinion or preference. For example, you should not digress or go off topic and write about something that does not support the topic and your opinion. (See the score rating explanation for Answer C in the "Example Essay Responses, Scores, and Score Explanations" above for an example of a digression.)

Writing Skill 3: Outlining the Independent Essay

The outlining format for Independent Task 2 is different from the Integrated Task 1. In Task 1 you must outline what the professor says in the lecture; the organization is provided for you. However, in Task 2, you must come up with your outline. There are different styles of outlining you will need to use for Independent Task 2 depending on the topic in the prompt.

Outlining based on reasons for your opinion:

I. **Brief Introduction:** your opinion about the question

II. **Reason #1**—first reason to support your opinion and any examples that support the opinion you have chosen

III. **Reason #2**—second reason to support your opinion and supporting examples

IV. **Reason #3**—third reason to support your opinion and supporting examples

V. **Brief Conclusion:** paraphrase, or summarize the reasons for your opinion

Outlining based on advantages and/or disadvantages of the choices:

In addition to creating an outline to organize your essay according to the reasons that support your opinion or preference, some essay question topics may require you to make an outline according to the advantages and/or disadvantages.

I. Introduction: advantages to both choices, but choice #2 is better **II. Advantages of choice #1 + examples** **III. Advantages of choice #2 + reasons & examples for choosing choice #2** **IV. Conclusion:** paraphrase, or summarize advantages of choice #2 and your reasons for choosing it	**I. Introduction:** disadvantages of choice #1 & advantages of choice #2, so you prefer choice #2 **II. Disadvantages of choice #1 + examples** **III. Advantages of choice #2 + reasons & examples for choosing choice #2** **IV. Conclusion:** paraphrase, or summarize advantages of choice #2

SKILL BUILDER

A. *Read the following question. Then fill in the outline in the blanks provided below. (Save your outline notes to use in the Skill Builder activity for Skill 4.)*

Question: Do you agree or disagree with the following statement? **The first impression is the most important one.** Use specific reasons and examples to support your opinion.

I. Introduction: [your opinion (OP)] OP – ______________________________

____

II. [reason #1] R1– ______________________________

____

III. [reason #2] R2– ______________________________

____

IV. [reason #3] R3– ______________________________

____

V. Conclusion: [OP / paraphrase or summarize R1–R3] CCL – ______________________________

____

B. *Work with a partner. Compare your outlines. What is similar and what is different?*

C. *Read the following question. Then fill in the outline in the blanks provided below.*

Question: Is it better to work for a large company or is it better to work for a small company? Use specific reasons and examples to support your opinion.

[Note: The opinion ("It is better to work for a small company") has been chosen for you in the outline below; however, you can choose to support the opposite opinion ("Working for a large company is better") if you wish.]

I. Introduction: [sm co more advantages than lrg co] ____________________

____

II. [advantages of lrg co] adv lrg co + [examples] ex – ____________________

____

III. [advantages of sm co] adv sm co + [reasons and examples for sm co] r & ex sm co –

____

____

IV. Conclusion: [paraphrase / summarize advantages of sm co w/ reasons for] CCL –

____

D. *Work with a partner. Compare your outlines. What is similar and what is different?*

EXPRESS TIP

Type your outline directly in the space provided on the computer screen for your essay instead of writing it on the paper that is provided for you during the test. Leave a few lines between each part of your outline, and then go back and fill in the information. This will make it easier and faster for you to write your essay.

Skill Builder Sample Answers: (Please see "Note-Taking Skills" on pages 87–91 for more information on symbols and abbreviations.)

A: (This is only an example; answers will vary based on your individual opinion and experience.)

I. Introduction OP– 1st impress = very imprt b/c base of success relatnshps
II. R1– social – make new frds –spcl/lng frdshps
III. R2– university – imprt fr academ success § support from prof ex: give ++ time § get into clss
IV. R3– work –1 chance to impress @job interview, bad impress → no job
V. Conclusion CCL– 1st impress – only 1 get = affect future frndshps, school § career

C: (This is only an example; answers will vary based on your individual opinion and experience.)

I. Intro: advs lrg co & sm co– lrg co= some advs, but sm co = many too, sm co better
II. adv lrg co– ++ salary, ++ benefit (health insure) § ++ resources → human resource dept. – help w/benefit and career
III. adv sm co– sm = ++chance 2 b noticed → faster promo § $ raises, not enough skill, but do many dif project → ++experience = get better skills
IV. r & ex sm co– ex: personally = not much wrk experience – sm co better 4 me b/c learn more, faster
IV. Conclusion: CCL– lrg co advs = +++salary § ++benefits § resources, but sm have better advs, but b/c young § inexperienced, sm co better 4 me to get ++experience § improve skills

(Note: Here is an example of an alternative outlining according to advantages and disadvantages for the same question as addressed in the outline in C above.)

I. **Intro:** sm co ++disads, but lrg co has ++ads, prefer lrg co

II. disadv of sm co = ↓salary, ↓ benefits § ↓job positions to be promote 2

III. advs of lrg co = ++salary, ++benefits § ++ jobs 2 be promote 2
r & ex lrg co = lrg co better 4 me b/c ++stdt loans 2 pay bck after grad ∴ want make ++$ @job, want family in future ∴ med. benefits § promo imprt

IV. **Conclusion:** CCL– sm = ++ disadvs, but lrg co = better b/c $$, benefit § opportunity 4 promote 2 pay loans quick § 4 ++secure future]

PRACTICE

A. *Read the prompts carefully to make sure you understand the questions completely.*

B. *Choose one opinion or preference for each question and be sure to provide at least three points to support it. Create an outline for each question on a separate piece of paper for each question.* ***Save your outlines as you will need to refer to them for Skills 4 and 5.***

1. Some people prefer to take trains or subways when they commute to work. Other people like to take buses to get to their jobs. Which do you prefer? Use specific reasons and examples to support your choice. (*Hint:* Think about organizing your outline according to the advantages or the disadvantages of each choice.)
2. Do you agree or disagree with the following statement? **The best things in life are free.** Use specific reasons and examples to support your opinion.
3. Many people today are concerned about the damage humans have done to the Earth. What do you think can be done to help create a better and cleaner environment? Use specific reasons and examples to support your answer.

C. *Work with a partner. Read and compare your outlines. How are they different? How are they the same?*

D. *Complete the chart below. How well do you feel you did these things? Rank questions 1–5 from 1 to 5. Then answer questions 6–8.*

Self-Evaluation: Skill 3

	1 = low, 5 = high
1. Understand the prompts	
2. Include your opinion or preference or whether you will write about the advantages and/or disadvantages of each choice in your outline introductions	
3. Include three reasons and advantages and/or disadvantages in your outlines	
4. Include examples or personal experiences in your outlines	
5. Include a paraphrase or a summary of the main points in your outline conclusions	
6. What is something you did especially well?	

continued . . .

7. What one or two things would you like to improve on?
8. How do you plan to improve those things?

Writing Skill 4: Organizing the Introduction and Conclusion

An essay that receives the best score on the TOEFL iBT Test should include an introduction and conclusion. However, it is extremely important that you keep the introduction and the conclusion very brief: two or three sentences. The majority of your essay should focus on supporting your opinion or preference with reasons and examples.

Because conclusions generally paraphrase or summarize the introduction, they are being addressed here together.

INTRODUCTION

Begin your essay by stating your opinion or preference and explaining clearly what you plan to discuss so the raters will have a "road map" to guide them through your essay.

This will also help *you* to stay organized and focused on the points you will be discussing.

See Speaking Skill 4, pages 171–172 and Speaking Skill 12, pages 223–224 for more information on using the following expressions to state opinions and preferences:

In my opinion . . .
From my point of view / In my view . . .
I agree / disagree with . . .
I prefer . . .
I believe . . .
I think . . .
I feel that . . .

Note that the superlative forms of adjectives can be used to indicate which choice you prefer:

In my opinion, X is *the adjective + ~est* (*best, worst*) choice because . . .
I believe that X is *the most adjective* (*important, intelligent*) choice because . . .

The following examples are based on the prompt from the computer screen example above:

Do you agree or disagree with the following statement? ***The first impression is the most important one.*** *Use specific reasons and examples to support your opinion.*

Purpose	Examples
Provide a **general statement** of the reasons you will write about to support your opinion or preference:	***In my opinion,*** *first impressions are extremely important because they can significantly affect our relationships with people in many aspects of our lives.*
Provide a **specific list** or **summary** of the two or three reasons you will write about to support your opinion or preference:	***I completely agree that*** *a first impression is the most significant one. How we first perceive someone or how someone first feels about us affects us socially, academically, and professionally.*

continued . . .

Purpose	Examples
Provide a brief statement about **the disadvantages of the other side of the issue** as a way of indicating why you prefer one choice or the other and will be discussing your preference:	***I strongly believe that*** *first impressions are the most powerful ones. Some people think that this isn't true because they believe you can change someone's first impression later. However, in many situations, you only have one opportunity to make an impression and it will be the one that stays in other people's mind forever.*
Try to include an engaging first sentence that gets the raters' attention and makes them want to read your essay. This is not absolutely necessary, but it may raise your score as long as the sentence clearly relates to your opinion or preference. You can use your personal experience or knowledge.	
Use your personal experience:	*A few years ago, I was twenty minutes late for a job interview. When the interview finally started, the person interviewing me said, "Being late for your job interview does not make a very good impression." She was right because I didn't get the job.* ***So, in my own personal experience****, first impressions really do count!*

CONCLUSION

Conclude your essay by briefly paraphrasing or summarizing the main reasons for your opinion or preference. It is perfectly acceptable to refer back to the information you included in your introduction as long as you restate it in different words.

Use the following expressions to signal your conclusion:

In conclusion, . . .
To summarize, . . .
In summary, . . .
For the following reasons, 1, 2, and 3, I have come to the conclusion that . . .
Although X does have some advantages / benefits, I disagree with / I prefer Y because . . .

Purpose	Examples
Paraphrase:	***In conclusion****, first impressions can make the difference between creating good relationships or bad relationships with people in all parts of our lives.*
Summary:	***In summary****, a first impression is definitely the most significant one because it has the ability to shape forever our social, academic, and professional lives.*
Reference to personal information in the introduction:	***Although*** *some people believe first impressions aren't that important,* ***I strongly disagree****. Making a negative first impression has taught me personally that it can result in something as serious as not getting a job you really want.*

EXPRESS TIP

- Do **not** try to define or explain the question in your introduction; it has already been described in the prompt.
- Do **not** introduce new information in your conclusion that is not related to reasons and examples you provided for your opinion or preference in your essay.

SKILL BUILDER

A. *Read the following questions (they are the same ones from Skill 3, Practice). Use your outlines from Skill 3, Practice to write an introduction and a conclusion for an essay based on the questions. Be sure to use the information and expressions from the charts above. If possible, add your own personal experience.* ***Save your introductions and conclusions as you will need to refer to them for Skill 5.***

1. Some people prefer to take trains or subways when they commute to work. Other people like to take buses to get to their jobs. Which do you prefer? Use specific reasons and examples to support your choice.

Introduction:	**Conclusion:**

2. Do you agree or disagree with the following statement? **The best things in life are free.** Use specific reasons and examples to support your opinion.

Introduction:	**Conclusion:**

3. Many people today are concerned about the damage humans have done to the Earth. What do you think can be done to help create a better and cleaner environment? Use specific reasons and examples to support your answer.

Introduction:	**Conclusion:**

B. *Work with a partner. Read and compare your introductions and conclusions.*

EXPRESS TIP

Do **not** write a long introduction or conclusion that uses up your time but does not provide necessary or relevant information.

Skill Builder Sample Answers:

1. **Introduction:** *When I got a part-time job in a city near my town last summer, I tried taking both the subway and the buses to work. I can definitely say that I prefer to take the subway because it has so many more advantages than riding on the city buses.*
Conclusion: *In summary, I would much rather take the subway than a bus because I know it provides more options and means getting to work faster in a cleaner environment.*

2. **Introduction:** *Many people spend all of their time and energy trying to make as much money as they possibly can, but it doesn't always bring them happiness or success. They are so busy working that they forget that some of the best things in life—love, friendship, and peace of mind—are free.*
Conclusion: *In conclusion, having the love of our family, supportive friendships, and peace of mind are not things that money can buy. Therefore, I strongly agree that the best things are free because they lead to happiness and success in way that money just can't.*

3. **Introduction:** *While stopping the destruction of our environment is a complicated and global issue, each one of us has the power to help save our planet. We can start in small and practical ways in our daily lives by doing simple things, such as walking more, recycling, and doing volunteer clean-up work.*
Conclusion: *Although reversing the course of environmental destruction will require global governmental and business solutions, if we all work together on a personal and local level by getting out of our cars and walking, recycling, and volunteering to clean up, we can begin to save the Earth for future generations.*

PRACTICE

A. *Read the prompts and make brief outline notes on a separate piece of paper for each one.*

B. *Then* ***write introductions and conclusions*** *for the questions in the prompts on a separate piece of paper. Use the information and expressions from Skill 4.*

1. Do you agree or disagree with the following statement? **All textbooks should be available online.** Use specific reasons and examples to support your opinion.
2. Some people prefer to eat only organic fruit and vegetables grown without chemicals. Other people care more about getting the best price for their produce. Which do you think is better? Use specific reasons and examples to support your answer.
3. What is the **most** important skill students need to succeed at a university and obtain a degree? Choose **one** skill and use specific reasons and examples to support your choice.

C. *Work with a partner. Read and compare your introductions and conclusions. How are they different? How are they the same?*

D. *Complete the self-evaluation chart below. How well do you feel you did these things? Rank questions 1–6 from 1 to 5. Then answer questions 7–9.*

Self-Evaluation: Skill 4

	1 = low, 5 = high
1. State your opinion or preference or advantages and/or disadvantages in the introductions using appropriate expressions	
2. State clearly what you plan to discuss in the introductions	
3. Include personal information to engage the raters in your introductions	
4. Briefly paraphrase, or summarize the main reasons for your opinion or preference in your conclusions	
5. Use the appropriate expressions for signaling your conclusions.	
6. Refer to personal information in your conclusions	
7. What is something you did especially well?	
8. What one or two things would you like to improve on?	
9. How do you plan to improve those things?	

EXPRESS TIP

Remember to start each paragraph in the body of your essay with a good topic sentence. A topic sentence should clearly state what the paragraph is going to be about, and it should create a smooth transition from one paragraph to another.

Writing Skill 5: Using Transitions to Connect Ideas in the Body of the Essay

Your Independent essay will be rated, in part, on how well it is organized, and how smoothly and logically it moves from one point to the next. If there are no clear or appropriate connections between your ideas, it will make the body of your essay unclear and confusing to the raters. This will result in a lower score. Therefore, it is essential to use transitions to connect your ideas.

When writing the body of your essay, use specific transitional words and expressions for connecting the paragraphs and main points in your essay:

Purpose	Transitional Words and Expressions	Examples
Moving from the first, to the second, and to the last supporting reasons	*first, my first reason is, in the first place, to begin with* *second, the second reason is* *third, the next point is* *finally, my last reason is*	Paragraph 1: ***To begin with***, *first impressions determine future friendships.* Paragraph 2: ***The second reason*** *I believe first impressions are so important is that they help to determine academic success.* Paragraph 3: ***Finally***, *how someone perceives you the first time they meet you in the workplace will affect your career.*
Introducing and adding new information	*not only, but also* *in addition, furthermore, also, as well as*	Paragraph 1: *First impressions are extremely important in our social lives.* Paragraph 2: ***Not only*** *do first impressions matter in our social life,* ***but*** *they* ***also*** *have an important impact in our academic lives.* Paragraph 3: ***In addition***, *if the person who interviews you for a job has a bad impression of you, you probably won't get the job.*
Showing contrast and comparison between main ideas (See Integrated Task 4 on pages 274–276 for more information on contrast and comparison.)	**contrast:** *although, even though, instead, unlike, in contrast / contrary to, on the other hand, however* **comparison:** *like, the same as / in the same way, equally, similar to / similarly, as well as, more [adjective] than / [adjective + ~er], the most [adjective] / the [adjective + ~est]*	Paragraph 1: *First impressions are extremely important in our social lives.* Paragraph 2: *Making a good first impression in your academic life is essential* ***in the same way*** *that it is when you meet people for the first time.* Paragraph 3: ***Although*** *first impressions matter in both our social and academic lives, they are even* ***more important*** *for our future careers.*

continued . . .

Purpose	Transitional Words and Expressions	Examples
Providing examples	*for instance, for example, let me give you an example, here's a case in point:*	Paragraph 1: *First impressions are extremely important in our social lives.* ***For example,*** *the first time I met someone who is now my best friend, I was in a bad mood, so she didn't like me at all. It took me a long time to persuade her that I wasn't a bad person.* Paragraph 2: *Making a good first impression in your academic life is essential.* ***Here's a case in point:*** *Because I was polite and respectful of my English professor in the first class I took from her, she allowed me to enroll in another one of her classes the next semester that was already full.* Paragraph 3: *Furthermore, first impressions can also affect your potential employment.* ***For instance,*** *if you communicate with customers in an inappropriate way, it could have a very negative impact on the business you work for and that could mean losing your job.*
Showing results or what happens because of a specific event or action	*as a result,* *therefore* *consequently / as a consequence* *and so*	Paragraph 1: *First impressions are extremely important in our social lives;* ***therefore,*** *we should all remember to "put our best foot forward" when we meet new people.* Paragraph 2: ***As a result*** *of making a good first impression with your classmates, you will benefit from their willingness to cooperate in group projects.* Paragraph 3: *Furthermore, first impressions can also affect your potential employment. For instance, if you communicate with customers in an inappropriate way, it could have a very negative impact on business.* ***Consequently,*** *that could lead to being fired from your job.*

EXPRESS TIP

The words and expressions used to introduce, make transitions, and conclude your essay have different grammatical functions. For example, some such as *although* are used to connect an independent clause to a dependent clause. If you are unsure how to use these words and expressions, study them in a grammar textbook or look them up in a dictionary.

SKILL BUILDER

A. *In Writing Skill 4, you wrote introductions and conclusions for the questions below. Now, you will write topic sentences for these questions to support your opinions or preferences.*

Read the questions below again. Using the three main points from the outlines you wrote for the same questions in Writing Skill 3, Practice (page 271), write a topic sentence for each. ***Be sure to use the transitional words and expressions from the chart on pages 279–280.*** *Note: Depending on how you chose to organize your essay (by reasons or by advantages/disadvantages) in Writing Skill 3, Practice, you may only need to write two topic sentences.*

EXAMPLE:

(**Introduction:** I completely agree that a first impression is the most significant one. How we first perceive someone or how someone first feels about us affects us socially, academically, and professionally.)

Para #1—topic sentence: ***To begin with***, *first impressions determine future friendships.*
Para #2—topic sentence: ***Not only*** *do first impressions matter in our social life,* ***but*** *they* ***also*** *have an important impact in our academic lives.*
Para #3—topic sentence, example, and result: ***Furthermore***, *first impressions can also affect your potential employment.* ***For instance***, *if you communicate with customers in an inappropriate way, it could have a very negative impact on business.* ***Consequently***, *that could lead to being fired from your job.*
(**Conclusion:** In summary, a first impression is definitely the most significant one because it has the ability to shape forever our social, academic, and professional lives.)

1. Some people prefer to take trains or subways when they commute to work. Other people like to take buses to get to their jobs. Which do you prefer? Use specific reasons and examples to support your choice.

   Para #1 – topic sentence:

   Para #2 – topic sentence:

   Para #3 – topic sentence (if needed):

2. Do you agree or disagree with the following statement? **The best things in life are free.** Use specific reasons and examples to support your opinion.

   Para #1 – topic sentence:

   Para #2 – topic sentence:

   Para #3 – topic sentence (if needed):

3. Many people today are concerned about the damage humans have done to the Earth. What do you think can be done to help create a better and cleaner environment? Use specific reasons and examples to support your answer.

   Para #1 – topic sentence:

   Para #2 – topic sentence:

   Para #3 – topic sentence (if needed):

B. *Work with a partner. Read and compare your topic statements for each of the questions.*

Skill Builder Sample Answers:

1. **Para #1—topic sentence:** *Let me begin by explaining why riding the bus to work was such a miserable experience for me. In the heavy, morning rush-hour traffic, the city buses were so slow and noisy, and most of the time, they were incredibly dirty.*
Para #2—topic sentence: *On the other hand, the subway was so much faster, cleaner, and offered many more stations where I could get off at to walk to work than the city buses.*
Para #3—topic sentence: not needed for this "disadvantage / advantage" organization

2. **Para #1—topic sentence:** *First, the most precious thing to me in life that money can't buy is the love your family gives to you.*
Para #2—topic sentence: *In addition, friendship can't be bought, but it is essential for happiness in our daily lives as well as success in our professional lives.*
Para #3—topic sentence: *Not only are the best things in life free in our relationships with other people, but finding peace of mind for ourselves doesn't have to cost us a thing.*

3. **Para #1—topic sentence:** *To begin with, the simple act of getting out of our cars and walking can have a huge impact on our environment and can provide additional health benefits.*
Para #2—topic sentence: *Not only will walking help to reduce the damage we are doing to the environment, but recycling at home can also save valuable resources and energy.*
Para #3—topic sentence: *Finally, volunteering for organized projects to help clean up in your local area can make a big difference in the quality of life for both humans and the plants and animals in our environment.*
Conclusion: *In summary, a first impression is definitely the most significant one because it has the ability to shape forever our social, academic, and professional lives.*

EXPRESS TIP

If you want to make a specific point stronger, you can use the following expressions for emphasis: *in fact, indeed, actually.*

PRACTICE

A. *Read the prompts.*

B. *Opinions and preferences on both sides of each issue have been provided for you. Choose one opinion or preference and points to support it. On a separate piece of paper,* ***write topic statements for two to three paragraphs to support your opinions or preferences****. Use the transitional words and expressions from Skill 5. (Note: If you can think of other supporting points for your opinion, please feel free to use them.)*

1. A large outdoor concert has been planned for the park next to your house. There will be a wide variety of music and many popular musicians for the three-day event from Friday to Sunday. Do you support or oppose this plan? Why? Use specific reasons and examples to support your position.

Oppose:	**Support:**
- noisy - increased traffic & parking problems - garbage left behind in the park & neighborhood	- opportunity to hear great music - chance for people to relax in a natural setting - business opportunities for nearby stores & restaurants

2. Some people believe that parents should not take very young children out to restaurants. Other people think children should go to restaurants when they are young. What is your opinion? Use specific reasons and examples to support your answer.

Do not take young children to restaurants:	**Should take young children to restaurants:**
- children are noisy & bother other diners - children are messy; extra work for restaurant employees to clean up - children are active and get bored; not fair to them - parents cannot relax and enjoy a night out	- teaches children how to behave in public - families should do things together - parents may not have money for babysitters or someone to watch them, so should be allowed to bring them

3. "Believe and act as if it were impossible to fail." Do you agree or disagree with this quotation from the American inventor Charles F. Kettering? Use specific reasons and examples to support your opinion.

Agree:	**Disagree:**
- if feel confident, you will become confident - others are more confident in you if you believe in yourself - gives you courage to do things you might be afraid to	- should not attempt to do things you know you can't do; focus on being good at what you can do - should accept failure as a natural part of life and learn from it - makes other people think you are too proud and you may not succeed if others don't like your attitude

C. *Work with a partner. Read and compare your topic statements. How are they different? How are they the same?*

D. *Complete the self-evaluation chart on the next page. How well do you feel you did these things? Rank questions 1–4 from 1 to 5. Then answer questions 5–7.*

Self-Evaluation: Skill 5

	1 = low, 5 = high
1. Use transitions for moving from the first, to the second, and to the last supporting reasons	
2. Use transitions for introducing and adding new information	
3. Use transitions to show contrast and comparison between main ideas	
4. Use transitions to provide examples	
5. What is something you did especially well?	
6. What one or two things would you like to improve on?	
7. How do you plan to improve those things?	

EXPRESS TIP

Remember that a good essay is around 300 words, but there is no maximum word limit, so you can write as much as you want in the time given. However, don't write just to make your essay longer; don't repeat ideas or add new ones at the end. The number of ideas you include in your essay is important, but the quality of what you write and the way in which you express your ideas is more important to the raters.

The raters will score your essay based on how well it is organized; how well you addressed the topic and provided details, support, and examples for your opinion; and how well and accurately you used language.

SKILLS REVIEW

Independent Writing Skills 3–5 for Task 2, Opinion–Preference Essay: Outlining for the Independent Essay, Organizing the Introduction and Conclusion, and Using Transitions to Connect Ideas in the Body of the Essay

EXPRESS TIP

Don't stop writing your essay before the 30 minutes given is up. If you have enough time left, use it wisely to expand on your ideas and provide additional examples. However, be *especially* careful to save some time to review and edit your essay.

Directions: *This task requires you to write an essay in response to a question that asks you to state, explain, and support your opinion on an issue.*

You have 30 minutes to plan, write, and revise your essays. Write your essays on a separate piece of paper.

Essay Topic 1:
If your parents decided to pay for you to travel for a few weeks, would you prefer to visit places in your own country that you have not seen or to travel in a foreign country? Why? Use specific reasons and examples to support your answer.

Response Time: 30 minutes

Begin timing yourself.

Essay Topic 2:
What do you think is the *most* important quality a person needs to work effectively in a group: open-mindedness, respect for others, or problem-solving abilities? Choose *one* quality and use specific reasons and examples to support your choice.

Response Time: 30 minutes

Begin timing yourself.

Self-Evaluation: Review of Skills 3–5

Read your essays from the Skills Review for Skills 3–5 and complete the self-evaluation chart below. How well do you feel you did these things? Rank questions 1–14 from 1 to 5. Then answer questions 15–17.

	1 = low, 5 = high
1. Understand the prompt	
2. Make brief outline notes to organize your essays appropriate to the topic	
3. State your opinion or preference or advantages and / or disadvantages in the introductions using appropriate expressions	
4. Explain clearly what you plan to discuss in the introductions	
5. Include personal information to engage the raters in your introductions	
6. Use transitions for moving from the first, to the second, and to the last supporting reasons	
7. Use transitions for introducing and adding new information	
8. Use transitions to show contrast and comparison between main ideas	
9. Use transitions to provide examples	
10. Briefly paraphrase or summarize the main reasons for your opinion or preference in your conclusions	
11. Use the appropriate expressions for signaling your conclusions	
12. Refer to personal information in your conclusions	
13. Use correct sentences structures, appropriate vocabulary, good grammar, and a variety of sentence structures	
14. Review and revise your essays	
15. What is something you did especially well?	
16. What one or two things would you like to improve on?	
17. How do you plan to improve those things?	

EXPRESS TIP

When you edit your essay, be sure to look for the mistakes that are commonly made. For example:

- singular / plural agreement errors
- incorrect usage of articles (*a, an, the*)
- incorrect verb tense or form
- pronoun errors
- parallel structure mistakes (*adverb, adverb,* and *adverb* = parallel)
- two sentences that are not connected properly with a coordinator (*and, or, but*) or a subordinator (*because, although, since*)
- digressions (going off the main topic)

Note: Scoring information for this Writing Post-Test is available on page 328. If you are able to have a teacher or another English language speaker score the Writing Post-Test for you, keep track of your score on this Writing Post-Test and add it to your scores for the Reading, Listening, and Speaking Post-Tests. The Writing Post-Test can also be taken on the CD-ROM, where it is combined with the other Post-Tests into one full test. It can be taken on the CD-ROM in either the "Practice Mode" (not timed; you can work at your own pace) or the "Timed Mode" (TOEFL iBT® Test timing; you will not be able to pause). If you want to see how you would score on an authentic TOEFL iBT® Test, take the test on the CD-ROM in the "Timed Mode."

WRITING POST-TEST

Directions:

The Writing section of the TOEFL iBT® Test measures your ability to write academically appropriate texts. There are two writing tasks.

Task 1 is an integrated reading-listening-writing task. You will first have 3 minutes to read a short passage. You may take notes while you read. Then the passage will disappear, and you will listen to a short lecture on the same topic. You will hear the passage only once. You may take notes while you listen. After that, the reading will reappear. Then you will hear and read a question. You will have 20 minutes to plan and write a response to the question. You may use your notes to make your response.

A sufficient response will generally be 150–225 words long. Your writing will be rated on both the content of your response and the overall quality of your writing.

Task 2 is an independent writing task. You will be asked a question about your opinion on a general issue. You will have 30 minutes to plan and write your response.

A sufficient response will generally be at least 300 words long. Your writing will be rated on the expression and support of your ideas, the organization of your response, and the overall quality of your writing.

When you take the actual TOEFL iBT Test, and if you take the Writing section of the Test on the CD-ROM, an on-screen clock will count down your preparation time and writing time.

Time yourself or have your instructor time your writing. For Task 1, stop after 20 minutes. For Task 2, stop after 30 minutes.

When you have finished reading these directions, go on to the first writing task. Write your responses on your own paper or type them on a computer or word processor.

Integrated Task 1

Directions: *This task requires you to read a passage on an academic topic and then listen to a lecture about the same topic. You may take notes while you read and listen. Then write a response to a question that asks you to relate the lecture to the reading. You are not asked to give your personal opinion. You may look at the reading passage while you write, and you may use your notes to help you.*

First, read the passage for 3 minutes:

An increasing concern over both water costs and water availability has challenged North Americans, especially those in the arid west and southwest regions of the United States, to reconsider common landscaping methods and especially the once-popular lawn—a large expanse of grass. Although people enjoy walking and playing on lawns, these areas can be difficult and costly to maintain, often requiring chemical fertilizers and an inordinate amount of water. Homeowners in the desert regions of the continent trying to re-create the look of a golf course find themselves paying enormous bills, while at the same time depleting a precious resource.

Enter xeriscaping, a bold new method of landscape design that uses significantly less water. By some estimates, xeriscaping can reduce the amount of water used for landscapes by 50 to 75 percent. In addition to amending and improving the soil, xeriscaping moves away from a dependence on lawns. Instead, gardeners plant hardy, drought-resistant cacti and succulents, and also use paving stones, paths, and patios in the yard design, which not only serve as areas for people to gather but of course don't need any water at all. Mulch—layers of leaves, tree bark, or even sand and gravel—is spread between plants to keep weeds down, lessen the need for watering, and keep existing water in the soil from evaporating in the strong sunlight. Xeriscapers plant similar types of plants in the same area so that some areas can be given more water and other areas less water, depending on the different species of plants.

Reading Time: 3 minutes

Now listen to part of a lecture on the same topic. 3-29

Essay topic:

Summarize the points made in the lecture, being sure to explain how they contradict claims made in the reading passage.

You now have 20 minutes to plan, write, and revise your essay. You may check the reading again and use your notes.

Response Time: 20 minutes

Independent Task 2

Directions: *This task requires you write an essay in response to a question that asks you to state, explain, and support your opinion on an issue.*

Essay Topic:

The world you live in today is not the same as it was for your parents a generation ago; there have been significant changes. How is your life different from your parents' life when they were the same age as you are now? Use specific reasons and examples to support your answer.

You now have 30 minutes to plan, write, and revise your essay.

Response Time: 30 minutes

THIS IS THE END OF THE WRITING POST-TEST.

Record your score: ______

PRACTICE TEST

Note: Scoring information for each section of this Practice Test is available on pages 329 (Reading), 330 (Listening), 327 (Speaking), and 328 (Writing). If you are able to have a teacher or another English language speaker score the Speaking and Writing sections for you, add these scores to your Reading and Listening scores. The Practice Test can also be taken on the CD-ROM in either the "Practice Mode" (not timed; you can work at your own pace) or the "Timed Mode" (TOEFL iBT® Test timing; you will not be able to pause). On the CD-ROM, the Reading and Listening sections will automatically be scored for you. If you want to see how you would score on an authentic TOEFL iBT® Test, take the test on the CD-ROM in the "Timed Mode."

READING

Directions:

The Reading Section of the TOEFL iBT® Test measures your understanding of academic passages and your ability to answer questions about them. It contains three passages and a set of questions about each passage. You have 60 minutes in which to complete the Reading Section.

The majority of questions are worth 1 point; however, the last question (summary or table completion) for each passage is worth more than 1 point. Please read the directions for the last question so you know how many points are possible.

When words or phrases are blue and underlined, definitions appear at the end of the reading in the glossary.

(Note: On the actual TOEFL iBT Test, the words will be blue and underlined, and definitions for them will appear when you click on them.)

As soon as you have finished one question, move on to the next one. You may skip questions and come back to them later, and change your answers if you want.

When you have finished reading these directions, go on to the first reading.

Reading Passage 1

Questions 1–13

Read the following passage and mark the correct answers.

Monarch Migration

1 The Monarch butterfly (*Danaus plexippus*), which inhabits regions from the northern area of South America through the United States to southern Canada in North America, is a well-known garden butterfly. It is easily spotted because of its bright orange and black coloring and large size; its popular name means "king," in fact. Adult Monarch butterflies lay eggs on the milkweed plant, which provides food for the newly hatched **caterpillars** when they emerge.

2 The Monarch is perhaps best known for its unusual life cycle and dramatic migration habits. Not only do Monarchs go through the four stages of life typical for a butterfly—the egg; the larva, or caterpillar; the pupa, or **chrysalis**; and the adult butterfly—but they also go through four generations in one year.

3 The first generation of Monarchs hatches from eggs in March and April. The caterpillars eat the milkweed plant and do little else; in about two weeks, the caterpillars are ready to create a chrysalis. Once inside the chrysalis, the former caterpillar transforms into the adult butterfly, a process that takes about ten days. After the adult butterflies have emerged from the chrysalis, they lay eggs for the next generation. An adult Monarch butterfly lives for only two to six weeks.

4 In May and June, the second generation of Monarchs is born, and the third comes in July and August. In September and October, though, comes the most interesting generation, the fourth. While the first three parts of the life cycle are the same as those of the other three generations, the fourth generation of Monarchs does not die in two to six weeks but instead enters a non-reproductive phase known as diapause, during which they do not lay eggs, and during this phase, the Monarchs make an incredible migration.

5 Great clouds of fourth-generation Monarchs migrate from the cold regions in the north and east to warmer regions in the south and west. Although they are not the only butterflies to do so, migration is more commonly associated with birds. In fact, most other adult butterflies in North America die in the winter, leaving their chrysalises to winter over. This fourth generation of Monarchs, though, lives not for a few weeks but for six to eight months, long enough to lay the eggs for the new first generation.

6 7A Monarchs actually have two reasons for migrating: One is because they could not survive the cold winter temperatures, and the second is because milkweed plants also die in winter. 7B While Monarchs are the only butterfly to migrate both south in the fall and back north in the spring, the generation that moves north is not the same one that flew south, but rather the first generation of the next year. 7C No one is sure how the new generation of Monarchs knows the way back north—current theories include the notion that flight patterns are inherited from previous generations, and also that the insects are guided by the sun or by magnetic fields from the Earth's surface—but they do, and the next cycle of four generations begins again. 7D

continued . . .

7 The migration path of the Monarchs can stretch for 2,500 miles (4,023 kilometers). Monarchs in the United States that live to the west of the Rocky Mountains migrate to southern California, while those that live to the east winter in Mexico. Interestingly, the Monarchs settle in the same trees in their winter spots every year—even though it is different butterflies that make the trip each year. How this happens is not yet fully understood. However, a major threat to Monarch butterflies is the removal of these perennial nesting trees for roads, housing, and other development projects.

8 In warmer areas of the world, such as Bermuda, Monarchs live year round and do not migrate; in Australia, Monarchs living in cooler areas migrate and others, in warmer regions, don't.

Glossary

caterpillar: A stage in the lifecycle of a butterfly; a creature with a wormlike body that can be smooth or covered with hair.

chrysalis: A stage of a butterfly's life where it forms a hard, protective covering around itself before emerging as a butterfly.

1. The word spotted in paragraph 1 could best be replaced by
   Ⓐ noticed
   Ⓑ removed
   Ⓒ marked
   Ⓓ understood

2. The word which in paragraph 1 refers to
   Ⓐ eggs
   Ⓑ the milkweed plant
   Ⓒ adult butterflies
   Ⓓ caterpillars

3. What is implied about butterflies other than the Monarch in paragraph 2?
   Ⓐ They do not go through four stages of life.
   Ⓑ They have interesting migration habits.
   Ⓒ They are not as well-known as the Monarch.
   Ⓓ They do not go through four generations in a year.

4. Which of the sentences below best expresses the essential information in the highlighted sentence in paragraph 4?
   Ⓐ Monarchs from the fourth generation die more quickly than ones from the first three generations.
   Ⓑ The fourth generation of Monarchs is special because they do not lay eggs, a phenomenon known as diapause.
   Ⓒ Fourth-generation Monarchs are unusual because they live long enough to migrate.
   Ⓓ If the other generations of Monarchs could migrate, then they would not die so quickly.

5. Why does the author use the phrase "great clouds" in paragraph 5?
   Ⓐ To indicate that Monarchs prefer to travel in cool weather
   Ⓑ To show that Monarchs travel in large groups
   Ⓒ To explain that Monarchs travel together with birds
   Ⓓ To show that Monarchs travel first in one direction, and then in another

6. The word so in paragraph 5 refers to
   Ⓐ associate with birds
   Ⓑ migrate
   Ⓒ die in the winter
   Ⓓ leave their chrysalises to winter over

7. Look at the four squares [■] that indicate where the following sentence could be added to paragraph 6.

   If the fourth generation of Monarchs behaved as the first three did, then when their eggs hatched, the emerging caterpillars would have nothing to eat.

   Where would the sentence best fit? Circle the square 7A, 7B, 7C, or 7D where the sentence should be added to the paragraph.

(Note: On the actual TOEFL iBT Test, the directions would ask you to "Click on a square to add the sentence to the passage." On the computer, you will then **click on** the correct square [■] and the sentence will appear in that location.)

8. According to paragraph 6, what is true about how Monarchs migrate north?
   Ⓐ The flight path is taught from one generation to the next.
   Ⓑ No one has directly observed the northern migration.
   Ⓒ The butterflies that migrate north have never made the trip before.
   Ⓓ The route is different from the southern migration path.

9. The word notion in paragraph 6 could best be replaced by
   Ⓐ idea
   Ⓑ direction
   Ⓒ proof
   Ⓓ discovery

10. According to paragraph 7, what is a danger for Monarchs?
   Ⓐ Their short lifespan
   Ⓑ A lack of food
   Ⓒ Loss of habitat
   Ⓓ Climate change

11. The word perennial in paragraph 7 is closest in meaning to

Ⓐ safe for insects
Ⓑ not well understood
Ⓒ typical of warm climates
Ⓓ used again and again

12. Which of the following is NOT mentioned as an area where Monarchs live?

Ⓐ England
Ⓑ Canada
Ⓒ Australia
Ⓓ Mexico

13. **Directions:** *Select the appropriate phrases from the answer choices, and match them to the Monarch generation they describe. TWO of the answers will not be used.* **This question is worth 3 points** (3 points for 5 correct answers, 2 points for 4 correct answers, 1 point for 3 correct answers, and 0 points for 2, 1, or 0 correct answers).

first generation	• •
second generation	•
fourth generation	• •

Answer choices: (choose 5)

1. Migrates from north to south
2. Migrates from south to north
3. Is born in March and April
4. Is born in May and June
5. Lives for six or more months
6. Is born in the south or west
7. Spends two to six weeks in a chrysalis

Reading Passage 2

Questions 14–25

Read the following passage and mark the correct answers.

Eclipses

1 It is no surprise that the origin of the word *eclipse* is related to "abandonment" and "darkening." Today's meaning of the word describes an event whereby an object in space such as a planet or a moon is hidden temporarily by either another object moving in front of it—that is, between it and its viewer—or by the shadow of another such object. While eclipses can occur with any planet, moon, or star, the types we're most familiar with as observers are solar eclipses and lunar eclipses.

2 A solar eclipse occurs when the Moon passes between the Earth and the Sun, from the point of view of someone standing on the Earth. There are three types of solar eclipses: partial, annular, and total. A partial eclipse occurs when only some of the of the Sun is covered, so that a portion of the Sun can still be seen. An annular eclipse is caused when the Moon passes completely in front of the Sun, but because of its observed size does not totally cover the Sun, so around the edges of the Moon a ring of light from the Sun can still be seen (note that *annular* comes from the Latin *annularis*, meaning "ring-shaped"). Partial and annular eclipses are dangerous to look at directly, since the Sun's light is not completely blocked. A total eclipse refers to an event in which the perceived size of the Moon is the same as or larger than that of the Sun, so that the body of the Sun is completely blocked—although light from the Sun's corona (a gaseous area surrounding the Sun) is still visible.

3 A solar eclipse can occur only at the time of a new moon. Between two and five solar eclipses occur each year, and of these between zero and two will be total. It's important to remember, too, that because the effect of an eclipse depends on where the viewer is standing, such an event is visible only for a short time—about seven and a half minutes—and along a track no wider than 250 kilometers, or about 155 miles. Eclipse enthusiasts, known as "eclipse chasers" or "umbraphiles" (literally, shadow lovers), travel great distances in order to be able to observe such an event. Solar eclipses can be predicted years in advance of their occurrence.

4 22A, During a lunar eclipse, the Moon passes through the Earth's shadow, which blocks the light from the Sun. 22B, This can only occur during a full moon, when the Moon is on the far side of the Earth. 22C, A lunar eclipse can last from thirty minutes up to a maximum of one hour and forty minutes, and can be seen from about half of the Earth at a time. 22D

continued . . .

5 The Earth's shadow is comprised of two distinct sections: the umbra and the penumbra. The umbra is the darkest part of a shadow, caused by the total blocking of light. The penumbra, on the other hand, refers to a shadow caused when only part of the light source is blocked. The resulting shadow is dark, but not as dark as the umbra. Lunar eclipses can be categorized as three types: penumbral, partial, and total. A penumbral (from the Latin for "almost shadow") eclipse is the result of the Moon passing through the Earth's penumbra, which causes the Moon's surface to look darker. When part of the Moon passes through the Earth's umbra, it causes a partial eclipse. A total lunar eclipse is the name given to the event when the Moon lies entirely inside the Earth's umbra. A total eclipse, however, does not mean that total darkness occurs: light from the Sun refracts through the Earth's atmosphere, and the bent light waves can cast a red glow, earning the term "Blood Moon" for the event.

---

14. Which of the sentences below best expresses the essential information in the highlighted sentence in paragraph 1?
    Ⓐ People see more solar and lunar eclipses than any other type.
    Ⓑ It isn't possible to see a solar and lunar eclipse at the same time.
    Ⓒ People learn a lot more about eclipses by actually seeing one occur.
    Ⓓ Solar and lunar eclipses occur at the same time as other, more distant eclipses.

15. The word portion in paragraph 2 is closest in meaning to
    Ⓐ section
    Ⓑ serving
    Ⓒ shadow
    Ⓓ reflection

16. What is true about an annular eclipse?
    Ⓐ It causes total darkness for the person viewing it.
    Ⓑ It happens no more than once a year.
    Ⓒ It occurs when the Moon is between the Sun and the Earth.
    Ⓓ It is caused by the shadow of the Earth.

17. What can be inferred from paragraph 2 about the Sun's light?
    Ⓐ It is brighter during an annular eclipse than during a partial eclipse.
    Ⓑ None of it is visible during a total eclipse.
    Ⓒ It causes the Sun to look larger than it really is.
    Ⓓ It is dangerous to look at it directly.

18. The word that in paragraph 2 refers to
    Ⓐ a total eclipse
    Ⓑ an event
    Ⓒ the perceived size
    Ⓓ the body

19. How many total solar eclipses occur in a year?
Ⓐ between zero and two
Ⓑ between zero and five
Ⓒ between two and five
Ⓓ more than five

20. Why does the author say, "It's important to remember, too, that because the effect of an eclipse depends on where the viewer is standing" in paragraph 3?
Ⓐ To show that solar eclipses can only occur at certain times of the month
Ⓑ To explain why seeing a solar eclipse is a rare event
Ⓒ To demonstrate the difference between three different types of solar eclipse
Ⓓ To explain why different people have different perceptions of solar events

21. According to paragraph 3, what can be inferred about eclipse chasers?
Ⓐ They know in advance when a solar eclipse is going to occur.
Ⓑ They prefer solar eclipses to lunar eclipses.
Ⓒ They travel 250 kilometers to see the entire eclipse.
Ⓓ They spend a great deal of time trying to witness an eclipse.

22. Look at the four squares [■] that indicate where the following sentence could be added to paragraph 4.

More people, therefore, have seen a lunar eclipse than a solar eclipse.

Where would the sentence best fit? Circle the square **22A**, **22B**, **22C**, or **22D** where the sentence should be added to the paragraph.

23. The word which in paragraph 4 refers to
Ⓐ a lunar eclipse
Ⓑ the Moon
Ⓒ the Earth's shadow
Ⓓ the Sun's light

24. The phrase comprised of in paragraph 5 could best be replaced by
Ⓐ covered by
Ⓑ at least
Ⓒ changed into
Ⓓ made up of

25. **Directions:** *Select the appropriate phrases from the answer choices, and match them to the type of eclipse to which they relate. TWO of the answers will not be used.* **This question is worth 3 points** (3 points for 5 correct answers, 2 points for 4 correct answers, 1 point for 3 correct answers, and 0 points for 2, 1, or 0 correct answers).

solar eclipse	• • •
lunar eclipse	• •

Answer choices: (choose 5)

1. Occurs at the time of a full moon
2. Occurs at the time of a new moon
3. Occurs every two to five years
4. Lasts less than eight minutes
5. Cannot be seen from both hemispheres of the Earth
6. Has a penumbral eclipse
7. Has an annular eclipse

Reading Passage 3

Questions 26–38

Read the following passage and mark the correct answers.

Graphene

1 In 2010, two Russian-born scientists, Andre Geim and Konstantin Novoselov, shared the Nobel Prize in physics for their work on a carbon-based compound called graphene. Not since the invention of plastics or silicon computer chips has a compound had so much potential to dramatically change our lives for generations to come. Yet, despite graphene's far-reaching impact, creating it requires only the most basic tools. Graphene can be extracted from graphite, the substance used in pencils; therefore, technically, anyone with tape and a pencil can create the compound at home. It can be formed by first using a clear, sticky tape to peel off thin layers from a small flake of graphite and then pressing the tape back and forth until thinner and thinner layers are split off. Eventually, a nearly transparent, gray layer of graphene will be left on the tape. Based on the work of Geim and Novoselov, scientists throughout the world are now racing to find new ways to use graphene, a material so simply created yet with so many extraordinary properties.

continued . . .

2 One of the reasons graphene is considered revolutionary is that it is the strongest material ever discovered, yet is flexible and ultra-light. In fact, it is 200 times stronger than steel, while still being the thinnest material scientists are now able to create. Further, because graphene is pliable, devices in a variety of unique shapes could be constructed that are more compact and less easily damaged when they are dropped or abused. As a result of all these unique properties, graphene is considered the perfect material for various applications in the aerospace and automotive industries. Consider the possibilities, for example, of building nearly indestructible and lightweight satellites, airplanes, and cars.

3 The use of graphene could also provide benefits on a more personal level. Stronger and lighter medical implants, such as artificial hips, are already in the early stages of development at a research facility in California. While not quite as vital, air-tight plastic containers could be produced by embedding graphene in the plastic, thus allowing food to stay fresh for weeks. Even our leisure activities could become more enjoyable and efficient as graphene is used to build better recreational sports equipment; for instance, feather-light but incredibly durable tennis racquets or golf clubs.

4 Furthermore, graphene is transparent: it lets in 98 percent of the light. **32A** Because of this unique quality, innovations in many types of electronic devices are possible, including transparent touch screens and more efficient solar cells for heating homes and businesses. **32B** Therefore, graphene's transparency, coupled with its strength and flexibility, holds the promise of inexpensively manufactured and paper-thin television and computer screens. At major manufacturing and electronic corporations worldwide, the pace of investment in research into graphene-based products has significantly increased in the past few years. **32C** In fact, developments are under way in Sweden to produce large television screens using graphene. **32D**

5 Among graphene's other remarkable qualities is its ability to resist heat and to be an excellent conductor of electricity. This has major implications for producing new computer chips that are smaller than silicon chips, more powerful, and yet will not cause an increase in temperature. The reason for this is that electricity can move through graphene computer chips very quickly without generating too much heat that would otherwise disrupt the connections between the chips. The result is that not only would computer chips made of graphene be only one atom thick, but they could also be up to 1,000 times faster than the silicon chips used today. This would allow nearly limitless processing power to be stored on extremely tiny chips, further reducing the size of devices such as computers and smartphones. Some scientists predict that one day we may be carrying around devices the size of credit cards that have as much processing power as the current smartphones. And these futuristic devices could be folded up and put in your pocket.

6 The miraculous properties of graphene open a world of limitless possibilities for every area of science, industry, and manufacturing. Consequently, while it may take some time for its full potential to be realized, there is no doubt that in the near future graphene will be as common as plastic is today.

---

26. Which of the sentences below best expresses the essential information in the highlighted sentence in paragraph 1?

Ⓐ Graphene will be more difficult to create in the future than creating plastics and silicon computer chips was in the past.

Ⓑ Plastics and silicon computer chips have not had as much of an effect on our lives as graphene will have.

Ⓒ The possibilities for graphene to significantly alter our existence is comparable to the impact plastics and silicon computer chips have had.

Ⓓ Graphene, plastics, and computer chips have significantly changed our world for many years.

27. The word extracted in paragraph 1 is closest in meaning to

Ⓐ composed

Ⓑ removed

Ⓒ grown

Ⓓ absorbed

28. The word pliable in paragraph 2 could best be replaced by

Ⓐ uniform

Ⓑ bendable

Ⓒ unusual

Ⓓ complex

29. According to paragraph 2, why is graphene a potentially good material for constructing satellites?

Ⓐ It is as strong as steel and thinner than any substance known.

Ⓑ It is extremely light, which helps it to resist changing shape.

Ⓒ It is very thin, strong, and can be packed tightly together.

Ⓓ It is thin, nearly see-through, and weighs very little.

30. The word leisure in paragraph 3 is closest in meaning to

Ⓐ athletic

Ⓑ open-air

Ⓒ professional

Ⓓ free-time

31. According to the passage, what is true about graphene?

Ⓐ No consumer goods using it are currently on the market.

Ⓑ It is 2,000 times stronger than steel.

Ⓒ Researchers in Sweden and California are producing it.

Ⓓ It is twice as thin as silicon.

32. Look at the four squares [■] that indicate where the following sentence could be added to paragraph 4.

In terms of such advanced applications, it is important to note that research is already at the point where laboratories can cheaply produce the material in large quantities.

Where would the sentence best fit? Circle the square 32A, 32B, 32C, or 32D where the sentence should be added to the paragraph.

33. The phrase under way in paragraph 4 could best be replaced by
Ⓐ in order
Ⓑ in demand
Ⓒ in a hurry
Ⓓ in progress

34. It is implied in paragraph 5 that
Ⓐ silicon computer chips are unable to conduct electricity because they aren't strong enough
Ⓑ when graphene computer chips are made small enough, they will be as fast as silicon chips currently are
Ⓒ devices using silicon computer chips must be very large to function properly
Ⓓ if silicon computer chips were reduced to the same size as graphene chips, they would create excess heat

35. The word they in paragraph 5 refers to
Ⓐ connections between chips
Ⓑ silicon chips
Ⓒ graphene computer chips
Ⓓ computers

36. The author of the passage mentions in paragraph 5 that some devices "could be folded up and put in your pocket" in order to
Ⓐ demonstrate the extraordinary strength of graphene
Ⓑ illustrate how flexible and small graphene devices might be
Ⓒ suggest a new credit card design using graphene
Ⓓ imply that graphene-based devices are lighter than smartphones

37. All of the following are mentioned in the passage as potential applications of graphene EXCEPT
Ⓐ aircraft and automobiles
Ⓑ transparent lights
Ⓒ well-sealed storage containers
Ⓓ specialized computer screens

38. **Directions:** *Below is an introductory sentence for a brief summary of the passage. Complete the summary by choosing the THREE answer choices that represent the most important ideas of the passage. Some of the answer choices are incorrect because they express ideas that are not given in the passage or because they express only details from the passage.* **This question is worth 2 points** (2 points for 3 correct answers, 1 point for 2 correct answers, and 0 points for 1 or 0 correct answers).

Graphene has many amazing qualities that may change our lives in the future.

•
•
•

Answer choices: (choose 3)

1. More powerful and smaller computers can be built with graphene.
2. Electricity is easily attracted to graphene, but it maintains a low temperature.
3. Graphene is extremely light, and the most durable and flexible material in the world.
4. Because graphene is lightweight and strong, it is cheap to produce in large quantities.
5. Graphene is a clear material that allows nearly 100 percent of the light to enter it.
6. All of graphene's properties are useful for the electronics industry.

STOP. THIS IS THE END OF THE READING SECTION OF THE TOEFL iBT PRACTICE TEST.

Record your score: _______

LISTENING

Directions:

The Listening Section of the TOEFL iBT® Test measures your understanding of English conversations and lectures and your ability to answer questions about them. It contains six passages and a set of five or six questions about each passage. You have 60 minutes in which to complete the Listening Section.

You will hear each conversation and lecture **only one time**.

You can take notes as you listen. You can use your notes to help you answer the questions.

When you see the icon 🔊 in the replay questions, it indicates that you will hear part of the talk again, but on the actual TOEFL iBT Test the conversation or lecture will not be shown on the computer screen.

The majority of questions are worth 1 point; however, some questions are worth more than 1 point. If the question is worth more than 1 point, it will have additional directions that indicate how many points are possible.

When you have finished reading these directions, go on to the first listening passage.

Listing Passage 1

Questions 1–5

Now get ready to listen. You may take notes. 3-30

Now get ready to answer the questions. You may use your notes to help you answer the questions.

1. Why does the student want to talk to the advisor? 3-31
   Ⓐ He wants to know how to raise his grade.
   Ⓑ He isn't able to meet with his professor.
   Ⓒ He wants to drop one of his classes.
   Ⓓ He wants to change his grading option.

2. Which of these was NOT a reason for the student's problem in class? 3-32
   Ⓐ He didn't attend some lectures.
   Ⓑ He didn't take an important test.
   Ⓒ He did poorly on an exam.
   Ⓓ He failed to complete some required work.

3. Listen again to part of the conversation. Then answer the question. 3-33
   What does the advisor imply when she says this?
   Ⓐ The roommate is not an art major.
   Ⓑ The roommate gave good advice.
   Ⓒ The student should have spoken to the professor instead.
   Ⓓ The student shouldn't try to major in art.

4. What is the student's current major? 3-34
   Ⓐ History
   Ⓑ Business
   Ⓒ Economics
   Ⓓ Art history

5. What is true about taking a class Pass / No Pass instead of for a letter grade? 3-35
   Ⓐ A student needs a higher grade in order to receive credit.
   Ⓑ A student can choose either option at any time.
   Ⓒ The professor needs to approve a change from one system to the other.
   Ⓓ The Pass / No Pass option will raise a student's grade point average.

Listening Passage 2

Questions 6–11

Now get ready to listen. You may take notes. 4-1

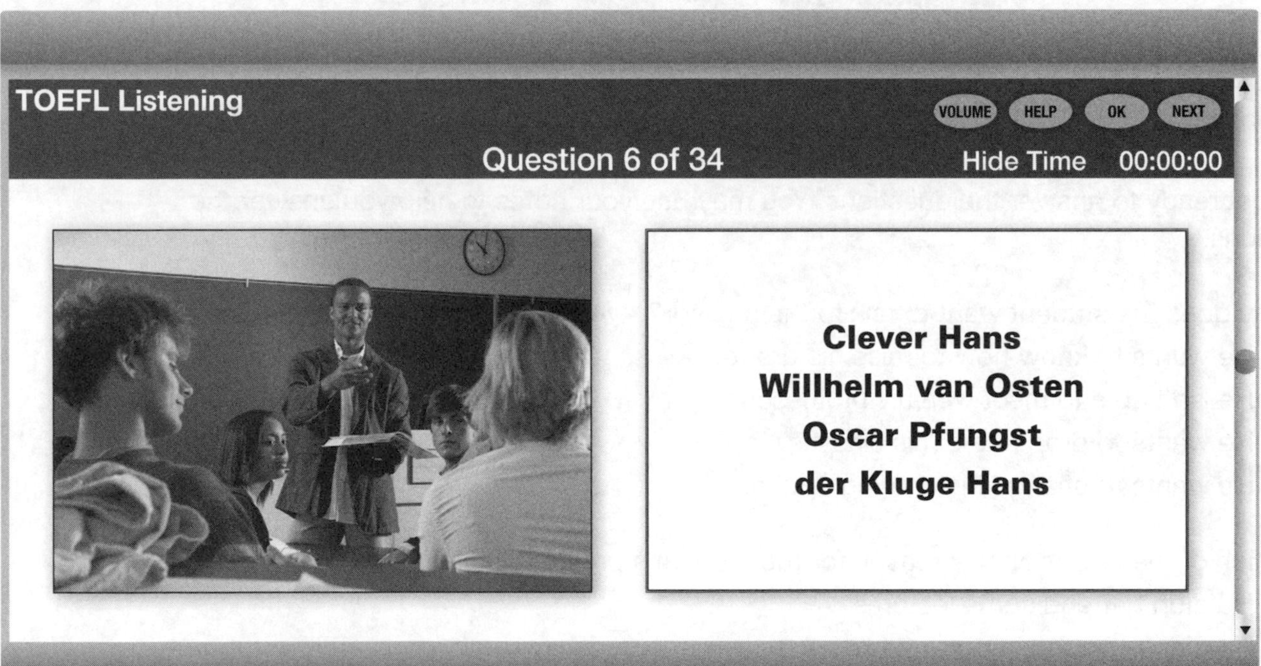

Now get ready to answer the questions. You may use your notes to help you answer the questions.

6. What is the discussion mainly about? 4-2

Ⓐ How scientific results can be tested
Ⓑ Whether animals can think
Ⓒ A famous scientific trick
Ⓓ How animals can be taught

7. How is the information in the discussion organized? 4-3

Ⓐ As a series of chronological events
Ⓑ As a list of causes and effects
Ⓒ As a classification of different tests
Ⓓ As a series of problems and answers

8. Why does the woman tell a story about her dog? 4-4

Ⓐ To show that dogs are smarter than horses
Ⓑ To prove that dogs don't understand what they hear
Ⓒ To demonstrate that her dog is intelligent
Ⓓ To explain why some people believe animals can think

9. Clever Hans answered all of these types of questions EXCEPT 4-5

Ⓐ how to spell a word
Ⓑ ones that required an opinion
Ⓒ ones that required an answer of "yes" or "no"
Ⓓ math questions with fractions

10. Listen again to part of the discussion. Then answer the question. 4-6
What does the professor mean when he says this?

Ⓐ The professor doesn't know if anyone else tested the horse.
Ⓑ The horse wasn't really able to perform the calculations.
Ⓒ The professor wants the student to provide some additional information.
Ⓓ It's important to test scientific theories in several ways.

11. When did Clever Hans get answers wrong? **This question is only worth 1 point** (1 point for 2 correct answers and 0 points for 1 or 0 correct answers). 4-7

Choose 2 answers.

[A] When the questioner didn't know the answers either
[B] When the questioner stood far away
[C] When the questioner didn't ask questions in German
[D] When the questioner was not his owner

Listening Passage 3

Questions 12–17

Now get ready to listen. You may take notes. 4-8

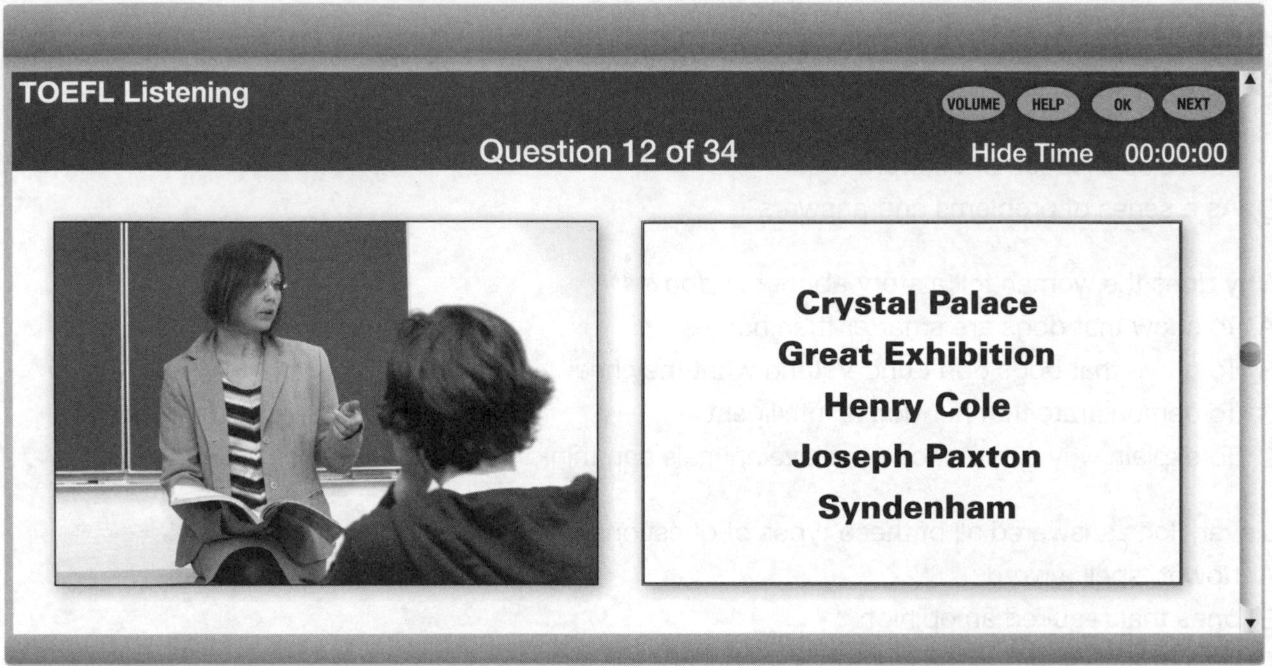

12. What does the professor NOT mention as something remarkable about the Crystal Palace? 4-9
    - (A) Why it was built
    - (B) How much it cost
    - (C) Who designed it
    - (D) What it was made of

13. What does the professor imply about the schedule Henry Cole made for the Exhibition of 1851? 4-10
    - (A) The timeframe from start to completion was unusually short.
    - (B) It was copied by Cole from the exhibition in Paris.
    - (C) It was changed to accommodate supplies of building materials.
    - (D) It was made without the approval of other members of his committee.

14. Listen again to part of the lecture. Then answer the question. 4-11
What does the professor mean when she says this?
Ⓐ A different design would have been more practical.
Ⓑ The Crystal Palace burned down because it wasn't well built.
Ⓒ The committee didn't select the winning design in a fair way.
Ⓓ It didn't seem likely that Paxton's design would work.

15. Are these features of plate glass? **This question is worth 2 points** (2 points for 4 correct answers, 1 point for 3 correct answers, and 0 points for 2, 1, or 0 correct answers). 4-12

For each answer, put a check mark (✓) in the **YES** or **NO** column.		
	YES	**NO**
Was developed in France		
Cools quickly		
Needs polishing		
Made on small tables		

16. What is important about the taxes on glass at the time the Crystal Palace was built? 4-13
Ⓐ Paxton had to pay high taxes to use glass as a building material.
Ⓑ Taxes were raised as a result of all the glass that Paxton used.
Ⓒ Prince Albert said Paxton's builders didn't have to pay the whole tax.
Ⓓ Removal of the taxes meant that Paxton had cheaper materials.

17. Why does the professor mention elm trees? 4-14
Ⓐ Because elm tree branches posed a threat to the panes of glass
Ⓑ Because trees were cut down to provide building materials
Ⓒ To show that the Palace was large enough for trees to be inside it
Ⓓ To show that they were taller than the Crystal Palace

Listening Passage 4

Questions 18–22

Now get ready to listen. You may take notes. 4-15

Now get ready to answer the questions. You may use your notes to help you answer the questions.

18. What can be inferred about the woman? 4-16

    Ⓐ She needs directions to get to the Italian section.

    Ⓑ She is sorry about interrupting the man.

    Ⓒ She doesn't understand the lab procedures.

    Ⓓ She is embarrassed about her poor language skills.

19. Listen again to part of the conversation. Then answer the question. 4-17

    What does the man mean when he says this?

    Ⓐ He is uncertain whether or not the university website is working properly.

    Ⓑ He doesn't think her plan was a very good one.

    Ⓒ He thinks that she should have gone to the new-student orientation.

    Ⓓ He doesn't have much time to help her right now.

20. According to the man, what will the special software program allow the woman to do? 4-18

    Ⓐ Send her assignments and weekly updates of her course progress to her professor

    Ⓑ Listen to a native speaker, review and store recordings of her own voice, and send them to her professor

    Ⓒ Download web-based recordings and a review device onto her laptop computer at home

    Ⓓ Listen to a native speaker, record her own voice, and play back both

21. What does the man tell the woman about printing out materials? 4-19
Ⓐ There are limitations on what can be printed.
Ⓑ It is typically required for students to print out course textbooks.
Ⓒ Students are allowed to print up to six pages from the materials.
Ⓓ The Lab Assistants are the only ones who can print.

22. According to the man, what are some of the materials available in the Language Laboratory? **This question is only worth 1 point** (1 point for 2 correct answers and 0 points for 1 or 0 correct answers). 4-20

Choose 2 answers.

[A] Musical recordings
[B] Online video materials
[C] Individual CDs
[D] Movies on DVDs

Listening Passage 5

Questions 23–28

Now get ready to listen. You may take notes. 4-21

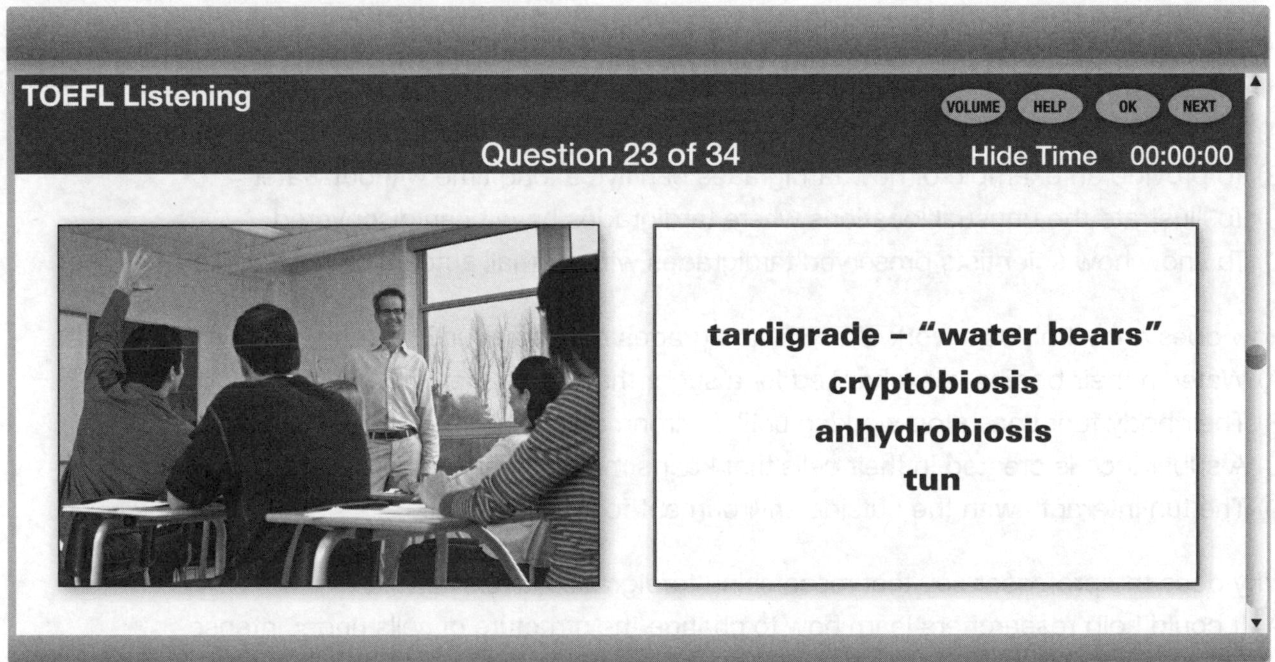

Now get ready to answer the questions. You may use your notes to help you answer the questions.

23. According to the discussion, all of the following are features of water bears EXCEPT 4-22

Ⓐ Four claws per leg

Ⓑ Bodies composed of sections

Ⓒ Six legs

Ⓓ Microscopic size

24. According to the professor, what are some of the harsh conditions that water bears can tolerate? **This question is only worth 1 point** (1 point for 2 correct answers and 0 points for 1 or 0 correct answers). 4-23

Choose 2 answers.

A Freezing

B Rotten soil

C Bright sunlight

D Lack of air

25. Listen again to part of the discussion. Then answer the question. 4-24

What does the professor mean when he says this?

Ⓐ He believed the students knew the answer to the question.

Ⓑ He suspected that the discovery might be possible.

Ⓒ He doubted that the article was accurate.

Ⓓ He thought the results were unusual.

26. For what purpose does the professor mention a 100-year-old piece of moss in a museum? 4-25

Ⓐ To define the cryptobiosis that occurs when tardigrades are brought back to life

Ⓑ To provide an example of how tardigrades can live a long time without water

Ⓒ To illustrate the unusual locations where tardigrades have been discovered

Ⓓ To show how scientists preserved tardigrades with a small amount of water

27. How does anhydrobiosis work after the tardigrades roll into a tun? 4-26

Ⓐ Water in their bodies is exchanged for a sugar that keeps them from harm.

Ⓑ Their body functions stop working until environmental conditions improve.

Ⓒ A substance is created in their cells that keeps moisture inside their bodies.

Ⓓ The tun interacts with the outside environment to protect them.

28. Why does the professor say that researching tardigrades is relevant? 4-27

Ⓐ It could help researchers learn how to change the structure of cells under intense conditions.

Ⓑ Scientists might be able to create new techniques for understanding tardigrade behavior.

Ⓒ It could help scientists find ways to save and defend living things from hostile environments.

Ⓓ Researchers hope to find a way to use tardigrades to protect humans during space flights.

Listening Passage 6

Questions 29–34

Now get ready to listen. You may take notes. 4-28

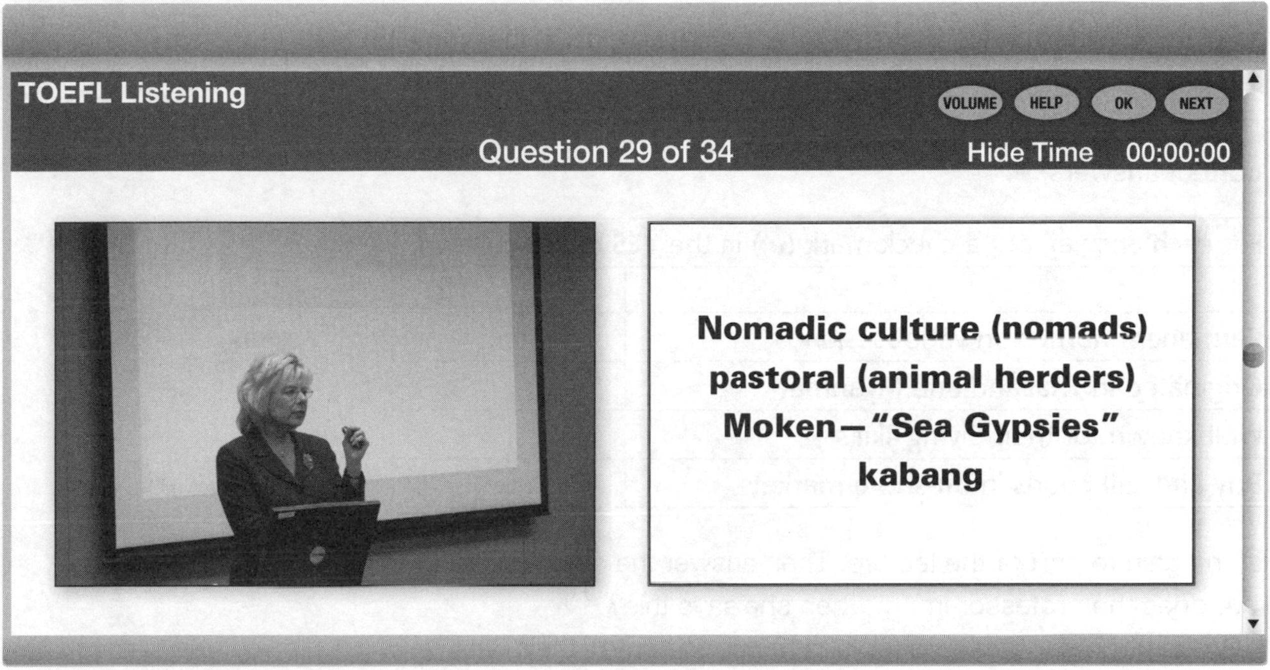

Now get ready to answer the questions. You may use your notes to help you answer the questions.

29. For what purpose does the professor mention tribes in Africa and Central Asia? 4-29
   Ⓐ To provide a definition of nomads
   Ⓑ To illustrate that nomadic cultures vary
   Ⓒ To contrast a farming culture with a nomadic culture
   Ⓓ To explain how nomadic societies function

30. According to the lecture, which of the following best describes the role of the *kabang* in Moken culture? 4-30
   Ⓐ Its enclosed section protects the family during periods of heavy rain and winds.
   Ⓑ It provides everything necessary for carrying on the functions of daily life.
   Ⓒ It serves as the main means of transportation to large family gatherings.
   Ⓓ Its structure and design reflect the traditional Moken system of beliefs.

31. When is the major fishing season for the Moken people? 4-31
   Ⓐ From June to October
   Ⓑ Between the dry season and the wet season
   Ⓒ From November to May
   Ⓓ During the dry season and the beginning of the wet season

32. According to the professor, why are the Moken people "environmentally smart"? 4-32

Ⓐ They fish in a way that maintains a steady supply of marine life.

Ⓑ They build houses high above the ground out of natural materials.

Ⓒ They collect wild plants and hunt for wild animals.

Ⓓ They harvest fresh fish and dry it for storage.

33. Based on the information in the lecture, indicate which of the following are characteristics of Moken society. **This question is worth 2 points** (2 points for 4 correct answers, 1 point for 3 correct answers, and 0 points for 2, 1, or 0 correct answers). 4-33

For each answer, put a check mark (✓) in the **YES** or **NO** column.		
	YES	**NO**
Permanent homes on various islands		
Originated in Thailand and Myanmar		
Well known for their diving skills		
Buy and sell goods in on-shore markets		

34. Listen again to part of the lecture. Then answer the question. 4-34

What does the professor imply when she says this?

Ⓐ Groups of older Moken people continue to control their lives.

Ⓑ Life for the Moken will remain the same over time.

Ⓒ The Moken people have an important place in history.

Ⓓ The future is uncertain for the Moken.

STOP. THIS IS THE END OF THE LISTENING SECTION OF THE TOEFL iBT PRACTICE TEST.

Record your score: _______

SPEAKING

Directions:

The Speaking section of the TOEFL iBT® Test measures your ability to speak about a variety of subjects. There are six tasks in this section. You may take notes while you listen and read, and use your notes to make your responses.

Tasks 1 and 2 are independent speaking tasks. After you hear and read the question, you will have 15 seconds to prepare a response. After you hear a beep, you will have 45 seconds to record your response.

Tasks 3 and 4 are integrated reading-listening-speaking tasks. You will first have 45 seconds to read a short passage. Then you will listen to a short conversation or lecture on the same topic. You will hear the passage only once. Then you will hear and read a question, after which you will have 30 seconds to prepare a response. After you hear a beep, you will have 60 seconds to record your response.

Tasks 5 and 6 are integrated listening-speaking tasks. You will first listen to a short conversation or lecture. You will hear it only once. Then you will hear and read a question, after which you will have 20 seconds to prepare a response. After you hear a beep, you will have 60 seconds to record your response.

Time your recorded responses or have your instructor time your responses for you. For Task 1 and 2, stop after 45 seconds. For Tasks 3, 4, 5, and 6, stop after 60 seconds.

When you take the actual TOEFL iBT Test, and if you take the Speaking section of the Practice Test on the CD-ROM, an on-screen clock will count down your preparation time and response time.

You may take notes on a separate piece of paper.

When you have finished reading these directions, go on to the first speaking task.

Speaking Task 1

1. *You will now be asked to give your opinion about a familiar topic. After you hear the question, you have 15 seconds to prepare your response and 45 seconds to answer.* 4-35

1. Describe a family member who has influenced you. What have you learned from this person? Use specific details in your response.

Preparation Time: 15 Seconds

Response Time: 45 Seconds

Speaking Task 2

2. *You will now be asked to give your opinion about a familiar topic. After you hear the question, you have 15 seconds to prepare your response and 45 seconds to answer.* 4-36

2. Some college students prefer to take night classes. Others prefer to take classes only in the daytime. Which class schedule would you prefer and why?

Preparation Time: 15 Seconds

Response Time: 45 Seconds

Speaking Task 3

3. *You will now read a short passage and then listen to a conversation on the same subject. You will then hear a question about the topic. After you hear the question, you will have 30 seconds to prepare your response and 60 seconds to speak.* 4-37

Reading Time: 45 Seconds

INFO SESSION: Literature Term in Edinburgh, Spring Term
Thursday, November 20 • 1:00–2:30 P.M. • Jackson International Center

Interested in spending spring term in Scotland? Spring is a great season in Edinburgh: not yet too touristy and many events, shows, and things to do. This spring, English literature professor George Ricklin will offer two courses (one on tone and style in the poetry of Robert Burns and one on Scottish novelists of the 18th and 19th centuries). In addition, a professor from Edinburgh National University will teach a course on the works of Robert Louis Stevenson as well as courses in theater and art history. Eligible juniors and seniors may also choose to replace one course with a custom-designed independent study course. The program's fee includes supervised cultural outings, a long weekend excursion to London, and much more! Stay for the summer program, too, and take courses on literary criticism and creative writing. Join us Wednesday to learn more about this wonderful opportunity!

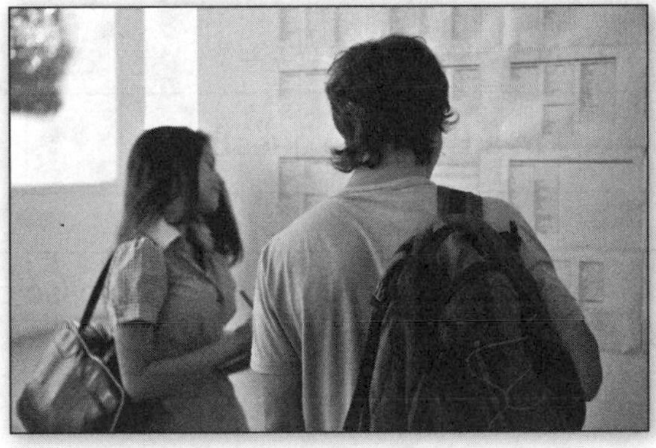

Now listen to a conversation on this topic between two students.

Now get ready to answer the question.

3. The woman expresses her opinion about the opportunity described in the notice. State her opinion and explain her reasons for that opinion.

Preparation Time: 30 Seconds
Response Time: 60 Seconds

Speaking Task 4

4. You will now read a short passage and then listen to a lecture on the same academic subject. You will then hear a question about them. After you hear the question, you will have 30 seconds to prepare your response and 60 seconds to speak. 4-38

Reading Time: 45 Seconds

Keynesianism

Keynesianism is an economic theory proposed by the British economist John Maynard Keynes in 1936. The central concept of his theory is that the most important force for economic growth is the total demand for goods and services created by individual households, businesses, and government. Therefore, economic progress is *not* achieved by unregulated or free markets. According to Keynes, markets do not balance themselves in a way that leads to full employment. For example, if car manufacturers perceived that demand for new products was dropping, they wouldn't hire new workers. Keynesian economics supports government involvement through public policies. The goals of these governmental policies are to achieve full employment, which stabilizes the prices of goods and services because employed people have more money to spend. An example of this would be increasing government spending to stimulate the economy in periods of weak economic growth.

Now listen to part of a lecture on this topic in an economics class.

Now get ready to answer the question.

4. Explain how Milton Friedman's Chicago School of Economics discussed by the professor differs from Keynesianism as described in the reading.

Speaking Task 5

5. You will now listen to a conversation. You will then be asked a question about it. After you hear the question, you will have 20 seconds to prepare your response and 60 seconds to speak. 4-39

Listen to a conversation between the president of the Student Government Association and the Dean of Student Affairs.

Now get ready to answer the question.

5. The speakers discuss two possible solutions to the problem. Briefly summarize the problem and the two solutions. Then explain what you think the man should recommend and why.

Preparation Time: 20 Seconds

Response Time: 60 Seconds

Speaking Task 6

6. You will now listen to a lecture. You will then be asked a question about it. After you hear the question, you will have 20 seconds to prepare your response and 60 seconds to speak. 4-40

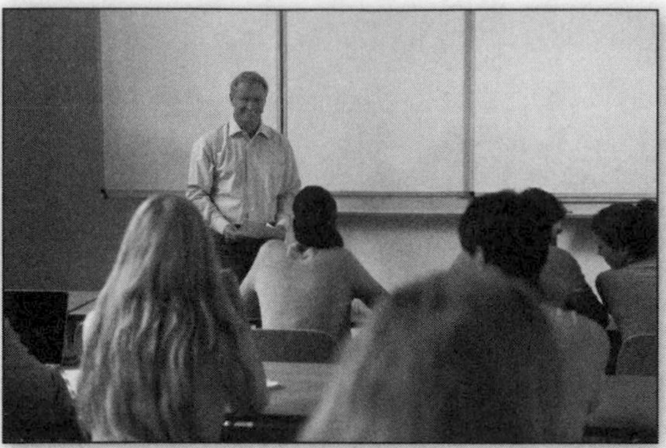

Listen to part of a lecture from a meteorology class.

Now get ready to answer the question.

6. Using information from the lecture, explain the causes and effects of a sirocco.

Preparation Time: 20 Seconds

Response Time: 60 Seconds

STOP. THIS IS THE END OF THE SPEAKING SECTION OF THE TOEFL iBT PRACTICE TEST.

Record your score: ________

WRITING

Directions:

The Writing section of the TOEFL iBT® Test measures your ability to write academically appropriate texts. There are two writing tasks.

Task 1 is an integrated reading-listening-writing task. You will first have 3 minutes to read a short passage. You may take notes while you read. Then the passage will disappear, and you will listen to a short lecture on the same topic. You will hear the passage only once. You may take notes while you listen. After that, the reading will reappear. Then you will hear and read a question. You will have 20 minutes to plan and write a response to the question. You may use your notes to make your response.

A sufficient response will generally be 150–225 words long. Your writing will be rated on both the content of your response and the overall quality of your writing.

Task 2 is an independent writing task. You will be asked a question about your opinion on a general issue. You will have 30 minutes to plan and write your response.

A sufficient response will generally be at least 300 words long. Your writing will be rated on the expression and support of your ideas, the organization of your response, and the overall quality of your writing.

When you take the actual TOEFL iBT Test, and if you take the Writing section of the Practice Test on the CD-ROM, an on-screen clock will count down your preparation time and writing time.

Time yourself or have your instructor time your writing. For Task 1, stop after 20 minutes. For Task 2, stop after 30 minutes.

When you have finished reading these directions, go on to the first writing task. Write your responses on your own paper or type them on a computer or word processor.

Integrated Writing Task 1

Directions:

This task requires you to read a passage on an academic topic and then listen to a lecture about the same topic. You may take notes while you read and listen. Then write a response to a question that asks you to relate the lecture to the reading. You are not asked to give your personal opinion. You may look at the reading passage while you write, and you may use your notes to help you.

First, read the passage for three minutes.

The *Mary Celeste*

Nearly 150 years later, the *Mary Celeste* still stands as one of the great maritime mysteries. On November 5, 1872, Captain Benjamin Briggs, his wife and two-year-old child, and a crew of seven sailed from Staten Island, New York, en route to Genoa, Italy, in the American merchant ship *Mary Celeste*. It never arrived.

On December 5 of the same year, the crew of the ship *Dei Gratia*, sailing from Canada to the Mediterranean, found the *Mary Celeste* about 600 miles west of Portugal. The ship was mostly undamaged, although the sails were somewhat torn. When the crew from the *Dei Gratia* boarded the *Mary Celeste*, they found no one on board. There was water between the decks, but the ship was not sinking. Several of the ship's navigational instruments were missing, as well as one lifeboat.

Although the mystery was never solved, over the years several theories have been put forth. Some speculate that the crew could have been attacked by pirates, known to have been active in those waters. Pirates could have boarded the vessel, killed the crew members, and left. Another theory holds that a seaquake—an earthquake that occurs at sea—could have frightened the crew, who might have worried that the ship was sinking. They might then have escaped in the lifeboat, but perished in the high waves resulting from the seaquake. A third hypothesis is that of mutiny—that is, the crew members turning against the captain, either killing him or taking him prisoner, and leaving the ship in the lifeboat, which was subsequently lost at sea.

Reading Time: 3 minutes

Now listen to part of a lecture on the same topic. 4-41

Essay topic:
Summarize the points made in the lecture, being sure to explain how they respond to claims made in the reading passage.

You now have 20 minutes to plan, write, and revise your essay. You may check the reading again and use your notes.

Response Time: 20 minutes

Independent Writing Task 2

Directions:

This task requires you write an essay in response to a question that asks you to state, explain, and support your opinion on an issue.

Essay Topic:
Some students prefer to live with their parents after high school. Others prefer to live in an apartment or a dormitory room. Which do you prefer? Use specific reasons and examples to support your answer.

You now have 30 minutes to plan, write, and revise your essay.

Response Time: 30 minutes

STOP. THIS IS THE END OF THE WRITING SECTION AND THE TOEFL iBT PRACTICE TEST.

Record your score: ________

SCORING THE READING POST-TEST

To determine a scaled score on the Reading Post-Test, you must first determine the number of points you received in the section. You must determine the number of points you receive on the last question of each reading passage before you can determine the total number of points out of a possible 45 points. When you know the total points you received on the Reading Post-Test, you can refer to the following chart to determine your scaled score out of 30 for this section.

TOTAL POINTS	READING SCALED SCORE	TOTAL POINTS	READING SCALED SCORE
45	30	22	9
44	29	21	8
43	28	20	8
42	27	19	7
41	26	18	7
40	25	17	6
39	24	16	6
38	23	15	5
37	22	14	5
36	21	13	4
35	20	12	4
34	19	11	3
33	18	10	3
32	17	9	3
31	16	8	2
30	16	7	2
29	15	6	2
28	14	5	1
27	13	4	1
26	12	3	1
25	11	2	0
24	10	1	0
23		0	0

SCORING THE LISTENING POST-TEST

To determine a scaled score on the Listening Post-Test, you must first determine the number of points you received in the section. You must determine the number of points you receive on the three questions that are worth more than one point before you can determine the total number of points out of a possible 37 points. When you know the total points you received on the Listening Post-Test, you can refer to the following chart to determine your scaled score out of 30 for this section.

TOTAL POINTS	LISTENING SCALED SCORE	TOTAL POINTS	LISTENING SCALED SCORE
37	30	18	9
36	29	17	9
35	28	16	8
34	27	15	8
33	26	14	7
32	25	13	6
31	24	12	6
30	23	11	5
29	22	10	4
28	21	9	4
27	20	8	3
26	19	7	3
25	18	6	3
24	17	5	2
23	16	4	2
22	15	3	1
21	14	2	1
20	13	1	0
19	12	0	0

SCORING THE SPEAKING POST-TEST AND THE SPEAKING PRACTICE TEST

The following chart shows how a score of 0 through 4 on a Speaking task is converted to a scaled score out of 30.

SPEAKING SCORE (0–4)	SPEAKING SCALED SCORE (0–30)
4.00	30
3.83	29
3.66	28
3.50	27
3.33	26
3.16	24
3.00	23
2.83	22
2.66	20
2.50	19
2.33	18
2.16	17
2.00	15
1.83	14
1.66	13
1.50	11
1.33	10
1.16	9
1.00	8
0.83	6
0.66	5
0.50	4
0.33	3
0.16	1
0.00	0

Scaled scores on each of the Speaking tasks on a test are averaged to determine the scaled score for the test.

SCORING THE WRITING POST-TEST AND THE WRITING PRACTICE TEST

The following chart shows how a score of 0 through 5 on a Writing task is converted to a scaled score out of 30.

WRITING SCORE (0–5)	WRITING SCALED SCORE (0–30)
5.00	30
4.75	29
4.50	28
4.25	27
4.00	25
3.75	24
3.50	22
3.25	21
3.00	20
2.75	18
2.50	17
2.25	15
2.00	14
1.75	12
1.50	11
1.25	10
1.00	8
0.75	7
0.50	5
0.25	4
0.00	0

Scaled scores on each of the Writing tasks on a test are averaged to determine the scaled score for the test.

SCORING THE READING SECTION OF THE PRACTICE TEST

To determine a scaled score on the Reading section of the Practice Test, you must first determine the number of points you received in the section. You must determine the number of points you receive on the last question of each reading passage before you can determine the total number of points out of a possible 43 points. When you know the total points you received on the Reading section of the Practice Test, you can refer to the following chart to determine your scaled score out of 30 for this section.

TOTAL POINTS	READING SCALED SCORE	TOTAL POINTS	READING SCALED SCORE
43	30	21	9
42	29	20	8
41	28	19	8
40	27	18	7
39	26	17	7
38	25	16	6
37	24	15	6
36	23	14	5
35	22	13	5
34	21	12	4
33	20	11	4
32	19	10	3
31	18	9	3
30	17	8	2
29	16	7	2
28	16	6	1
27	15	5	1
26	14	4	1
25	13	3	1
24	12	2	0
23	11	1	0
22	10	0	0

SCORING THE LISTENING SECTION OF THE PRACTICE TEST

To determine a scaled score on the Listening section of the Practice Test, you must first determine the number of points you received in the section. You must determine the number of points you receive on the six questions that are worth more than one point before you can determine the total number of points out of a possible 38 points. When you know the total points you received on the Listening section of the Practice Test, you can refer to the following chart to determine your scaled score out of 30 for this section.

TOTAL POINTS	LISTENING SCALED SCORE	TOTAL POINTS	LISTENING SCALED SCORE
38	30	18	10
37	29	17	9
36	28	16	9
35	27	15	9
34	26	14	8
33	25	13	7
32	24	12	6
31	23	11	6
30	22	10	5
29	21	9	4
28	20	8	4
27	19	7	3
26	18	6	3
25	17	5	3
24	16	4	2
23	15	3	2
22	14	2	1
21	13	1	0
20	12	0	0
19	11		

SINGLE-USER LICENSE AGREEMENT

THESE TERMS APPLY TO ALL LICENSED SOFTWARE ON THE DISK EXCEPT THAT THE TERMS FOR USE OF ANY SHAREWARE OR FREEWARE ON THE DISKETTES ARE AS SET FORTH IN THE ELECTRONIC LICENSE LOCATED ON THE DISK:

1. GRANT OF LICENSE and OWNERSHIP: The enclosed computer programs ("Software") are licensed, not sold, to you by Pearson Education, Inc. ("We" or the "Company") and in consideration of your payment of the license fee, which is part of the price you paid, and your agreement to these terms. We reserve any rights not granted to you. You own only the disk(s) but we and/or our licensors own the Software itself. This license allows you to use and display your copy of the Software on a single computer (i.e., with a single CPU) at a single location, so long as you comply with the terms of this Agreement. You may make one copy for back up, or transfer your copy to another CPU, provided that the Software is usable on only one computer.

2. RESTRICTIONS: You may not transfer or distribute the Software or documentation to anyone else. Except for backup, you may not copy the documentation or the Software. You may not network the Software or otherwise use it on more than one computer or computer terminal at the same time. You may not reverse engineer, disassemble, decompile, modify, adapt, translate, or create derivative works based on the Software or the Documentation. You may be held legally responsible for any copying or copyright infringement which is caused by your failure to abide by the terms of these restrictions.

3. TERMINATION: This license is effective until terminated. This license will terminate automatically without notice from the Company if you fail to comply with any provisions or limitations of this license. Upon termination, you shall destroy the Documentation and all copies of the Software. All provisions of this Agreement as to limitation and disclaimer of warranties, limitation of liability, remedies or damages, and our ownership rights shall survive termination.

4. LIMITED WARRANTY AND DISCLAIMER OF WARRANTY: Company warrants that for a period of 30 days from the date you purchase this Software, the Software, when properly installed and used in accordance with the Documentation, will operate in substantial conformity with the description of the Software set forth in the Documentation, and that for a period of 30 days the disk(s) on which the Software is delivered shall be free from defects in materials and workmanship under normal use. The Company does not warrant that the Software will meet your requirements or that the operation of the Software will be uninterrupted or error-free. Your only remedy and the Company's only obligation under these limited warranties is, at the Company's option, return of the disk for a refund of any amounts paid for it by you or replacement of the disk. THIS LIMITED WARRANTY IS THE ONLY WARRANTY PROVIDED BY THE COMPANY AND ITS LICENSORS, AND THE COMPANY AND ITS LICENSORS DISCLAIM ALL OTHER WARRANTIES, EXPRESS OR IMPLIED, INCLUDING WITHOUT LIMITATION, THE IMPLIED WARRANTIES OF MERCHANTABILITY AND FITNESS FOR A PARTICULAR PURPOSE. THE COMPANY DOES NOT WARRANT, GUARANTEE OR MAKE ANY REPRESENTATION REGARDING THE ACCURACY, RELIABILITY, CURRENTNESS, USE, OR RESULTS OF USE, OF THE SOFTWARE.

5. LIMITATION OF REMEDIES AND DAMAGES: IN NO EVENT, SHALL THE COMPANY OR ITS EMPLOYEES, AGENTS, LICENSORS, OR CONTRACTORS BE LIABLE FOR ANY INCIDENTAL, INDIRECT, SPECIAL, OR CONSEQUENTIAL DAMAGES ARISING OUT OF OR IN CONNECTION WITH THIS LICENSE OR THE SOFTWARE, INCLUDING FOR LOSS OF USE, LOSS OF DATA, LOSS OF INCOME OR PROFIT, OR OTHER LOSSES, SUSTAINED AS A RESULT OF INJURY TO ANY PERSON, OR LOSS OF OR DAMAGE TO PROPERTY, OR CLAIMS OF THIRD PARTIES, EVEN IF THE COMPANY OR AN AUTHORIZED REPRESENTATIVE OF THE COMPANY HAS BEEN ADVISED OF THE POSSIBILITY OF SUCH DAMAGES. IN NO EVENT SHALL THE LIABILITY OF THE COMPANY FOR DAMAGES WITH RESPECT TO THE SOFTWARE EXCEED THE AMOUNTS ACTUALLY PAID BY YOU, IF ANY, FOR THE SOFTWARE OR THE ACCOMPANYING TEXTBOOK. BECAUSE SOME JURISDICTIONS DO NOT ALLOW THE LIMITATION OF LIABILITY IN CERTAIN CIRCUMSTANCES, THE ABOVE LIMITATIONS MAY NOT ALWAYS APPLY TO YOU.

6. GENERAL: This agreement shall be construed in accordance with the laws of the United States of America and the State of New York, applicable to contracts made in New York, and shall benefit the Company, its affiliates and assignees. This agreement is the complete and exclusive statement of the agreement between you and the Company and supersedes all proposals or prior agreements, oral, or written, and any other communications between you and the Company or any representative of the Company relating to the subject matter of this agreement. If you are a U.S. government user, this Software is licensed with "restricted rights" as set forth in subparagraphs (a)-(d) of the Commercial Computer-Restricted Rights clause at FAR 52.227-19 or in subparagraphs (c)(1)(ii) of the Rights in Technical Data and Computer Software clause at DFARS 252.227-7013, and similar clauses, as applicable.

Should you have any questions concerning this agreement or if you wish to contact the Company for any reason, please contact in writing:

Customer Service
Pearson Education, Inc.
10 Bank Street
White Plains, NY 10606

To the Teacher:	To the Student:
HOW TO VIEW YOUR STUDENTS' DATA ON THE WEBSITE	**HOW TO SEND YOUR DATA FROM THE CD-ROM**
Follow these steps to view your students' data on **www.longmantestprep.com**.	Get your class name and teacher's e-mail address from your teacher. Then follow these steps.
STEP 1: Choose a class name and e-mail address. Decide on a unique class name, such as TOEFL 101 or Prep 07. Then choose an e-mail address or create a new one only for student data. Give this information to your students.	**STEP 1: Start the process.** To start the process, click on SEND DATA on the Main Menu.
STEP 2: Go to www.longmantestprep.com. After your students have submitted their data, go to this website: **www.longmantestprep.com.**	**STEP 2: Select recordings (if you have made any).** When you send data, your Results Reports and written responses will be sent automatically. However, you must select your recordings (if you have any).
STEP 3: Enter information. Type the information requested in each box: *E-mail Address* and *Password*. You must use the same e-mail address that you gave your students. You can use any password.	**STEP 3: Enter information.** Type the information requested in each box: *Your Name*, *Your E-mail Address*, *Your Teacher's E-mail Address*, and *Your Class Name*. Then click on CONTINUE to send the data.
STEP 4: Click on "Login" to enter the website. After you enter the website, you can choose REVIEW BY STUDENTS to see the results of an individual student.	**STEP 4: Wait for data to send.** You will see a message when the computer connects to the Internet and starts sending data. You will also see a message when the data has been sent.

Express to the TOEFL iBT® Test CD-ROM

INSTALLING AND LAUNCHING THE PROGRAM

PLEASE NOTE:

- If you plan to use this program in a computer lab, contact the lab administrator early.
- To begin the program, please read the instructions completely before proceeding.
- After you install the program, the CD-ROM must be in the CD-ROM drive when you use the program.

WINDOWS: ONE-STEP INSTALLATION

- Insert the Express to the TOEFL iBT® Test CD-ROM into the CD-ROM drive. On most computers, the installation will begin automatically.
- If the installation does not begin, follow these instructions:
  - Open My Computer.
  - Right-click on the CD-ROM drive icon (the symbol that looks like a CD).
  - Click on Open.
  - Double-click on the "Install.exe."
- Follow the instructions on the screen to complete the installation.
- When you complete the installation, the program will start automatically.
- To launch the Express to the TOEFL iBT® Test CD-ROM program each following session:
  - Click on Start.
  - Select Programs (or All Programs).
  - Select Express to the TOEFL iBT® Test
  - Click on the Express to the TOEFL iBT® Test icon.

STARTING THE PROGRAM

The first screen of the Express to the TOEFL iBT® Test CD-ROM offers three ways to start the program.

1. New User: if you have never used the program before
2. Local User: if you have already used the program on this computer
3. Disk User: if you have used the program on this computer or on a different computer and have your score data stored on a floppy disk or other portable storage device.

USING THE PROGRAM

You can use this program in two ways.

1. One person on the same computer for each session. For this method, a floppy disk or other portable storage device is NOT necessary, and you do not need to do anything to save your score data when you exit the program. The computer will automatically save your scores and your completed questions.

- Start your first session by selecting "New User."
- Start each following session by selecting "Local User."
- At the end of each session, your data will automatically be saved on the computer.

PLEASE NOTE: Starting a session as a New User or as a Disk User will delete all previously saved data on the computer.

2. More than one person on the same computer or one person on different computers. A floppy disk or other portable storage device is necessary for saving score data if more than one person uses the program on the same computer. A person who uses the software on different computers will also need a floppy disk or flash drive for saving data.

- Insert a floppy disk or attach another portable storage device.
- Start your first session by selecting "New User."
- Start each following session by selecting "Disk User."
- At the Log Out screen, click on the "Copy Data" button to save your data to the floppy disk or another portable storage device.

TECHNICAL SUPPORT

For Technical Product Support, please visit our support website at www.PearsonELTSupport.com.